# SQL and NoSQL Database

## Fourth Edition

Lucy Scott

ISBN-13: 979-8-2957-6248-2

## DISCLAIMER



## DEDICATION

TO LISA.

## NOTICE OF LIABILITY



## ACKNOWLEDGMENTS

We are grateful to Dr. Youlong Zhuang for reviewing this edition.

# CONTENTS

# Chapter 1: Introduction to Database

## Chapter Learning Objectives

1.1 Recognize the different types of database.
1.2 Interpret database environment.
1.3 Compare database schema and database state.
1.4 Execute SQL scripts.
1.5 Recall the major usage of DML and DDL commands.

## 1.1 Data and Information

Businesses need data for their day to day operations as well as for decision making. When you checkout at a local grocery store, the business stores your payment information unless you are paying with cash. Even if you are paying with cash, the business updates their inventory items so that they know when to reorder from their suppliers. Data is used for daily operations.

Data on what you buy can also be used for decision making. It shows what sells well and what does not sell, or which products contribute most to profits and which ones don't. This type of data is especially useful when accumulated at large, into what is called 'big data.' Companies can use big data to do analysis and discover trends and patterns for the business. Many business decisions are made based on big data.

Data is everywhere, and has all sorts of applications. At school, data about you is stored in a database. At the end of the semester, your instructor would enter your grade for this course into the database. Data on your grade could look something like this:

| Student Name | Course Title | Final Grade |
|---|---|---|
| Lucy | Introduction to Database | A |

Table 1.1 Grade data

In a grocery store, if you buy two gallon-size bottles of milk at three dollars each, what counts as data? At its simplest, the data includes the products you buy (gallon-size bottles of milk,) the quantity of the product you buy (two,) and the unit price for the product ($3.00.) Data of the transaction will look like this (actual data will also usually include a timestamp, showing date and time of transaction):

| Product | Quantity | Unit Price |
|---|---|---|
| Gallon milk | 2 | 3.00 |

Table 1.2 Sales data

If you pay with a credit card, the data will also include your name, card number, and card expiration date, among other pieces of data. However, regardless of payment form, the inventory of that specific product will be updated, as such:

| Product | On Hand | Unit Cost | Supplier |
|---|---|---|---|
| Gallon milk | 198 | 3.00 | Diary Wholesaler |

Table 1.3 Inventory data

Thus, as demonstrated by the examples, data is defined as raw fact that has meaning and is measurable. Raw fact means that data is specific, stating "five bottles of milk" instead of "a few bottles of milk." By stating "five bottles of milk," one is giving meaningful data that is measurable. Not meaningful data could include age, which is calculated differently in certain parts of Asia, and thus loses meaning due to its variability. Data on date of birth would be more meaningful. For data to be measurable, it must have a specific quantity, such as "seven bottles of milk" instead of "five to ten bottles of milk."

Information is processed data that has value and meets the need of the user. The database should be designed to store all data that a business needs, meaning it should include unprocessed raw data, and be able to provide information that the user needs. For example, as an employee in a company, you can store the date of birth into a database, because the data is raw fact and can be used to calculate the age.

As you can see in Table 1.2, you recorded all the purchases, which is raw data. With raw data, you can get information for the user, including today's sale, this week's sale, this month's sale, etc.

| | Today's sale | This week's sale | This month's sale |
|---|---|---|---|
| Gallon Milk | 120 | 800 | 3120 |
| Cheese (lb) | 21 | 155 | 610 |

Table 1.4 Sales information

As shown in Table 1.1, you recorded data of all students' grade for courses which is raw fact. Even though a complete database would have an overwhelming amount of data, the database should be able to easily output information, such as a list of students who are enrolled in a particular course.

Information is the result from processing raw data to reveal meaning. Information can be used as the foundation for decision making. For example, based on the sales information, the manager can decide to reorder more or less of a certain product. Based on course enrollment information, a school administrator can decide whether to cancel a class or add more sections.

As a database developer, it is important for you to understand that data must be properly stored so that meaningful information can be created from the data. You may have noticed that, based on the sales data in Table 1.2, you cannot generate the sales information in Table 1.4. You will need to add the date of transaction to Table 1.2 so that each sale transaction can be correctly summed to each category (today, this week, this month).

In this book, you will learn how to develop a database to store raw data, and how to produce information by processing the data. You will learn database development and query languages.

Review Question 1.1
The data can be defined as ____________.
a. raw fact that has meaning and can be measured
b. information we use daily
c. numbers
d. numbers or strings

Review Question 1.2
Information is the result of ____________.
a. hard work
b. processing raw data to reveal its meaning.
c. calculation
d. computer power

Review Question 1.3
The database should be designed to store all ______ that a business needs and be able to provide ______ that the user needs.
a. data, data
b. information, information
c. data, information
d. information, data

Review Question 1.4
In this book, you will learn how to develop a database to store raw data, and how to produce information by processing the data. you will learn ______ and ______.
a. database design, query languages
b. database development, query languages
c. database design, information production
d. database development, information production

## 1.2 The Need for Organizing Data: Database

Data is everywhere, and how we organize it makes a huge difference in how useful it becomes. A grocery store manager writes down inventory in a notebook. A college instructor tapes a sheet of student grades to the office door, sorted by student ID. These are examples of raw data being tracked, but they're not very efficient. What happens when the notebook gets lost, or when a student wants to know how their grades compare across different semesters?

That's where databases come in. A database is simply a collection of organized data. Think of it as a digital filing cabinet where information is stored in a structured way so you can find, update, and use it easily. There are several ways to organize a database, and each approach has its strengths and weaknesses.

The simplest form is a flat-file database, which stores data in a plain table (often like a spreadsheet). Each line, or row, represents one record. For example, a flat file of sales transactions might list each purchase with a product, quantity, and unit price. Flat-file databases are still common in small businesses and personal projects. For example, a store owner may track sales in an Excel sheet.

While flat files are easy to set up, they quickly become inconvenient. If you want to find one specific record, you may have to scan the entire file. Even worse, there's no built-in way to represent relationships, like which customer bought which product, without repeating information over and over.

To overcome these limitations, databases evolved into more structured designs. A hierarchical database organizes data in a tree-like structure with parent tables and child tables. For example, consider student information. The parent table could store each student's basic details:

| Student Id | First Name | Last Name |
|---|---|---|
| 1001 | John | White |
| 1002 | Larry | Green |

Table 1.5: Hierarchical database, parent table

From there, the database branches into child tables. One table might store course enrollments and grades:

| Student Id | Course Number | Grade |
|---|---|---|
| 1001 | CS101 | A |
| 1001 | CS102 | C |
| 1002 | CS101 | B |

Table 1.6: Hierarchical database, child table

Another table might store club memberships:

| Student Id | Club Name | Date Joined |
|---|---|---|
| 1001 | Squall watch | 3/12/2017 |
| 1002 | Chess Master | 4/23/2017 |

Table 1.7: Hierarchical database, child table

```
Student
├── Courses
│   ├── CS101: A
│   └── CS102: C
└── Clubs
    └── Chess Masters
```

Figure 1.1: Hierarchical database structure

In this setup, each student (the parent) can connect to many records in the child tables, such as multiple courses or multiple clubs. However, each child record belongs to only one parent. Hierarchical databases are popular in the early days of banking and government record systems, where tree-like structures matched organizational charts. Some older systems still use them today.

While hierarchical databases improved organization, they were still somewhat rigid. This inflexibility stemmed from their tree-like structure, which forced data into strict parent-child relationships that were difficult to modify or expand. For example, if a company wanted an employee to belong to multiple departments, the hierarchical model would require duplicating the employee's record in each department branch, leading to data inconsistency and wasted storage. That's why the relational database became the most widely used approach today.

Relational databases organize data into multiple related tables, but unlike strict parent-child hierarchies, they allow flexible connections between tables. The first half of book will focus mainly on relational databases, since they are the foundation of most modern business systems -- from online shopping carts to hospital patient records to social media platforms.

The second half of the book will focus on NoSQL databases, which offer a flexible alternative to relational models. Unlike tables with fixed structures, NoSQL systems are designed to handle unstructured data and massive scale efficiently. This is essential for understanding how modern businesses manage big data and rapid growth that often exceed the capabilities of traditional systems.

Review Question 1.5

According to the author, a database is _____________.
a. a collection of data
b. a collection of organized data
c. any computer file
d. a collection of numbers and text

Review Question 1.6
Which of the following databases is the most popular and the focus of the first half of this book?
a. flat-file
b. spreadsheet
c. hierarchical
d. relational

Review Question 1.7
What type of database is not structured, and has no apparent relationships between records, thus making it necessary to read the entire file in order to find a specific record?
a. flat-file
b. spreadsheet
c. hierarchical
d. relational

Review Question 1.8
Data is organized into a tree-like structure. The relationship allows a parent table to have multiple children tables but a child table can only have one parent table. This is describing which type of database?
a. flat-file
b. spreadsheet
c. hierarchical
d. relational

Review Question 1.9
Unlike relational databases, _____ systems are designed to handle unstructured data and massive scale efficiently.
a. NoSQL
b. spreadsheet
c. hierarchical
d. SQL

## 1.3 Mini-world

Databases contain data that is related to some part of the real world. The part of the real world the data is related to is known as the mini-world. For example, if you build a database about a library, then the mini-world is the library. Another example, if the database is for a tutoring center of a university, then the mini-world is the tutoring center.

The database should be an abstract of the mini-world. Take for example building of a database for a library. When a borrower checks out a book, the inventory for that specific book should be one less in the database. The copies available recorded in the database should reflect the physical number of copies in the library (mini-world.)

The first step for a database designer is to understand the mini-world. A database that doesn't relate to a mini-world has no purpose. The process of understanding the mini-world is a part of database requirements determination, a topic often covered in system analysis and design books. We will continue talking about this process in the next chapter.

Review Question 1.10
If a database is for a tutoring center of a university, then the mini-world is the ______.
a. tutoring center
b. university
c. database
d. tutors

Review Question 1.11
A database should be a(n) ______ of the mini-world.
a. data center
b. abstract
c. storage
d. organizer

Review Question 1.12
The first step for a database designer is to understand the ______.
a. users
b. designers
c. mini-world
d. whole world

Review Question 1.13
The part of the real world the database is related to is known as the ___________.
a. partial database
b. partial world
c. mini-world
d. mini-database

## 1.4 Database Management System (DBMS)

We learned that data is ubiquitous and is organized into databases. The next natural question would be what tools are available for creating, maintaining, and using the databases.

Like how you use a word processor to write your term paper, you use DBMS to create a database and access the data. A Database Management System is a computer system that allows the user to develop, maintain, and use the database. This book will cover both how to develop and use the database. Instead of following the sequence of how to develop the database first and then how to use it later, this book will cover aspects of both in each chapter. This way, readers will have more exposure to the use of databases.

Examples of DBMSs include: Oracle, SQL Server, MySQL, DB2, SQLite, and MongoDB, among others. In this book, you will learn how to use SQL Server, but the knowledge can be easily applied to other DBMSs.

Review Question 1.14
Word processor software to your term paper is like ___________ to databases.
a. table
b. data
c. DBMS
d. spreadsheet

Review Question 1.15
Which of the following is NOT a DBMS?
a. Oracle
b. MySQL
c. SQL server
d. IBM

## 1.5 User Data and Metadata

The DBMS will need two types of data: user data and Metadata. The user data includes data that users are interested in. For example, customer data (customer name, address, and contact information) is of interest to business users.

Metadata includes data that describes the user data. Metadata makes it easier for a DBMS to search and work on the user data. For example, CustomerName is a column name that describes the data in that column, such as *Skyler Johnson,* which is the user data. So CustomerName is considered metadata and *Skyler Johnson* is user data. CustomerName has to be alphanumeric. It cannot be integers. Therefore, the data type of the column describes what user data is acceptable for the column. Data type is another example of metadata.

The DBMS uses metadata for the structure of the user data. The metadata is data about data.

Review Question 1.16
The ___________ is the data that users are interested in.
a. user data
b. interest data
c. metadata
d. database

Review Question 1.17
The DBMS uses _________ for the structure of the user data. It is data about data.
a. user data
b. interest data
c. metadata
d. database

## 1.6 The Relational DBMS (RDBMS)

The word "relational" in relational databases refers to a table. So, the RDBMS organizes user data into tables. A table contains one or more records and each record contains one or more fields. For example, a student table may have thousands of individual student records and each student has a first name, last name, and date of birth field. The most popular way of organizing data is through the relational database.

| StudentId | First Name | Last Name | Date of Birth |
|---|---|---|---|
| 1234567 | Skyler | Johnson | 2001-03-21 |
| 2234567 | Lucy | Scott | 2002-11-25 |
| 3234567 | Linda | Smith | 2001-09-22 |

Review Question 1.18
The word "relational" in relational databases refers to a _________.
a. relationship
b. link
c. table
d. record

Review Question 1.19
In relational databases, a table contains one or more ____________.
a. records

b. tables
c. fields
d. relations

Review Question 1.20
In relational databases, a record contains one or more ___________.
a. records
b. tables
c. fields
d. relations

## 1.7 Database System

The database system includes the DBMS software together with the data itself. Sometimes, the applications are also included. It defines the structure and the relationship between the database and the DBMS. It aims at the synchronization of the two for the purpose of better user experience.

It is important to differentiate the database system from a DBMS. A DBMS is the tool that is required for working with a database. But it is the database system that the business uses for day to day operations or decision making.

Review Question 1.21
A ______ is the tool that is required for working with a database.
a. DBMS
b. MBA
c. DBA
d. programming language

Review Question 1.22
The _____ includes the DBMS software together with the data itself. Sometimes, the applications are also included.
a. database system
b. database
c. system
d. RDBMS

## 1.8 Database Environment

Let's have a high-level view of what a database environment looks like:

The user works on the application program written in a programming language such as C# or Java. The application program, in turn, works with the DBMS, which can include SQL Server, or Oracle, by issuing SQL statements. And, the DBMS manipulates the database via metadata.

Think of the database as the stuffed animals in a claw machine. The player has no interaction with these stuffed animals unless if the claw, analogous to the application, selects a stuffed animal, analogous to a specific piece of data, for the user.

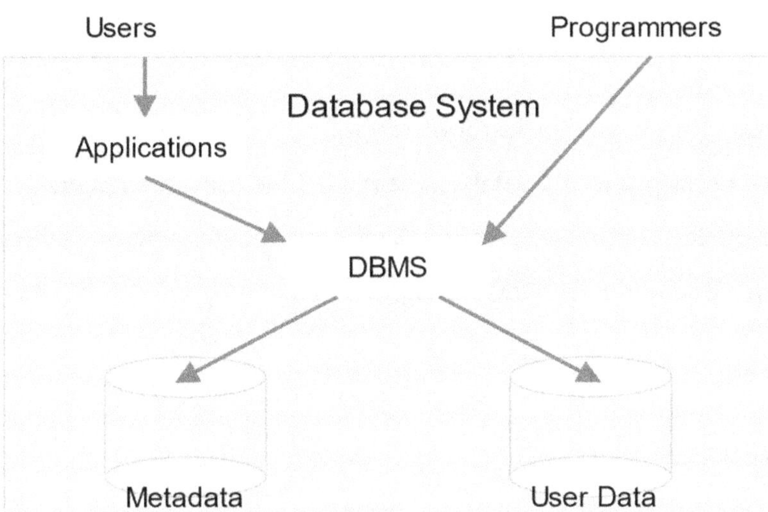


Figure 1.2 Database Environment

Users typically interact with databases through user-friendly interfaces, which abstract the complexity of database operations. On the other hand, programmers often engage directly with SQL to write intricate queries, optimize their performance, and develop applications that rely on databases.

For example, a business user opens the application program (e.g. a web browser) and enters a customer name, then clicks on a button to display the orders by this customer. The application program will communicate with the DBMS to find all orders of this customer by issuing SQL statements and send the data back to the application to be displayed. In this process, the DBMS depends on the metadata (e.g. table and field names) to find the user data.

Review Question 1.23
Which of the following is a typical sequence when a user works with a database?
a. user -> applications -> DBMS -> metadata (via user data)
b. user -> applications -> DBMS ->user data (via metadata)

c. user -> DBMS -> applications -> metadata (via user data)
d. user -> DBMS -> applications -> user data (via metadata)

Review Question 1.24
In relational database, the ______ usually works with DBMS directly by issuing ______ statements.
a. users, SQL
b. users, NOSQL
c. programmers, SQL
d. programmers, NOSQL

## 1.9 Schema

The term schema usually has two meanings. One is often used in textbooks to refer to the entire structure of the database. The database schema shows the description of a database. It is the blueprint of a database. It defines tables, fields, relationships, and other objects. Suppose, a simple database contains only two tables, a course table and an instructor table. The database schema diagram will look like this:

COURSE

| CourseID | CourseTitle | Location | InstructorID |
|---|---|---|---|

INSTRUCTOR

| InstructorID | FirstName | LastName | Office |
|---|---|---|---|

The database schema is different from the database state. The database state is a snapshot of all the data in the database at a particular moment in time.

| CourseID | CourseTitle | Location | InstructorID |
|---|---|---|---|
| 1001 | Introduction to Database | Classroom Building 201 | 101 |
| 1002 | Introduction to SQL | Classroom Building 202 | 101 |

| InstructorID | FirstName | LastName | Office |
|---|---|---|---|
| 101 | Lucy | Scott | CB401 |
| 102 | Linda | Smith | CB405 |

The schema is relatively stable while the state is constantly changing. When the database state changes, the schema must be respected.

The second meaning of schema is a container that holds one or more database objects, such as tables and views. Along this line of thinking, the smallest unit of meaningful data is a field. One or more fields are grouped into a record. One or more records are grouped into a table. One or more tables are grouped into a schema. And one or more schemas are grouped into a database. In the SQL sections of the book, you will see how schema is used under this meaning.

Review Question 1.25
What are the two meanings of schema in database concepts?
a. structure and command
b. structure and container
c. command and container
d. command and SQL

Review Question 1.26
When a database state changes, the database _______ must be respected.
a. designers
b. developers
c. containers
d. schemas

Review Question 1.27
A database schema is the _______ of the relational database.
a. art
b. blueprint
c. requirement
d. end result

Review Question 1.28
One meaning of schema is a container that holds one or more _____.
a. databases
b. fields
c. relationships
d. database objects, such as tables and views

## 1.10 A Brief History of Relational Database

Before the RDBMS era, the use of databases was too costly due to the complexity of database management, which in turn required a high level of training for programmers. Plus, a single program could only be tied to a single database, which made it difficult to have another program use the same data.

The relational database era began with the publication of a paper by E. F. Codd of IBM in 1970 on *Communications of the ACM*, titled "A Relational Model of Data for Large Shared Data Banks." In the paper, he proposed to build databases with tables of rows and columns.

The next major event came when D. D. Chamberlin and R. F. Boyce published in 1974 a paper called "SEQUEL: A Structured English Query Language" from *Proceedings of the 1974 ACM SIGFIDET Workshop on Data Description, Access and Control.*

The first commercial RDBMS was introduced by Oracle (then called Relational Software Inc.) in 1979, followed by many so-called RDBMS that were not really "relational". In 1985, Codd developed twelve rules (actually thirteen counting from 0 to 12) as a campaign to prevent the original relational database ideas from being diluted.

Today, relational databases are popular, although they are challenged all the time. The first major challenge was Object-Oriented Database Management Systems (OODBMS) in the 1980s, followed by Object-Relational Database Management Systems (ORDBMS) in the early 1990s. Next, the XML database came into existence in the year 2000. Currently, a new technique called NoSQL is becoming popular, although none of the challenges have taken the place of relational databases.

Review Question 1.29
Before the RDBMS era, the use of databases was very ___________.
a. easy
b. simple
c. costly
d. convenient

Review Question 1.30
Which of the following was a problem for using databases before the RDBMS era?
a. businesses were not interested in using databases
b. there was no digital data in business
c. it required highly trained programmers
d. not many businesses could afford the hardware

Review Question 1.31
Which of the following was a problem for using databases before the RDBMS era?
a. a single program could only be tied to a single database, which made it difficult to have another program use the same data
b. there was not much digital data in business
c. a database could not be connected to the internet

d. not many businesses could afford the hardware

Review Question 1.32
Who is usually considered the founder of the relational database?
a. the president of IBM
b. the president of Oracle
c. the president of Microsoft
d. Dr. E.F. Codd of IBM

Review Question 1.33
The first commercial RDBMS was introduced by ____________.
a. IBM
b. Microsoft
c. Oracle
d. Google

Review Question 1.34
Which of the following is not a modern, popular challenger of the relational database?
a. Object-Oriented Database Management System
b. Object-Relational Database Management System
c. XML database
d. hierarchical database

## 1.11 Install Microsoft Visual Studio Community 2026

Before you can practice the SQL sections of this book, you need Microsoft SQL Server installed on your local computer. Download and install Visual Studio Community 2026, ensuring you select the "Data storage and processing" workload during setup. If you miss this step, you can add it later using the Visual Studio Installer.

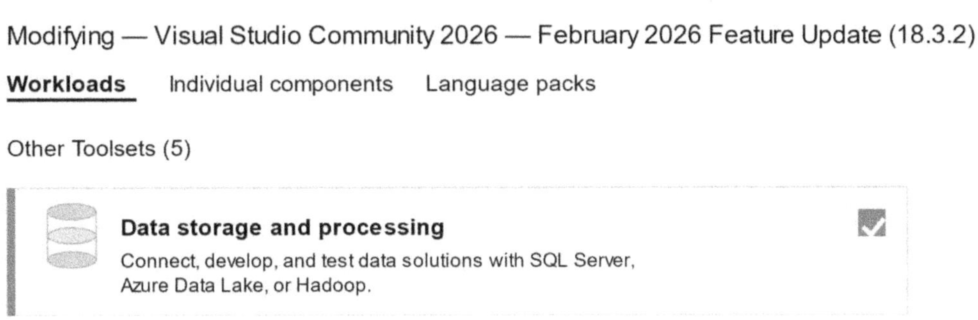


Figure 1.3 Install SQL Server Express (DBMS) on your local computer

## 1.12 Install Database for Practice:

After you install the DBMS, you will need a database, which you can download the script from goo.gl/ftzOxl

Follow the steps below to install the database:

Open Visual Studio. On the Visual Studio start window, click on "continue without code ->"

On the new window, click "Tools" on the menu, then "SQL Server", then "New Query"

A connect window will pop up as shown in Figure 1.4. Type "(LocalDB)\MSSQLLocalDB" into the Server Name field and click on the "connect" button.

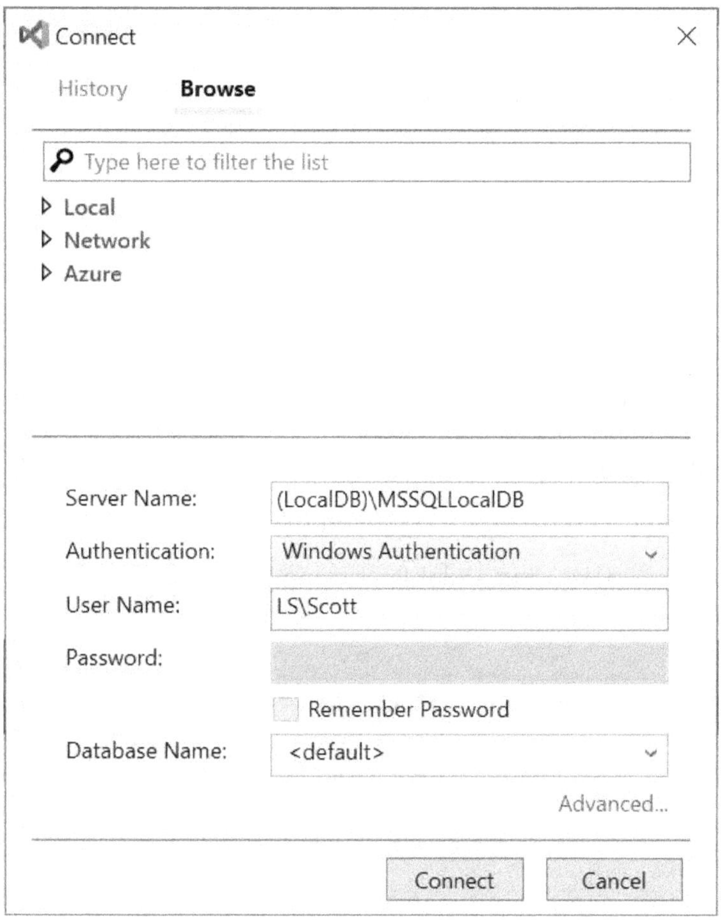


Figure 1.4 Connect to the SQL Server

An SQL Editor will be displayed. Copy the script from our website (goo.gl/ftzOxl) and paste it into the SQL editor. Click on the "Execute (Ctrl+Shift+E)" button in the top left to install the database into your local DBMS. Refer to Figure 1.5 for an example.

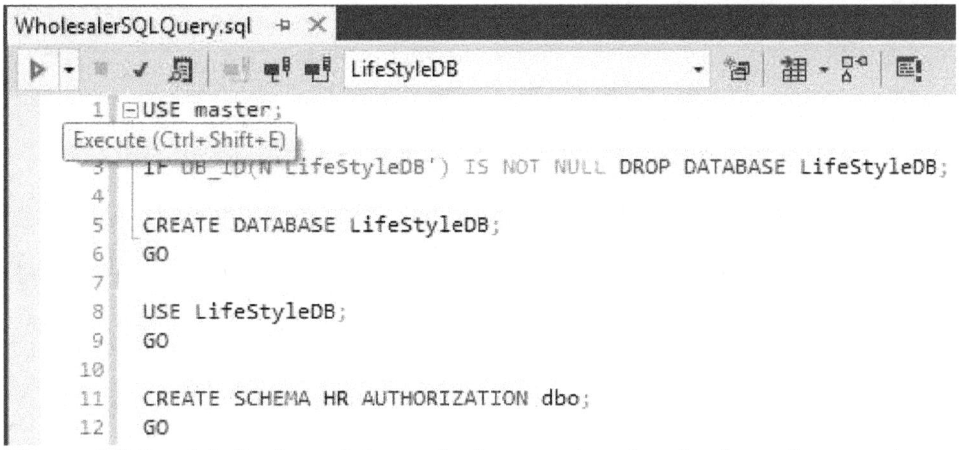

Figure 1.5 Partial display of the code for creating the database for practice

Next you will learn how to issue a simple SQL statement. You will follow these same steps when you practice SQL for the rest of the book.

Close the SQL editor. Do not close the Visual Studio. Then start a new SQL editor by following the steps listed below:

Click on “Tools” => “SQL Server” => “New Query” again to open a new SQL Editor. Enter (LocalDB)\MSSQLLocalDB again as shown in Figure 1.4. Type in the following line of SQL into the SQL editor:

```
SELECT * FROM Sales.Customers;
```

Change “Available Database” dropdown from the default “master” to “LifeStyleDB” and click on the “Execute” button to run the SQL statement. The result should look like Figure 1.6:

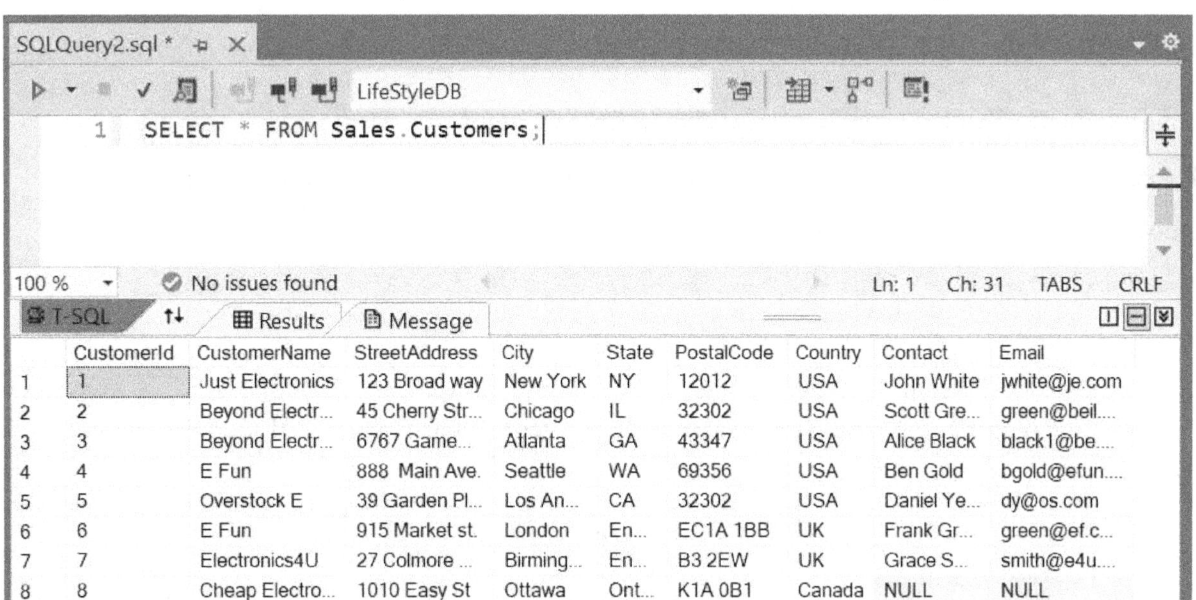

Figure 1.6 Windows for SQL statements and output

## 1.13 Types of SQL Statement

In this book, you will learn two types of SQL statements. The first one is Data Manipulation Language (DML). It will allow you to use the statements SELECT (strictly speaking, this is not a DML, we include it here for convenience,) INSERT, UPDATE, DELETE, and MERGE to manipulate data. These statements affect the data stored in the database.

SELECT will retrieve zero or many rows or columns from one or more tables in SQL Server. You will spend most of your time on this command in this book.

INSERT will add one or more new records to a table or a view in SQL Server.
UPDATE will change existing data in one or more columns in a table or a view.
DELETE will remove zero or many rows from a table or a view.
MERGE will perform insert, update, or delete operations on a target table based on the results of a source table.

The second type of SQL statement is Data Definition Language (DDL). It enables a database administrator to create database objects like schemas, tables, constraints, and stored procedures. You can either create these objects through a graphical user interface or by issuing DDL script statements. This book will only cover the latter. DDL statements define the data structure of the database. We will cover the following three DDL commands:

ALTER will change an existing object, such as by adding a field to a table.
CREATE will form a new SQL Server database object such as a table, view, or stored procedure.
DROP will remove an object from the database.

Review Question 1.35
Adding one or more new records to a table or a view in SQL Server is what type of SQL command?
a. DML
b. DDL
c. ADD
d. NoSQL

Review Question 1.36
Creating a new SQL Server database object such as a table, view, or stored procedure is related to what type of SQL command?
a. DML
b. DDL
c. NEW
d. NoSQL

## 1.14 Chapter Summary

In this chapter, you learned the basic concepts that are necessary to understand the database environment. The major concepts include, data, field, record, table, schema, and database. You also learned how to run SQL statements on SQL Server through Visual Studio Community Edition. This chapter ends with an introduction of different types of SQL commands that you will learn the details of in the rest of the book.

## 1.15 Discussion Questions

Discussion 1.1
Many people agree that the concepts of data and information are different, but use the terms interchangeably anyway. What is your opinion?

Discussion 1.2
Database focuses on the user data. Why does it also include the metadata?

Discussion 1.3
What's the difference between DBMS and database systems?

## 1.16 References

Chamberlin, D. D., & Boyce, R. F. (1974, May). SEQUEL: A structured English query language. In Proceedings of the 1974 ACM SIGFIDET (now SIGMOD) workshop on Data description, access and control (pp. 249-264).
Codd, E. F. (1970). A relational model of data for large shared data banks. Communications of the ACM, 13(6), 377-387.

## 1.17 Solutions to the Review Questions

1.1 A; 1.2 B; 1.3 C; 1.4 B; 1.5 B; 1.6 D; 1.7 A; 1.8 C; 1.9 A; 1.10 A; 1.11 B; 1.12 C; 1.13 C; 1.14 C; 1.15 D; 1.16 A; 1.17 C; 1.18 C; 1.19 A; 1.20 C; 1.21 A; 1.22 A; 1.23 B; 1.24 C; 1.25 B; 1.26 D; 1.27 B; 1.28 D; 1.29 C; 1.30 C; 1.31 A; 1.32 D; 1.33 C; 1.34 D; 1.35 A; 1.36 B;

# Chapter 2: Data Model and SQL SELECT Statement

## Chapter Learning Objectives

2.1 Extract business rules from business descriptions.
2.2 Identify entities from business rules.
2.3 Identify relationships from business rules.
2.4 Execute SQL SELECT ... FROM statement.

## 2.1 Data Model

We build models to better understand more complex real-world objects or events. A model is an abstraction of a mini-world. There are three characteristics of a good model: first, the model must map the mini-world object. For example, a 3D model for a ten-story building that has yet to be built must resemble a ten-story building, and not something irrelevant. Secondly, the model should be an abstract, meaning smaller details are forgone so the focus can be centered on the more important base details. For example, the 3D model may lack color in order to focus on structure. The purpose of the model is to function as a communication tool for stakeholders, and so some minor details may be dropped. The third characteristic is that the model must fit its purpose and intended audience. For example, the 3D model of the building would be intended for potential investors rather than engineers, who would need a blueprint for a model instead.

Figure 2.1 Different models are built for different purposes.

A data model is a specific form of a model, so all three characteristics of a model apply. However, a data model also has its own characteristics. A data model has to include constructs, which is the structure of the database, operations that work on these constructs, and constraints for the data.

Constructs are entities and the relationships among the entities. You will learn more about entities and relationships later in this chapter. Operations are specifications for how to insert or update a construct. You will learn the SQL statements concerning that throughout the book. Constraints are restrictions on data that allow the data to reflect the mini-world more accurately.

For example, suppose we are interested in a mini-world about teacher assignments (who teaches what course) in a small school. The constructs or the entities would be INSTRUCTOR and COURSE. The relationship would be "an instructor teaches multiple courses and each course is taught by exactly one instructor." The operations would be how to add a new course or update a course. A constraint can be that an instructor must teach at least three courses per semester.

In this book, we focus on one particular relational data model, called the Entity-Relationship (ER) model. An ER model contains three major concepts: entity, relationship, and attribute. These concepts will be introduced in this chapter and further explained throughout the following chapters.

Review Question 2.1
According to the author of the book, why do we build models?
a. to better understand more complex real-world objects or events.
b. to have a hobby for students.
c. because model building is a required skill for college students.
d. because model building is a good way to learn the concepts of databases.

Review Question 2.2
A model is ______ a mini-world.
a. similar to
b. an abstraction of
c. a detailed reflection of
d. an entity of

Review Question 2.3
Which of the following is a characteristic of a good model?
a. The model must map the mini-world objects.
b. The model should provide all the details of the mini-world.
c. The model should always be smaller than the real object.
d. The model should be fun to build.

Review Question 2.4
Which of the following is a characteristic of a good model?
a. The model is just a map for directions.
b. The model is just an abstract; certain details are purposely ignored.
c. The model should always be smaller than the real object.
d. The model should provide learning purposes.

Review Question 2.5
Which of the following is a characteristic of a good model?
a. The model is just a map for directions.
b. The model is just a detailed mini-world.
c. The model should always be smaller than the real object.
d. The model should fit its purpose.

Review Question 2.6
A data model has to include ______, which is the structure of the database, ______ that work on these constructs, and ______ for the data.
a. constructs, operations, constraints
b. structure, operations, constructs
c. operations, constraints, constructs
d. modules, packages, sources

Review Question 2.7
In a data model, the ______ are entities and the relationships among the entities.
a. constructs
b. operations
c. constraints
d. modules

Review Question 2.8
In a data model, the ______ are specifications for how to insert or update a construct.
a. constructs
b. operations
c. constraints
d. modules

Review Question 2.9
Which of the following is NOT a concept of ER model?
a. entity
b. relationship
c. attribute
d. blueprint

# 2.2 Business Description

Before modeling for a mini-world, you will receive a document known as a business description from the user you are modeling for. The business description contains information on what the user wants of the database, including expectations and specific criteria that must be met in order to receive the user's approval. The expectations serve as a roadmap for the endeavor of database development. The criteria serve as a user acceptance checklist.

In other textbooks, the process of documenting business description is often called systems analysis or gathering requirements. An important aspect of the business description is that it strictly contains what the business wants, not how to develop it. In other words, it is not a technology document. For example, a business document can say that they want to display an employee's age when the employee's data is displayed on a form, but the document should not say the age must be stored in a database table, because that's a technical decision for the database designer.

The business description is a communication tool, not a contract. So, if the database designers do not understand an object or event, they should ask. The designers should never tell the business manager how to run the business. The purpose of the document is that both sides, the business manager and the database designer, understand the requirements in the way they are intended to. It is a good idea that both sides learn the language used by the other. For example, the meaning of 'customer' may be pretty obvious to many people, but in a company that serves truck drivers for shipping, the term can be confusing. It can mean the truck drivers who use the company's service, or the customers who want the goods to be shipped. If the database designers are unsure what group in that scenario counts as the 'customer,' they need to ask.

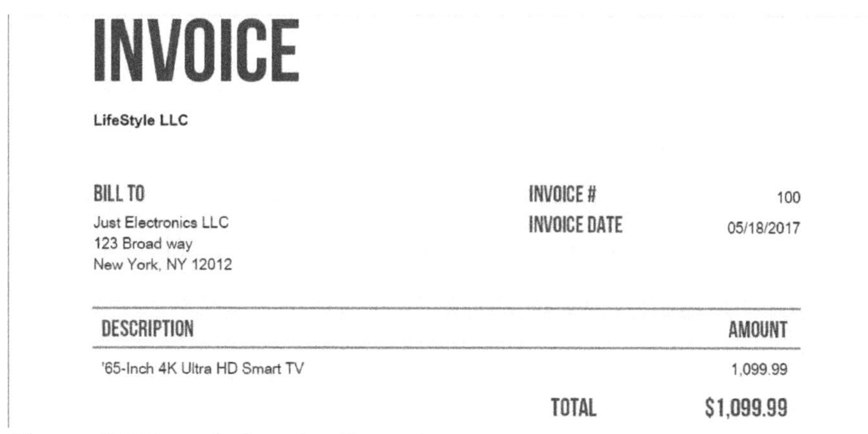
# INVOICE

LifeStyle LLC

BILL TO
Just Electronics LLC
123 Broad way
New York, NY 12012

INVOICE # 100
INVOICE DATE 05/18/2017

| DESCRIPTION | AMOUNT |
| --- | --- |
| '65-Inch 4K Ultra HD Smart TV | 1,099.99 |
| TOTAL | $1,099.99 |

Figure 2.2 Sample invoice from the customer

A business description is mainly based on an interview with the business users. However, do not forget to collect supporting documents, such as forms, reports, notes, and screenshots that may contain sample data. These documents are important because not many people can remember all items on a form or a report. By looking at the forms and reports, you can see what sort of data the user plans on keeping. Figure 2.2 shows a sample invoice from our fictitious company, LifeStyle LLC. From the invoice, you can see that customer name and address are musts for an invoice, so your database needs to be able to store those data.

Here are two examples of business description:

*Case Example 1*

ContinueEducation is a small online school. It offers courses that reflect current job market demands. It has small class sizes which allow good interaction between the students and the instructors.

A course is taught by just one instructor while an instructor can teach multiple courses. A student can register for zero or many courses. A course must have at least 5 students and at most 20 students. At the end of the semester, the student will receive a letter grade for the course he or she registered for. Students are allowed to register for the same course in different semesters.

*Case Example 2*

LifeStyle LLC is a small electronic wholesaler. Even though the company has a small number of employees, it has suppliers and customers all over the world, thanks to the internet.

The company needs an inventory management system which will help the managers determine the inventory at any time. For each product, the company wants to know the product name, supplier, and deliveries. Each product comes from just one supplier while one supplier can provide multiple products. A delivery should show the date, quantity, and unit price. A product can have zero or many deliveries while a delivery is about exactly one product.

The company wants to keep a sales record for each customer. The record includes the customer's name, the employee who served the customer for that order, the product, quantity, unit price, and the date the order was placed. An order may include more than one product.

Some employees supervise other employees. Each employee has just one boss. Certain employees have no boss (e.g. the CEO).

Review Question 2.10
According to the text, the first step in data modeling is ________.
a. writing the business rules
b. documenting the business description

c. identifying constructs
d. determining operations on objects

Review Question 2.11
The business description document usually includes ___________.
a. the detailed budget and the schedule for the new system
b. the list of tables in the new database
c. user expectations and criteria to measure success
d. the names of the tables in the new database

Review Question 2.12
The business description serves as a ___________.
a. contract between the customers and the developers
b. communication tool between the customers and the developers
c. strategic plan for the development team
d. measure of how well the development team is doing

Review Question 2.13
A business description in database design usually includes __________.
a. names from top management
b. no more than one page of paper
c. supporting documents
d. database name

## 2.3 Business Rules

Business rules are derived from the business description and focus on the policies and rules of the mini-world. Business rules should also serve as a communication tool. When writing these rules, you may ask the users for clarification or additional information on the business description.

For Case Example 1 (Section 2.2), sample business rules that focus on entities and their relationships are:

Each student can take up to six courses as a full-time student ("six courses" is not in the original description. It is added with the approval of the users).
Each course must have at least five students and no more than 20 students.
Each course is taught by exactly one instructor.
Each instructor can teach zero or several courses.
Each student will receive a letter grade for each course he or she took by the end of the semester.

For Case Example 2 (Section 2.2), sample business rules are:

A product is supplied by just one supplier.
Each supplier can provide several products.
A customer can place many orders.
Each order is from just one customer.
An order must be completed by an employee.

An employee can help complete multiple orders.
Each order must have at least one product.
Each product can appear in zero or many orders.
A manager can supervise multiple employees.
An employee can have only one manager.

You may notice that business rules begin with a singular noun such as "a product" or "each supplier". Can you identify the issues with the following business rules?

A customer can place many orders.

Many orders can be placed by a customer.

If you realize that these two rules are actually one, you get the correct answer.

You may also notice that most business rules are paired with two objects. Such as this:

A customer can place many orders.

Each order is from just one customer.

Here, the two objects are customer and order. The two rules show the relationship from each object to the other.

Review Question 2.14
The ____ is/are derived from the business description and focus on the policy and rules of the mini-world.
a. abstracts
b. business rules
c. business policies
d. mini-world

Review Question 2.15
Each business rule typically starts with ____.
a. singular verb
b. singular noun
c. plural verb
d. plural noun

Review Question 2.16
Most business rules are paired with _____.
a. one object
b. two objects
c. three objects
d. four objects

## 2.4 Entity

To develop a data model with Entity-Relationship Diagram (ERD), you need to identify the entities, relationships, and attributes from the business rules. In this section, you will learn how to identify the entities. An entity is a person, place, object, event, or concept in the mini-world about which you wish to develop the database. Read the business rules carefully. Focus on the nouns in the business rules that may be the entities.

For the Case Example 1 (Section 2.2), there are the following entities:

*STUDENT (persons who want to take courses)*

*COURSE (objects offered by ContinueEducation)*

*INSTRUCTOR (persons who teach courses)*

You may have a question. How about the staff? They are the employees who help the students register for courses. Shouldn't they be an entity? It all depends on if the customer (ContinueEducation) wants to keep records on assistant staff, such as whether a staff member helped a student. If yes, then include them.

What about the name of the school? Should we make it an entity? Usually no. We don't need to make a table (entity) just to store the school's name, which rarely changes and typically does not affect the areas of interest of the user. This is the mini-world, not an entity of the mini-world.

For Case Example 2 (Section 2.2), you may find the following entities:

*CUSTOMER (retailers that place orders from LifeStyle LLC)*

*EMPLOYEE (people who work for LifeStyle)*

*SUPPLIER (companies that supply products to LifeStyle)*

*PRODUCT (items LifeStyle buys and sells)*

*ORDER (transactions retailers conduct with LifeStyle)*

Do not feel bad if your list of entities is different from the above. For example, some of you may think that we should have a MANAGER entity. In fact, it's not wrong to have a MANAGER entity. We just decided that we won't add a MANAGER entity because we consider a manager an employee. Also, the MANAGER entity could get complicated when there are middle managers in the company (you would have to add another entity called MIDDLEMANAGER). In summary, do not think of the example as the final answer. The example just gives you a direction so that you can think in the right way.

Another question you may have is, what of "delivery?" If you think of delivery as an entity, you are correct. At this time, though, we will consider delivery as an attribute of PRODUCT.

Still another question is, how about "LifeStyle LLC?" It is the mini-world, not an entity.

The entities we identified above are all called entity types. The specific data within those entities are called entity instances. For example, in Case Example 1, 'EMPLOYEE' is considered an entity type, while a row of data for an employee, including name, date of birth, and so on, is considered an entity instance.

Note that sometimes the word 'entity' is used interchangeably with 'entity instance' and 'entity type.' Under most situations, it is not difficult to differentiate the meaning when we say 'entity'.

A weak entity type is a special type of entity. Sometimes you may find that one entity's existence will completely depend on another's. For example, in a company, if you keep data about each employee's dependents, the DEPENDENT can be a separate entity, but completely depends on the EMPLOYEE entity. So, the DEPENDENT entity is a weak entity. Another example can be a BUILDING entity and a CLASSROOM entity. A classroom completely depends on a building so we say that the CLASSROOM entity is a weak entity.

Entities are represented as a rectangle in ERD with the entity name inside the rectangle. A weak entity has dashed border line.

Figure 2.3 Regular entity and weak entity in ERD.

Review Question 2.17
A(n) ______________ is a person, place, object, event, or concept in the mini-world about which we wish to develop the database.
a. entity
b. relationship
c. attribute
d. table

Review Question 2.18
A single occurrence of an entity type is __________
a. a single entity

b. a sole entity
c. an attribute
d. an entity instance

Review Question 2.19
The _____ is an entity type whose existence completely depends on another entity.
a. database
b. object
c. strong entity
d. weak entity

Review Question 2.20
A department has several student clubs. The department needs a database to keep data about the clubs and students. Which of the following is NOT an entity in ERD?
a. department
b. club
c. student
d. department, club, and student are all entities

## 2.5 Relationship

A relationship is an association between the instances of one or more entity types. For example, Tom Smith (an instance of INSTRUCTOR) teaches Introduction to Computer Science (an instance of COURSE) is an example of a relationship between two entities, the INSTRUCTOR and COURSE entities. Larry Smith (an instance of INSTRUCTOR) teaches sports psychology (an instance of COURSE) is another example of a relationship between the INSTRUCTOR and the COURSE entities.

A relationship type is a collection of the same type of relationships between the same entities. The above two relationship examples are both the relationship type of "INSTRUCTOR teaches COURSE."
The number of entity types in a relationship is called the degree of relationship. If only one entity type participates in the relationship, the degree of relationship is unary. For example, a course (an instance) has a prerequisite of another course (an instance). Both courses are from the COURSE entity. The "a course may have one or more prerequisites" is a unary relationship.

Figure 2.4 Unary Relationship

Another example of a unary relationship is "a manager manages other employees." In this example, both managers and employees are from the EMPLOYEE entity. Still another example is "a person is married to another person." Both are from the PERSON entity. A unary relationship is also called a recursive relationship.

A binary relationship is a relationship between instances of two entity types. For example, "an instructor teaches zero or more courses" is a binary relationship. The instructor is an instance of the INSTRUCTOR entity type and the course is an instance of the COURSE entity type. Binary relationships are the most popular form of relationships. You will see many examples of binary relationships throughout the book.

Figure 2.5 Binary relationship

A ternary relationship is a relationship among instances of three entity types. For example, a supplier ships a product to a retailer. This is a relationship among the instances of three entity types: SUPPLIER, PRODUCT, and RETAILER.

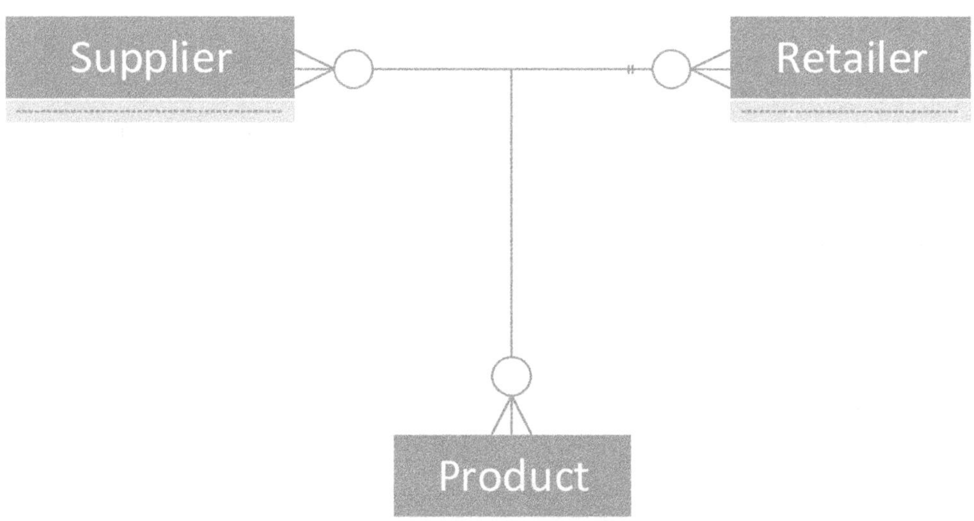


Figure 2.6 Ternary relationship.

The connectivity of a relationship explains the specifics of how two entity types are related. There are three major types of connectivity. The first is one-to-many (1:M). For example, if an instructor can teach many courses and each course can be taught by only one instructor, this is a one-to-many (1:M) relationship. Figure 2.5 shows a one-to-many connectivity between INSTRUCTOR and COURSE. As another example, a customer can place zero or many orders while an order comes from exactly one customer. The connectivity is again 1:M.

Figure 2.7 One-to-many (1:M) relationship.

The second type of connectivity is a many-to-many relationship (M:N). For example, a student can take zero or many courses and each course must have at least one student. This is a many-to-many (M:N) relationship.

Figure 2.8 Many-to-many (M:N) relationship.

The third type of connectivity is a one-to-one relationship (1:1). For example, each student has one computer lab account and each computer lab account belongs to at most one student is an example of a one-to-one (1:1) relationship.

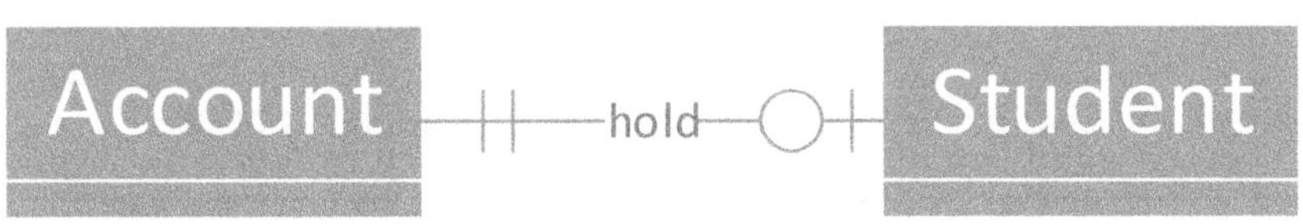


Figure 2.9 One-to-one (1:1) relationship.

If an entity can have zero instances in the relationship, it is optional. It is shown as a small circle in ERD. If an entity has one or many instances in the relationship, it is mandatory. It is shown as a short vertical line in ERD. For example, if each student can take zero or many courses, the course entity is optional. This is shown in Figure 2.8. If each course must have at least one student, the student entity is mandatory.

If you change the above business rule to "each student must take at least one course (mandatory) and each course must have at least one student (mandatory,)" the relationship will be mandatory on both sides as shown below:

Figure 2.10 Mandatory connectivity on both sides of a relationship.

The cardinality of a relationship is similar to the connectivity, but with more details. It shows the minimum and maximum entity instances possible in the relationship. Continue the above example. If each course is taught by exactly one instructor and each instructor can teach between zero to four courses, then on the INSTRUCTOR side, you add (1, 1). And you add (0, 4) on the COURSE side as shown:

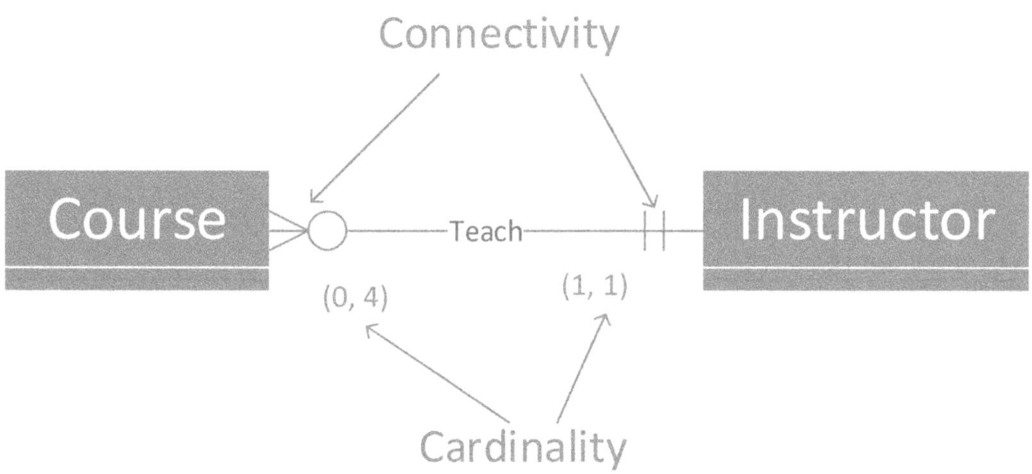


Figure 2.11 Connectivity vs. cardinality.

The cardinality added to which side can be a little bit confusing. While an instructor can teach between 0 and 4 courses, the cardinality is added to the COURSE side. Such notation makes it easy to read the relationship as "Each instructor can teach zero or up to four courses". If there's no upper limit, you can use the letter N to indicate it. For example, if an instructor can teach as many courses as he or she likes, the cardinality would be (0, N).

Knowing the cardinality is very useful for application software programmers. Cardinality cannot be implemented at the table level. As a database developer, you may write triggers to handle it (a topic which will be covered in our next book).

Business rules and connectivity must match. Each business rule shows one side of the connectivity. We recommend two business rules for each relationship. The following example shows 16 possible cases between Instructor and Course entities. The purpose is for you to see the match between rules and ERD, not which university has the rules.

| | |
|---|---|
| Case 1:<br>Each course is taught by at most one instructor.<br>Each instructor teaches at most one course. | 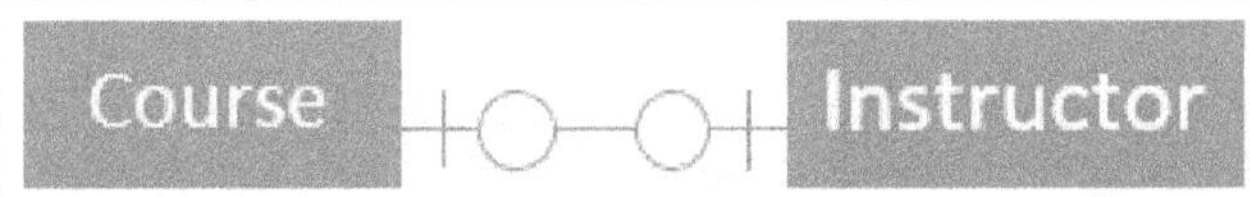 |
| Case 2:<br>Each course is taught by at most one instructor.<br>Each instructor teaches exactly one course. | 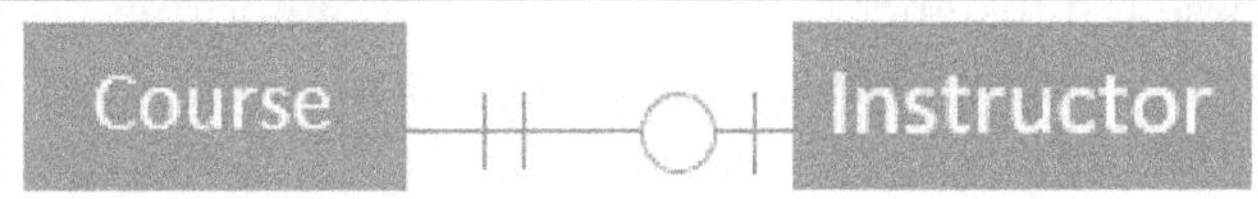 |
| Case 3:<br>Each course is taught by at most one instructor.<br>Each instructor teaches zero or more courses. | 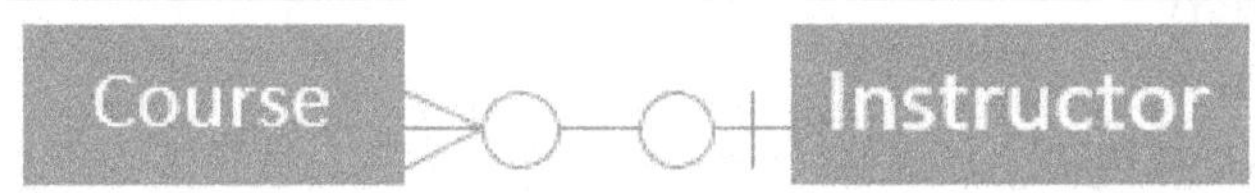 |
| Case 4:<br>Each course is taught by at most one instructor.<br>Each instructor teaches at least one course. | 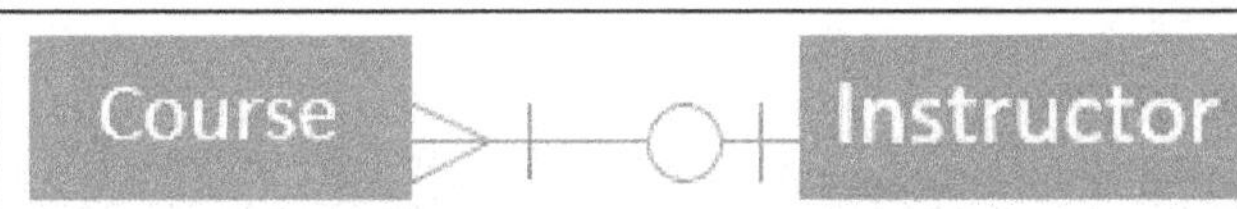 |
| Case 5:<br>Each course is taught by exactly one instructor.<br>Each instructor teaches at most one course. | 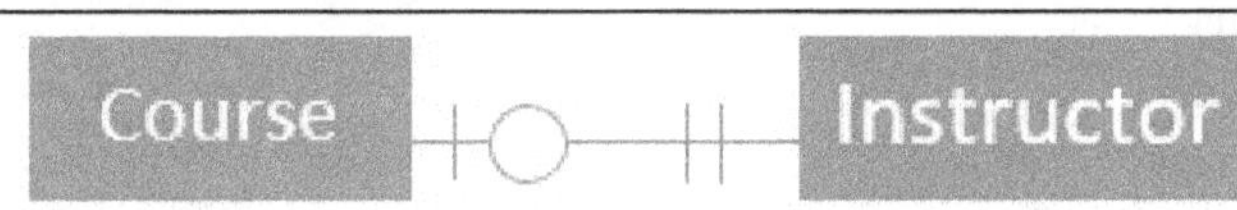 |
| Case 6:<br>Each course is taught by exactly one instructor.<br>Each instructor teaches exactly one course. | 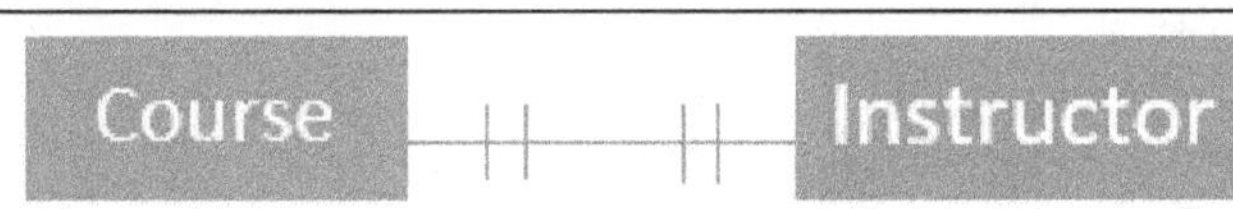 |
| Case 7:<br>Each course is taught by exactly one instructor.<br>Each instructor teaches zero or more courses. | 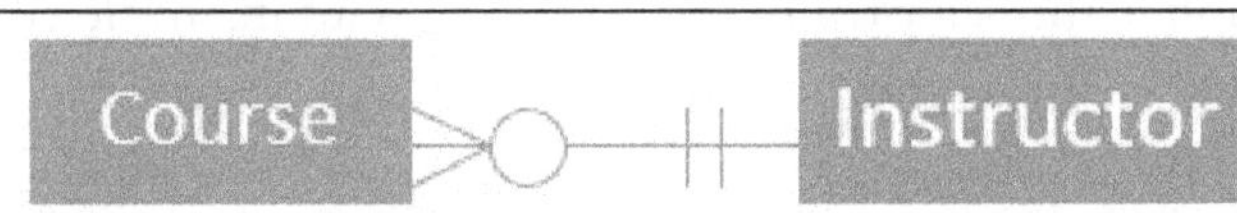 |
| Case 8:<br>Each course is taught by exactly one instructor.<br>Each instructor teaches at least one course. | 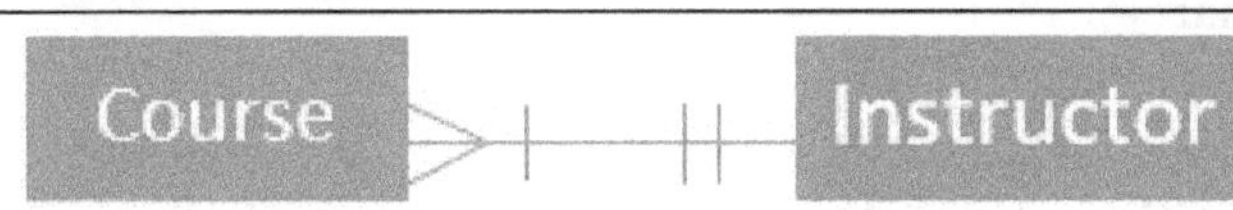 |
| Case 9:<br>Each course is taught by zero or more instructors.<br>Each instructor teaches at most one course. | 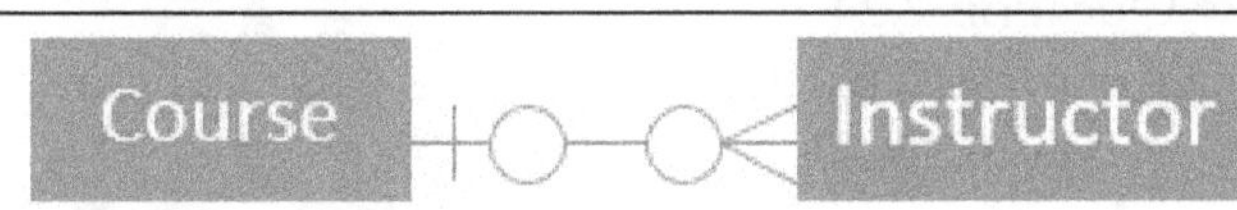 |
| Case 10:<br>Each course is taught by zero or more instructors.<br>Each instructor teaches exactly one course. | 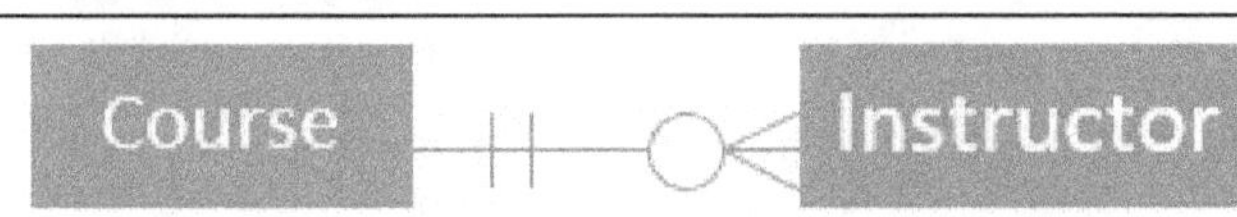 |
| Case 11:<br>Each course is taught by zero or more instructors.<br>Each instructor teaches zero or more courses. | 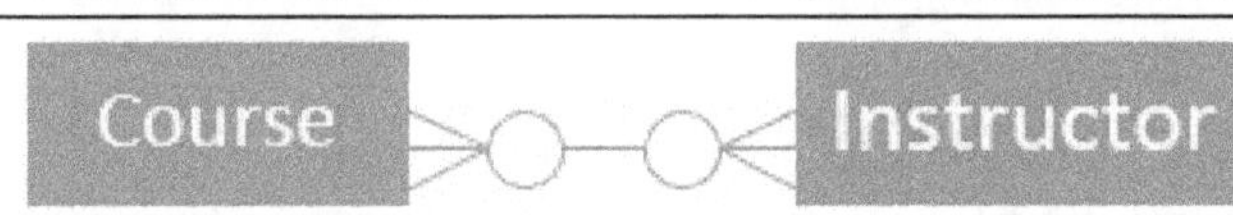 |
| Case 12:<br>Each course is taught by zero or more instructors.<br>Each instructor teaches at least one course. | 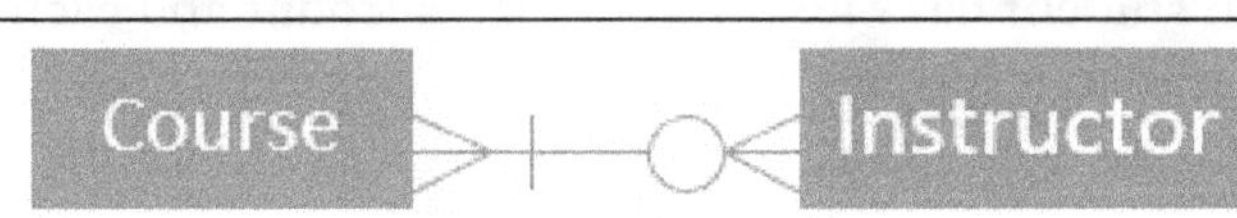 |

| Case 13:<br>Each course is taught by at least one instructor.<br>Each instructor teaches at most one course. |  |
|---|---|
| Case 14:<br>Each course is taught by at least one instructor.<br>Each instructor teaches exactly one course. |  |
| Case 15:<br>Each course is taught by at least one instructor.<br>Each instructor teaches zero or more courses. |  |
| Case 16:<br>Each course is taught by at least one instructor.<br>Each instructor teaches at least one course. |  |

Review Question 2.21
A course (an instance) has a prerequisite of another course (an instance). Both courses are from the COURSE entity. The "a course may have one or more prerequisites" is a ______ relationship.
a. unary
b. binary
c. ternary
d. hierarchical

Review Question 2.22
An example of a ______ relationship is "an instructor teaches zero or more courses."
a. unary
b. binary
c. ternary
d. hierarchical

Review Question 2.23
A supplier ships a product to a retailer is an example of ________ relationship.
a. unary
b. binary
c. ternary
d. hierarchical

Review Question 2.24
If an instructor can teach many courses and each course can be taught by only one instructor, this is a ______ relationship.
a. 1:1
b. 1:M
c. M:N
d. I:C

Review Question 2.25
If each student has one computer lab account and each computer lab account belongs to at most one student is an example of a ______ relationship.
a. 1:1
b. 1:M

c. M:N
d. I:C

Review Question 2.26
If an entity can have zero instances in the relationship, it is ______. It is shown as ______ in ERD.
a. 1:M, vertical line
b. mandatory, vertical line
c. zero, a small circle
d. optional, a small circle

Review Question 2.27
If an entity has one or many instances in the relationship, it is ______. It is shown as ______ in ERD.
a. 1:M, a short vertical line
b. mandatory, a short vertical line
c. zero, a small circle
d. optional, a small circle

Review Question 2.28
How many entity types are in the relationship is called the __________ of relationship. Examples include unary, binary, or ternary.
a. degree
b. connectivity
c. cardinality
d. optional/mandatory

Review Question 2.29
The _________ of a relationship is about how many instances of an entity are associated with each instance of the participating entity. For example, 1:1, 1:M, M:N.
a. degree
b. connectivity
c. cardinality
d. optional/mandatory

Review Question 2.30
The ________ of a relationship shows the minimum and maximum entity instances possible in the relationship.
a. degree
b. connectivity
c. cardinality
d. optional/mandatory

Review Question 2.31
A department has several student clubs. A student can join any number of clubs. A club must have at least three students. The department needs a database to keep data about the clubs and students. What is the connectivity of the relationship between the Club and Student entities in ERD?
a. 1:1
b. 1:M
c. M:1
d. M:N

## 2.6 Attribute

Attributes are the properties used to describe an entity or a relationship. For example, an INSTRUCTOR entity may have an instructor ID, First name, and last name. The instructor ID, first name, and last name are called attributes of the INSTRUCTOR entity. A relationship such as "a STUDENT takes a COURSE" can have an attribute called final grade. The final grade cannot be an attribute for the STUDENT entity because a student can take many courses. The final grade cannot be an attribute for the COURSE entity because a course can have many students.

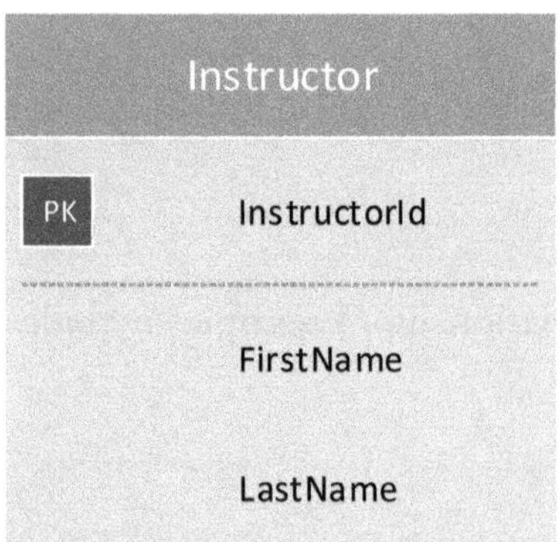

Figure 2.12 The attributes of an entity.

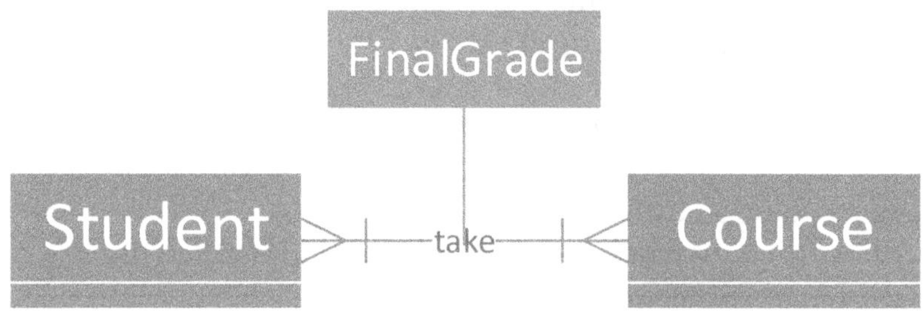

Figure 2.13 The attribute of a relationship.

Each attribute has a value set (data type) associated with it. For example, an instructor ID may be an integer, and the first name and last name should be a string of letters.

Review Question 2.32
A relationship such as "a STUDENT takes a COURSE" can have a(n) ______ called final grade.
a. attribute
b. entity
c. exam
d. time

Review Question 2.33
The ___________ are the properties used to describe an entity or a relationship. For example, an INSTRUCTOR entity may include the instructor ID, first name, and last name.
a. attributes
b. entities
c. relations
d. domains

## 2.7 Abstract Levels of Data Model

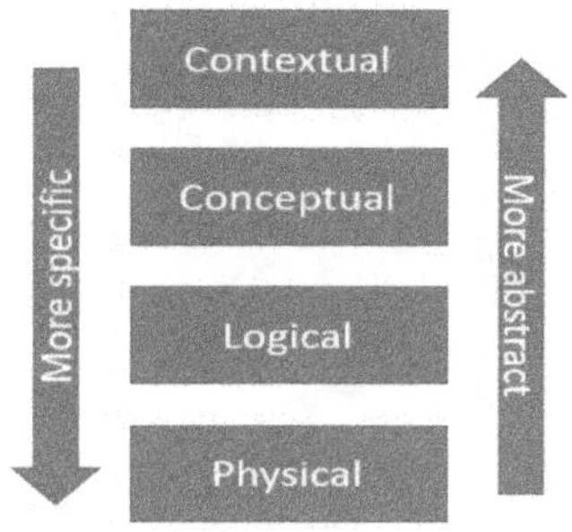


Figure 2.14 Four levels of abstract.

Data models can have different levels of abstraction, which means how much detail we need for the data. Different levels of abstraction can serve different purposes. Business users usually just need a conceptual and logical model, and don't need a physical model, which is less abstract than a conceptual or logical model. A conceptual model will help the users and developers to define the scope of the project. A logical model will help users determine if all data needed are in the model and if no extra data is included in the model. There is no clear line between the levels of abstraction. For example, some books will place both conceptual and logical models on the same level of abstraction, while others won't. All models serve the purpose of communication between the developers and the customers. This book will introduce four levels of abstraction: contextual, conceptual, logical, and physical.

The contextual level brings together all business stakeholders with their vision and strategy and their resulting priorities into a set of principles. The model is mainly used during requirement collection. It focuses on why we need to model the data; e.g. student records must be accurate and kept for a long time. This book won't further discuss this level because it is typically covered in systems analysis books.

The conceptual level focuses on data requirements with entities and relationships. It answers 'what' questions, such as 'what are the entities/objects you are going to model? What are the relationships between the entities? What is a course? (Do two sections of the same course count as one or two courses?)' The conceptual model includes all the entities and their relationships.

Based on case example 1 described earlier in the chapter (Section 2.2), you may develop a conceptual model that looks like this:

Figure 2.15 A conceptual model of case example 2 (Section 2.2).

At the logical level, you start to add attributes to each entity and relationship. Determine attribute domains. Decide which attribute(s) can uniquely identify each record. Resolve any many to many relationships, check integrity constraints, convert entities into relations, and finally normalize the relations. More about attributes, keys, and constraints will be explained in Chapter 3, so do not worry if you don't understand the terms used in this paragraph. A logical model of case example 1 (Section 2.2) may look like this:

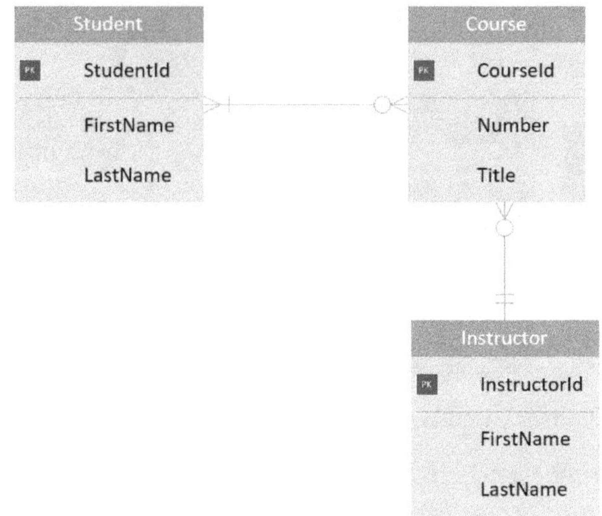


Figure 2.16 A logical model of case example 1.

At the physical level, you first select the DBMS. In this book, you will use SQL Server. Then, add the data type for each field. At this point you may perform denormalization. These topics will be covered in later chapters. You may note that a new entity called enrollment is added in the above model. We will explain this in Chapter 5.

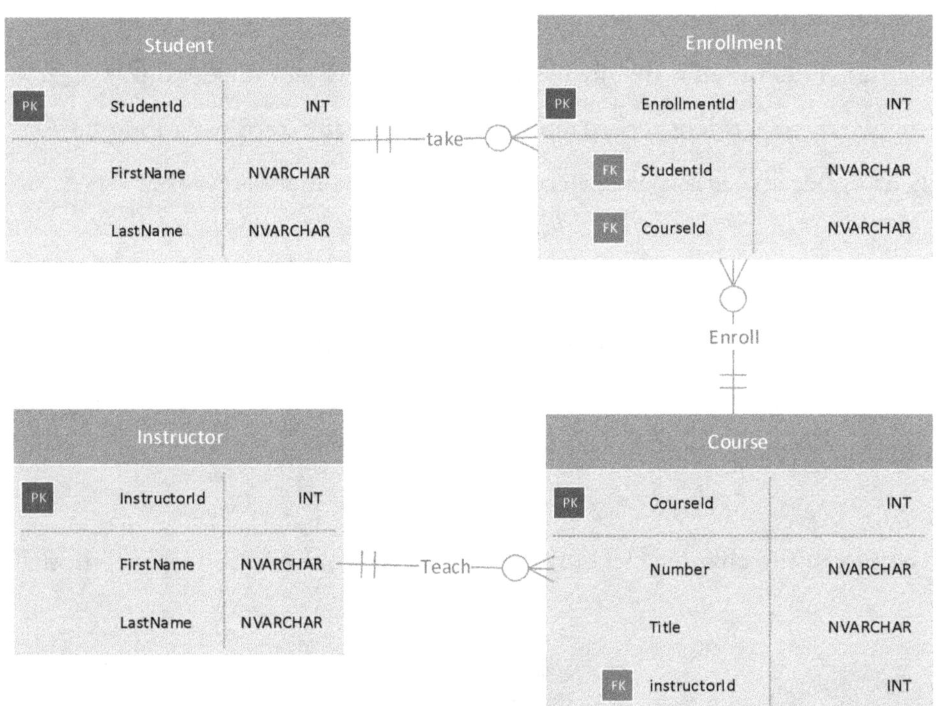


Figure 2.17 A physical model of case example 1.

Review Question 2.34
Different levels of abstraction can serve different purposes. Business users usually just need a ______ and ______ model, and don't need a ______ model.
a. contextual, conceptual, logical

b. conceptual, logical, physical
c. logical, physical, contextual
d. physical, contextual, conceptual

Review Question 2.35
A ______ model will help the users and developers to define the scope of the project.
a. contextual
b. conceptual
c. logical
d. physical

Review Question 2.36
A ______ model will help users determine if all data needed are in the model and if no extra data is included in the model.
a. contextual
b. conceptual
c. logical
d. physical

Review Question 2.37
All data models serve the purpose of ______.
a. communication between the developers and the customers
b. having a solid foundation for a robust database design
c. complete requirements from the business users
d. simple coding for the application developers

Review Question 2.38
A model at the _____________ level focuses on data requirements with entities and relationships, answering "what" questions, such as 'what are the entities/objects you are going to model?'
a. contextual
b. conceptual
c. logical
d. physical

Review Question 2.39
In a model at the _____________ level, you first select the DBMS. In this book, you will use SQL Server. Then, add the data type for each field.
a. contextual
b. conceptual
c. logical
d. physical

## 2.8 Conceptual Model

This chapter focuses on the conceptual model of database design. In Section 2.7, you learned that conceptual models have a high level of abstraction. It focuses on the entities and their relationships. Details such as attributes are on purposely omitted to ensure the relationships between entities are correctly modeled from the business description and business rules.

*Conceptual model (ERD) Example 1:*

The Career Center of Jefferson County offers in-demand IT skill courses to adult learners. They want to keep records of students and courses. Write possible business rules and construct conceptual ERD.

Business rules:

1. A student can take zero or many courses.
2. A course must have at least one student.

Conceptual ERD:

You may notice that the career center is not an entity. It is the mini-world.

*Conceptual model (ERD) Example 2:*

The Career Center of Jefferson County offers in-demand IT skill courses to adult learners. They want to keep records of students, instructors, and courses. Write possible business rules and construct conceptual ERD.

Business rules:

1. A student can take zero or many courses.
2. A course must have at least one student.
3. An instructor can teach zero or many courses
4. A course has exactly one instructor.

Conceptual ERD:

*Conceptual model (ERD) Example 3:*

*The* Career Center of Jefferson County offers in-demand IT skill courses to adult learners. They want to keep records of students, instructors, courses, and classrooms. Write possible business rules and construct conceptual ERD.

Business rules:

1. A student can take zero or many courses.
2. A course must have at least one student.
3. An instructor can teach zero or many courses
4. A course has exactly one instructor.
5. A course is assigned to exactly one classroom.
6. A classroom can be assigned to zero or many courses.

Conceptual ERD:

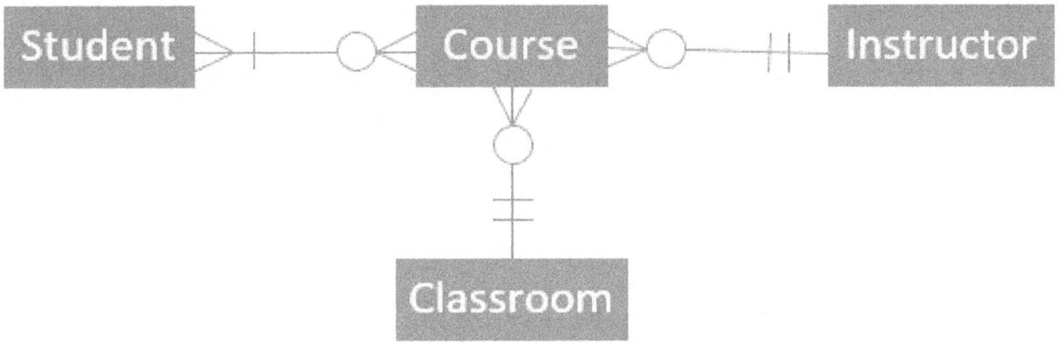


*Conceptual model (ERD) Example 4:*

Based on the business description and business rules of Case Example 2 (Section 2.2), write possible business rules and construct conceptual ERD.

Business Rules:

An employee may manage zero or many employees.
An employee may be managed by zero or one boss/employee.
An employee can complete zero or many orders.
An order must be completed by exactly one employee.
A customer can place zero or many orders.
An order must come from exactly one customer.
An order contains at least one product.
A product can appear in zero or many orders.
A product is provided by exactly one supplier.
A supplier may provide zero or many products.

Conceptual ERD:

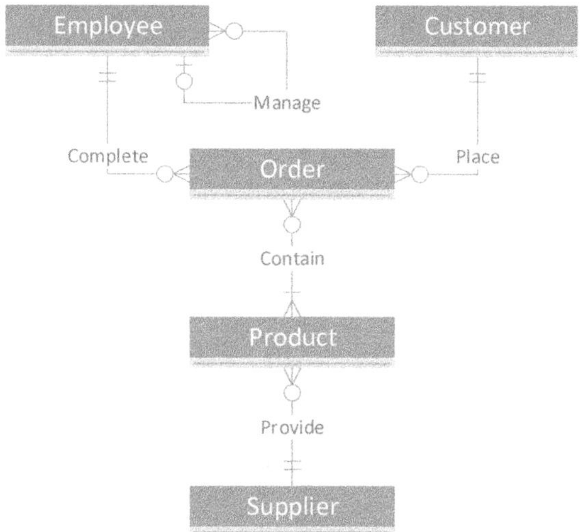

Figure 2.18 Conceptual model for case example 2.

You use this conceptual ERD and the business rules to communicate with the business users, and see whether they agree with you.

## 2.9 SQL SELECT... FROM Statement

To retrieve data from one or more tables in a database, you can use SELECT ... FROM statement. For example: SELECT CustomerName, Contact FROM Sales.Customers allows you to retrieve data from the CustomerName and Contact columns of the Customers table in the Sales schema. Where you retrieve the data from should be written 'schema'.'table name'. In this case, the Customers table is in the Sales schema.

In the last chapter, you tested the database you installed with the following SQL command:

```
SELECT * FROM Sales.Customers;
```

This is an SQL SELECT statement that tells the DBMS (SQL Server in our case) to return all rows and all columns from the customers table.

The SQL SELECT statement allows you to select one or more columns of all rows from a table. The syntax for a simple SELECT statement is:

```
SELECT ColumnName1, ColumnName2, ...
FROM TableName;
```

SQL statements are case insensitive. However, in this book, we follow the following convention:

SQL keywords are all caps, such as SELECT, FROM.

Table names and column names are capitalized on the first letter of each word, such as Customers, CompanyName.

Note: when working with the examples and exercises, you need to take a look at the list of tables in Appendix B of this book to familiarize yourself with the table structure and the data.

To practice SQL statements, you must open the editor and connect it to the LifeStyleDB as you did in Chapter 1.

SQL Example 2.1

Display all customers' names from the Customers table.

SQL Example 2.1 Analysis

Go to Appendix B and find the Customers table. The column name is CustomerName, the table name is Customers, and the schema name is Sales, so you have all input for the SELECT statement.

SQL Example 2.1 statement

```
SELECT CustomerName
FROM Sales.Customers;
```

SQL Example 2.1 Output (Type the above two lines in the editor, highlight both lines, and click on the "execute" button on the top left side to display the following in the output):

| | CustomerName |
|---|---|
| 1 | Just Electronics |
| 2 | Beyond Electronics |
| 3 | Beyond Electronics |
| 4 | E Fun |
| 5 | Overstock E |
| 6 | E Fun |
| 7 | Electronics4U |
| 8 | Cheap Electronics |

SQL Example 2.2

Display all customers' names and email addresses from the Customers table.

SQL Example 2.2 Analysis

According to Appendix B, the CustomerName and Email are in the Sales.Customers table. Just add one column to the statement in Example 2.1. Remember to add a comma between column names.

SQL Example 2.2 statement

```
SELECT CustomerName, Email
FROM Sales.Customers;
```

SQL Example 2.2 Output:

| | CustomerName | Email |
|---|---|---|
| 1 | Just Electronics | jwhite@je.com |
| 2 | Beyond Electronics | green@beil.com |
| 3 | Beyond Electronics | black1@be.com |
| 4 | E Fun | bgold@efun.com |
| 5 | Overstock E | dy@os.com |
| 6 | E Fun | green@ef.com |
| 7 | Electronics4U | smith@e4u.com |
| 8 | Cheap Electronics | NULL |

SQL Example 2.3

Display all employee's first names, last names, and phone numbers from the Employees table.

SQL Example 2.3 Analysis

According to Appendix B, the column names are FirstName, LastName, and Phone and the table name is HR.Employees, so you have all input for the SELECT statement.

SQL Example 2.3 statement

```
SELECT FirstName, LastName, Phone
FROM HR.Employees;
```

SQL Example 2.3 Output:

| | FirstName | LastName | Phone |
|---|---|---|---|
| 1 | Alex | Hall | (434) 290-3322 |
| 2 | Dianne | Hart | (434) 290-1122 |
| 3 | Maria | Law | (434) 531-5673 |
| 4 | Alice | Law | (434) 531-1010 |
| 5 | Black | Hart | (434) 531-1034 |
| 6 | Christina | Robinson | NULL |
| 7 | Nicholas | Pinkston | NULL |

SQL Example 2.4

Display all data from the suppliers table.

SQL Example 2.4 Analysis

For column names, you can either go to Appendix B to write down all column names or just use the wildcard, *, to represent all columns. The table name is Suppliers and the schema is Purchasing, so you have all input for the SELECT statement.

SQL Example 2.4 statement

```
SELECT *
FROM Purchasing.Suppliers;
```

SQL Example 2.4 Output:

| | SupplierId | SupplierName | StreetAddress | City | State | PostalCode | Country |
|---|---|---|---|---|---|---|---|
| 1 | 1 | Pine Apple | 1 Pine Apple St. | Idanha | CA | 87201 | USA |
| 2 | 2 | IMB | 123 International Blvd | Los Angeles | CA | 89202 | USA |
| 3 | 3 | Lonovo | 33 Beijin Square | Beijing | Beijing | 100201 | China |
| 4 | 4 | Samsong | 1 Electronics Road | Yeongtong | Suwon | 30174 | South Korea |
| 5 | 5 | Canan | 12 Camera St | Ota | Tokyo | 100-0121 | Japan |

Review Question 2.40
An SQL SELECT… FROM statement allows you to select ______ from a table.
a. one or more rows
b. one or more columns
c. one or more rows or columns
d. any number of cells

Review Question 2.41
What does the following SQL statement do?

```
SELECT FirstName, LastName, GPA
FROM Admission.Student;
```

a. Retrieve all students' first names, last names, and G.P.As from the student table.
b. Select only the first student's first name, last name, and G.P.A from the student table.
c. Retrieve all students who provided their first name, last name, and G.P.A.
d. Select all students' first names, last names, and G.P.As from the admission table.

Review Question 2.42
The * in the SELECT clause of an SQL statement indicates selecting ______.
a. all rows
b. all columns

c. all rows with the * in them
d. all columns with the * in them

## 2.10 DISTINCT Keyword

Sometimes, the SQL command result may contain duplicated rows. For example, if you want to know all the different first names for students at a university, you are sure to see many duplications. To remove all duplications, just add the DISTINCT keyword in the SELECT clause as shown in example 2.5.

SQL Example 2.5

Display all suppliers who have products in LifeStyle's products table. List the product's supplier ID.

SQL Example 2.5 Analysis

Supplier ID appears in two tables. One is the product table and the other is the suppliers table. Since not all suppliers provide a product for LifeStyle, only the products table should be used. The SupplierID is a column in the Products table, so we have all the input to issue the SELECT statement. However, if you execute the following statement:

```
SELECT SupplierId
FROM Purchasing.Products;
```

You will get the following output:

| SupplierId |
|---|
| 4 |
| 4 |
| 3 |
| 5 |
| 2 |
| 2 |
| 4 |
| 2 |
| 5 |

We don't want to see the supplier ID more than once. To remove all duplicate rows, you can use the DISTINCT keyword in SQL as shown in the following statement.

SQL Example 2.5 statement

```
SELECT DISTINCT SupplierId
FROM Purchasing.Products;
```

SQL Example 2.5 Output:

| | SupplierId |
|---|---|
| 1 | 2 |
| 2 | 3 |
| 3 | 4 |
| 4 | 5 |

Review Question 2.43
What does the following SQL statement do?

```
SELECT DISTINCT FirstName, LastName
FROM Admission.Student;
```

a. Retrieve all students' first names and last names.
b. Retrieve all students' first names and last names without duplicates for first names.
c. Retrieve all students' first names and last names without duplicates for both first and last names.
d. Retrieve all students' first names and last names without duplicates for the first name, but duplications may appear for the last name.

## 2.11 ORDER BY Clause

When a DBMS generates output, there is no guarantee that the result rows will appear in a certain order. You can use the ORDER BY clause to sort results in the column(s) you specified. You can decide whether the results are presented as ascending (default) or descending (for example, in a list of names, whether you prefer it to be alphabetical, or reverse alphabetical.) You may sort multiple columns. In that case, the sorting would be first decided by the first column. If the first column is unable to decide which of two pieces of data should go first, it sorts according to the second column, and so on. In the case of sorting names in alphabetical order, for example, two people could have the same last name (the first column,) and so the ORDER BY clause will move on to the next column, first names, to decide which result goes first.

SQL Example 2.6

Display all employees' first names, last names, and date of births. Sort them from the oldest to the youngest.

SQL Example 2.6 Analysis

By now, it should be easy for you to display all employees' first names, last names, and date of births. The new stuff is the ORDER BY clause which will sort the result in ascending order by default, which is from the oldest to the youngest in this case. This may sound odd, but you sort by the date of birth, not age.

SQL Example 2.6 statement

```
SELECT FirstName, LastName, BirthDate
```

```
FROM HR.Employees
ORDER BY BirthDate;
```

SQL Example 2.6 Output:

| | FirstName | LastName | BirthDate |
|---|---|---|---|
| 1 | Nicholas | Pinkston | 1977-10-05 |
| 2 | Christina | Robinson | 1978-07-13 |
| 3 | Dianne | Hart | 1978-12-03 |
| 4 | Black | Hart | 1982-11-09 |
| 5 | Maria | Law | 1988-07-13 |
| 6 | Alice | Law | 1988-12-13 |
| 7 | Alex | Hall | 1990-02-03 |

SQL Example 2.7

Display all employees' first names, last names, and date of births. Sort them from the youngest to the oldest.

SQL Example 2.7 Analysis

This is almost the same as Example 2.6. You just need to reverse the order from the ascending to descending by adding the keyword DESC.

SQL Example 2.7 statement

```
SELECT FirstName, LastName, BirthDate
FROM HR.Employees
ORDER BY BirthDate DESC;
```

SQL Example 2.7 Output:

| | FirstName | LastName | BirthDate |
|---|---|---|---|
| 1 | Alex | Hall | 1990-02-03 |
| 2 | Alice | Law | 1988-12-13 |
| 3 | Maria | Law | 1988-07-13 |
| 4 | Black | Hart | 1982-11-09 |
| 5 | Dianne | Hart | 1978-12-03 |
| 6 | Christina | Robinson | 1978-07-13 |
| 7 | Nicholas | Pinkston | 1977-10-05 |

SQL Example 2.8

Display all employees' first names and last names. Sort them by how much time he or she has worked for the company, from the longest to the shortest.

SQL Example 2.8 Analysis

The purpose of this example is to demonstrate that you can sort a column that does not appear in the SELECT column list. In the example, you do not list the hire date, but use it in the ORDER BY clause.

SQL Example 2.8 statement

```
SELECT FirstName, LastName
FROM HR.Employees
ORDER BY HireDate;
```

SQL Example 2.8 Output:

| | FirstName | LastName |
|---|---|---|
| 1 | Dianne | Hart |
| 2 | Alice | Law |
| 3 | Maria | Law |
| 4 | Nicholas | Pinkston |
| 5 | Christina | Robinson |
| 6 | Black | Hart |
| 7 | Alex | Hall |

Review Question 2.44
When the DBMS generates output, there is no guarantee that the result rows will appear in a certain order. You can use ________ clause to fix the problem.
a. ORDER
b. SORT
c. ORDER BY
d. SORT BY

## 2.12 The TOP Keyword

The TOP keyword will select the first however many pieces of data you wish to obtain on the list. TOP is almost always used with an ORDER BY clause so that the results are meaningful, since the ORDER BY clause will sort the list into a meaningful order.

SQL Example 2.9

Display the first two employees who worked for the company and who are still employed now. Show their first names and last names.

SQL Example 2.9 Analysis

This solution needs to use the keyword TOP to limit the results. You should sort the list by hire date before picking the first 2 rows. You can also add PERCENT after the number 2 to limit the number to two percent instead of 2 units.

SQL Example 2.9 statement

```
SELECT TOP 2 FirstName, LastName
FROM HR.Employees
ORDER BY HireDate;
```

SQL Example 2.9 Output:

| | FirstName | LastName |
|---|---|---|
| 1 | Dianne | Hart |
| 2 | Alice | Law |

SQL Example 2.10

Display all employees' first names and last names. Sort the results by last name. In the case if two or more last names are the same, sort by the first name.

SQL Example 2.10 Analysis

You just need to add the secondary sort column to the ORDER BY clause. When more than one column is in the ORDER BY clause, they should be separated by a comma.

SQL Example 2.10 statement

```
SELECT firstName, LastName
FROM HR.Employees
ORDER BY LastName, FirstName;
```

SQL Example 2.10 Output:

| | FirstName | LastName |
|---|---|---|
| 1 | Alex | Hall |
| 2 | Black | Hart |
| 3 | Dianne | Hart |
| 4 | Alice | Law |
| 5 | Maria | Law |
| 6 | Nicholas | Pinkston |
| 7 | Christina | Robinson |

Review Question 2.45
What does the following SQL statement do?

```
SELECT FirstName, LastName
FROM Admission.Student;
ORDER BY gpa
```

a. Display all students' first names, last names, and GPAs from the student table.
b. Display all students' first names and last names and sort by GPAs with the highest GPA first.
c. Display all students' first names and last names and sort by GPAs with the lowest GPAs first.
d. It has a syntax error because the GPA column was in ORDER BY but not in SELECT.

Review Question 2.46
Write an SQL statement to display the student with the highest GPA. Show their first name, last name, and GPA.
a. SELECT FirstName, LastName, TOP 1 gpa FROM Admission.Student ORDER BY gpa;
b. SELECT FirstName, LastName, TOP 1 gpa FROM Admission.Student ORDER BY gpa DESC;
c. SELECT TOP 1 FirstName, LastName, gpa FROM Admission.Student ORDER BY gpa;
d. SELECT TOP 1 FirstName, LastName, gpa FROM Admission.Student ORDER BY gpa DESC;

## 2.13 Chapter Summary

In this chapter, you learned the first few steps for building a data model. You started with writing business descriptions and then extracted business rules from business descriptions. Next, you determined the entities and the relationships among the entities and built the conceptual data model. You also learned how to display data with certain columns from a table of our LifeStyle Electronic wholesaler by using the SELECT ... FROM statement. You learned how to remove duplication in the output by using the DISTINCT keyword. You applied the ORDER BY clause to sort the result of the SELECT. Finally, you used the TOP keyword to limit the number of rows displayed.

## 2.14 Discussions

Discussion 2.1.
Think of a model you are familiar with in the real world. Explain the three characteristics of the model.

Discussion 2.2.
Compare and contrast connectivity and cardinality of a relationship in an ERD.

Discussion 2.3.
Why do you need to have different levels of abstraction when modeling data?

## 2.15 Database Design Exercises

Exercise One:
A small publisher wants to keep data about its books and authors. What are possible business rules (must come from the real world)? Draw a conceptual ERD for the publisher.

Exercise Two:
TourUSA is a small tourism company. It needs a database to store data described here. Its main customers are visitors from other countries. It offers many tours. Each tour includes a list of cities, number of days for the whole tour, and the manager who will be in charge of the tour.

For each city, it lists a brief description of the city and a list of attractions. Each attraction also includes a description and the weather forecast.

Each tour can have zero or many trips. Each trip includes a specific start date and end date, the price, and the guide. The guide information includes first name, last name, date hired, gender, and what languages he or she speaks and with what level of fluency.

A customer can book one or more trips that are announced on TourUSA's website. Each customer provides his or her first name, last name, date of birth, gender, and payment data.

Payment data required by TourUSA includes the name on the credit card, card expiration date, card number, and security code.

Your task:
1. Extract all possible business rules.
2. Construct the conceptual model for the TourUSA.

## 2.16 SQL Exercises

Exercise 2.1 Display all suppliers' names so the result look like this:

| SupplierName |
|---|
| Pine Apple |
| IMB |
| Lonovo |
| Samsong |
| Canan |

Exercise 2.2 Display all suppliers' names and country of origin:

| SupplierName | Country |
|---|---|
| Pine Apple | USA |
| IMB | USA |
| Lonovo | China |
| Samsong | South Korea |
| Canan | Japan |

Exercise 2.3 Display all customers' names, emails, and country.

| | CustomerName | Email | Country |
|---|---|---|---|
| 1 | Just Electronics | jwhite@je.com | USA |
| 2 | Beyond Electronics | green@beil.com | USA |
| 3 | Beyond Electronics | black1@be.com | USA |
| 4 | E Fun | bgold@efun.com | USA |
| 5 | Overstock E | dy@os.com | USA |
| 6 | E Fun | green@ef.com | UK |
| 7 | Electronics4U | smith@e4u.com | UK |
| 8 | Cheap Electronics | NULL | Canada |

Exercise 2.4 Display all data from the products table.

| ProductId | ProductName | supplierid |
|---|---|---|
| 1 | 65-Inch 4K Ultra HD Smart TV | 4 |
| 2 | 60-Inch 4K Ultra HD Smart LED TV | 4 |
| 3 | 3200 Lumens LED Home Theater Projector | 3 |
| 4 | Wireless Color Photo Printer | 5 |
| 5 | 6Wireless Compact Laser Printer | 2 |
| 6 | Color Laser Printer | 2 |
| 7 | 10" 16GB Android Tablet | 4 |
| 8 | GPS Android Tablet PC | 2 |
| 9 | 20.2 MP Digital Camera | 5 |

Exercise 2.5 Display all IDs of employees who have ever made a sale

| EmployeeId |
|---|
| 2 |
| 3 |
| 4 |
| 5 |
| 6 |
| 7 |

Exercise 2.6 Display all orders sorted by order date, from the earliest to the most recent.

| OrderId | CustomerId | EmployeeId | OrderDate |
|---|---|---|---|
| 7 | 5 | 7 | 2016-11-08 |
| 8 | 7 | 2 | 2016-12-23 |
| 1 | 1 | 5 | 2017-01-03 |
| 3 | 2 | 5 | 2017-02-23 |
| 2 | 1 | 3 | 2017-03-05 |
| 4 | 4 | 5 | 2017-04-13 |
| 5 | 1 | 4 | 2017-05-03 |
| 6 | 3 | 6 | 2017-05-08 |

Exercise 2.7 Display all orders sorted by order date, from the most recent to the earliest.

| OrderId | CustomerId | EmployeeId | OrderDate |
|---|---|---|---|
| 6 | 3 | 6 | 2017-05-08 |
| 5 | 1 | 4 | 2017-05-03 |
| 4 | 4 | 5 | 2017-04-13 |
| 2 | 1 | 3 | 2017-03-05 |
| 3 | 2 | 5 | 2017-02-23 |
| 1 | 1 | 5 | 2017-01-03 |
| 8 | 7 | 2 | 2016-12-23 |
| 7 | 5 | 7 | 2016-11-08 |

Exercise 2.8 Display products delivered with the product ID and quantity of each delivery. Sort from the most recent to the oldest.

| ProductId | Quantity |
|---|---|
| 1 | 5 |
| 7 | 18 |
| 7 | 12 |
| 6 | 25 |
| 5 | 15 |

| 4 | 20 |
|---|---|
| 3 | 10 |
| 2 | 10 |
| 1 | 2 |

Exercise 2.9 Display the three most recent deliveries with the product ID and quantity.

| ProductId | Quantity |
|---|---|
| 1 | 5 |
| 7 | 18 |
| 7 | 12 |

Exercise 2.10 Display all customers' names and contacts. Sort by the customer name. In the case where two or more customers have the same name, sort by contact.

| | CustomerName | Contact |
|---|---|---|
| 1 | Beyond Electronics | Alice Black |
| 2 | Beyond Electronics | Scott Green |
| 3 | Cheap Electronics | NULL |
| 4 | E Fun | Ben Gold |
| 5 | E Fun | Frank Green |
| 6 | Electronics4U | Grace Smith |
| 7 | Just Electronics | John White |
| 8 | Overstock E | Daniel Yellow |

# 2.17 Solutions to the Review Questions

2.1 A; 2.2 B; 2.3 A; 2.4 B; 2.5 D; 2.6 A; 2.7 A; 2.8 B; 2.9 D; 2.10 B; 2.11 C; 2.12 B; 2.13 C; 2.14 B; 2.15 B; 2.16 B; 2.17 A; 2.18 D; 2.19 D; 2.20 A; 2.21 A; 2.22 B; 2.23 C; 2.24 B; 2.25 A; 2.26 D; 2.27 B; 2.28 A; 2.29 B; 2.30 C; 2.31 D; 2.32 A; 2.33 A; 2.34 B; 2.35 B; 2.36 C; 2.37 A; 2.38 B; 2.39 D; 2.40 B; 2.41 A; 2.42 B; 2.43 C; 2.44 C; 2.45 C; 2.46 D;

# Chapter 3: Logical Model and SQL WHERE Clause

## Chapter Learning Objectives

3.1 Construct logical ERD with attributes and primary keys
3.2 Differentiate types of attributes
3.3 Interpret entity existence dependence and relationship strength
3.4 Use WHERE clause to retrieve rows that meet certain criteria
3.5 Use BETWEEN and IS NULL operators
3.6 Use AND, OR, and NOT logical operators

## 3.1 Attributes of an Entity and a Relationship

As you learned in the last chapter, an attribute is a named property or characteristic of an entity or a relationship that is of interest to the user.

After you build the conceptual model of a database, you can move on to the logical design by adding the attributes to the entities and relationships. For example, the INSTRUCTOR entity has the attributes of instructor ID, first name and last name, the COURSE entity has a course ID, course number and course title. In the ERD, you can add them inside the entity box as in Figure 3.1:

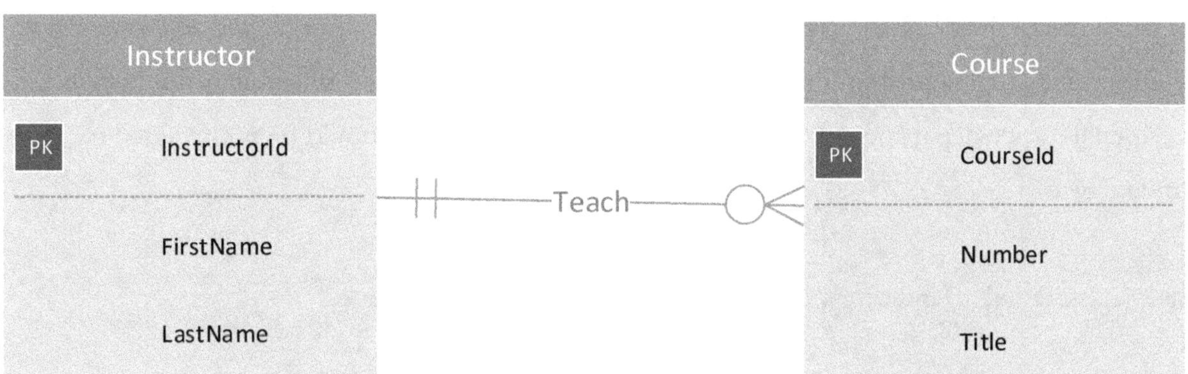


Figure 3.1 ERD entities with attributes added (we will cover PK attribute later in the chapter).

Do not add an attribute to an entity that is an entity in itself. For example, we say every course has an instructor, but we don't add instructor as an attribute to the course entity because an instructor is an entity.

There are many types of attributes you need to know when creating a data model.

A *simple attribute* has a single atomic value that cannot be subdivided. For example, an instructor's first name is a simple attribute because it cannot be subdivided without losing meaning.

A *composite attribute* is an attribute that can be further subdivided to yield additional attributes. For example, an instructor's full name is a composite attribute that can be further subdivided into first name, middle initial, and last name, each of which can be its own attribute. Another example is a mailing address, which usually contains street address, city, state, and zip code. Therefore, we can say that a mailing address is a composite attribute.

A *single-valued attribute* can have only one value for each record. For example, a course can have only one course number. A person can have only one date of birth. Course number and date of birth are single-valued attributes. Do not confuse a simple attribute with a single-valued attribute. Sometimes an attribute can be both, and other times not. For instance, a person's full name is a single-valued attribute, but not a simple attribute.

A *multivalued attribute* can hold more than one value for a single record. For example, an instructor's phone number attribute might store multiple values, such as home, work, and cell numbers. While many attributes can be multivalued, you must consider the specific circumstances of the mini-world. Ask yourself: Is the attribute truly multivalued in this particular context? For instance, in an ordinary business mini-world, is an employee's last name multivalued? No, even though employees may change their last names due to marriage or divorce. If this occurs, simply update the current last name; there is no need to track historical names. However, in a criminal justice department mini-world, the last name attribute should be multivalued to maintain a complete history.

In ERD, you use {LastName} to indicate a multivalued attribute called LastName.

A *derived attribute* or *computed attribute* is obtained from other attributes. For example, the student age attribute can be calculated from the date of birth attribute. Storing derived attributes takes storage, so it is preferred to store normal attributes. However, there will be cases in which both a normal attribute and a derived attribute are necessary. For example, if a school wanted to look up the age for one student, they would use a normal attribute. However, if the school frequently needed to look up ages for many students, calculation would take up time, and so it would be more convenient to use a derived attribute.

A *required attribute* is an attribute that must have a value for every entity instance. For example, an employee's ID, first name, and last name are all required fields to insert a new employee. In ERD, it is often shown as bold.

On the contrary, an *optional attribute* is an attribute that may not have a value for every entity instance. For example, not all employees will fill out a second phone number for a company's database. In ERD, an optional attribute is often shown as regular text.

Not only can an entity type have attributes, but a relationship type can have attributes as well. For example, there's a relationship between EMPLOYEE and PROJECT. An employee can work on multiple projects and each project has several employees. But then how do you record the hours each employee works on each project? The hours worked on a project is not an attribute of the EMPLOYEE because he or she can work on multiple projects. But, it cannot be an attribute of the project either, because each project has multiple employees. In this case, the attribute actually belongs to the relationship type of "work on project". As shown in Figure 3.2, hoursWorked is an attribute of the "work on project" relationship. Just like in this example, most relationship attributes apply to M:N relationships.

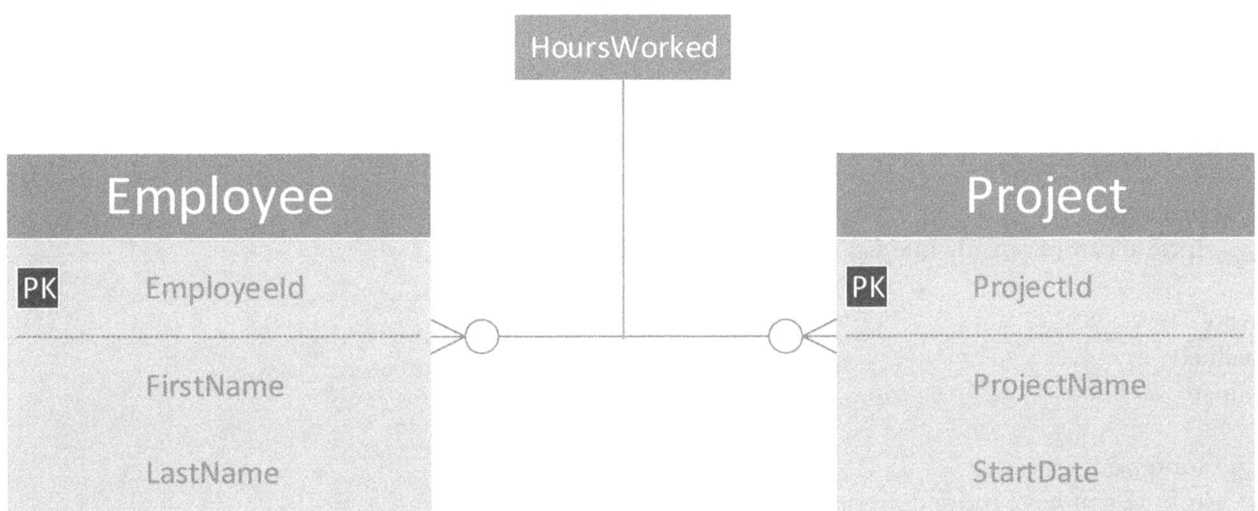


Figure 3.2 An attribute can belong to a relationship.

Review Question 3.1
A(n) ______ is a named property or characteristic of an entity or a relationship that is of interest to the user.
a. attribute
b. variable
c. function
d. piece of data

Review Question 3.2
After you build the conceptual model of a database, you can move on to the logical design by adding the ______ to the entities and relationships.
a. attributes
b. variables
c. tables
d. data

Review Question 3.3
In ERD, you use {LastName} to indicate a(a) ______ attribute called LastName.
a. optional
b. required
c. derived
d. multivalued

Review Question 3.4
A ______ attribute has a single atomic value that cannot be subdivided.
a. simple
b. composite
c. single-valued
d. multivalued

Review Question 3.5
A _______ attribute is the one that can be further subdivided to yield additional attributes.
a. simple
b. composite
c. single-valued
d. multivalued

Review Question 3.6
A ______ attribute can have only one value for each record.
a. simple
b. composite
c. single-valued
d. multivalued

Review Question 3.7
A ______ attribute can have more than one value for each record.
a. simple
b. composite
c. single-valued
d. multivalued

Review Question 3.8
If the STUDENT entity has an attribute called age, what type of attribute is it most likely to be?
a. composite
b. derived
c. required
d. optional

Review Question 3.9
If the STUDENT entity has an attribute called LastName, what type of attribute is it most likely to be?
a. composite
b. derived
c. required
d. optional

## 3.2 Attribute Domains

The domain of an attribute is all possible values that are allowed for the attribute. For example, if you have an attribute called GPA, the domain for that attribute would be [0, 4]. In another example, a student's first name is an attribute of the student entity. The domain of that attribute is a set string of alphabetical letters. In ERD, you usually don't display the domain directly. In the physical model, you will display the data type in the ERD, which partially reflects the domain. A constraint may be added to the physical model due to the attribute domain. For example, you will use DECIMAL data type for the GPA attribute and NVARCHAR data type for FirstName attribute. You may use the CHECK constraint to ensure that a PGA is within the range of 0 and 4.

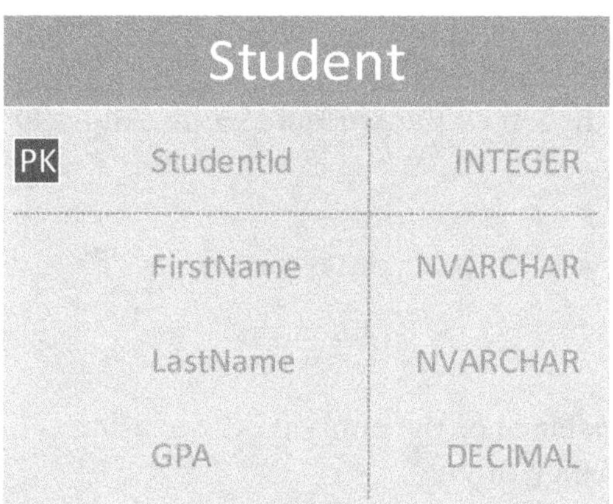

Figure 3.3 Data types are shown in ERD at physical level.

Review Question 3.10
All possible values for an attribute are called the attribute's ______________.
a. possibility
b. possible values
c. range
d. domain

Review Question 3.11
If GPA is an attribute of the STUDENT entity and can be values from 0 to 4, what is the set of possible GPA values called?
a. special range

b. possible range
c. domain
d. special domain

Review Question 3.12
If GPA is an attribute of the STUDENT entity and can be values from 0 to 4, you will see a _______ constraint in the physical model if using SQL Server.
a. GPA
b. DOMAIN
c. LIMIT
d. CHECK

## 3.3 Primary Key (PK)

An entity may have one or more attributes that can uniquely identify each instance of the entity type. Such an attribute is called a key of the entity, or an identifier. For example, student ID or social security number is a key of the STUDENT entity. The one key chosen by the database developer is called the primary key (PK). Note that a primary key of an entity does not have to be a single attribute, it can be a few attributes, in which case it is called a composite primary key.

In ERD, primary keys are indicated by underlining or just the PK on the left of the attribute name. All ERD in this book adopts the latter method.

There are a few rules to follow when you choose a primary key.

1. One attribute primary key is better than a composite primary key.
2. A good primary key will not change its value over the life of each instance of the entity type. So, using name and address for primary key is a bad choice because they can change often.
3. A primary key should not have null value. Not even part of the primary key can be null. A null value means no value for the record. For example, not all people have middle names, so middle names should not be included as part of a primary key.
4 A good primary key avoids using an intelligent identifier, meaning parts of the attribute value can be decoded for meaning. For example, some companies use products that contain parts that indicate the manufacturer location, such as US12345 for a product made in the USA, CN23456 for a product made in China.
5. A good primary key uses a single attribute surrogate for large composite identifiers. A surrogate key is a label used to serve as identification that may not have any meaning. For example, companies and schools may use a series of numbers (an ID) to represent an individual. These numbers have no meanings in the mini-world.
6. A good primary key should not use an attribute that can have security or privacy concerns, such as social security number.

When determining the primary key for a weak entity, the primary key of the identifying entity should be included as part of the weak entity's primary key. For example, DEPENDENT is a weak entity. Its identifying entity is EMPLOYEE. Suppose employee ID is the primary key of the EMPLOYEE entity, then the DEPENDENT entity should contain the employee ID as partial key. Then, the primary key for the DEPENDENT can be (EmployeeId, FirstNameOfDependent).

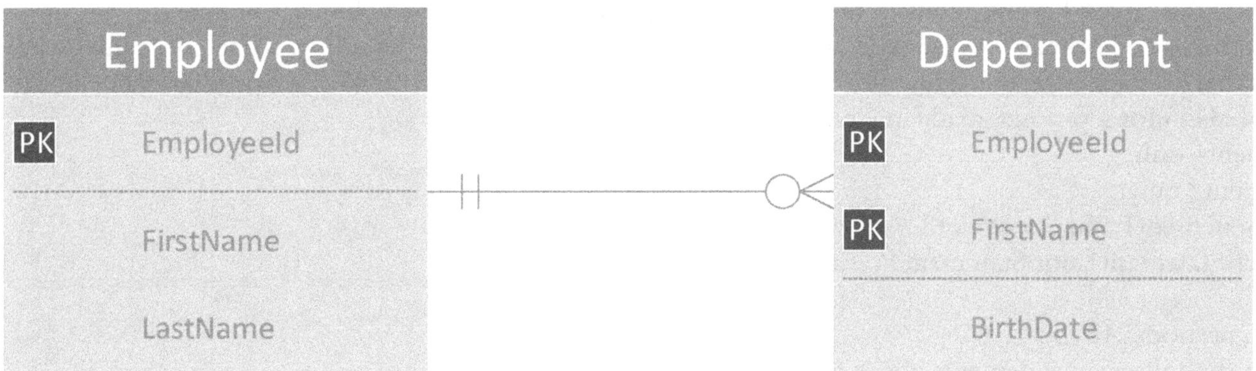

Figure 3.4 Primary key of a weak entity is a composite key.

Review Question 3.13
An entity may have one or more attributes that can uniquely identify each instance of the entity type. Such attribute(s) are called _______ attributes.
a. unique
b. key
c. primary key
d. foreign key

Review Question 3.14
An entity may have multiple keys. The one key chosen by the database developer is called the __________.
a. chosen key
b. major key
c. primary key
d. foreign key

Review Question 3.15
Which of the following statements about primary key is correct?
Statement1: One attribute primary key is better than a composite primary key.
Statement2: A good primary key will not change its value over the life of each instance of the entity type.
a. Statement1 only.
b. Statement2 only.
c. Both Statement1 and Statement2.
d. Neither Statement1 nor Statement2.

Review Question 3.16
Which of the following statements about primary key is correct?

Statement1: A good primary key will not change its value over the life of each instance of the entity type.
Statement2: A primary key may contain null value as long as the value for the column is unique.
a. Statement1 only.
b. Statement2 only.
c. Both Statement1 and Statement2.
d. Neither Statement1 nor Statement2.

Review Question 3.17
Which of the following statements about primary keys is correct?
Statement1: A primary key may contain null value as long as the value for the column is unique.
Statement2: A good primary key is made up of meaningful components. For example, some companies use products that contain parts indicating the manufacturer location, such as US12345 for a product made in the USA, CN23456 for a product made in China.
a. Statement1 only.
b. Statement2 only.
c. Both Statement1 and Statement2.
d. Neither Statement1 nor Statement2.

Review Question 3.18
Which of the following statements about primary key is correct?
Statement1: A good primary key is made up of meaningful components. For example, some companies use products that contain parts indicating the manufacturer location, such as US12345 for a product made in the USA, CN23456 for a product made in China.
Statement2: In the USA, a social security number is a good choice as the primary key for an employee entity because it is always unique.
a. Statement1 only.
b. Statement2 only.
c. Both Statement1 and Statement2.
d. Neither Statement1 nor Statement2.

Review Question 3.19
Sometimes, database developers add a new attribute that is meaningless in the mini-world to an entity to avoid using a large composite primary key. Such a primary key is called ___________.
a. simplified key
b. meaningless key
c. single key
d. surrogate key

Review Question 3.20
Which of the following statements about primary key is correct?
Statement1: In the USA, a social security number is a good choice as the primary key for an employee entity because it is always unique.
Statement2: One attribute primary key is better than a composite primary key.
a. Statement1 only.
b. Statement2 only.
c. Both Statement1 and Statement2.
d. Neither Statement1 nor Statement2.

# 3.4 Existence Dependence

In Chapter 2, you learned that if an entity can exist in the database only when an associated entity exists, then the entity is called a weak entity. The DEPENDENT of EMPLOYEE is an example of a weak entity because a dependent cannot exist without the associated employee in the database. Such an entity is also called an existence-dependent entity.

On the other hand, if an entity can exist by itself, the entity is called existence-independent, also called a strong entity or simply a regular entity. An example of such entity can be STUDENT in a university setting.

Review Question 3.21
An ERD contains the BUILDING and CLASSROOM entities. A classroom is always inside a building. What is the CLASSROOM entity called?
a. strong entity
b. existence-dependent entity
c. existence-independent entity
d. regular entity

Review Question 3.22
An ERD contains the BUILDING and CLASSROOM entities. A classroom is always inside a building. What is the CLASSROOM entity called?
a. strong entity
b. weak entity
c. existence-independent entity
d. regular entity

# 3.5 Relationship Strength

A weak relationship, also known as a non-identifying relationship, exists if the primary key of one entity does not overlap with a primary key of the other entity. For example, the relationship between the INSTRUCTOR and the COURSE is a weak relationship because the COURSE entity's primary key is CourseID, which does not contain the primary key of the INSTRUCTOR entity.

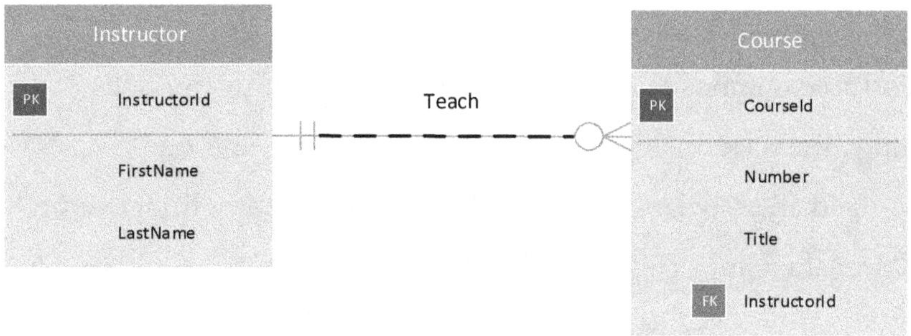


Figure 3.5 A weak relationship using a dashed line.

A strong relationship, or identifying relationship, exists between a strong entity and its associated weak entity. The relationship between EMPLOYEE and DEPENDENT demonstrates a strong relationship.

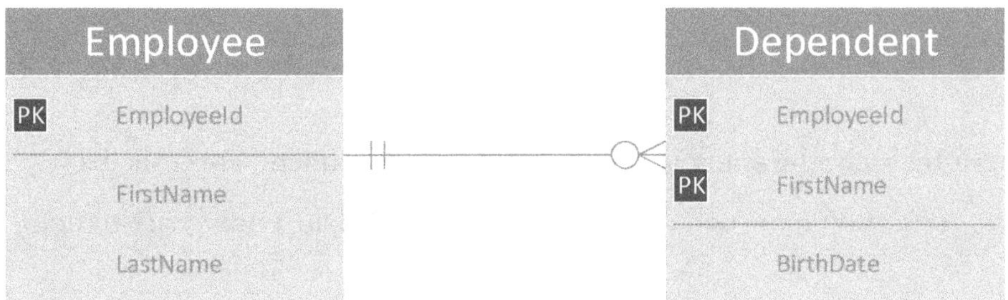

Figure 3.6 A strong relationship between a strong entity and a weak entity.

A strong relationship exists between the strong and weak entity because the primary key of the DEPENDENT entity contains EmployeeID, which is the primary key of the EMPLOYEE entity.

Review Question 3.23
An ERD contains the BUILDING and CLASSROOM entities. A classroom is always inside a building. What is the relationship strength between the BUILDING and CLASSROOM called?
a. a strong relationship
b. a weak relationship
c. a regular relationship
d. a special relationship

## 3.6 Many-to-Many Relationship

A many-to-many relationship (M:N) is special in relational databases. Some designers choose to keep the relationship until mapping the entities to relations (Chapter 5). Others decide to replace the M:N relationship with two 1:M relationships in the logical model by adding an associative entity.

An associative entity, also known as bridge entity or composite entity, is a relationship that the modeler chooses to model as an entity type. For example, the relationship between the STUDENT and the COURSE is a M:N relationship. We choose to add an associative entity called Enrollment as a bridge entity that makes one M:N relationship into two 1:M relationships (Figure 3.7).

The primary key of the associative entity is usually composed of the primary keys of each of the entities to be connected. In such a case, the primary key of the associative entity has a composite primary key.

As stated earlier, you may just keep the M:N relationship in the logical model. We will show you how to map the relationship to a relation in Chapter 5.

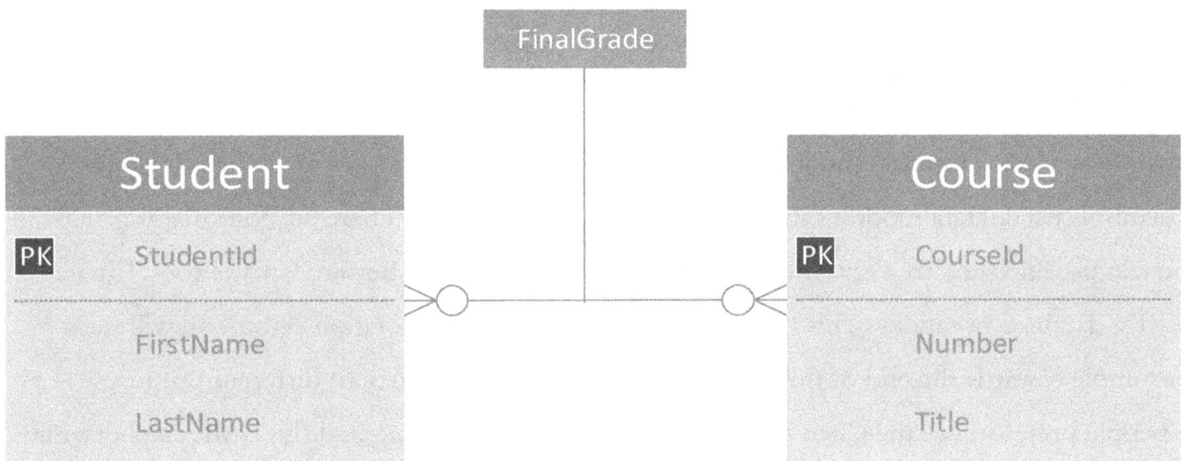


Part A) A many-to-many relationship

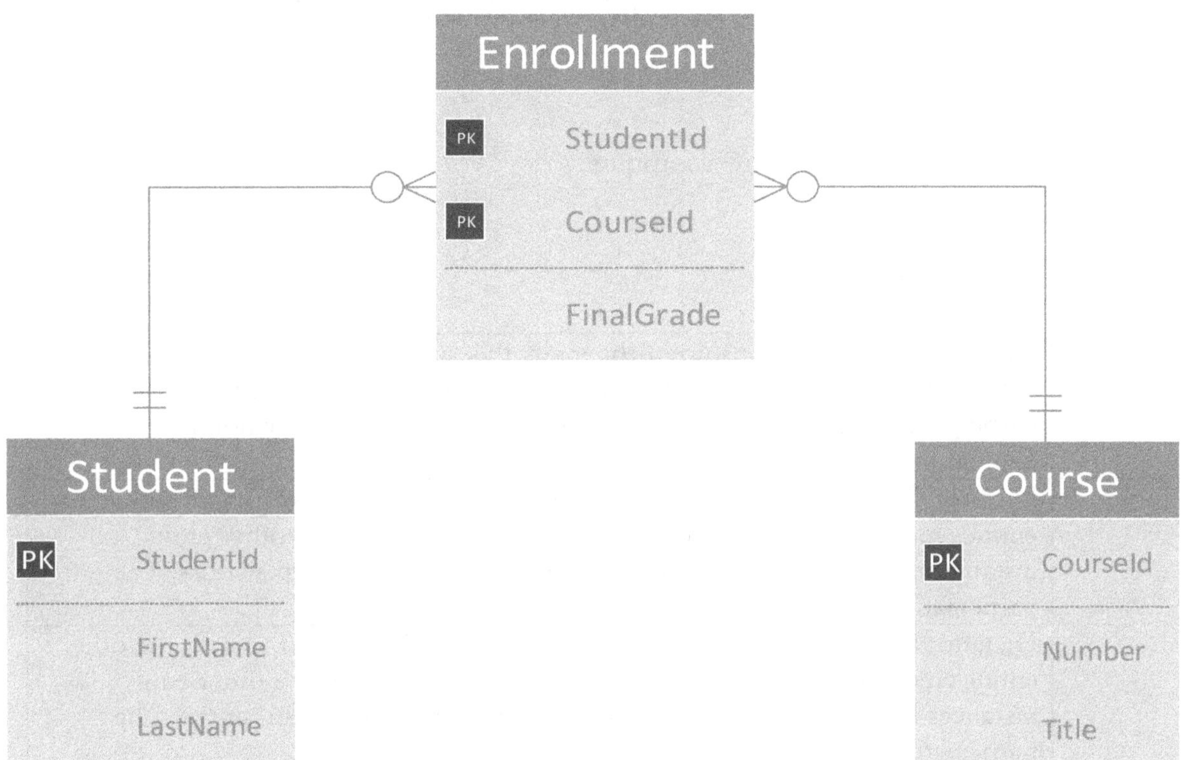


Part B) Two one-to-many relationship

Figure 3.7 Convert a many-to-many relationship into two one-to-many relationships.

Review Question 3.24
A(n) ___________ entity is a relationship that the modeler chooses to model as an entity type.
a. relationship
b. special
c. simple
d. associative

## 3.7 Entity-Relationship Diagram (ERD)

So far, you learned how to develop data models by using entities, relationships, and attributes. It is time to summarize the symbols used. Data models can be represented in many ways. There are four major groups of notations you can use and they are very similar in the ideas behind them. They are Crow's foot, Chen, UML, and IDEF1X database notations. This book will use the Crow's foot notation only. You will see a Chen notation example towards the end of this section. Different notations may fit different purposes. For example, some people prefer to use the Chen notation for conceptual modeling and the UML class diagram for Entity Framework used in .net application development.

| Symbol | Meaning |
|---|---|
| 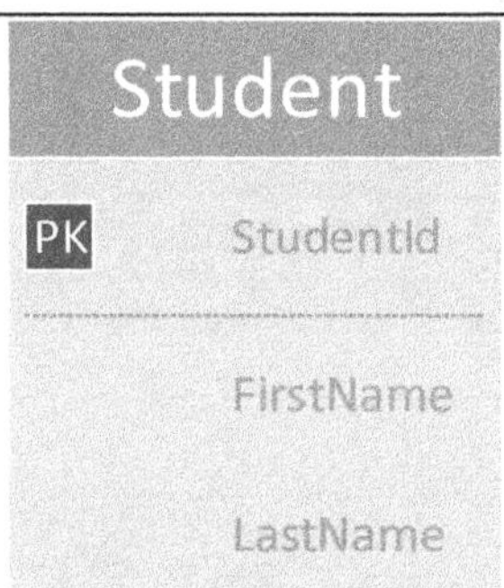 | A rectangle shape shows the entity. An entity contains three parts, the entity name is on the top, followed by the primary key attribute(s), and ends with the list of attributes.<br><br>PK stands for Primary Key attribute. |
| 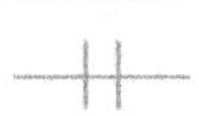 | Dictates that the relationship of the entity this symbol is next to with the other entities must be 1: M or 1:1. It must be true that there is one and only one participant from the entity this symbol is next to. The participation is mandatory. |
| 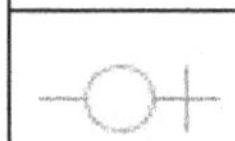 | Dictates that the relationship of the entity this symbol is next to with the other entities must be 1: M or 1:1, but with the possibility that the other entity instances may not have any relationship to the instances of this entity. The participation is optional. |
| 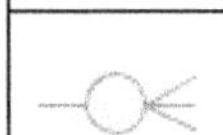 | Dictates that the relationship of the entity this symbol is next to with the other entities must be 1: M or M:N, but with the possibility that the other entity instances may not have any relationship to the instances of this entity. The participation is optional. |
| 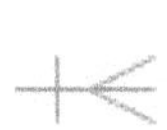 | Dictates that the relationship of the entity this symbol is next to with the other entities must be 1: M or M:N. It must be true that there is at least one participant from the entity this symbol is next to. The participation is mandatory. |

Table 3.1: Crow's foot notation

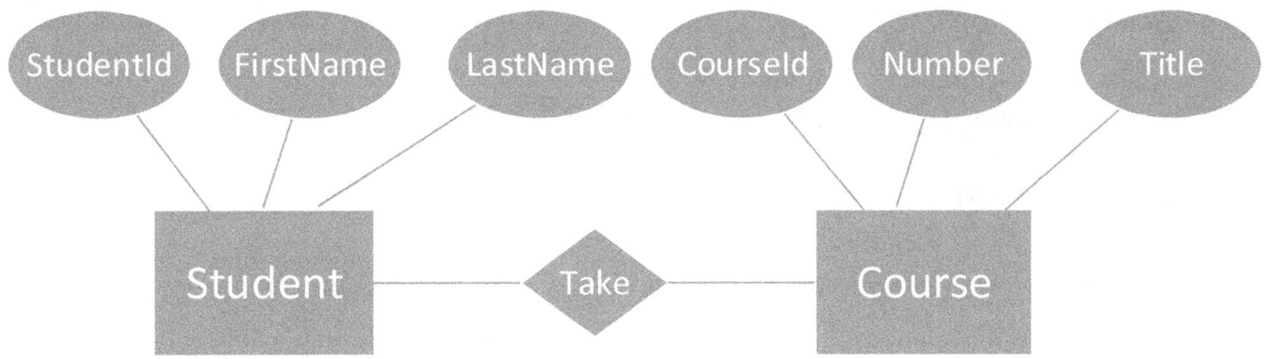


Figure 3.8 Chen's database notation example.

Review Question 3.25
Which of the following is NOT a popular database modeling notation?
a. Bigfoot
b. Chen
c. UML
d. IDEFX1X

## 3.8 Documentation

A data model should be accompanied by a document, sometimes called a data dictionary. Good documentation serves at least three purposes. One is as a communication tool between the developers and the customers. The second serves as a facilitator for the deployment of the system to production. The third serves as help to reduce the cost and effort during the maintenance stage of the system.

You should name an entity type so that both the users and developers can understand and interpret it in the same way. Keep in mind that an entity name is typically a noun. A description can help give a better understanding of the entities and the data model as a whole. An alias is also important when different users use different terms to mean the same thing. Finally, how an entity relates with another entity will help the understanding of the entity itself. A sample entity documentation is shown below:

| Entity | Description | Alias | Relationship |
|---|---|---|---|
| Customer | All retail customers who buy from LyfeStyle or just registered to be a customer. | Client, Buyer | Each customer place zero or many orders. |
| Employee | All persons who work at LyfeStyle and still employed | Staff, Manager, Associate | Each employee assists zero or many orders. |

Similarly, you should name relationship types so that both users and developers can understand. It usually is a verb or verb phrase. The document typically includes the relationship type names, participating entities and their corresponding cardinalities.

| Entity | Cardinality | Relationship | Cardinality | Entity |
|---|---|---|---|---|
| Customer | (1, 1) | Place | (0, N) | Order |
| Employee | (1, 1) | Assist | (0, N) | Order |
| Employee | (0, 1) | Manage | (0, N) | Employee |

Finally, you should name an attribute appropriately, organizing them under their entity or relationship. The document should include entity/relationship name, attribute name, description, aliases, data type and size, and attribute type. For ease of reading, the attribute type is often under several columns such as required, composite, multiple value, derived. The following table shows an example:

| Customer Entity | | | | | | |
|---|---|---|---|---|---|---|
| Attribute | Description | Alias | Date Type | Domain | Allow null | Multi-valued |
| CustomerId | Uniquely identify a customer | Company ID | Integer auto generated by the system | Any integer | No | No |
| CustomerName | Customer's registered company name | Company name | Up to 50 variable characters | Any alpha-numeric | No | No |
| StreetAddress | Customer's headquarter street address | Address | Up to 50 variable characters | Any alpha-numeric | Yes | No |
| City | Customer's headquarter city | Town | Up to 20 variable characters | Any alpha-numeric | Yes | No |
| State | Customer's headquarter state | Province | Up to 20 variable characters | Any alpha-numeric | Yes | No |
| PostalCode | Customer's headquarter postal code | Zip code | Up to 10 variable characters | Any alpha-numeric | Yes | No |
| Country | Customer's headquarter country | Nation | Up to 50 variable characters | Any alpha-numeric | Yes | No |
| Contact | Customer's liaison person full name | customer | Up to 50 variable characters | Any alpha-numeric | Yes | No |
| Email | Liaison person's email address | Contact email | Up to 50 variable characters | Any alpha-numeric | Yes | No |

Table 3.2 Sample attribute documentation

Note: Many data modeling tools include documentation more or less similar to the one shown. Some companies have their own specific format for collecting data.

Review Question 3.26
Which of the following is NOT a purpose good database modeling documentation can serve?
a. as a communication tool between the developers and the customers.
b. as a facilitator for the deployment of the system to production.
c. as a contract between developers and the customers
d. as help to reduce the cost and effort during the maintenance stage of the system.

## 3.9 Logical Model

The two major activities in constructing ERD of logical modeling are adding attributes to the entities and relationships and picking primary key for each entity.

In Section 2.8 Conceptual Model of the last chapter, you practiced 4 examples. In this section, you will see how you can make those conceptual models into logical models by adding attributes to each entity and relationship and selecting the primary key for each entity.

*Logical model (ERD) Example 1:*

The Career Center of Jefferson County offers in-demand IT skill courses to adult learners. They want to keep records of students and courses. A student has an ID, first name, and last name. A course has an ID, number, title, begin date and end date, and class time. Same course may be offered at the same time with different IDs. Each student will receive a grade when the student completes a course. Construct a logical model by adding attributes and selecting PK to the conceptual model example 1 of Chapter 2 (Section 2.8).

Business rules:

1. A student can take zero or many courses.
2. A course must have at least one student.
3. A student has an ID, first name, and last name.
4. A course has an ID, number, title, begin date, end date, and class time.
5. The relationship between a student and a course has a grade.

Logical ERD:

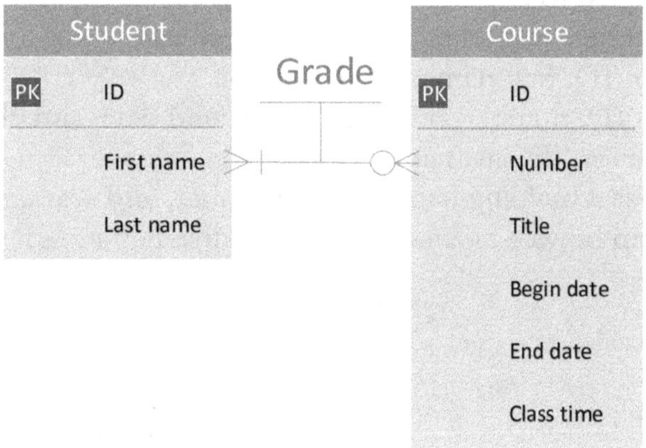

*Conceptual model (ERD) Example 2:*

The Career Center of Jefferson County offers in-demand IT skill courses to adult learners. They want to keep records of students, instructors, and courses. Write possible business rules and construct conceptual ERD.

Business rules:

1. A student can take zero or many courses.
2. A course must have at least one student.
3. An instructor can teach zero or many courses
4. A course has exactly one instructor.
5. A student has an ID, first name, and last name.
6. A course has an ID, number, title, begin date, end date, and class time.
7. An instructor has an ID, last name, and office.
8. The relationship between a student and a course has a grade.

Logical ERD:

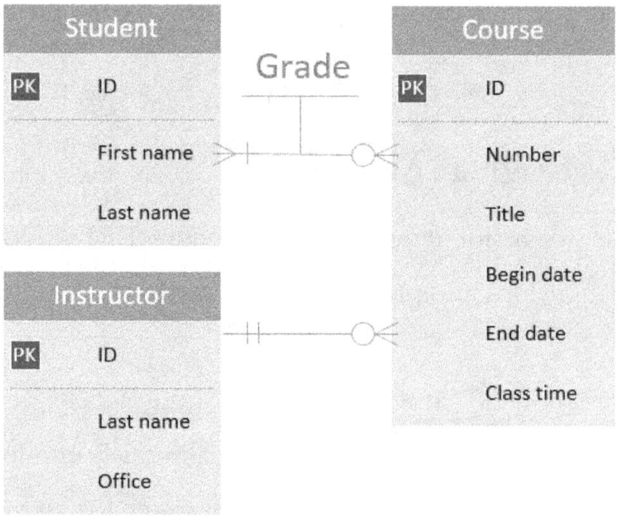


*Conceptual model (ERD) Example 3:*

The Career Center of Jefferson County offers in-demand IT skill courses to adult learners. They want to keep records of students, instructors, courses, and classrooms. Write possible business rules and construct conceptual ERD.

Business rules:

1. A student can take zero or many courses.
2. A course must have at least one student.
3. An instructor can teach zero or many courses
4. A course has exactly one instructor.
5. A course is assigned to exactly one classroom.
6. A classroom can be assigned to zero or many courses.
7. A student has an ID, first name, and last name.
8. A course has an ID, number, title, begin date, end date, and class time.
9. An instructor has an ID, last name, and office.
10. A classroom has a building name, room number, and seat capacity.
11. The relationship between a student and a course has a grade.

Logical ERD:

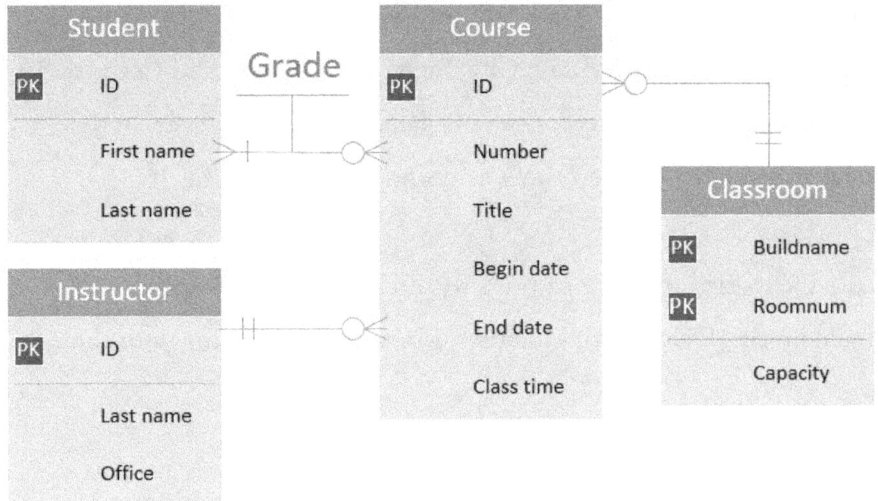


*Conceptual model (ERD) Example 4:*

Based on the business description and business rules of Case Example 2 (Section 2.2), write possible business rules and construct conceptual ERD.

Business Rules:

An employee may manage zero or many employees.
An employee may be managed by zero or one boss/employee.
An employee can complete zero or many orders.
An order must be completed by exactly one employee.
A customer can place zero or many orders.
An order must come from exactly one customer.
An order contains at least one product.
A product can appear in zero or many orders.
A product is provided by exactly one supplier.
A supplier may provide zero or many products.
An employee has employee ID, first name, last name, birth date, hire date, address, phone, and manager ID.
An order has an order ID and an order date.
A customer has an ID, name, address, contact, and email.
A product has an ID, name, and several deliveries. A delivery has an ID, quantity, price, and delivery date.
A supplier has an ID, name, and address.
The relationship between order and product has quantity and price.

Logical ERD:

Add all attributes and resolve the many-to-many relationship between ORDER and PRODUCT by adding an associative entity called ORDERDETAIL as shown in Figure 3.9. If you prefer, you can keep the M:N relationship between ORDER and PRODUCT. In Figure 3.9, omit the ORDERDETAIL entity and add "price" and "quantity" as attributes to the relationship between ORDER and PRODUCT.

In Figure 3.9, the Address attribute of the EMPLOYEE, CUSTOMER, and SUPPLIER entities are composite attributes which have the components of StreetAddress, City, State, PostalCode, and Country. In reality, you should replace the Address attribute with the five components listed above. However, in this book, we want the ERD to fit on one page, and so we just keep them as composite attributes.

Also, in Figure 3.9, you may notice that the Deliveries attribute of the PRODUCT entity is a composite multiple valued attribute. A delivery is made up of {DeliveryId, Quantity, Price, DeliveryDate} with the {} indicating that it is a multivalued attribute.

The many-to-many relationship between the ORDER and the PRODUCT is now replaced with two 1:M relationships. The following four business rules explain the two relationships:

An ORDER includes at least one ORDERDETAIL.
Each ORDERDETAIL must be included in exactly one ORDER.
A PRODUCT is contained in zero or many ORDERDETAIL.
Each ORDERDETAIL contains exactly one PRODUCT.

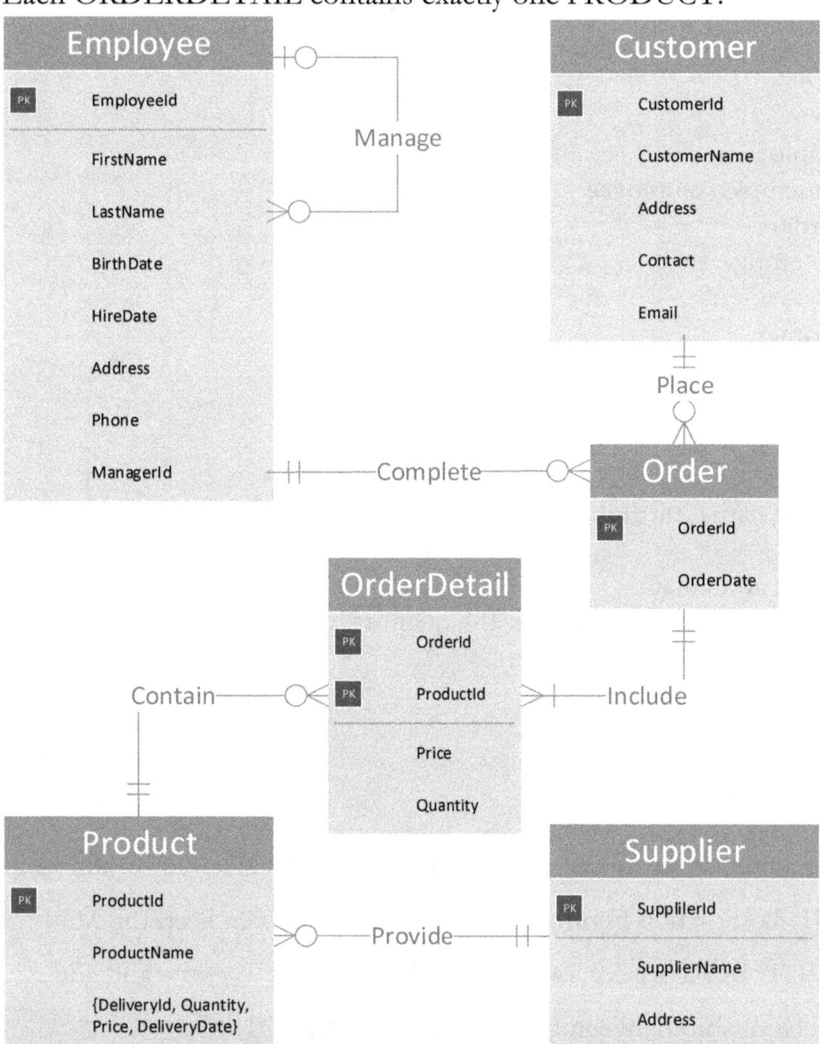


Figure 3.9 Logical model for case example 1 of Chapter 2

Review Question 3.27
What are the two major activities in constructing ERD of logical modeling?
a. Add attributes to entities and relationships and pick the primary key for each entity.
b. Add attributes to entities and pick the primary key for each relationship.
c. Add a primary key and pick foreign key for each relationship.
d. Add a primary key and pick foreign key for each entity.

Review Question 3.28
The many-to-many relationship between two entities can be replaced with ______ 1:M relationships.
a. one
b. two
c. three
d. four

## 3.10 SQL Filtering Data with WHERE Clause

In Chapter 2, you learned how to use the SELECT ... FROM statement to retrieve specific column(s) from a table. In this chapter, you will learn how to retrieve specific rows that meet certain criteria by using the WHERE clause. The syntax for the SELECT statement with WHERE clause is:

```
SELECT Column1, Column2, ...
FROM Table
WHERE condition is true;
```

SQL Example 3.1

Display all products that only sold one unit in an order. Show product ID.

SQL Example 3.1 Analysis

The column that you want to display is ProductID. The table is OrderDetails. The condition for the WHERE clause is quantity equals one.

You just want to know what products customers buy, so you may want to eliminate the duplicates by using the DISTINCT keyword.

SQL Example 3.1 statement

```
SELECT DISTINCT ProductId
FROM Sales.OrderDetails
WHERE quantity = 1;
```

SQL Example 3.1 Output:

| | ProductId |
|---|---|
| 1 | 1 |
| 2 | 2 |
| 3 | 6 |
| 4 | 7 |
| 5 | 8 |
| 6 | 9 |

SQL Example 3.2

Display all products that sold five or more units in an order. Show product ID.

SQL Example 3.2 Analysis

This is almost the same as Example 3.1 except that the filtering condition is different. Instead of finding "quantity = 1", you find "quantity >= 5".

You just want to know what products customers buy, so you may want to eliminate the duplicates by using the DISTINCT keyword.

SQL Example 3.2 statement

```
SELECT DISTINCT ProductId
FROM Sales.OrderDetails
WHERE quantity >= 5;
```

SQL Example 3.2 Output:

| | ProductId |
|---|---|
| 1 | 3 |
| 2 | 4 |
| 3 | 6 |

SQL Example 3.3

Display all USA customers. Show customer name and email. Sort by customer name in alphabetic order.

SQL Example 3.3 Analysis

In order to find customers from the USA, you use the WHERE clause condition country = 'USA'. Note that the quotation mark indicates the value is a string. In the previous two examples, the conditions involved numbers, and didn't use quotation marks. Also note that it is a single quotation mark. You cannot use double quotation marks or no quotation marks.

The ORDER BY clause must appear after the WHERE clause.

SQL Example 3.3 statement

```
SELECT CustomerName, Email
FROM Sales.Customers
WHERE Country = 'USA'
ORDER BY CustomerName;
```

SQL Example 3.3 Output:

| | CustomerName | Email |
|---|---|---|
| 1 | Beyond Electronics | green@beil.com |
| 2 | Beyond Electronics | black1@be.com |
| 3 | E Fun | bgold@efun.com |
| 4 | Just Electronics | jwhite@je.com |
| 5 | Overstock E | dy@os.com |

Review Question 3.29
The use of the WHERE clause allows you to ___________.
a. retrieve specific rows(s) of a table
b. retrieve specific column(s) of a table
c. insert data in a specific row(s) of a table
d. insert data in a specific column(s) of a table

Review Question 3.30
What's wrong with the following SQL statement:

```
SELECT CustomerName, Email
FROM Sales.Customers
WHERE Country = "Mexico"
```

a. Mexico is not one of the countries for the practice database.
b. The double quotation marks should be removed.
c. Single quotation marks should replace the double quotation marks.
d. No errors.

# 3.11 SQL BETWEEN and IS NULL Operators

You can use the BETWEEN operator for the WHERE condition if you want to select just those rows with a column value between two values, such as selecting all rows with a GPA between 3.0 and 4.0.

SQL Example 3.4

Display all employees who were born in the 1980s. Show first name, last name, and date of birth.

SQL Example 3.4 Analysis

The WHERE clause condition is between January 1, 1980 and December 31, 1989. You can use the BETWEEN operator. The BETWEEN operator includes both ending dates, but only to 12am of the last day, effectively excluding the day. The operator will not cause any problems with the DATE data type. However, if the data type is DATETIME2, you should add an additional day for the ending date. Note how the date is treated like a string with quotation mark and format of 'yyyymmdd', such as '19891231' for December 31, 1989. How do you know if a data type is DATE or DATETIME2? Go to Appendix B and check the value, does it include the time part in the value? If yes, then it is DATETIME2. Otherwise, it is DATE.

SQL Example 3.4 statement

```
SELECT FirstName, LastName, BirthDate
FROM HR.Employees
WHERE BirthDate BETWEEN '19800101' AND '19891231';
```

SQL Example 3.4 Output:

| | FirstName | LastName | BirthDate |
|---|---|---|---|
| 1 | Maria | Law | 1988-07-13 |
| 2 | Alice | Law | 1988-12-13 |
| 3 | Black | Hart | 1982-11-09 |

SQL Example 3.5

Display all products with sale prices between $100.00 and $200.00. Show the product ID and sale price.

SQL Example 3.5 Analysis

This is just another example of using the BETWEEN operator.

SQL Example 3.5 statement

```
SELECT DISTINCT ProductId, Price
FROM Sales.OrderDetails
WHERE price BETWEEN 100.00 AND 200.00;
```

SQL Example 3.5 Output:

| | ProductId | Price |
|---|---|---|
| 1 | 3 | 149.99 |
| 2 | 3 | 159.99 |
| 3 | 6 | 189.99 |
| 4 | 6 | 199.99 |
| 5 | 7 | 109.99 |

SQL Example 3.6

Display all customers that do not provide a contact name. Show customer name.

SQL Example 3.6 Analysis

When a customer does not provide a contact name, the value is NULL. You cannot use the equal sign (=) to compare if a column is NULL. You use the IS NULL operator.

SQL Example 3.6 statement

```
SELECT CustomerName
FROM Sales.Customers
WHERE contact IS NULL;
```

SQL Example 3.6 Output:

| | CustomerName |
|---|---|
| 1 | Cheap Electronics |

SQL Example 3.7

Display all customers that provide an email. Show customer name and email.

SQL Example 3.7 Analysis

The condition for this example is just the opposite of that in Example 3.6. You can use the IS NOT NULL operator.

SQL Example 3.7 statement

```
SELECT CustomerName, Email
FROM Sales.Customers
WHERE email IS NOT NULL;
```

SQL Example 3.7 Output:

| | CustomerName | Email |
|---|---|---|
| 1 | Just Electronics | jwhite@je.com |
| 2 | Beyond Electronics | green@beil.com |
| 3 | Beyond Electronics | black1@be.com |
| 4 | E Fun | bgold@efun.com |
| 5 | Overstock E | dy@os.com |
| 6 | E Fun | green@ef.com |
| 7 | Electronics4U | smith@e4u.com |

Review Question 3.31
Select the SQL clause that is equivalent to the following SQL clause:
WHERE Price BETWEEN 100.0 And 200.0
a. WHERE Price >= 100.0 AND <= 200.0
b. WHERE Price >= 100.0 AND Price <= 200.0
c. WHERE Price > 100.0 AND < 200.0
d. WHERE Price > 100.0 AND Price < 200.0

Review Question 3.32
Which of the following SQL WHERE clause is correct for retrieving rows without email provided?
a. WHERE Email = NULL
b. WHERE Email IS NULL
c. WHERE Email = “”
d. WHERE Email = “ “

Review Question 3.33
Suppose a student’s date of birth is “2010-01-01 01:02:03 000001” in a database table. Which of the following filters correctly selects the rows of all students who were born in the first 10 days of 2011?
a. BETWEEN ‘2011-01-01’ AND ‘2011-01-10’
b. BETWEEN ‘2010-12-31’ AND ‘2011-01-10’
c. BETWEEN ‘2011-01-01’ AND ‘2011-01-11’
d. BETWEEN ‘2010-12-31’ AND ‘2011-01-11’

## 3.12 SQL Logical Operators, AND, OR, NOT.

When you have more than one condition in the WHERE clause, you can use a logical operator, such as AND, OR, and NOT to combine the conditions. Here’s a list to show the result of the operator:

The result of the AND operator is TRUE only if both condition expressions are TRUE.
The result of the OR operator is TRUE if either condition expression is TRUE.
The result of the NOT operator reverses the value of the condition expression.

SQL Example 3.8

Display all products that are sold with unit price under $100.00 and over $1000.00. Show Product ID and sales price.

SQL Example 3.8 Analysis

There are two conditions in the problem. One is the price under $100 and the other is the price over $1000. You want the row if either condition is met. The logical OR operator will combine both in the result set.

SQL Example 3.8 statement

```
SELECT DISTINCT ProductId, Price
FROM Sales.OrderDetails
WHERE Price < 100.00 OR Price > 1000;
```

SQL Example 3.8 Output:

| | ProductId | Price |
|---|---|---|
| 1 | 1 | 1499.99 |
| 2 | 2 | 1599.99 |
| 3 | 4 | 99.99 |
| 4 | 7 | 79.99 |
| 5 | 8 | 59.99 |
| 6 | 8 | 69.99 |
| 7 | 9 | 1449.99 |

SQL Example 3.9

Display all employees who were born before January 1, 1990 and hired after January 1, 2014. Show the employee's first name and last name.

SQL Example 3.9 Analysis

There are two conditions expressed in this problem. The first one was born before January 1, 1990 and the second one was hired after January 1, 2014. To meet both conditions, you use the AND logical operator.

SQL Example 3.9 statement

```
SELECT FirstName, LastName
FROM HR.Employees
WHERE BirthDate < '19900101' AND HireDate > '20140101';
```

SQL Example 3.9 Output:

| | FirstName | LastName |
|---|---|---|
| 1 | Black | Hart |
| 2 | Christina | Robinson |

SQL Example 3.10

Display all products sold more than 1 unit in an order and that the sales price is either under $100.00 or over $1000.00. Show the product ID, units sold, and unit price.

SQL Example 3.10 Analysis

First, you want to retrieve all products sold from the OrderDetails with a quantity greater than one. Next, you filter out the rows by the price. Keep only those with prices less than $100 or over $1000. If you just put the three conditions expressed like this,

```
SELECT ProductId, Price, Quantity
FROM Sales.OrderDetails
WHERE Quantity > 1 AND Price < 100 OR Price > 1000;
```

You will get the wrong answer as shown below:

| | ProductId | Price | Quantity |
|---|---|---|---|
| 1 | 1 | 1499.99 | 1 |
| 2 | 1 | 1499.99 | 1 |
| 3 | 2 | 1599.99 | 1 |
| 4 | 4 | 99.99 | 6 |
| 5 | 8 | 69.99 | 2 |
| 6 | 9 | 1449.99 | 1 |
| 7 | 4 | 99.99 | 2 |
| 8 | 1 | 1499.99 | 1 |
| 9 | 8 | 59.99 | 2 |

You know the result is incorrect because several of them have a quantity equal to one. The problem is that the "AND" operator is higher ranked than the "OR" operator, which means the DBMS will execute the "AND" before executing the "OR". To solve this problem, you can use a parenthesis to force the OR operator to be performed first as shown below.

SQL Example 3.10 statement

```
SELECT ProductId, Price, Quantity
FROM Sales.OrderDetails
WHERE Quantity > 1 AND (Price < 100 OR Price > 1000);
```

SQL Example 3.10 Output:

| | ProductId | Price | Quantity |
|---|---|---|---|
| 1 | 4 | 99.99 | 6 |
| 2 | 8 | 69.99 | 2 |
| 3 | 4 | 99.99 | 2 |
| 4 | 8 | 59.99 | 2 |

Review Question 3.34
What is the result of the following:
(5<3) AND (3<2) OR (4>3)
a. TRUE
b. FALSE
c. Cannot tell
d. an error

Review Question 3.35
What is the difference between the following two WHERE clause condition:
```
WHERE Quantity > 1 AND Price < 100 OR Price > 1000
WHERE Quantity > 1 AND (Price < 100 OR Price > 1000)
```
a. You must add a pair of parentheses when logical AND is in the clause.
b. You must add a pair of parentheses when logical OR is in the clause.
c. A pair of parentheses are always required for complicated conditions in the WHERE clause.
d. The "AND" operator is higher ranked than the "OR" operator.

## 3.13 Chapter Summary

In this chapter, you learned about logical data modeling. After you show the conceptual model to the user, you now add attributes to the entities and relationships, set the primary key to each entity, and optionally, you can result in any many-to-many relationship with two one-to-many relationships. You also learned how to use SQL WHERE clause to retrieve rows that meet certain criteria. You learned how to use BETWEEN, IS NULL, AND, OR, NOT operators in the WHERE clause.

## 3.14 Discussion Questions

Discussion 3.1
When developing data models, some people suggest that you should have all entities identified before you add attributes to each entity, while others suggest that you include the attributes in each entity when you start the conceptual model. Explain the pros and cons for each approach.

Discussion 3.2
When determining the primary key for an entity, some people suggest that you should just use a surrogate key to save time. For example, for a STUDENT entity, just use StudentId as the primary key. For a BUILDING just use a BuildingId as a primary key. What are the pros and cons of such an approach?

Discussion 3.3
Many students do not like documentation for data modeling. What are the pros and cons of data modeling documentation?

## 3.15 Database Design Exercises

Exercise One:
A small publisher wants to keep data about its books and authors. A book has an ISBN, title, author(s), page count, genre(s), edition, retail price, and publishing year. An author has an author ID, first name, last name, and bio. ISBN is unique for books and author ID is unique for authors. Also, royalties are kept for each book and author(e.g. $100 for Book 1 and Author 1, $80 for Book 1 and Author 2). Write all business rules, build a conceptual mode, and draw a logical ERD for the publisher.

Exercise Two:
TennisAcademy is a small local tennis club that trains players from all skill levels and ages. The club needs a system to handle its player data.

A player has first name, last name, age, skill level, the date he or she joined the club, and, for some older players, their email and phone number.
A family has at least one player in the club. A family needs to pay an annual membership of $450.00, and provide a contact's first name, last name, email, and phone number.

There are different types of activities a player can participate in and each activity includes a practice fee. For example, a three-time-per-week activity costs $100 a month. An advanced private lesson costs $50 per hour. All coaches at TennisAcademy are part time employees. They are paid different hourly rates based on their experience and their time with the club. A coach may be qualified to coach one or more activities and each activity may have more than one qualified coach.

Most players also participate in different types of tournaments. Each tournament can have none or multiple players in it. A tournament includes a name, start date and end date, fee, and location. The club also keeps record of the points (e.g. the first place in a more competitive tournament may earn 500 points while a local tournament champion may only count for 100 points) a player earns for a tournament.

Finally, the club encourages all players to play with each other for practice at a location and time of their own choice. However, one of the players needs to report the winner and date played.

Your task:
1. Extract all possible business rules.
2. Build the conceptual model for the TennisAcademy.
3. Construct the logical model for the TennisAcademy.

## 3.16 SQL Exercises

Exercise 3.1

Display all products sold with the unit price of $149.99. Show product ID and unit price.

| | ProductId | Price |
|---|---|---|
| 1 | 3 | 149.99 |

Exercise 3.2

Display all products that are delivered more than 10 units at a time. Show product ID and units delivered in that delivery.

| | ProductId | Quantity |
|---|---|---|
| 1 | 4 | 20 |
| 2 | 5 | 15 |
| 3 | 6 | 25 |
| 4 | 7 | 12 |
| 5 | 7 | 18 |

Exercise 3.3

Display all UK customers. Show customer name and email. Sort customer name in alphabetic order.

| | CustomerName | Email |
|---|---|---|
| 1 | E Fun | green@ef.com |
| 2 | Electronics4U | smith@e4u.com |

Exercise 3.4

Display all products delivered in the first 9 days of October, 2016. Show product ID, quantity, and date.

| | ProductId | Quantity | DeliveryDate |
|---|---|---|---|
| 1 | 1 | 2 | 2016-10-01 09:30:00.0000000 |
| 2 | 2 | 10 | 2016-10-02 11:10:00.0000000 |
| 3 | 3 | 10 | 2016-10-05 09:15:00.0000000 |
| 4 | 4 | 20 | 2016-10-07 14:00:00.0000000 |
| 5 | 5 | 15 | 2016-10-07 15:30:00.0000000 |

Exercise 3.5

Display all products with supplier price between $100.00 and $200.00. Show the product ID, quantity, and price.

| | ProductId | Quantity | Price |
|---|---|---|---|
| 1 | 3 | 10 | 129.99 |
| 2 | 5 | 15 | 139.99 |
| 3 | 6 | 25 | 169.99 |

Exercise 3.6

Display all employees who do not provide a phone number. Show the employee's first name and last name.

| | FirstName | LastName |
|---|---|---|
| 1 | Christina | Robinson |
| 2 | Nicholas | Pinkston |

Exercise 3.7

Display all employees who provide a phone number. Show the employee's first name, last name, and phone number.

| | FirstName | LastName | Phone |
|---|---|---|---|
| 1 | Alex | Hall | (434) 290-3322 |
| 2 | Dianne | Hart | (434) 290-1122 |
| 3 | Maria | Law | (434) 531-5673 |
| 4 | Alice | Law | (434) 531-1010 |
| 5 | Black | Hart | (434) 531-1034 |

Exercise 3.8

Display all products with supplier unit price under $100.00 or over $1000.00. Show Product ID and supplier price.

| | ProductId | Price |
|---|---|---|
| 1 | 1 | 1099.99 |
| 2 | 1 | 1199.99 |
| 3 | 2 | 1199.99 |

| | | |
|---|---|---|
| 4 | 4 | 79.99 |
| 5 | 7 | 69.99 |
| 6 | 7 | 79.99 |

Exercise 3.9

Display all customers who placed orders before January 1, 2017 and are served by Employee ID 1. Show the customer ID and order date.

| | CustomerId | OrderDate |
|---|---|---|
| 1 | 5 | 2016-11-08 |
| 2 | 7 | 2016-12-23 |

Exercise 3.10

Display all products that are delivered more than 5 units at a time and the supplier price is either under $100.00 or over $1000.00. Show the product ID, supplier price, and delivery date.

| | ProductId | Price | DeliveryDate |
|---|---|---|---|
| 1 | 2 | 1199.99 | 2016-10-02 11:10:00.0000000 |
| 2 | 4 | 79.99 | 2016-10-07 14:00:00.0000000 |
| 3 | 7 | 79.99 | 2016-10-11 11:10:00.0000000 |
| 4 | 7 | 69.99 | 2016-10-12 09:50:00.0000000 |

## 3.17 Solutions to Review Questions

3.1 A; 3.2 A; 3.3 D; 3.4 A; 3.5 B; 3.6 C; 3.7 D; 3.8 B; 3.9 C; 3.10 D; 3.11 C; 3.12 D; 3.13 B; 3.14 C; 3.15 C; 3.16 A; 3.17 D; 3.18 D; 3.19 D; 3.20 B; 3.21 B; 3.22 B; 3.23 A; 3.24 D; 3.25 A; 3.26 C; 3.27 A; 3.28 B; 3.29 A; 3.30 C; 3.31 B; 3.32 B; 3.33 C; 3.34 A; 3.35 D;

# Chapter 4: Enhanced Data Model and SQL Function

## Chapter Learning Objectives

4.1 Construct enhanced entity relationship diagrams (EERD).
4.2 Use LIKE operator with single character and multiple character wildcards.
4.3 Use concatenations and aliases in the SELECT clause.
4.4 Use calculated fields in the SELECT clause.
4.5 Use functions to handle numbers, strings, data, and time.

## 4.1 Enhanced Entity Relationship Diagram (EERD)

In the last two chapters, you learned how to model a database with an Entity Relationship Diagram (ERD). However, sometimes you may find the attributes and relationships to have many duplications. It is wise, then, to use an enhanced entity relationship diagram (EERD). EERD is an extension of ERD and allows you to model more complex data requirements than ERD can do.

Suppose there are two types of students in the mini-world: GRADUATE and UNDERGRADUATE. You have three options to model the mini-world.

The first option is to use just a STUDENT entity that includes both undergraduate students and graduate students. There will be two issues in this approach. One is that there will be many null values. For example, if you have an attribute called GRE score (Graduate Record Examination), then the field value will be null for all undergraduate students. Another issue pertains to relationships. For example, a certain relationship may only exist for undergraduate students, which also results in more null values.

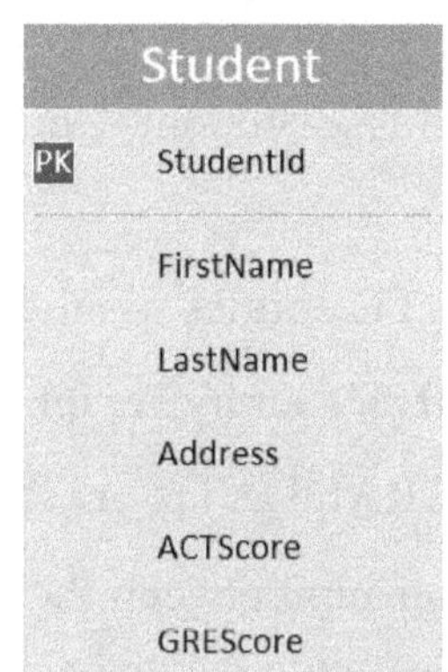

Figure 4.1 Student entity.

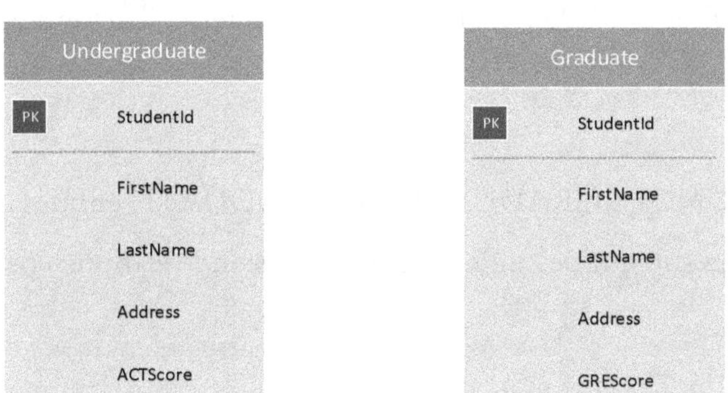

Figure 4.2 Use Undergraduate and graduate entities.

The second option is to replace the STUDENT entity with two entities, UNDERGRADUATE and GRADUATE? If you use this two-entity approach, you will have a model like this:

The problem for this approach is that there are many duplicated fields. As shown in Figure 4.2, you see that both entities contain FirstName, LastName, and Address attributes. In reality, there would be even more duplications. Duplication is often the major problem for maintenance.

To solve this problem, you can have a third option of modeling by choosing a third entity with all the common fields from UNDERGRADUATE and GRADUATE and put them in this new third entity. The new three-entity model looks like Figure 4.3. The duplication problem is solved because you have only one place to update.

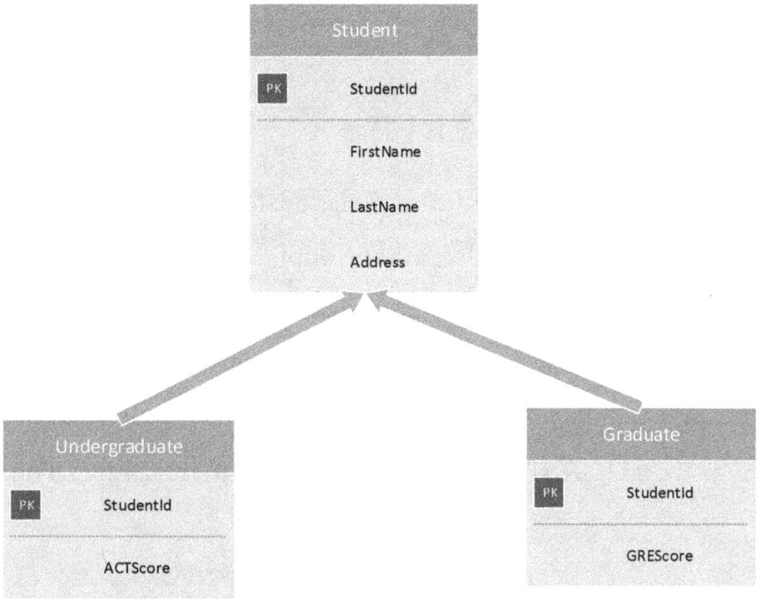

Figure 4.3 Use Student, Undergraduate, and Graduate entities.

Compare the model in Figure 4.3 and Figure 4.2. You can see that the duplicated attributes are all gone. The common/duplicated attributes are now only in the STUDENT entity. The UNDERGRADUATE and GRADUATE entities have their own unique attributes (except for the primary key, in this case student ID, which is expected to be shared.)

Such an arrangement allows the UNDERGRADUATE and GRADUATE entities to inherit attributes from the STUDENT entity. Both attributes and relationships of the STUDENT entity are inherited by UNDERGRADUATE and GRADUATE entities. And, the UNDERGRADUATE or GRADUATE entity can have its own relationship with other entities.
The relationship between the STUDENT and the UNDERGRADUATE and GRADUATE entities is called an "IS-A" relationship. In other words, an undergraduate student is a student, and a graduate student is a student, therefore allowing the UNDERGRADUATE and GRADUATE entities to inherit all attributes and relationships from the STUDENT entity.

The STUDENT entity is called the super entity and the UNDERGRADUATE and GRADUATE entities are called sub entities. Thus, in an "IS-A" relationship, the sub entities inherit all attributes and relationships of the super entity.

In EERD modeling, when you start with several entities that have common characteristics and put all those common characteristics in a new entity, the process is called generalization. The original entities become the sub entities and the newly formed entity becomes the super entity.

When you start with the super entity type and add unique characteristics to form sub entities, the process is called specialization.

In this book, we will use the term generalization/specialization to indicate the relationship between the super type and subtypes.

Review Question 4.1
Suppose there are UNDERGRADUATE and GRADUATE entities in the mini-world. What might be a problem if you combine the two entities into just one entity called STUDENT?
a. not enough entities to hold all attributes.
b. there may be many null values.
c. more entities are better than fewer entities.
d. too many attributes in just one entity.

Review Question 4.2
Suppose there are UNDERGRADUATE and GRADUATE entities in the mini-world. What might be a problem if you combine the two entities into just one entity called STUDENT?
a. There are not enough entities to hold all attributes.
b. This is not possible when a relationship is unique to the UNDERGRADUATE entity.
c. More entities are better than fewer entities.
d. There are too many attributes in just one entity.

Review Question 4.3
Suppose there are UNDERGRADUATE and GRADUATE entities in the mini-world. What might be a problem if you model with just the two entities?
a. There are not enough entities to hold all attributes.
b. This is not possible when a relationship is unique to the UNDERGRADUATE entity.
c. More entities are better than fewer entities.
d. Many duplicated attributes can cause maintenance issues.

Review Question 4.4
Suppose there are UNDERGRADUATE and GRADUATE entities in the mini-world. What might be an advantage if you model with three entities: UNDERGRADUATE, GRADUATE, and STUDENT?
a. There are fewer null values.
b. More attributes can be held with three entities.
c. More entities are better than fewer entities.
d. Three is a good number.

Review Question 4.5

Suppose there are UNDERGRADUATE and GRADUATE entities in the mini-world, and you pick all common attributes from both UNDERGRADUATE and GRADUATE entities and put them into a new entity called STUDENT. What do you call this new STUDENT entity?
a. associative entity
b. super entity
c. sub entity
d. composite entity

Review Question 4.6
Suppose there are UNDERGRADUATE and GRADUATE entities in the mini-world. You pick all common attributes from both UNDERGRADUATE and GRADUATE entities and put them into a new entity called STUDENT. What do you call the UNDERGRADUATE entity?
a. associative entity
b. super entity
c. sub entity
d. composite entity

Review Question 4.7
If you start with several entities that have common characteristics and put all those common characteristics in a new entity, the process is called ___________.
a. common flow
b. one-to-many relationship
c. generalization
d. specialization

Review Question 4.8
If you start with the super entity type and add unique characteristics to form sub entities, the process is called ____________.
a. common flow
b. one-to-many relationship
c. generalization
d. specialization

Review Question 4.9
When you model two entities as supertype and subtype, the subtype entity inherits _________.
a. all attributes and relationships of the super type entity.
b. some attributes and relationships of the super type entity.
c. all attributes of the super type entity.
d. all relationships of the super type entity.

Review Question 4.10
Suppose there are UNDERGRADUATE and GRADUATE entities in the mini-world. You pick all common attributes from both UNDERGRADUATE and GRADUATE entities and put them into a new entity called STUDENT. What is the relationship between the STUDENT the UNDERGRADUATE entities called?
a. EERD relationship
b. ERD relationship
c. STUDENT relationship
d. IS-A relationship

Review Question 4.11
Which of the following statements about EERD is correct?
a. A supertype is always a subtype
b. A subtype is always a supertype
c. A supertype is a subtype if you generalize
d. A subtype is a supertype if you generalize

## 4.2 Constraints

There are two types of constraints, or limitations, that can apply to a specialization/generalization between supertype and subtype entities. They are the disjointness constraint and the completeness constraint.
The *disjointness* constraint has two possible values: disjoint (specified by a character "d" in the circle in the diagram) or overlapping (specified by a character "o" in the circle in the diagram.) For a disjoint constraint, a super type entity instance can be a member of at most one of the subtypes of the relationship, while for an overlapping constraint, a super type entity instance can be a member of more than one subtype of the relationship.

For example, if a student cannot be considered as both an undergraduate and graduate at the same time, then the constraint is disjoint. If a student can be considered as both an undergraduate and graduate at the same time, then the constraint is overlapping (some universities allow 5$^{th}$ year undergraduate students to be counted as both an undergraduate or graduate student.)

A *completeness* constraint is about whether a supertype instance must be one of the subtype instances. There are two possibilities. If a super type instance must be one of the subtype instances, the constraint is called total completeness, specified by a double line under the circle in the diagram. On the other hand, if a super type instance can be none of the subtype instances, the constraint is called partial completeness, specified by a single line under the circle in the diagram. For example, if a student must be one or both undergraduate and graduate, then the constraint is total completeness. On the other hand, if a student is a non-degree student, they are neither an undergraduate nor graduate student, and so the constraint is partial completeness.

An example of EERD is displayed below assuming the following business rules: A student cannot be both an undergraduate and a graduate at the same time (this is a disjoint constraint and is indicated as a letter "d" inside the circle.) A student can also be neither undergraduate nor graduate, e.g. a non-degree student (this is a partial completeness constraint and is indicated as a single line under the circle in the figure.) Similar to regular ERD, EERD should also be based on business rules.

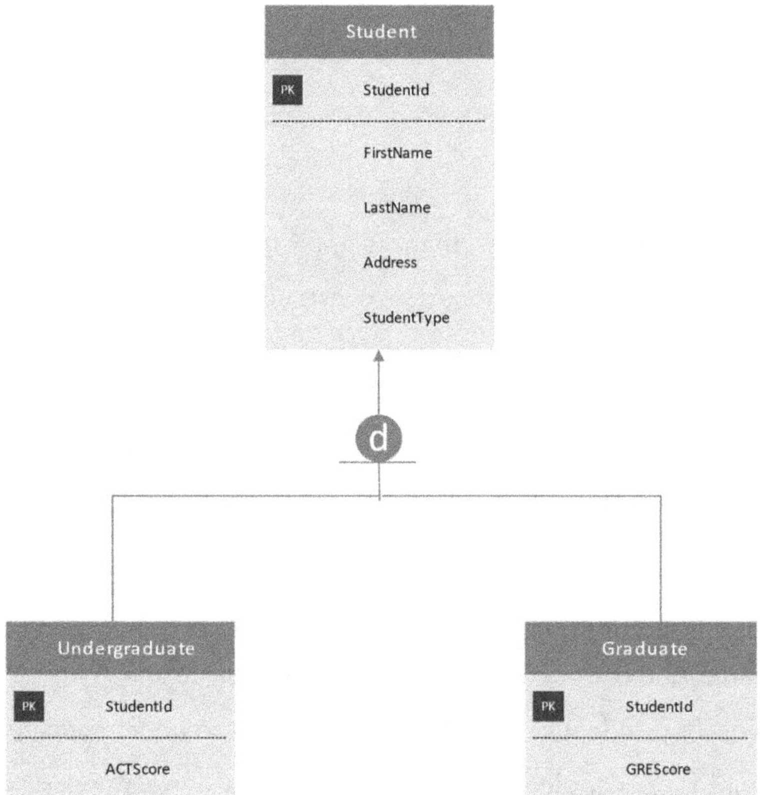


Figure 4.4 A simple EERD example with Student, Undergraduate, and Graduate entities.

Review Question 4.12
A student cannot be both an undergraduate and a graduate in a mini-world. This constraint is called _____.
a. disjoint
b. overlapping
c. total completeness
d. partial completeness

Review Question 4.13
A student can be both an undergraduate and a graduate in a mini-world. This constraint is called ________.
a. disjoint
b. overlapping
c. total completeness
d. partial completeness

Review Question 4.14
A student can be neither an undergraduate nor a graduate in a mini-world. This constraint is called ______.
a. disjoint
b. overlapping

c. total completeness
d. partial completeness

Review Question 4.15
A student must be an undergraduate or a graduate in a mini-world. This constraint is called ________.
a. disjoint
b. overlapping
c. total completeness
d. partial completeness

Review Question 4.16
Which of the following are types of constraints that can apply to a specialization/generalization between supertype and subtype entities?
a. disjointness
b. completeness
c. both disjointness and completeness
d. neither disjointness nor completeness

Review Question 4.17
A super type entity instance can be a member of at most one of the subtypes of the specialization/generalization. This constraint is called ________.
a. disjoint
b. overlapping
c. total completeness
d. partial completeness

Review Question 4.18
A super type entity instance can be a member of more than one subtype of the specialization/generalization relationship. This constraint is called __________.
a. disjoint
b. overlapping
c. total completeness
d. partial completeness

Review Question 4.19
If a super type instance must be one of the subtype instances, the constraint is called ____________.
a. disjoint
b. overlapping
c. total completeness
d. partial completeness

Review Question 4.20
If a super type instance can be none of the subtype instances, the constraint is called ___________.
a. disjoint
b. overlapping
c. total completeness
d. partial completeness

Review Question 4.21
In EERD, a double line under the circle indicates ____________.

a. disjoint
b. overlapping
c. total completeness
d. partial completeness

Review Question 4.22
In EERD, a single line under the circle indicates ___________.
a. disjoint
b. overlapping
c. total completeness
d. partial completeness

## 4.3 Subtype Discriminator

One problem with creating a supertype is that it can be hard to identify which subtype a supertype instance belongs to. For example, along with the undergraduate/graduate example, an instance under the student entity gives the student's name and identification, but does not indicate which subtype the student belongs to, undergraduate or graduate. Therefore, you need a discriminator, which is an attribute for the supertype entity used to identify which subtype an instance belongs to. In the student example, the discriminator could be an attribute under the student entity called StudentType, in which the student is either shown to be an 'undergraduate', 'graduate', both or neither. In the case of Figure 4.4, the domain for the student type is "undergraduate" and "graduate".

The connectivity between the supertype and each subtype is 1:1. This 1:1 relationship only exists between the supertype and each subtype. In other words, we cannot label relationships between the supertype and multiple subtypes. Thus, a student who is both an undergraduate and a graduate experiences two connectivity relationships: a 1:1 between student and undergraduate, and a 1:1 between student and graduate.

A discriminator is a single attribute when the disjointness constraint between the supertype and subtype is disjoint. The discriminator is a multivalued attribute when the disjointness constraint is overlapping. For example, if a student can only be an undergraduate or a graduate (a disjoint constraint,) a discriminator is a single attribute called studenttype with the attribute domain of "undergraduate" and "graduate". The example in Figure 4.4 illustrates the situation.

If a student can be both undergraduate and graduate at the same time (an overlapping constraint,) the discriminators are two attributes, an undergraduate attribute and a graduate attribute, in which both have the attribute domain of "yes" and "no".

Review Question 4.23
In order to know which subtype the supertype instance belongs to, the supertype needs a ______ as an attribute.
a. subtype indicator
b. supertype indicator
c. subtype discriminator
d. supertype discriminator

Review Question 4.24
The connectivity between the supertype and subtype is ____________.
a. one-to-one
b. one-to-many
c. many-to-many
d. one-to-two

Review Question 4.25
How many subtype discriminators are needed when the disjointness constraint between the supertype and subtype is disjoint?
a. 1
b. 2
c. 3
d. cannot tell

Review Question 4.26
Suppose a supertype has two subtypes. If the disjointness constraint is overlapping, how many subtype discriminators are needed?
a. 1
b. 2
c. 3
d. cannot tell

## 4.4 An Example of Using EERD

LearningByDoing University needs a database to keep track of its personnel. It has the following business description:

The university has several colleges, such as College of Business and College of Engineering. Each person is associated with only one college. There are three types of persons: employee, student, and alumni. A person can belong to one, two, or all three types. For example, an alumnus can be an employee of the university and also take courses as a student to update knowledge. A person must be at least one of the three. Each person has a name, social security number, address, date of birth, and email. Every person works for one of the colleges (Arts and Sciences, the engineering school, etc.)

There are two types of employees: faculty and staff. An employee must be either faculty or staff, but cannot be both. Each employee has a date hired. A faculty member has a rank level, such as full professor. A staff member has a staff position, such as student advisor. Staff members also have a salary.

An alumna/alumnus has a degree year, such as 2022.

There are two types of students, undergraduate and graduate. A student can be neither undergraduate nor graduate, for example, a non-degree student. A student can be undergraduate or graduate. And, a student can be both undergraduate and graduate. Each student has a GPA.

An undergraduate student has a class standing which determines what courses she or he can take. A graduate student has major research interests. A logical EERD may look like:

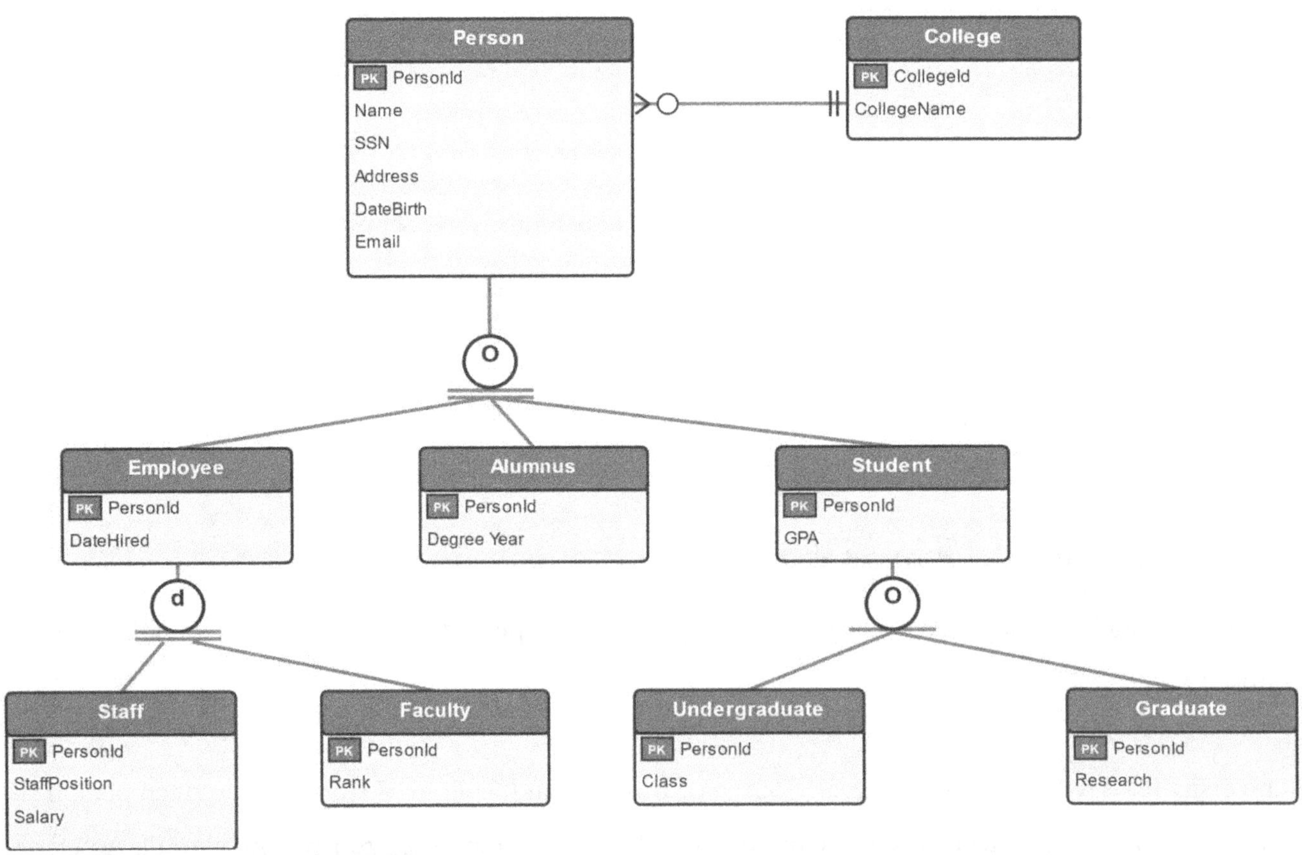


Figure 4.5. An example of EERD.

## 4.5 Figure 4.5 Example Explanation

A person has to be at least one of the three types (Employee, Alumnus, Student) which suggests that the disjointness constraint is overlapping (character “o” in the figure) and the completeness constraint is total completeness (double lines under the circle in the figure).

An employee has to be exactly one of the two types (staff and faculty) which suggests that the disjointness constraint is disjoint (character “d” in the figure) and the completeness constraint is total completeness (double lines under the circle in the figure).

A student can be neither or both types (undergraduate and graduate) which suggests that the disjointness constraint is overlapping (character “o” in the figure) and the completeness constraint is partial completeness (single line under the circle in the figure).

## 4.6 SQL LIKE Operator

Sometimes, the filtering condition in the WHERE clause may not be an exact match for a string. For example, if you search for a customer name, you may only know part of their name. In this case, you may still use the WHERE clause to filter the rows by using the LIKE operator.

SQL Example 4.1
Display all customers that have the word “Electronics” in their name. Show the customer name and country of origin.

SQL Example 4.1 Analysis
In the WHERE clause, instead of using WHERE CustomerName = ‘Electronics’, you can use WHERE CustomerName LIKE ‘%electronics%’. LIKE is a keyword that you use when you don’t have an exact string. The percentage % sign indicates that there may be any number of characters. So in this case, the rows with customer names containing anything before and after the word “electronics” will be displayed. The string is not case sensitive in SQL Server by default.

SQL Example 4.1 statement

```
SELECT CustomerName, Country
FROM Sales.Customers
WHERE CustomerName LIKE '%electronics%';
```

SQL Example 4.1 Output:

| | CustomerName | Country |
|---|---|---|
| 1 | Just Electronics | USA |
| 2 | Beyond Electronics | USA |
| 3 | Beyond Electronics | USA |
| 4 | Electronics4U | UK |
| 5 | Cheap Electronics | Canada |

SQL Example 4.2

Display all customers that are in the USA, and if their state abbreviation has an 'A' as the second letter. Show customer name and country.

SQL Example 4.2 Analysis

Similar to Example 4.1, this time you know exactly how many letters are missing and where the missing letter is (the first letter is missing). In this case, you can use an underscore (_) to indicate a missing letter. You can use an underscore to indicate one missing character in any string. You can use the underscore as many times as you like, each one indicating one unknown character.

SQL Example 4.2 statement

```
SELECT CustomerName, Country
FROM Sales.Customers
WHERE Country = 'USA' AND State LIKE '_A';
```

SQL Example 4.2 Output:

| | CustomerName | Country |
|---|---|---|
| 1 | Beyond Electronics | USA |
| 2 | E Fun | USA |
| 3 | Overstock E | USA |

Review Question 4.27

In the SQL SELECT statement, when the filtering condition in the WHERE clause is not an exact match for a string, you can use the ________ operator.

a. partial match

b. equal

c. wildcard

d. LIKE

Review Question 4.28
In the SQL SELECT statement, when the filtering condition in the WHERE clause has LIKE operator, the % stands for _______.
a. one unknown character
b. any number of unknown characters
c. percentage
d. really like

Review Question 4.29
In the SQL SELECT statement, when the filtering condition in the WHERE clause has LIKE operator, the "_" stands for _______.
a. one unknown character
b. any number of unknown characters
c. one variable
d. really like

## 4.7 SQL Concatenate Fields and Use Alias

Sometimes you may want to combine fields as you retrieve them. For example, you can combine the first name and last name of an employee and make it a full name. This is called concatenating. You use the + sign to concatenate, such as FirstName+ ' '+ LastName. You combine the first name and last name with a space in between. You are not limited to using a space. For example, FirstName+'-'+LastName will add a dash sign between the first name and last name

When you do the concatenation, you often need to rename the column head. In the above example, it is no longer appropriate to call the combined result either first name or last name. Instead, you may want to call it 'full name.' This is called using an alias. You use the keyword AS to add an alias. For example, FirstName + ' ' + LastName AS FullName.

If you want the column head to have more than one word, such as Full Name with a space in it, you will have to use either a quotation mark (either single or double) or a square bracket [] surrounding the alias words, for example FirstName + ' ' + LastName AS 'Full Name' or FirstName + ' ' + LastName AS "Full Name", or FirstName + ' ' + LastName AS [Full Name].

SQL Example 4.3
Display all employees' full names, which is the first name plus the last name with a space in between.

SQL Example 4.3 Analysis

You will need two columns, the FirstName and LastName columns. Then use a plus sign to combine them. Remember to add a space in the middle.

SQL Example 4.3 statement

```
SELECT FirstName + ' ' + LastName
FROM HR.Employees;
```

SQL Example 4.3 Output:

| | (No column name) |
|---|---|
| 1 | Alex Hall |
| 2 | Dianne Hart |
| 3 | Maria Law |
| 4 | Alice Law |
| 5 | Black Hart |
| 6 | Christina Robinson |
| 7 | Nicholas Pinkston |

SQL Example 4.4

Same as SQL Example 4.3, but this time use a more meaningful column head called "Full Name".

SQL Example 4.4 Analysis

The only thing new is that you add the alias by using the keyword AS. Note that the AS keyword is optional. We suggest that you use it to make it read easier.

SQL Example 4.4 statement

```
SELECT FirstName + ' ' + LastName AS "Full Name"
FROM HR.Employees;
```

SQL Example 4.4 Output:

| | Full Name |
|---|---|
| 1 | Alex Hall |
| 2 | Dianne Hart |
| 3 | Maria Law |
| 4 | Alice Law |
| 5 | Black Hart |
| 6 | Christina Robinson |
| 7 | Nicholas Pinkston |

Review Question 4.30

Suppose a table has a postalCode field, which is a five-digit string and a plus4 field which is a four-digit string. Write the SELECT clause that will display the zip+4 in the format of 12345-1234.
a. SELECT 12345-1234
b. SELECT postalCode, plus4
c. SELECT postalCode, -, plus4
d. SELECT postalCode + '-' + plus4

Review Question 4.31
Suppose a table has studentName and nickName fields. Write the SELECT clause that will display the name and nickname in the format of Lisa Smith (Liz).
a. SELECT studentName, nickName
b. SELECT studentName (nickName)
c. SELECT studentName + (nickName)
d. SELECT studentName + ' ('+nickName+')'

Review Question 4.32
Suppose a table has a postalCode field and you want the field header to display Postal Code. What is the correct SELECT clause?
a. SELECT postalCode
b. SELECT Postal Code
c. SELECT postalCode AS "Postal Code"
d. SELECT postalCode AS Postal Code

## 4.8 Calculated Fields

You not only can concatenate several fields into one with any strings (e.g. space) added, but you can also operate on these fields. For example, every product delivery includes the quantity and unit price. You can calculate the monetary value of each delivery by multiplying the quantity with the unit price.

SQL Example 4.5

Calculate the monetary value of each product delivery. Show all delivery IDs, product IDs, quantities, unit prices, and delivery monetary values (quantity x price.)

SQL Example 4.5 Analysis

Similar to the concatenation, you just add quantity * price AS "Monetary Value" in the column list of the SELECT. Remember to add the alias to make the display more meaningful. The keyword "AS" is optional.

SQL Example 4.5 statement

```
SELECT DeliveryId, ProductId, Quantity, Price, Quantity*Price AS "Monetary
Value"
FROM Purchasing.Deliveries;
```

SQL Example 4.5 Output:

| | DelieryId | ProductId | Quantity | Price | Monetary Value |
|---|---|---|---|---|---|
| 1 | 1 | 1 | 2 | 1099.99 | 2199.98 |
| 2 | 2 | 1 | 5 | 1199.99 | 5999.95 |
| 3 | 3 | 2 | 10 | 1199.99 | 11999.90 |
| 4 | 4 | 3 | 10 | 129.99 | 1299.90 |
| 5 | 5 | 4 | 20 | 79.99 | 1599.80 |
| 6 | 6 | 5 | 15 | 139.99 | 2099.85 |
| 7 | 7 | 6 | 25 | 169.99 | 4249.75 |
| 8 | 8 | 7 | 12 | 79.99 | 959.88 |
| 9 | 9 | 7 | 18 | 69.99 | 1259.82 |

SQL Example 4.6

The product 1's supplier decided to give Product 1 a 10% discount. Show delivery ID, product ID, regular price and discounted price.

SQL Example 4.6 Analysis

In the SELECT columns, you should add a new calculated column which is Price * 0.9.

SQL Example 4.6 statement

```
SELECT DeliveryId, ProductId, Price AS "Regular Price", Price *0.9 AS "Sale
Price"
FROM Purchasing.Deliveries
WHERE ProductId = 1;
```

SQL Example 4.6 Output:

| | DeliveryId | ProductId | Regular Price | Sale Price |
|---|---|---|---|---|
| 1 | 1 | 1 | 1099.99 | 989.99100 |
| 2 | 2 | 1 | 1199.99 | 1079.99100 |

Review Question 4.33
If a table has two numeric fields, X1 and X2, which of the following SELECT clauses is NOT valid?
a. SELECT X1+X2 AS Sum
b. SELECT 2X1 AS DoubleValue
c. SELECT X1-X2 AS DifferentValue
d. SELECT 2X1

## 4.9 Use Functions to Handle Number and String

In SQL Example 4.6's output, you may notice that the "Sale Price" contains five decimal places. To display only two decimal places, you may need a function called CAST(). There are many such functions in SQL. For example: An UPPER() function will change a string to all uppercase.

The CHARINDEX() function allows you to search for a specific expression in another expression. The return will be the starting position. For example, you can search for "go" in "go to a good school". The result will be 1. Every character counts, including the space. You can also specify where to start your search. In the above example, if you want to start the search from position 2, the result will be 9 because the first "go" will be ignored as it starts the search at position 2. By default, the search is case-insensitive.

Syntax:
CHARINDEX('expression to find', 'expression to search', start_location)

For example:
CHARINDEX('e', CustomerName, 3) will return the position of the first "e" in the customer's name beginning from the third letter. If the customerName is "electronic store", the returned value will be 3. If a match is not found, the returned value will be 0.

SUBSTRING() function can be used to return part of a character, binary, text, or image expression.

Syntax:
SUBSTRING('expression', start, length)

The 'expression' is the string you want to extract from.
The start is an integer number that specifies where the returned string starts.
The length is an integer number that specifies how many characters are in the returned string.

For example:
SUBSTRING('George Washington', 8, 10) will return the string of "Washington"
SUBSTRING('George Washington', 1, 6) will return the string of "George".

SQL Example 4.7
Same as SQL Example 4.6. This time, you should display only two decimal places for the "Sale Price" column.

SQL Example 4.7 Analysis

The syntax for CAST() function is

CAST(expression AS DataType)

In this example, you cast the sale price to a numeric data type that can take up to 7 digits with 2 decimal places.

SQL Example 4.7 statement

```
SELECT DeliveryId, ProductId, Price AS "Regular Price", CAST(Price *0.9 AS
NUMERIC(7, 2)) AS "Sale Price"
FROM Purchasing.Deliveries
WHERE ProductId = 1;
```

SQL Example 4.7 Output:

| | DeliveryId | ProductId | Regular Price | Sale Price |
|---|---|---|---|---|
| 1 | 1 | 1 | 1099.99 | 989.99 |
| 2 | 2 | 1 | 1199.99 | 1079.99 |

SQL Example 4.8

Display customer name and its headquarter country with the country name in all capital letters.

SQL Example 4.8 Analysis

Use UPPER() function to convert the country name to all capital letters.

SQL Example 4.8 statement

```
SELECT CustomerName, UPPER(Country) AS Country
FROM Sales.Customers;
```

SQL Example 4.8 Output:

| | CustomerName | Country |
|---|---|---|
| 1 | Just Electronics | USA |
| 2 | Beyond Electronics | USA |
| 3 | Beyond Electronics | USA |
| 4 | E Fun | USA |
| 5 | Overstock E | USA |
| 6 | E Fun | UK |
| 7 | Electronics4U | UK |
| 8 | Cheap Electronics | CANADA |

SQL Example 4.9

Find the position of the first "e" in a customer's name. Show customer name and the position of "e".

SQL Example 4.9 Analysis

Use the CHARINDEX() function to find the position. The search starts from the first position so you don't need to specify the starting position. Just provide the string to search for

SQL Example 4.9 statement

```
SELECT CustomerName, CHARINDEX('e', CustomerName) AS "Position of e"
FROM Sales.Customers;
```

SQL Example 4.9 Output:

| | CustomerName | Position of e |
|---|---|---|
| 1 | Just Electronics | 6 |
| 2 | Beyond Electronics | 2 |
| 3 | Beyond Electronics | 2 |
| 4 | E Fun | 1 |
| 5 | Overstock E | 3 |
| 6 | E Fun | 1 |
| 7 | Electronics4U | 1 |
| 8 | Cheap Electronics | 3 |

SQL Example 4.10

Find the position of the first "e" and second "e" in a customer's name. Show customer name and the position of the first "e" and second "e" in the customer's name. If the name does not contain one or two e's, show 0.

SQL Example 4.10 Analysis

Display the customer name and the position of the first "e" is the task of SQL Example 4.9. The only new task is to add a new column to display the position of the second "e". You will still use the CHARINDEX() function, but this time, you cannot begin the search from position 1. You have to start the search after the position of the first "e". You already know the location of the first "e", so just add a number 1 to it as CHARINDEX('e', CustomerName)+1 for start_location.

SQL Example 4.10 statement

```
SELECT CustomerName, CHARINDEX('e', CustomerName) AS "Position of e",
CHARINDEX('e', CustomerName, CHARINDEX('e', CustomerName)+1) AS "Position of
second e"
```

```
FROM Sales.Customers;
```

SQL Example 4.10 Output:

| | CustomerName | Position of e | Position of second e |
|---|---|---|---|
| 1 | Just Electronics | 6 | 8 |
| 2 | Beyond Electronics | 2 | 8 |
| 3 | Beyond Electronics | 2 | 8 |
| 4 | E Fun | 1 | 0 |
| 5 | Overstock E | 3 | 11 |
| 6 | E Fun | 1 | 0 |
| 7 | Electronics4U | 1 | 3 |
| 8 | Cheap Electronics | 3 | 7 |

SQL Example 4.11

Display all characters between the first two e's in a customer's name. For example, for the customer "Cheap Electronics", the characters between the first two e's are "ap ". Show customer name and the characters between the first two e's.

SQL Example 4.11 Analysis

Use SUBSTRING() function to extract all characters between the first two e's. You need to know the start location, which is the example in SQL Example 4.9. You also need the number of characters between the two e's which is the location of the second "e" minus the location of the first "e" minus 1.

For example, the number of characters between the two e's in "Cheap Electronics" is 3 (include a space). The location of the second "e" is 7. The location of the first "e" is 3. So the number of characters between the two e's are 7-3-1 = 3.

SQL Example 4.10 is about the location of the second "e".

You cannot show the characters between the two e's for customers who don't have two e's. So, you need to add a WHERE clause to filter out those who don't have two e's in the name by using

WHERE CustomerName LIKE '%e%e%';

SQL Example 4.11 statement

```
SELECT CustomerName, SUBSTRING(CustomerName, CHARINDEX('e', CustomerName)+1,
CHARINDEX('e', CustomerName, CHARINDEX('e', CustomerName)+1)-CHARINDEX('e',
CustomerName)-1 ) AS "Characters between the two e's"
FROM Sales.Customers
WHERE CustomerName LIKE '%e%e%';
```

SQL Example 4.11 Output (Note that it is difficult to see the ending space in the string)

| | CustomerName | Characters between the two e's |
|---|---|---|
| 1 | Just Electronics | l |
| 2 | Beyond Electronics | yond |
| 3 | Beyond Electronics | yond |
| 4 | Overstock E | rstock |
| 5 | Electronics4U | l |
| 6 | Cheap Electronics | ap |

Review Question 4.34
What is the purpose of the following WHERE clause?
WHERE CustomerName LIKE '%e%e%'
a. Retrieve only rows with a percentage sign in a customer name.
b. Retrieve only rows with three percentage signs in a customer name.
c. Retrieve only rows with two "e"s in a customer name.
d. Retrieve only rows with both "e"s and percentage signs in a customer name.

Review Question 4.35
What will be the result of the following function?
SUBSTRING('Lucy Scott', 1, 6)
a. Lucy
b. Lucy S
c. ucy S
d. ucy Sc

Review Question 4.36
What will be the result of the following function?
CHARINDEX('t', 'Lucy Scott', 3)
a. 2
b. 3
c. 9
d. 10

## 4.10 Use Functions to Handle Date and Time

The GETDATE() function will return today's date. You can often use it to calculate how many years/days/weeks have passed.

You can use the DATEDIFF() function to calculate the difference between two dates. The syntax is DATEDIFF(day, startdate, enddate)

The function will return the difference in days between the two dates. If you change the day to month, it will return the difference in number of months between the two dates. However, the calculation only considers the difference of months, not how much time is between. For example, between January 31st and February 1st, there is a one month difference. Between January 1st and January 31st, there is a zero month difference, so the actual time passed is not necessarily considered.

DATEDIFF(month, '20170601', '20170630') will return zero because the two dates are in the same month, while DATEDIFF(month, '20170630', '20170701') will return 1 because the two dates are in different months.

You can also change the day to year so that the function will return the number of years between two dates.

YEAR(date) will return the year of the date value. For example: YEAR('20160912') will return 2016. Similarly, MONTH('20160912') will return 9 and DAY('20160912') will return 12.

DATEFROMPARTS(year, month, day) function allows you to construct a new date from the three integers of year, month, and day as long as the three integers are valid (for example, you cannot insert 42 for the day value.)

SQL Example 4.12

Display today's date and the number of months the employee has worked for the company. Show the employee's first name, last name, today's date, and the number of months the employee has worked.

SQL Example 4.12 Analysis

In order to get today's date, you will use the GETDATE() function. To get the month difference between the date the employee was hired and today's date, you use the DATEDIFF() function.

SQL Example 4.12 statement

```
SELECT FirstName, LastName, HireDate, GETDATE() AS "Today's Date",
DATEDIFF(month, HireDate, GETDATE()) AS "Months Worked"
FROM HR.Employees;
```

SQL Example 4.12 Output (Note: the number of months worked will be different from yours because it depends on today's date)

| | FirstName | LastName | HireDate | Today's Date | Months Worked |
|---|---|---|---|---|---|
| 1 | Alex | Hall | 2015-08-09 | 2026-03-22 13:09:52.220 | 127 |
| 2 | Dianne | Hart | 2010-08-01 | 2026-03-22 13:09:52.220 | 187 |
| 3 | Maria | Law | 2012-08-21 | 2026-03-22 13:09:52.220 | 163 |
| 4 | Alice | Law | 2012-04-22 | 2026-03-22 13:09:52.220 | 167 |
| 5 | Black | Hart | 2015-04-12 | 2026-03-22 13:09:52.220 | 131 |
| 6 | Christina | Robinson | 2014-06-15 | 2026-03-22 13:09:52.220 | 141 |
| 7 | Nicholas | Pinkston | 2013-05-22 | 2026-03-22 13:09:52.220 | 154 |

SQL Example 4.13

Same as SQL Example 4.14. This time, show today's date without the time part.

SQL Example 4.13 Analysis

No new functions are necessary to accomplish this task. Recall the use of CAST() function in SQL Example 4.7. You just need to cast the data type to date.

SQL Example 4.13 statement

```
SELECT FirstName, LastName, HireDate, CAST(GETDATE() AS DATE) AS "Today's
Date", DATEDIFF(month, HireDate, GETDATE()) AS "Months Worked"
FROM HR.Employees;
```

SQL Example 4.13 Output (Note: the number of months worked will be different from yours because it depends on today's date)

| | FirstName | LastName | HireDate | Today's Date | Months Worked |
|---|---|---|---|---|---|
| 1 | Alex | Hall | 2015-08-09 | 2026-03-22 | 127 |
| 2 | Dianne | Hart | 2010-08-01 | 2026-03-22 | 187 |
| 3 | Maria | Law | 2012-08-21 | 2026-03-22 | 163 |
| 4 | Alice | Law | 2012-04-22 | 2026-03-22 | 167 |
| 5 | Black | Hart | 2015-04-12 | 2026-03-22 | 131 |
| 6 | Christina | Robinson | 2014-06-15 | 2026-03-22 | 141 |
| 7 | Nicholas | Pinkston | 2013-05-22 | 2026-03-22 | 154 |

SQL Example 4.14

Display all employees who were born in December of any year. Show the employee's first name, last name, and date of birth.

SQL Example 4.14 Analysis

To find out the month of an employee's date of birth, use the MONTH() function by passing the date of birth to the function.

SQL Example 4.14 statement

```
SELECT FirstName, LastName, BirthDate
FROM HR.Employees
WHERE MONTH(BirthDate) = 12;
```

SQL Example 4.14 Output:

| | FirstName | LastName | BirthDate |
|---|---|---|---|
| 1 | Dianne | Hart | 1978-12-03 |
| 2 | Alice | Law | 1988-12-13 |

SQL Example 4.15

Display all employees' birth month and year. Show employees' first name, last name, and the month and year of birth. To hide the day of birth, use the first day of the month for all employees.

SQL Example 4.15 Analysis

You can still use the BirthDate column of the employees table. Just replace the day of the month with the first day of the month and keep the actual month and year. The DATEFROMPARTS() function can be used.

SQL Example 4.15 statement

```
SELECT FirstName, LastName, DATEFROMPARTS(YEAR(BirthDate), MONTH(BirthDate),
1) AS BirthMonth
FROM HR.Employees;
```

SQL Example 4.15 Output:

| | FirstName | LastName | BirthMonth |
|---|---|---|---|
| 1 | Alex | Hall | 1990-02-01 |
| 2 | Dianne | Hart | 1978-12-01 |
| 3 | Maria | Law | 1988-07-01 |
| 4 | Alice | Law | 1988-12-01 |
| 5 | Black | Hart | 1982-11-01 |
| 6 | Christina | Robinson | 1978-07-01 |
| 7 | Nicholas | Pinkston | 1977-10-01 |

Review Question 4.37
Which T-SQL function returns today's date?
a. TODAY()
b. GETDATE()
c. CURRENT()

d. TODAYDATE()

## 4.11 Chapter Summary

In this chapter, you learned how to use an enhanced entity relationship diagram to model the mini-world with entities that allow inheritance of attributes and relationships. When you have two or more entities that share many attributes or relationships, you should consider using EERD.

You also learned how to use functions in the SQL SELECT clause. You can use t-sql functions to change data format, retrieve data, and manipulate fields for displaying. The functions covered in this chapter are only a small part of all t-sql functions. Also note that functions in SQL are one of the least versatile (it may or may not work with other DBMS).

## 4.12 Discussion Questions

Discussion 4.1
Compare the EERD you learned in this chapter with the ERD you learned in the previous chapters. What do you think are the advantages and disadvantages of EERD?

Discussion 4.2
Explain the differences between specialization and generalization in EERD design. Which one would you recommend under which situation? Why?

Discussion 4.3
A subtype discriminator is one or more attributes of the supertype. When would you just add one attribute for the discriminator and when would you add multiple attributes for the discriminator?

## 4.13 Database Design Exercises

Exercise One:
A small publisher wants to keep data about its books. A book has an ISBN, title, author(s), page count, genre(s), edition, retail price, and publishing year. An author has an author ID, first name, last name, and bio. Also, royalties are kept for each book and author. A book has three to four reviewers but only one editor. A reviewer is a volunteer who has a reviewer ID, first name, last name, and date that he or she reviews a book. An editor is an employee who has an employee ID, first name, last name, and all the books he or she edits. Write all business rules and draw a logical EERD for the publisher.

Exercise Two:
The following narrative describes a simplified version of a bank. There are about two dozen branches of the bank located in a Midwest state. Each branch has an address and a branch manager. Each branch also has 10 to 30 employees. Employee data includes name, office, and supervisor. Each branch offers several different types of accounts for its customers.

There are four different types of accounts. Three of them bear interest. They are savings accounts, money market deposit accounts (MMDAs), and certificates of deposits (CDs). The MMDA and CD includes a penalty if minimum requirements are not met. The non-interest account is the checking account.

All accounts have account numbers and balance. The interest-bearing accounts include the interest rate and the amount of interest earned. For the MMDA and CD account, the penalty amount is tracked. The checking account keeps track of each check written. A check has an amount and date. A CD account has a maturity date.

Each branch also offers several different types of loans for its customers. All loans have a loan amount and maturity date. A CD secured loan includes the CD account number. Vehicle loans have a VIN number and purchase amount. Customer data includes name, social security number, address, and phone.

Your tasks:
1. Extract all possible business rules.
2. Construct a logical EERD for the bank.

## 4.14 SQL Exercises

### Exercise 4.1

Display all products that have the word "LED" in its name. Show product ID and product name.

| | ProductId | ProductName |
|---|---|---|
| 1 | 2 | 60-Inch 4K Ultra HD Smart LED TV |
| 2 | 3 | 3200 Lumens LED Home Theater Projector |

### Exercise 4.2

Display all suppliers that have the letter "a" as its second letter in the name. Show supplier ID and supplier name.

| | SupplierId | SupplierName |
|---|---|---|
| 1 | 4 | Samsong |
| 2 | 5 | Canan |

### Exercise 4.3

Display all suppliers with the supplier name followed by the country in parentheses, such as Pine Apple (USA).

| | (No column name) |
|---|---|
| 1 | Pine Apple (USA) |
| 2 | IMB (USA) |
| 3 | Lonovo (China) |
| 4 | Samsong (South Korea) |
| 5 | Canan (Japan) |

### Exercise 4.4

Same as Exercise 4.3, but this time use a more meaningful column head called "Supplier (Country)".

| | Supplier (Country) |
|---|---|
| 1 | Pine Apple (USA) |
| 2 | IMB (USA) |
| 3 | Lonovo (China) |
| 4 | Samsong (South Korea) |
| 5 | Canan (Japan) |

Exercise 4.5

Calculate the monetary value of each order detail. Show order ID, product ID, price, quantity, and order detail monetary value (quantity x price.). Limit to the three highest monetary values.

| | OrderId | ProductId | Price | Quantity | Monetary Value |
|---|---|---|---|---|---|
| 1 | 2 | 2 | 1599.99 | 1 | 1599.99 |
| 2 | 1 | 1 | 1499.99 | 1 | 1499.99 |
| 3 | 2 | 1 | 1499.99 | 1 | 1499.99 |

Exercise 4.6

The LifeStyle manager decides to give customers who bought three or more units of the same product in the same order a 20 percent discount. Show order ID, product ID, price, quantity, and discounted price for those discounted in the orderdetails.

| | OrderId | ProductId | Price | Quantity | Discounted Price |
|---|---|---|---|---|---|
| 1 | 2 | 4 | 99.99 | 6 | 79.99200 |
| 2 | 2 | 6 | 189.99 | 5 | 151.99200 |
| 3 | 5 | 3 | 149.99 | 6 | 119.99200 |
| 4 | 5 | 6 | 199.99 | 3 | 159.99200 |

Exercise 4.7

Same as Exercise 4.6. This time, you should display only two decimal places for the "Discounted Price" column.

| | OrderId | ProductId | Price | Quantity | Discounted Price |
|---|---|---|---|---|---|
| 1 | 2 | 4 | 99.99 | 6 | 79.99 |
| 2 | 2 | 6 | 189.99 | 5 | 151.99 |
| 3 | 5 | 3 | 149.99 | 6 | 119.99 |
| 4 | 5 | 6 | 199.99 | 3 | 159.99 |

Exercise 4.8

Display employees' first name and last name with the last name in all capital letters.

| | FirstName | LastName |
|---|---|---|
| 1 | Alex | HALL |
| 2 | Dianne | HART |
| 3 | Maria | LAW |
| 4 | Alice | LAW |
| 5 | Black | HART |
| 6 | Christina | ROBINSON |
| 7 | Nicholas | PINKSTON |

Exercise 4.9

Find the position of the first blank space in a supplier's street address. Show supplier street address and the position of the first blank space.

| | StreetAddress | Position of space |
|---|---|---|
| 1 | 1 Pine Apple St. | 2 |
| 2 | 123 International Blvd | 4 |
| 3 | 33 Beijin Square | 3 |
| 4 | 1 Electronics Road | 2 |
| 5 | 12 Camera St | 3 |

Exercise 4.10

Find the position of the first blank space and second blank space in a supplier's street address. Show supplier's street address and the position of first blank space and second blank space in the supplier's street address.

| | StreetAddress | Position of space | Position of 2nd space |
|---|---|---|---|
| 1 | 1 Pine Apple St. | 2 | 7 |
| 2 | 123 International Blvd | 4 | 18 |
| 3 | 33 Beijin Square | 3 | 10 |
| 4 | 1 Electronics Road | 2 | 14 |
| 5 | 12 Camera St | 3 | 10 |

Exercise 4.11

Display the first word after the street number in a supplier's street address. For example, for the supplier "1 Pine Apple St", the first word after the street number is "Pine". Show the supplier's street address and the first word after the street number.

| | StreetAddress | First word after street number |
|---|---|---|
| 1 | 1 Pine Apple St. | Pine |
| 2 | 123 International Blvd | International |
| 3 | 33 Beijin Square | Beijin |
| 4 | 1 Electronics Road | Electronics |
| 5 | 12 Camera St | Camera |

Exercise 4.12

Display today's date and the number of days that have passed since the order date. Show order ID, customer ID, employee ID, order date, today's date, and the order's age in days.

| | OrderId | CustomerId | EmployeeId | OrderDate | Today's Date | Order's Age |
|---|---|---|---|---|---|---|
| 1 | 1 | 1 | 5 | 2017-01-03 | 2026-03-22 13:15:36.963 | 3365 |
| 2 | 2 | 1 | 3 | 2017-03-05 | 2026-03-22 13:15:36.963 | 3304 |
| 3 | 3 | 2 | 5 | 2017-02-23 | 2026-03-22 13:15:36.963 | 3314 |
| 4 | 4 | 4 | 5 | 2017-04-13 | 2026-03-22 13:15:36.963 | 3265 |
| 5 | 5 | 1 | 4 | 2017-05-03 | 2026-03-22 13:15:36.963 | 3245 |
| 6 | 6 | 3 | 6 | 2017-05-08 | 2026-03-22 13:15:36.963 | 3240 |
| 7 | 7 | 5 | 7 | 2016-11-08 | 2026-03-22 13:15:36.963 | 3421 |
| 8 | 8 | 7 | 2 | 2016-12-23 | 2026-03-22 13:15:36.963 | 3376 |

Exercise 4.13

Same as Exercise 4.12. This time, show today's date without the time part.

| | OrderId | CustomerId | EmployeeId | OrderDate | Today's Date | Order's Age |
|---|---|---|---|---|---|---|
| 1 | 1 | 1 | 5 | 2017-01-03 | 2026-03-22 | 3365 |
| 2 | 2 | 1 | 3 | 2017-03-05 | 2026-03-22 | 3304 |
| 3 | 3 | 2 | 5 | 2017-02-23 | 2026-03-22 | 3314 |
| 4 | 4 | 4 | 5 | 2017-04-13 | 2026-03-22 | 3265 |
| 5 | 5 | 1 | 4 | 2017-05-03 | 2026-03-22 | 3245 |
| 6 | 6 | 3 | 6 | 2017-05-08 | 2026-03-22 | 3240 |
| 7 | 7 | 5 | 7 | 2016-11-08 | 2026-03-22 | 3421 |
| 8 | 8 | 7 | 2 | 2016-12-23 | 2026-03-22 | 3376 |

Exercise 4.14

Display all orders placed in May of any year. Show the order's order ID, customer ID, employee ID, and order date.

| | OrderId | CustomerId | EmployeeId | OrderDate |
|---|---|---|---|---|
| 1 | 5 | 1 | 4 | 2017-05-03 |
| 2 | 6 | 3 | 6 | 2017-05-08 |

Exercise 4.15

Display all orders by month and year. Show the order's order ID, customer ID, employee ID, and order date as the first day of that month and year.

| | OrderId | CustomerId | EmployeeId | OrderMonth |
|---|---|---|---|---|
| 1 | 1 | 1 | 5 | 2017-01-01 |
| 2 | 2 | 1 | 3 | 2017-03-01 |
| 3 | 3 | 2 | 5 | 2017-02-01 |
| 4 | 4 | 4 | 5 | 2017-04-01 |
| 5 | 5 | 1 | 4 | 2017-05-01 |
| 6 | 6 | 3 | 6 | 2017-05-01 |
| 7 | 7 | 5 | 7 | 2016-11-01 |
| 8 | 8 | 7 | 2 | 2016-12-01 |

## 4.15 Solutions to Review Questions

4.1 B; 4.2 B; 4.3 D; 4.4 A; 4.5 B; 4.6 C; 4.7 C; 4.8 D; 4.9 A; 4.10 D; 4.11 B; 4.12 A; 4.13 B; 4.14 D; 4.15 C; 4.16 C; 4.17 A; 4.18 B; 4.19 C; 4.20 D; 4.21 C; 4.22 D; 4.23 C; 4.24 A; 4.25 A; 4.26 B; 4.27 D; 4.28 B; 4.29 A; 4.30 D; 4.31 D; 4.32 C; 4.33 B; 4.34 C; 4.35 B; 4.36 C; 4.37 B;

# Chapter 5: ERD to Relation Mapping and SQL Aggregate

## Chapter Learning Objectives

5.1 Exemplify ERD to relation mapping.
5.2 Use aggregate functions in SQL statements.
5.3 Use simple subquery in SQL statements.

## 5.1 What Is ERD to Relations Mapping?

The end product of database development is to have the tables constructed. Tables are called relations (that's where the word "relational" in relational databases comes from.) at the logical level. The purpose of mapping is to convert the entities and relationships in the ERD into relations/tables so that SQL statements can be written to actually create the database and the tables in the database server.

Under most situations, one entity will be mapped into one relation. The relationship between two entities will be represented as a foreign key. A foreign key is an attribute of one entity that is a primary key for another entity. Adding the foreign key allows the constraints of the relationship to be transferred to the relations.

An example of a constraint is the relationship between sales and employees of a commission-based retail store, in which every sale is handled by an employee and each employee can handle any number of sales. The ERD is shown in Figure 5.1a.

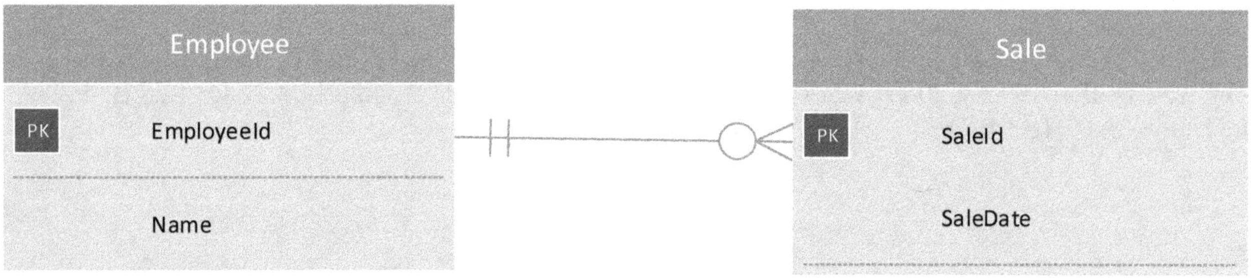

Figure 5.1a ERD of Employee and Sale.

In the example, you will use two tables, one to hold data about the employee, such as employee ID and name, and one to hold data about the sales, such as sale ID and sale date. However, we have yet to add a foreign key to represent the relationship between the two entities. This chapter will show you how to create relations to store the data and keep the constraints of the relationships.

There is more than one way to add a foreign key. Which way you use is dependent on the situation. Keep in mind that you should avoid or minimize null values (a null value is a value you do not know or a value that doesn't exist.) For example, an employee who just got hired and hasn't moved to the new town may not have a local address yet. The address for that employee is a null value.

In the rest of the chapter, you will learn the methods for mapping ERD to relations. No matter which method you use to map ERD to relations, the method must follow these three general rules:

1. All attributes of an entity are transferred over to the attributes of a relation.
2. Relationship constraints in ERD are kept in relations, which means that foreign keys are added.
3. Minimize null values whenever possible. This applies when you have more than one option for mapping.

In this book, we will represent a relation in three ways to help you understand the relations better. The first one is a table with two dimensional values (We show the column head row only for simplicity.):

Student Relation

| <u>StudentId</u> | FirstName | LastName | MiddleInitial |
|---|---|---|---|

The second way is a relational schema:
Student (<u>StudentId</u>, FirstName, LastName, MiddleInitial)

The schema starts with the relation name (Student in this case), and then all the attributes in the parentheses with the primary key underlined with a solid line and the foreign key underlined with a dash line. If an attribute is both a primary key and a foreign key, it will have both the solid and dashed underline (so two underlines.) For simplicity, we sometimes place 'PK' and 'FK' in parentheses after the corresponding attributes instead of underlining them, like this:
Student (StudentId(PK), FirstName, LastName, MiddleInitial)

The third way is to keep everything in the original ERD. You may see additional foreign key attributes added to a relation by following the mapping rules. A foreign key attribute will be labeled FK on the left side of an attribute.

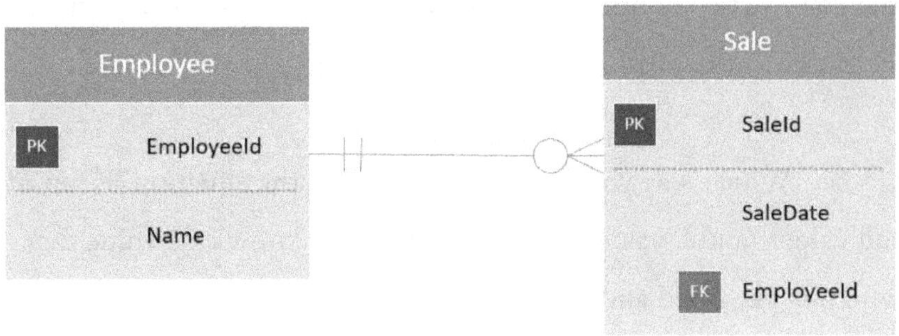


Figure 5.1b Relations of Employee and Sale.

Compared to Figure 5.1a, Figure 5.1b has an additional attribute called EmployeeId in the Sale relation with the FK labeled on the left. The added attribute is called foreign key (FK) because it is a primary key (PK) in the related relation of Employee. You will learn how to add FK in the following sections of this chapter.

Review Question 5.1
Tables are called ______ at the logical level.
a. spreadsheets
b. two dimensional tables
c. relations
d. logical tables

Review Question 5.2
Under most situations, one entity will be mapped into ______.
a. one relation
b. two relations
c. three relations
d. four relations

Review Question 5.3
Under most situations, a relationship between two entities will be represented as a ______.
a. primary key
b. foreign key
c. relation
d. mapped relation

Review Question 5.4
A foreign key is an attribute of one entity that is a ______ for another entity.
a. primary key
b. foreign key
c. relation
d. mapped relation

Review Question 5.5

Which of the following is a general rule for mapping ERD to relations?
a. All attributes of an entity are transferred over to the attributes of a relation.
b. Relationship constraints in ERD are kept in relations, which means that primary keys are added.
c. Minimize numeric values whenever possible. This applies when you have more than one option for mapping.
d. All primary keys of an entity are transferred over to the foreign keys of a relation.

Review Question 5.6
Which of the following is a general rule for mapping ERD to relations?
a. All attributes of an entity are transferred over to the primary keys of a relation.
b. Relationship constraints in ERD are kept in relations, which means that foreign keys are added.
c. Minimize numeric values whenever possible. This applies when you have more than one option for mapping.
d. All primary keys of an entity are transferred over to the foreign keys of a relation.

Review Question 5.7
Which of the following is a general rule for mapping ERD to relations?
a. All attributes of an entity are transferred over to the primary keys of a relation.
b. Relationship constraints in ERD are kept in relations, which means that primary keys are added.
c. Minimize null values whenever possible. This applies when you have more than one option for mapping.
d. All primary keys of an entity are transferred over to the foreign keys of a relation.

Review Question 5.8
What does "relational" in "relational database" mean?
a. relationship
b. database
c. table
d. column

Review Question 5.9
What is the "ERD to relations mapping"?
a. converting entities to relations
b. converting relationships to relations
c. converting entities and relationships in ERD to relations.
d. converting one ERD to one relation.

Review Question 5.10
What is a null value in relational database design?
a. an empty string value
b. a zero numeric value
c. an empty string value or a zero numeric value
d. an unknown value

Review Question 5.11
Which of the following is NOT one of the ERD to relation mapping objectives?
a. No data duplication.
b. All attributes in ERD are kept in relations.
c. Keep relationship constraints from ERD to relations.
d. Minimize the null values in the relations whenever possible.

Review Question 5.12
In a relation schema, how do you represent a primary key?
a. put the attribute as the first one in the list.
b. solid underline the attribute.
c. dash underlines the attribute.
d. put the attribute as the last one in the list.

Review Question 5.13
In a relation schema, how do you represent a foreign key?
a. put the attribute as the first one in the list.
b. solid underline the attribute.
c. dash underlines the attribute.
d. put the attribute as the last one in the list.

Review Question 5.14
What is the table name if you see the relation schema? Movie (MovieId, Title, Duration)
a. Movie
b. MovieId
c. Title
d. Duration

## 5.2 Mapping a Regular/Strong Entity in ERD to a Relation

This is the simplest case. One relation from one entity. All attributes of the entity become column headers in the relation. For example, to map a regular entity to a relation, just make the entity name to relation name and keep all attributes of the entity in the relation.

A corresponding relation/table would look like this:

Person Relation

| PersonId | Name | SSN | Address | DateBirth | Email |
|---|---|---|---|---|---|

A relation schema would look like this:
Person (PersonId, Name, SSN, Address, DateBirth, Email)

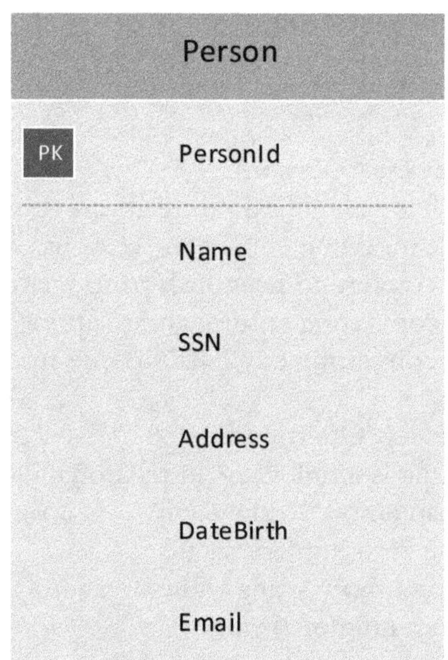

Figure 5.2 A regular entity.

There would be no changes in the original ERD when a regular entity is converted to a relation.

Review Question 5.15
How do you map a regular entity in the ERD to a relation?
a. The entity name becomes the relation name and the entity attributes become the relation column headers. There is no change in the primary key.
b. The relation is given no name, and entity attributes become relation column headers.
c. Each attribute in the entity becomes a relation.
d. Add the primary key of the owner entity as a foreign key to the entity and set both the owner primary key and current entity primary key as a composite primary key.

## 5.3 Mapping a Weak Entity in ERD to a Relation

In Chapter 2, you learned that a weak entity is a special type of entity in which its existence depends entirely on another entity. An example of a weak entity is the dependents of an employee. The DEPENDENT entity instance completely depends on the EMPLOYEE entity.

Let's see an example:

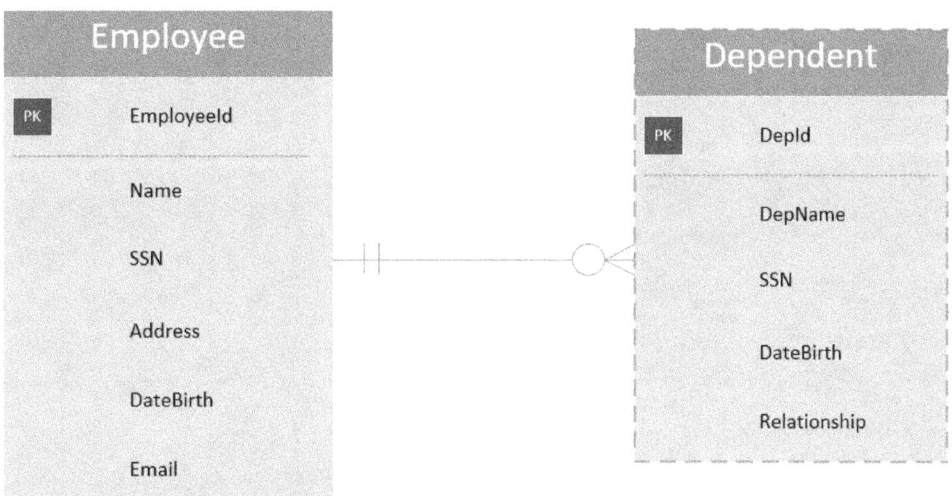


Figure 5.3 A weak entity mapping.

The Figure 5.3 shows the ERD of EMPLOYEE and the DEPENDENT. The EMPLOYEE is a strong entity and you learned how to map a strong entity to a relation in last section. The DEPENDENT is a weak entity. To map the DEPENDENT entity to a relation, 1) add the primary key of the owner entity (Employee in this case) as a foreign key in the weak entity, and 2) set both the primary keys of the owner entity and the weak entity as a composite primary key (EmployeeId and DepId in this case).
The following demonstrates the relations in three formats:

1) Table format:

Employee Relation

| <u>EmployeeId</u> | Name | SSN | Address | DateBirth | Email |
|---|---|---|---|---|---|

Dependent Relation

| <u>EmployeeId</u> | <u>DepId</u> | DepName | SSN | DateBirth | Relationship |
|---|---|---|---|---|---|

2) Schema format:

Employee (<u>EmployeeId</u>, Name, SSN, Address, DateBirth, Email)

Dependent (<u>EmployeeId</u>, <u>DepId</u>, DepName, SSN, DateBirth, Relationship)

3) ERD format:

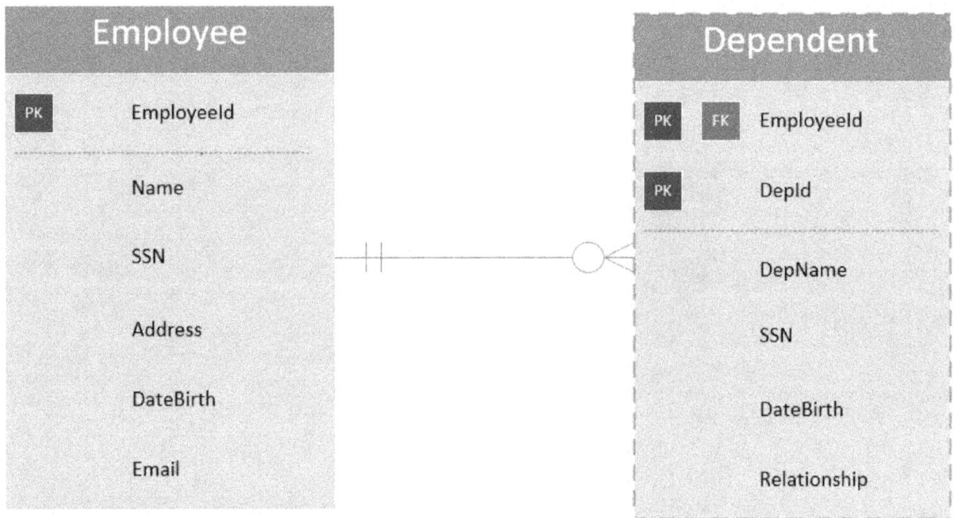


Figure 5.4 Relation for a weak entity.

Review Question 5.16
What is the rule for mapping a weak entity in an ERD to a relation?
a. Add the PK of the owner entity as a FK in the weak entity. Set the two keys as a composite PK.
b. Add the FK of the owner entity as a FK in the weak entity. Set the two keys as a composite PK.
c. Add the PK of the owner entity as a FK in the weak entity. Set the two keys as a composite FK.
d. Add the FK of the owner entity as a FK in the weak entity. Set the two keys as a composite FK.

Review Question 5.17
Suppose Dependent is a weak entity with the Employee entity as its owner. If EmployeeId is the primary key of the Employee entity and DependentName is the primary key of the Dependent entity, what is the primary key of the mapped relation of the Dependent entity?
a. EmployeeId
b. DependentName
c. EmployeeId, DependentName
d. None of the above

## 5.4 Map a Binary 1:M Relationship to Relations

The one-to-many relationship is perhaps the most popular relationship in the ERD. To map such a relationship, just add the primary key from the "one" side as a foreign key on the "many" side. Let's see an example:

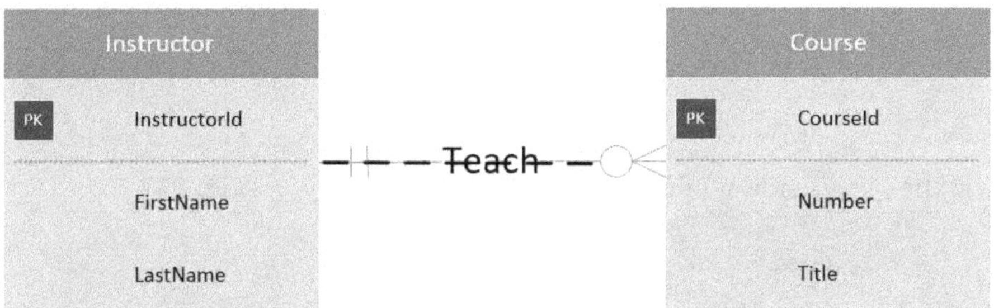


Figure 5.5 A one-to-many relationship (1:M).

The Instructor entity is on the one side while the Course entity is on the many side. The Instructor entity can be easily mapped to a relation by following section 5.2 on mapping a regular entity to a relation. When mapping the course entity to a relation, you should add the IntructorId as a foreign key. The relations are shown in three formats below.

Instructor Relation

| InstructorId | FirstName | LastName |
|---|---|---|

Course Relation

| CourseId | Number | Title | InstructorId |
|---|---|---|---|

Instructor (InstructorId, FirstName, LastName)

Course (CourseId, Number, Title, InstructorId)

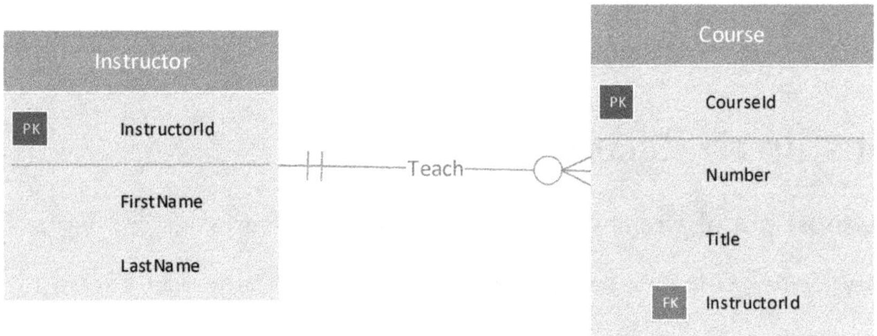


Figure 5.6 Relations for one-to-many relationships.

Review Question 5.18
Given the following ERD, the left side is the _____side while the right side is the ______ side.

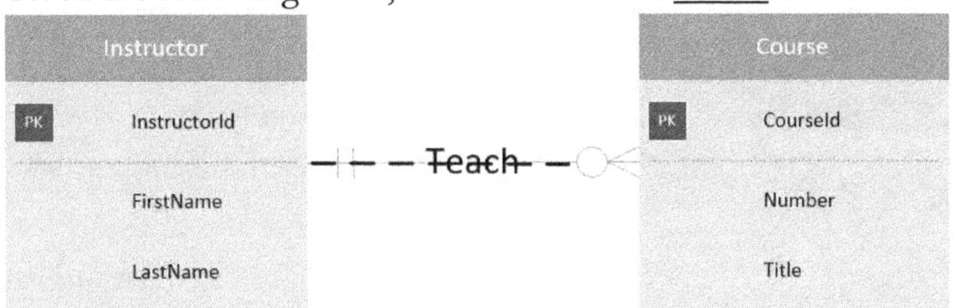


a. one, one
b. many, many
c. one, many
d. many, one

Review Question 5.19
To map a one-to-many relationship to relations, just add the primary key from the ___________ side as a foreign key on the _________ side
a. one, one
b. one, many
c. many, one
d. many, many

## 5.5 Map a Binary 1:1 Relationship to a Relation

Mapping a binary 1:1 relationship is very similar to mapping a binary 1:M relationship as in section 5.4. To map a binary one-to-one relationship to relations, add the primary key from the mandatory side as a foreign key to the optional side (remember that the mandatory side is the side with the two vertical dashes, while the optional side is the side with one circle and one vertical line.) Such mapping will reduce the number of null values (adding the primary key from the optional side as a foreign key to the mandatory side will result in more null values.) Let's see an example:

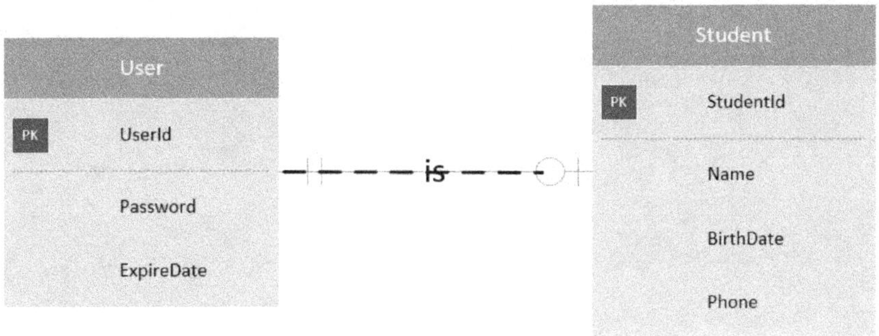


Figure 5.7 A one-to-one relationship.

A computer user in a university includes students, faculty, and staff, thus each user can be at most one student and each student must be a user. This relationship is 1:1. The mapping on the mandatory side (the user entity) simply follows section 5.2. To map on the optional side (the student entity,) add the primary key from the mandatory side (UserId) as a foreign key on the optional side (the student entity).

User Relation

| UserId | Password | ExpireDate |
|---|---|---|

Student Relation

| StudentId | Name | BirthDate | Phone | UserId |
|---|---|---|---|---|

User (UserId, Password, ExpireDate)

Student (StudentId, Name, BirthDate, Phone, UserId)

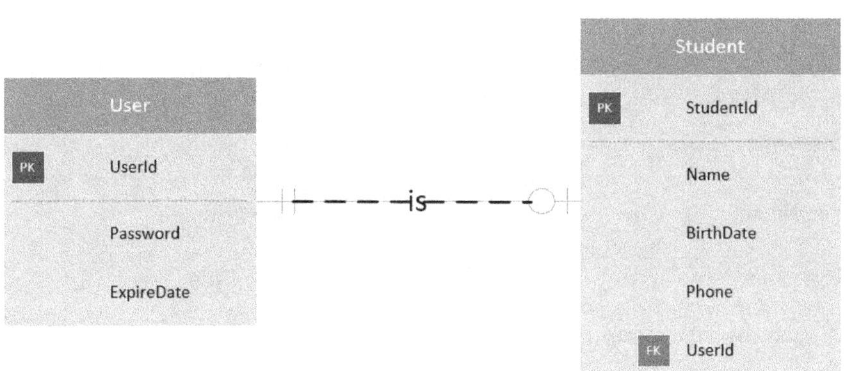


Figure 5.8 Relations for one-to-one relationship.

Review Question 5.20

Given the following ERD, the left side is the _____side while the right side is the ______ side.

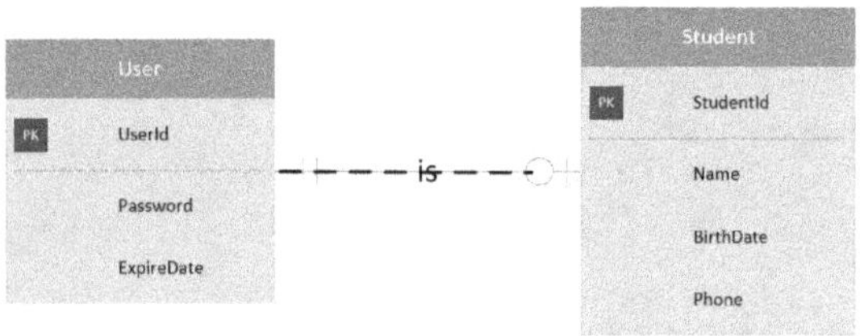


a. one, mandatory
b. one, optional
c. optional, mandatory
d. mandatory, optional

Review Question 5.21
To map a binary 1:1 relationship to relations, add the primary key from the __________ side as a foreign key to the _________ side.
a. optional, mandatory
b. mandatory, optional
c. optional, optional
d. mandatory, mandatory

Review Question 5.22
When mapping a binary 1:1 relationship to relations, adding the primary key from the optional side as a foreign key to the mandatory side results in ____.
a. more null values
b. fewer null value
c. more columns
d. fewer columns

# 5.6 Map a Binary M:N Relationship to a Relation

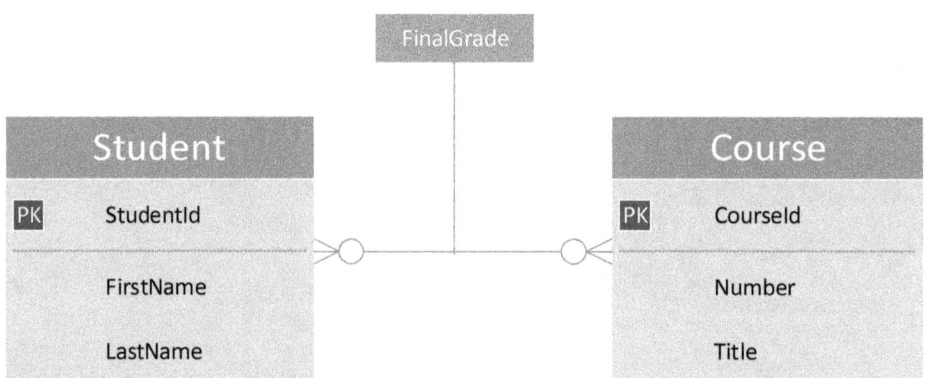


Figure 5.9 A many-to-many relationship.

To map a binary many-to-many relationship, you need to create three relations. For the two entities in the M:N relationship, simply create two relations as demonstrated in Section 5.2. Additionally, create a third relation (also known as an associative entity, as from Chapter 3) with at least two attributes -- the primary keys from each participating entity. The primary key of this new relation is a composite key of these two attributes. The two attributes also serve as foreign keys because they are primary keys of related relations. Add any attributes of the relationship to this new relation. Let's see the example in Figure 5.9:

There will be three relations mapped to the above M:N relationship

Student Relation

| StudentId | FirstName | LastName |
|---|---|---|

Course Relation

| CourseId | Number | Title |
|---|---|---|

Enrollment Relation

| StudentId | CourseId | FinalGrade |
|---|---|---|

Student (StudentId, FirstName, LastName)

Course (CourseId, Number, Title)

Enrollment (StudentId, CourseId, FinalGrade)

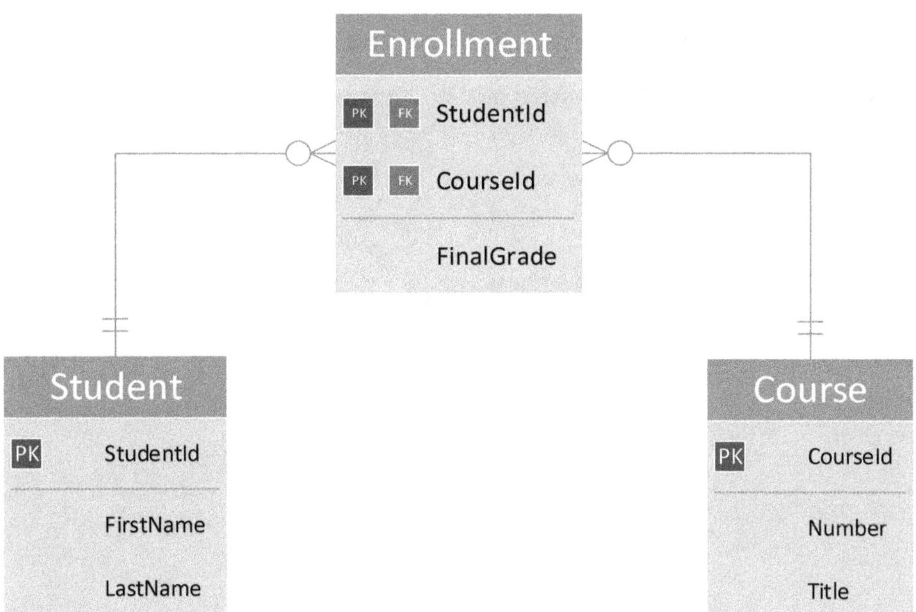

Figure 5.10 Relations for many-to-many relationships.

Review Question 5.23
To map a binary many-to-many relationship, you will create a total of __________ relation(s).
a. one
b. two
c. three
d. four

Review Question 5.24
To map a binary many-to-many relationship, you add a new relation to the database. This new relation is mapped to the __________.
a. associative entity
b. third entity
c. additional entity
d. backup entity

Review Question 5.25
The associative entity/relation added in a many-to-many relationship mapping contains at least two attributes _______________.
a. from one of the participating entities.
b. from both of the participating entities.
c. composite of the primary key attributes of the participating entities
d. composite of all attributes from both entities.

## 5.7 Map a Ternary Relationship to Relations

In Chapter 2, you learned that a ternary relationship is a relationship among three entities. To map a ternary relationship to relations, you map the three entities as you learned in Section 5.2. Then, add a new relation which includes the primary keys of all the three participating entities as a composite primary key for this new relation. Each attribute of the primary key is also a foreign key. Also add any attributes of the ternary relationship to this new relation.

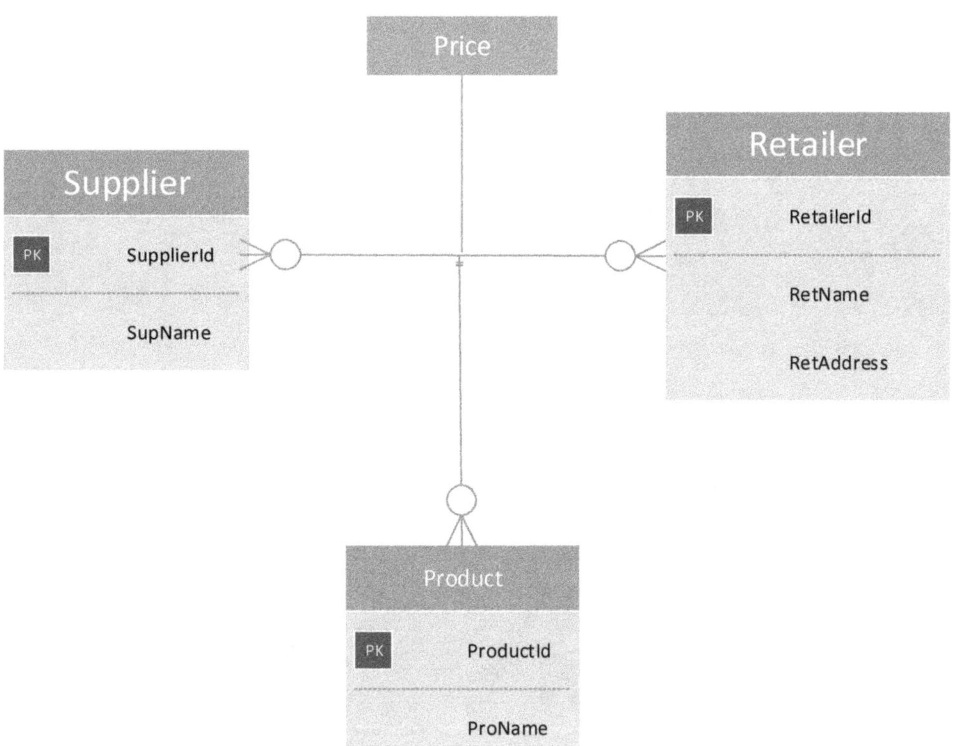


Figure 5.11 A ternary relationship.

This ERD shows that the mini-world includes data on which a supplier ships which products to which retailers. Each delivery includes the quote price. The mapped relations are as follows:

Supplier Relation

| SupplierId | SupName |
|---|---|

Retailer Relation

| RetailerId | RetName | RetAddress |
|---|---|---|

Product Relation

| ProductId | ProName |
|---|---|

Delivery Relation

| SupplierId | RetailerId | ProductId | Price |
|---|---|---|---|

Supplier (SupplierId, SupName)

Retailer (RetailerId, RetName, RetAddress)

Product (ProductId, ProName)

Delivery (SupplierId, RetailerId, ProductId, Price)

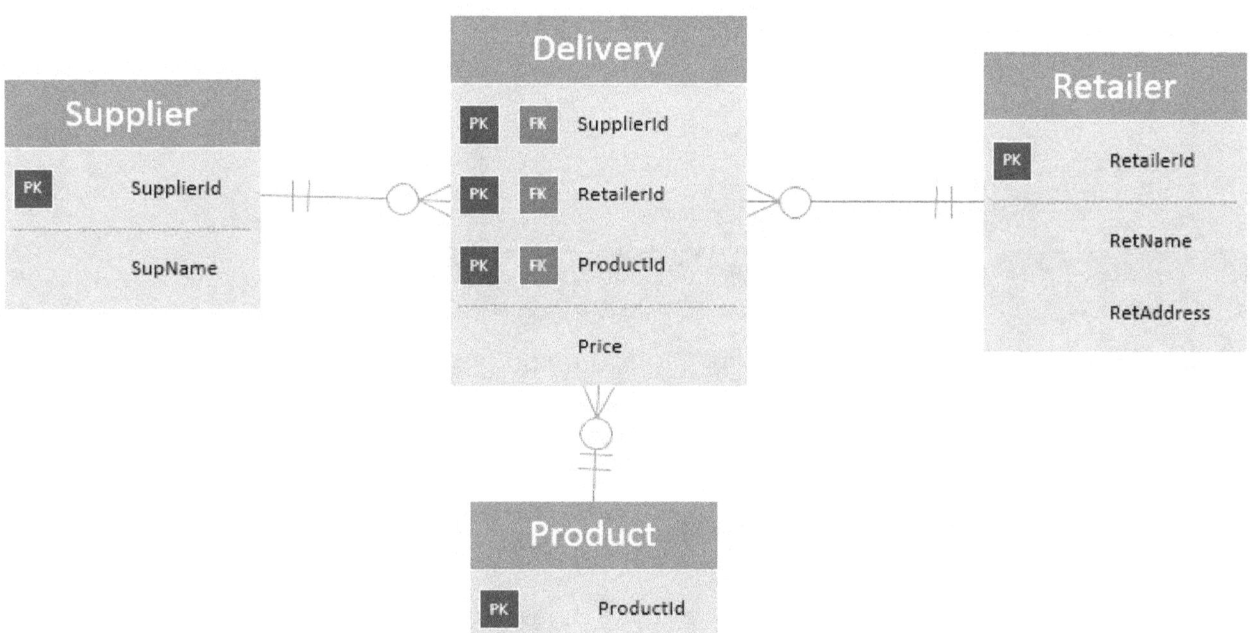


Figure 5.12 Relations for a ternary relationship.

Review Question 5.26
A ternary relationship will be mapped into a total of __________ relation(s).
a. one
b. two
c. three
d. four

## 5.8 Map Generalization/Specialization Relationship to Relations

You learned generalization/specialization relationships in Chapter 4. For generalization/specialization mapping, simply convert each entity into a relation, add the primary key of the super entity as a foreign key in each sub entity, then set the foreign key in the sub entity as also a primary key. Let's see an example:

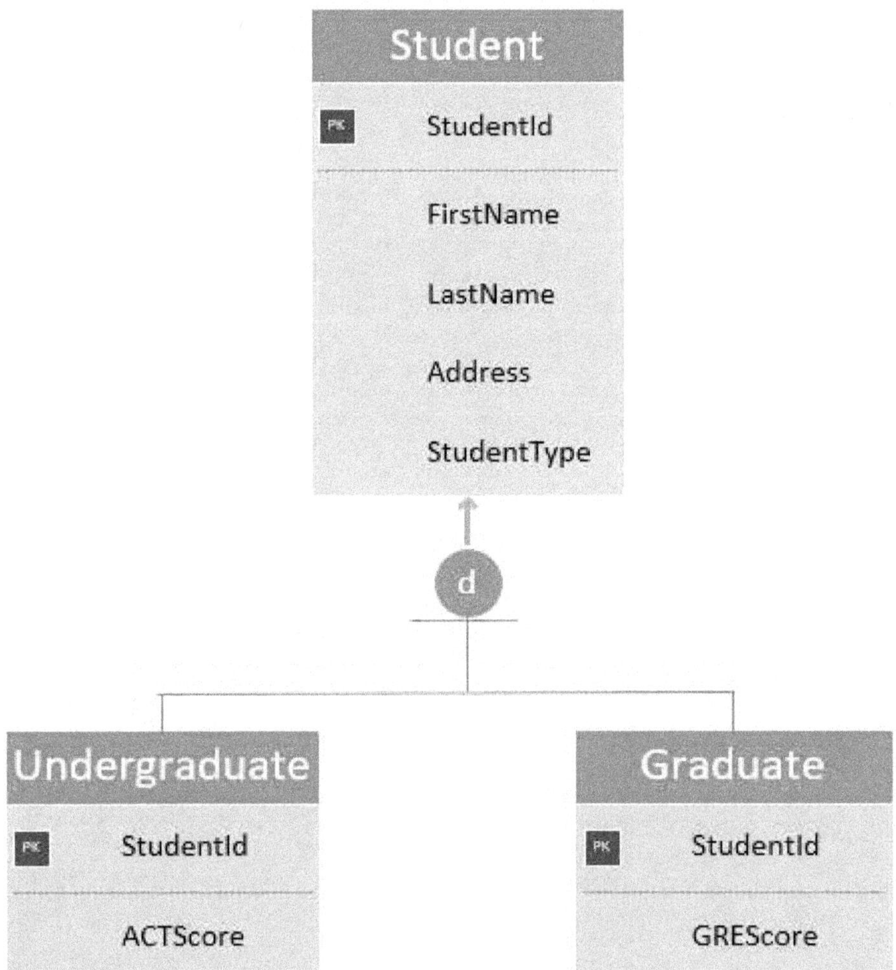


Figure 5.13 A generalization/specialization relationship.

The mapped relations are:

Student Relation

| StudentId | FirstName | LastName | Address | StudentType |
|---|---|---|---|---|

Undergraduate Relation

| StudentId | ACTScore |
|---|---|

Graduate Relation

| StudentId | GREScore |
|---|---|

Student (StudentId, FirstName, LastName, Address, StudentType)

Undergraduate (StudentId, ACTScore)

Graduate (StudentId, GREScore)

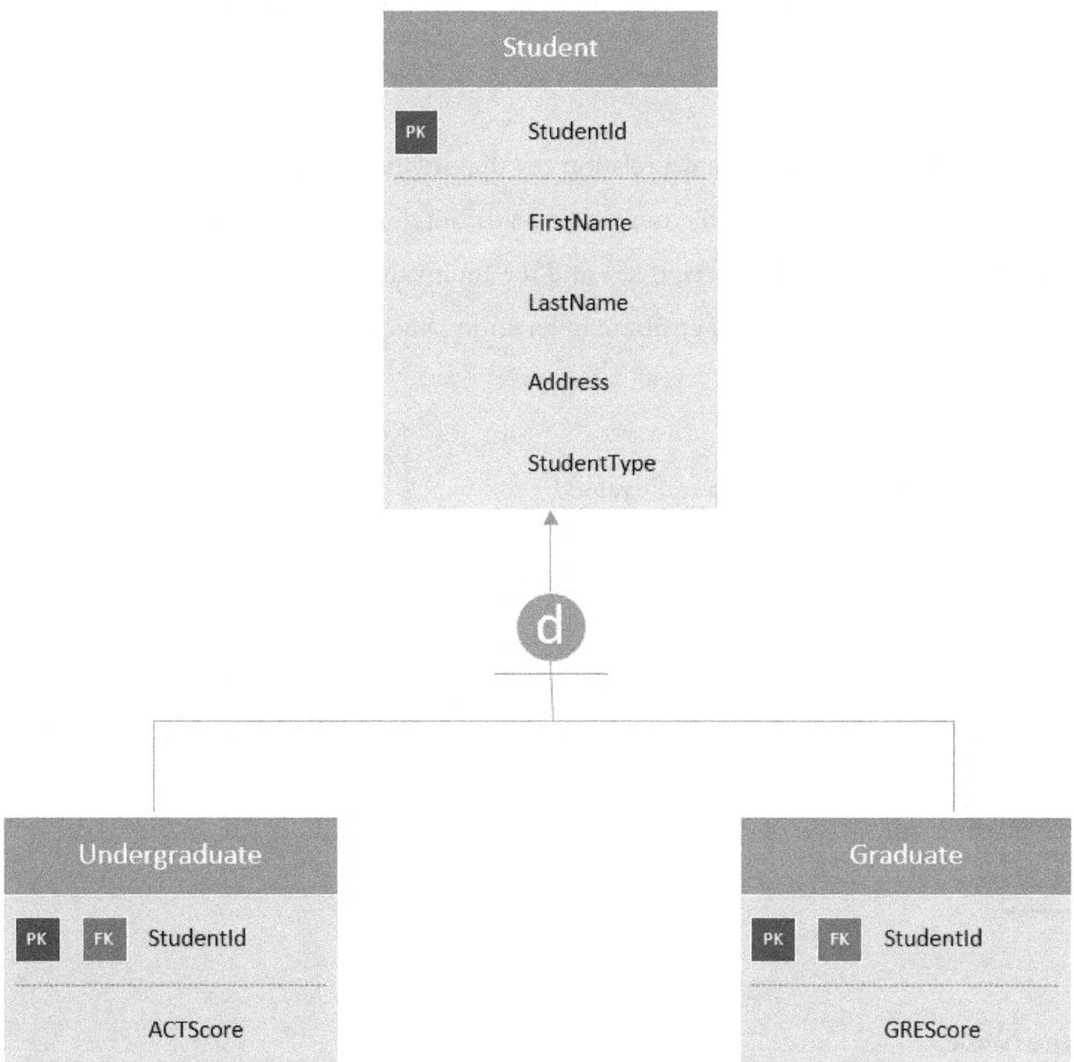


Figure 5.14 Relations for a generalization/specialization relationship.

Review Question 5.27
To map a generalization/specialization relationship to relations, create a relation for each entity, set the primary key of the _________ entity as a foreign key in each _______ entity, and then set the foreign key in the ______ entities as also the primary key.
a. sub, super, sub
b. super, sub, sub
c. super, super, sub
d. sub, super, super

## 5.9 Map a Multivalued-attribute Entity to a Relation

The multivalued attribute was introduced in Chapter 3. A multivalued attribute has more than one value. For example, if an employee has worked for a company and then left the company and then returned, what is the hire date? If the company wants to keep all hire dates, then hire date is a multivalued attribute. Multivalued attributes cannot be created in a DBMS. One solution to this then is to create a relation for the attribute(s).

To map an entity with a multivalued attribute, create a relation for the original entity without the multivalued attribute, then add a new relation for the multivalued attribute(s), with the primary key from the original entity as a foreign key, setting both this foreign key and the multivalued attribute as a composite primary key. If there is more than one multivalued attribute in an entity, you can group them in one new relation if they are related. Let's see an example:

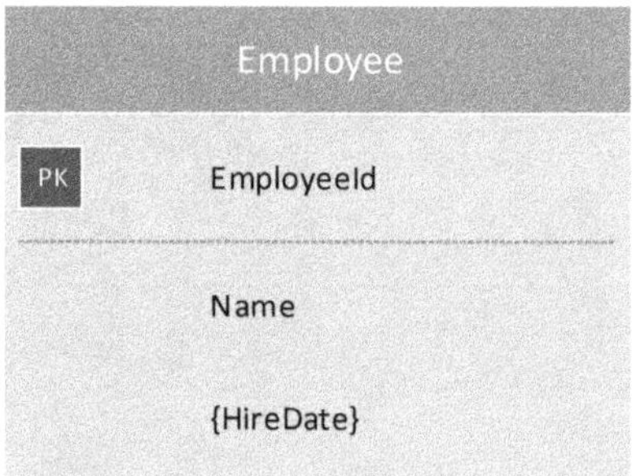

Figure 5.15 A multivalued entity.

The HireDate attribute of the Employee entity is a multivalued attribute. The two relations are:

Employee Relation

| EmployeeId | Name |
|---|---|

EmploymentHistory Relation

| EmployeeId | HireDate |
|---|---|

Employee (EmployeeId, Name)

EmploymentHistory (EmployeeId, HireDate)

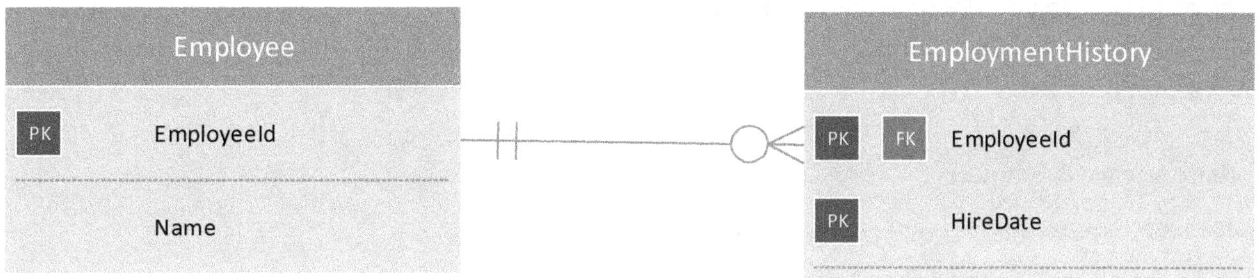


Figure 5.16 Relations for a multivalued entity.

Review Question 5.28
When mapping an entity with multivalued attributes, _____________.
a. there is no difference from mapping a strong entity.
b. there is no difference from mapping a weak entity.
c. add a new attribute for the multivalued attributes.
d. add a new relation for the multivalued attributes.

## 5.10 An Example of Mapping ERD to Relations

Given the ERD as shown in Figure 5.17, map it to relations by following the rules described in this chapter.

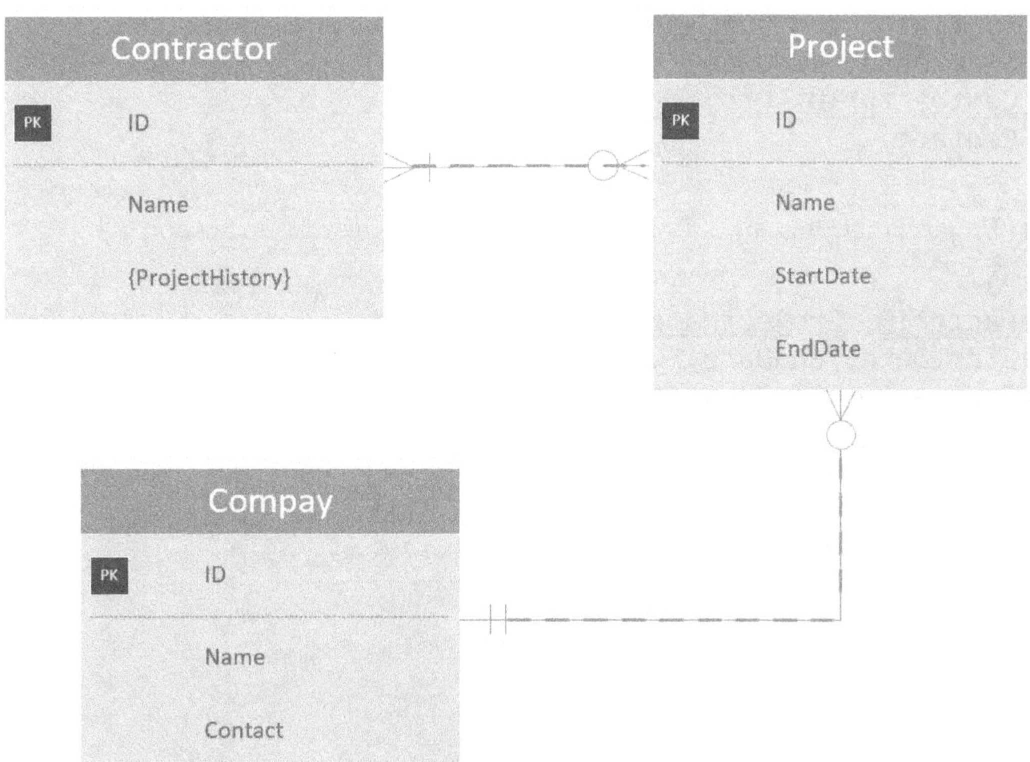


Figure 5.17 An example of mapping ERD to relations.

Step 1: Map each entity to a relation by keeping every attribute and PK.

```
Contractor (ID, Name, ProjectHistory)
Project (ID, Name, StartDate, EndDate)
Company (ID, Name, Contact)
```

Step 2: Is there any weak entities?

No. Skip this step.

Step 3: Is there any multi-value attribute?

Yes, ProjectHistory is one. Ask the client what data is in the project history. Suppose there is just a project name in this case. Add a new relation by following the rule described in Section 5.9:

```
Contractor (ID, Name)
ProjectHistory(ContractorID, ProjectName)
Project (ID, Name, StartDate, EndDate)
Company (ID, Name, Contact)
```

Step 4: Map each relationship

1. The relationship between Contractor and Project is a M:N relationship. Follow the rule described in Section 5.6:

```
Contractor (ID, Name)
ProjectHistory(ContractorID, ProjectName)
Project (ID, Name, StartDate, EndDate)
ContractorProject (ContractorID, ProjectID)
Company (ID, Name, Contact)
```

2. The relationship between Project and Company is 1:M relationship. Follow the rules in Section 5.4:

```
Contractor (ID, Name)
ProjectHistory(ContractorID, ProjectName)
Project (ID, Name, StartDate, EndDate, CompanyID)
ContractorProject (ContractorID, ProjectID)
Company (ID, Name, Contact)
```

The above five relations are the final mapped relations for the given ERD.

## 5.11 SQL Aggregate Functions

An aggregate function performs a calculation on a column and returns a single value. It includes one or more rows in a column as input and returns a single value as output. For example, if a table has a column called GPA, then AVG(GPA) will return the average GPA of all GPAs selected. The difference between the regular functions you learned in the last chapter and the aggregate functions you will learn in this section is that the former has one row value as input and the latter has one or more row values as input.

Aggregate functions ignore null values. So, if you have four students but only three of them have a GPA, then only three GPAs will be averaged even though you selected four students.

SQL Example 5.1

Display the average price of all products in the OrderDetails table.

SQL Example 5.1 Analysis

Use the AVG() function to show the average of all prices.

SQL Example 5.1 statement

```
SELECT CAST(AVG(Price) AS NUMERIC(7, 2)) AS "Average Price"
FROM Sales.OrderDetails;
```

SQL Example 5.1 Output:

| | Average Price |
|---|---|
| 1 | 536.31 |

SQL Example 5.2

Display number of customer emails in the customers table.

SQL Example 5.2 Analysis

Use the COUNT() function to show the number of customer emails. Note that the null value in the Email column won't count as one.

SQL Example 5.2 statement

```
SELECT COUNT(Email) AS "Number of customer emails"
FROM Sales.Customers;
```

SQL Example 5.2 Output:

| | Number of customer emails |
|---|---|
| 1 | 7 |

SQL Example 5.3

Display the total number of units of products in the order with the ID 3. From Appendix B Sales.OrderDetails table, you can find that the number is 2 units of Product Three +1 unit of Product Six +2 units of Product Seven + 2 units of Products Eight + 1 unit of Product Nine = 8 units of all products.

SQL Example 5.3 Analysis

Use the SUM() function to total all numbers in the quantity column of the OrderDetails table. Remember to keep this only to the order with ID 3.

SQL Example 5.3 statement

```
SELECT SUM(Quantity) AS "Total units in order id 3"
FROM Sales.OrderDetails
WHERE OrderId = 3;
```

SQL Example 5.3 Output:

| | Total units in order id 3 |
|---|---|
| 1 | 8 |

SQL Example 5.4

Display total sales value in the order with ID 3.

SQL Example 5.4 Analysis

In order to find out the total sales value, you need to use the OrderDetails table. The following table shows all items in the order with ID 3.

| | OrderId | ProductId | Price | quantity |
|---|---|---|---|---|
| 1 | 3 | 3 | 159.99 | 2 |
| 2 | 3 | 6 | 199.99 | 1 |
| 3 | 3 | 7 | 109.99 | 2 |
| 4 | 3 | 8 | 69.99 | 2 |
| 5 | 3 | 9 | 1449.99 | 1 |

The total value of the order with ID 3 will be 159.99×2 + 159.99×1 + 109.99×2 + 69.99×2 + 1449.99×1 = 2329.92. The SQL for calculating the total is SUM(Price*Quantity).

SQL Example 5.4 statement

```
SELECT SUM(Quantity*Price) AS "Total sales in order id 3"
FROM Sales.OrderDetails
```

```
WHERE OrderId = 3;
```

SQL Example 5.4 Output:

| | Total sales in order id 3 |
|---|---|
| 1 | 2329.92 |

SQL Example 5.5

Display the highest priced item sold. Show the price.

SQL Example 5.5 Analysis

Use the MAX() function to display the highest priced item from the OrderDetails table.

SQL Example 5.5 statement

```
SELECT MAX(Price) AS "Highest priced item"
FROM Sales.OrderDetails;
```

SQL Example 5.5 Output:

| | Highest priced item |
|---|---|
| 1 | 1599.99 |

Review Question 5.29
A(n) ___________ function performs a calculation on a column and returns a single value.
a. mathematic
b. aggregate
c. normal
d. single

Review Question 5.30
The difference between the regular functions you learned in the last chapter and the aggregate functions you will learn in this section is that the former has _______ as input and the latter has _______ as input.
a. one row value, one or more row values
b. one or more row values, one row values
c. one row value, zero or one row value
d. zero or one row value, one row value

Review Question 5.31
Which of the following is an aggregate function in Transact SQL?
a. UPPER()
b. SUBSTRING()
c. CAST()
d. MAX()

## 5.12 The GROUP BY Clause

The normal SELECT statement will return a result selected from rows. For example, if you want to return all students whose GPA are higher than 3.0, it will return, for example, 25 rows if there are 25 students whose GPA are higher than 3.0.

If you want to use the SELECT statement to return a result from a certain group of rows, you need to use the GROUP BY clause. For example, if you want to return the average GPA of all freshmen, you will need to group them by the class cohort using the GROUP BY clause as shown in the following example.

SQL Example 5.6

Display total number of units in each order. Show order ID and the corresponding total units in the order. Like this:

| OrderId | Total units in the order |
|---|---|
| 1 | 3 |
| 2 | 13 |
| 3 | 8 |
| 4 | 3 |
| 5 | 9 |
| 6 | 1 |
| 7 | 1 |
| 8 | 3 |

SQL Example 5.6 Analysis

In SQL Example 5.3, you learned how to retrieve the total number of units in order ID 3.

You may be tempted to try the following SQL statement:

```
SELECT OrderId, SUM(Quantity)
FROM Sales.OrderDetails;
```

You will get the following error:

```
"Msg 8120, Level 16, State 1, Line 28
Column 'Sales.OrderDetails.OrderId' is invalid in the select list because it is not contained in
either an aggregate function or the GROUP BY clause."
```

To put it simply, SQL Server won't allow you to select OrderId and an aggregate function, SUM() in this case, together. This is because OrderId is an individual row value while SUM() is a result of multiple row values. The solution is to add the GROUP BY clause so that the SQL Server knows which rows to add together and will use just one OrderId value for all those rows.

SQL Example 5.6 statement

```
SELECT OrderId, SUM(Quantity) AS "Total units in the order"
FROM Sales.OrderDetails
GROUP BY OrderId;
```

SQL Example 5.6 Output:

| | OrderId | Total units in the order |
|---|---|---|
| 1 | 1 | 3 |
| 2 | 2 | 13 |
| 3 | 3 | 8 |
| 4 | 4 | 3 |
| 5 | 5 | 9 |
| 6 | 6 | 1 |
| 7 | 7 | 1 |
| 8 | 8 | 3 |

SQL Example 5.7

Display one of the highest priced items on sale. Show the product ID and the price.

SQL Example 5.7 Analysis

SQL Example 5.5 asks for the highest price item sold. This time you need to show which product has that price. If you simply add the product ID in the SELECT, like this

```
SELECT ProductId, MAX(Price) AS "Highest priced item"
FROM Sales.OrderDetails;
```

You will receive an error message similar to the error message in SQL Example 5.6. The solution is to add the GROUP BY clause. Now the SQL statement will run and display all orders and their price as shown:

| | ProductId | Highest priced item |
|---|---|---|
| 1 | 1 | 1499.99 |
| 2 | 2 | 1599.99 |
| 3 | 3 | 159.99 |
| 4 | 4 | 99.99 |
| 5 | 6 | 199.99 |
| 6 | 7 | 109.99 |
| 7 | 8 | 69.99 |
| 8 | 9 | 1449.99 |

To display the highest price only, you can use ORDER BY with DESCENDING and then pick the first one with the TOP keyword. If there are more than one highest priced item, this method will only show one of them and SQL cannot guarantee which one. You will learn more in our second book on SQL.

SQL Example 5.7 statement

```
SELECT TOP 1 ProductId, MAX(Price) AS "Highest priced item"
FROM Sales.OrderDetails
GROUP BY ProductId
ORDER BY "Highest priced item" DESC;
```

SQL Example 5.7 Output:

| | ProductId | Highest priced item |
|---|---|---|
| 1 | 2 | 1599.99 |

SQL Example 5.8

Display the total value of each order. For example, with the following data of the order with Id 1

| | OrderId | ProductId | Price | quantity |
|---|---|---|---|---|
| 1 | 1 | 1 | 1499.99 | 1 |
| 2 | 1 | 3 | 149.99 | 2 |

The total value of Order id 1 is 1499.99×1 + 149.99×2 = 1799.97. Show order ID and total value.

SQL Example 5.8 Analysis

The total value of each item in an order is calculated as Price * Quantity. The total value of an order will be the sum of each item value in that order, which is SUM(Price*Quantity). You should also group the total value by order ID using the GROUP BY clause.

SQL Example 5.8 statement

```
SELECT OrderId, SUM(Price * Quantity) AS "Order total"
FROM Sales.OrderDetails
GROUP BY OrderId;
```

SQL Example 5.8 Output:

| | OrderId | Order total |
|---|---|---|
| 1 | 1 | 1799.97 |
| 2 | 2 | 4649.87 |
| 3 | 3 | 2329.92 |
| 4 | 4 | 269.97 |
| 5 | 5 | 1499.91 |
| 6 | 6 | 1499.99 |
| 7 | 7 | 999.99 |
| 8 | 8 | 199.97 |

Review Question 5.32
If you want to use the SELECT statement to return the result by a group of rows, you will use the __________ clause.

a. GROUP
b. WHERE
c. GROUP BY
d. ORDER BY

Review Question 5.33
What is the output of executing the following SQL statement on our LifeStyleDB database?

```
SELECT OrderId, SUM(Quantity)
```

```
FROM Sales.OrderDetails;
```

a. All order ID and the total number of quantities in that order.
b. All order ID and the total number of quantities in the Sales.OrderDetails table.
c. An error because the Sales.OrderDetails table does not have a column called Quantity.
d. An error because OrderId returns individual rows while SUM(Quantity) returns the aggregation value of multiple rows.

## 5.13 The HAVING Clause

In Chapter 3, you learned how to use the WHERE clause to filter out certain rows. For example, if you have a table called Students that holds data about all students, and you want to display only students with GPA of 3.5 or higher, you have something like this:

```
SELECT FirstName, LastName, GPA
FROM Students
WHERE GPA >= 3.5;
```

Suppose you want to display students' GPA average by cohort (that is, Freshman, Sophomore, Junior, and Senior) and only display the cohort with Average GPA of 3.5 or higher. You cannot use the WHERE clause. The following example won't work.

```
SELECT Cohort, AVG(GPA)
FROM Students
GROUP BY Cohort
WHERE AVG(GPA) >= 3.5;
```

To make it work, you will use HAVING clause like this:

```
SELECT Cohort, AVG(GPA)
FROM Students
GROUP BY Cohort
HAVING AVG(GPA) >= 3.5;
```

In short, WHERE is used to filter out individual rows while HAVING is used to filter out individual groups.

SQL Example 5.9

Display all orders with more than $2000.00 value. Display Order ID and corresponding order total.

SQL Example 5.9 Analysis

This is similar to SQL Example 5.8 except that you don't want any orders with a total of $2000.00 or less to be displayed. Because each order is a group of order items, you cannot use the WHERE clause to filter out the rows. Instead, you need to use the HAVING clause to filter out individual orders.

SQL Example 5.9 statement

```
SELECT OrderId, SUM(Price * Quantity) AS "Order total"
FROM Sales.OrderDetails
GROUP BY OrderId
HAVING SUM(Price * Quantity) > 2000;
```

SQL Example 5.9 Output:

| | OrderId | Order total |
|---|---|---|
| 1 | 2 | 4649.87 |
| 2 | 3 | 2329.92 |

SQL Example 5.10

Display any orders with a total number of more than 2 units in each order. Show order ID and the corresponding total units in the order.

SQL Example 5.10 Analysis

This is similar to SQL Example 5.6 except that you don't show any order with total units of 2 or less. As can be seen in the SQL Example 5.6 result table, there are 8 orders in all. Only 6 of those 8 orders have more than 2 units of items in them.

Because an order is a group, so you will use the HAVING clause instead of the WHERE clause to filter the groups.

SQL Example 5.10 statement

```
SELECT OrderId, SUM(Quantity) AS "Total units in order"
FROM Sales.OrderDetails
GROUP BY OrderId
HAVING SUM(Quantity) > 2;
```

SQL Example 5.10 Output:

| | OrderId | Total units in order |
|---|---|---|
| 1 | 1 | 3 |
| 2 | 2 | 13 |

| | | |
|---|---|---|
| 3 | 3 | 8 |
| 4 | 4 | 3 |
| 5 | 5 | 9 |
| 6 | 8 | 3 |

SQL Example 5.11

Display all products costing more than $1000.00 per unit with ten or more units delivered. Show product ID and the total units delivered.

SQL Example 5.11 Analysis

First, take a look at all deliveries from the deliveries table:

| | DeliveryId | ProductId | Quantity | Price | DeliveryDate |
|---|---|---|---|---|---|
| **1** | 1 | 1 | 2 | 1099.99 | 2016-10-01 09:30:00.0000000 |
| **2** | 2 | 1 | 5 | 1199.99 | 2016-11-01 10:20:00.0000000 |
| **3** | 3 | 2 | 10 | 1199.99 | 2016-10-02 11:10:00.0000000 |
| **4** | 4 | 3 | 10 | 129.99 | 2016-10-05 09:15:00.0000000 |
| **5** | 5 | 4 | 20 | 79.99 | 2016-10-07 14:00:00.0000000 |
| **6** | 6 | 5 | 15 | 139.99 | 2016-10-07 15:30:00.0000000 |
| **7** | 7 | 6 | 25 | 169.99 | 2016-10-10 10:30:00.0000000 |
| **8** | 8 | 7 | 12 | 79.99 | 2016-10-11 11:10:00.0000000 |
| **9** | 9 | 7 | 18 | 69.99 | 2016-10-12 09:50:00.0000000 |

Next, pick all rows with price of more than $1000.00, which gives the following table:

| | DeliveryId | ProductId | Quantity | Price | DeliveryDate |
|---|---|---|---|---|---|
| **1** | 1 | 1 | 2 | 1099.99 | 2016-10-01 09:30:00.0000000 |
| **2** | 2 | 1 | 5 | 1199.99 | 2016-11-01 10:20:00.0000000 |
| **3** | 3 | 2 | 10 | 1199.99 | 2016-10-02 11:10:00.0000000 |

Now, Product ID 1 has only 7 units delivered while Product ID 2 has 10 units. Only Product ID 2 meets the condition and should be displayed.

The reasoning above requires two steps. First is filtering out all prices lower than or equal to $1000.00. Second is filtering out all total units less than 10. The first filter is at the row level so you should use the WHERE clause and the second filter is at the group level (e.g. Product ID 1 is 7, not 2 and 5) so you should use the HAVING clause.

SQL Example 5.11 statement

```
SELECT ProductId, SUM(Quantity) AS "Total quantity"
FROM Purchasing.Deliveries
WHERE Price > 1000.0
GROUP BY ProductId
HAVING SUM(Quantity) >= 10;
```

SQL Example 5.11 Output:

| | ProductId | Total quantity |
|---|---|---|
| 1 | 2 | 10 |

SQL Example 5.12

Display products that are delivered between Oct 1, 2016 and Oct. 10, 2016. Show product ID, total quantity and average price (not weighted average price) of each product delivered during that time.

SQL Example 5.12 Analysis

First, you will use the WHERE clause to select products delivered between Oct. 1, 2016 and Oct. 10, 2016. Because the delivery date is a DateTime2 data type, you have to include one extra day in the ending date. Then, use the SUM() function for total quantity and AVG() function for average price. Finally, because there are aggregate functions used, you must GROUP BY all non-aggregate fields in the SELECT clause.

SQL Example 5.12 statement

```
SELECT ProductId, SUM(Quantity) AS "Total units", AVG(Price) AS "Average
price"
FROM Purchasing.Deliveries
WHERE DeliveryDate BETWEEN '20161001' AND '20161011'
GROUP BY ProductId;
```

SQL Example 5.12 Output:

| | ProductId | Total units | Average price |
|---|---|---|---|
| 1 | 1 | 2 | 1099.99 |
| 2 | 2 | 10 | 1199.99 |
| 3 | 3 | 10 | 129.99 |
| 4 | 4 | 20 | 79.99 |
| 5 | 5 | 15 | 139.99 |
| 6 | 6 | 25 | 169.99 |

SQL Example 5.13

Display products that are delivered between Oct 1, 2016 and Oct. 10, 2016 with total units delivered being 10 or more units during the time period. Show total quantity and average price of each product delivered during that time. Sort by total units delivered in descending order.

SQL Example 5.13 Analysis

This example is very similar to SQL Example 5.12 except that 1) you are only interested in products with a total unit of 10 or more and 2) you want to sort by total units. To answer 1) above, use the HAVING clause. To answer 2) above, use the ORDER BY clause.

Note that this example uses all clauses in the SELECT statement. Pay attention to the order in which each clause is presented, as shown in the left column below. Also note that the actual execution order differs from the written order, as shown in the right column:

| | |
|---|---|
| SELECT | FROM |
| FROM | WHERE |
| WHERE | GROUP BY |
| GROUP BY | HAVING |
| HAVING | SELECT |
| ORDER BY | ORDER BY |

Knowing the order of execution is important. For example, you can use the column alias in the ORDER BY clause, but cannot use the column alias in the GROUP BY nor HAVING clause. This is because ORDER BY is executed after the SELECT so that DBMS knows what the alias is, while GROUP BY and HAVING clauses are executed before the SELECT so the DBMS does not know what the alias is.

SQL Example 5.13 statement

```
SELECT ProductId, SUM(Quantity) AS "Total units", AVG(Price) AS "Average
price"
FROM Purchasing.Deliveries
WHERE DeliveryDate BETWEEN '20161001' AND '20161011'
GROUP BY ProductId
HAVING SUM(Quantity) >= 10
ORDER BY 'Total units' DESC;
```

SQL Example 5.13 Output:

| | ProductId | Total units | Average price |
|---|---|---|---|
| 1 | 6 | 25 | 169.99 |
| 2 | 4 | 20 | 79.99 |
| 3 | 5 | 15 | 139.99 |
| 4 | 2 | 10 | 1199.99 |
| 5 | 3 | 10 | 129.99 |

Review Question 5.34

In SQL, the WHERE clause is used to filter out individual rows while the __________ clause is used to filter out individual groups.
a. BOOLEAN
b. WHERE GROUP
c. LOGICAL AND
d. HAVING

Review Question 5.35
Which of the following is the correct execution sequence (not syntax sequence) of SQL statements?
a. SELECT, FROM, WHERE
b. FROM, WHERE, SELECT
c. SELECT, WHERE, FROM
d. FROM, SELECT, WHERE

Review Question 5.36
Which of the following is the correct execution sequence (not syntax sequence) of SQL statements?
a. FROM, WHERE, GROUP BY, HAVING, SELECT
b. SELECT, FROM, WHERE, GROUP BY, HAVING
c. SELECT, FROM, HAVING, GROUP BY, WHERE
d. SELECT, FROM, WHERE, HAVING, GROUP BY

Review Question 5.37
Which of the following is the correct execution sequence (not syntax sequence) of SQL statements?
a. SELECT, FROM, WHERE, GROUP BY, HAVING, ORDER BY
b. FROM, WHERE, GROUP BY, HAVING, ORDER BY, SELECT
c. FROM, WHERE, HAVING, GROUP BY, SELECT, ORDER BY
d. FROM, WHERE, GROUP BY, HAVING, SELECT, ORDER BY

## 5.14 Subquery

Subqueries are queries inside another query. The result of a SELECT statement is a table even though sometimes this table has only one value or even no values at all. You can use the result of a query in another query.

SQL Example 5.14

Display orders that contain product ID 1. Show Order ID.

SQL Example 5.14 Analysis

This is a simple SQL example to introduce a subquery.

SQL Example 5.14 statement

```
SELECT OrderId
```

```
FROM Sales.OrderDetails
WHERE ProductId = 1;
```

SQL Example 5.14 Output:

| | OrderId |
|---|---|
| 1 | 1 |
| 2 | 2 |
| 3 | 6 |

SQL Example 5.15

Display customers who placed the order ID 1, 2, or 6. Show customer ID.

SQL Example 5.15 Analysis

The OrderDetails table includes both customer ID and order ID. Use the WHERE clause and IN operator to filter the rows. The IN operator limits the column value to a set of values.

SQL Example 5.15 statement

```
SELECT DISTINCT CustomerId
FROM Sales.Orders
WHERE OrderId IN (1, 2, 6);
```

SQL Example 5.15 Output:

| | CustomerId |
|---|---|
| 1 | 1 |
| 2 | 3 |

SQL Example 5.16

Display customers whose orders contain product ID 1. Show customer ID.

SQL Example 5.16 Analysis

This is almost the same as Example 5.15. Just replace the literal OrderId inside the IN parentheses with the query from Example 5.14. You don't need to manually enter the order ID. Let the SQL SELECT statement do that. The SELECT statement inside the IN parentheses is called the subquery or inner query. Note that the subquery is executed before the outer query is executed.

SQL Example 5.16 statement

```
SELECT DISTINCT CustomerId
```

```
FROM Sales.Orders
WHERE OrderId IN (SELECT OrderId
            FROM Sales.OrderDetails
            WHERE ProductId = 1);
```

SQL Example 5.16 Output:

| | CustomerId |
|---|---|
| 1 | 1 |
| 2 | 3 |

SQL Example 5.17

Similar to Example 5.7, display all highest priced item(s) on sale. Show the product ID and the price.

SQL Example 5.17 Analysis

The subquery should find the highest price. The outer query displays all items that match that price.

SQL Example 5.17 Statement

```
SELECT ProductId, Price AS "Highest price"
FROM Sales.OrderDetails
WHERE Price = (SELECT Max(Price)
            FROM Sales.OrderDetails);
```

SQL Example 5.17 Output:

| | ProductId | Highest price |
|---|---|---|
| 1 | 2 | 1599.99 |

Review Question 5.38
In SQL statements, a query can be built on the result of another query. This is called ________.
a. query on query
b. subquery
c. result query
d. super query

## 5.15 Chapter Summary

In this chapter, you learned how to map entities and relationships in ERD to relations in databases. A relation is just another name for a table. You will learn more about relations in the next chapter. Mapping makes it possible to move models to databases. You also learned how to retrieve scale values by using aggregate functions in SQL. Usually these SELECT statements are accompanied by the GROUP BY clause and HAVING clause. You should pay more attention to the differences between the WHERE and HAVING clauses. This chapter introduces all the major clauses used in a SELECT statement. Finally, the concept of subquery was explained.

# 5.16 Discussion Questions

Discussion 5.1
If you compare an entity to a relation, you may notice there is almost no change most of the time. Yet, the mapping from ERD to relation is an important process. Explain what the significance of mapping is.

Discussion 5.2
This chapter introduces three formats of a relation. Which one is the easiest for beginners to understand? Why do you think so?

Discussion 5.3
One of the objectives for mapping from ERD to relations is the minimization of null values. In your opinion, what are some concerns of null values?

# 5.17 Database Design Exercise

Exercise One:
Map the following ERD into relations. Each customer can have many shipping addresses (including a name for each address). The account holder is just one of the many. Must include the final mapping list.

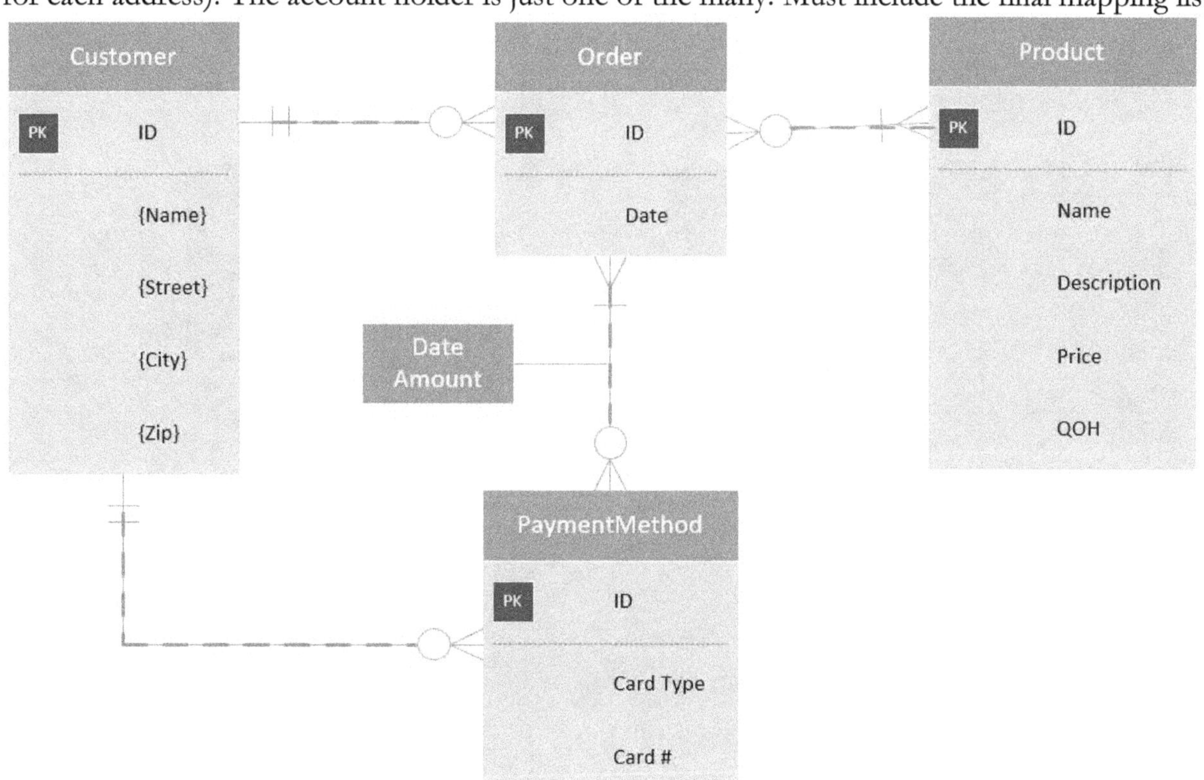

Exercise Two:
Map the following ERD into relations:

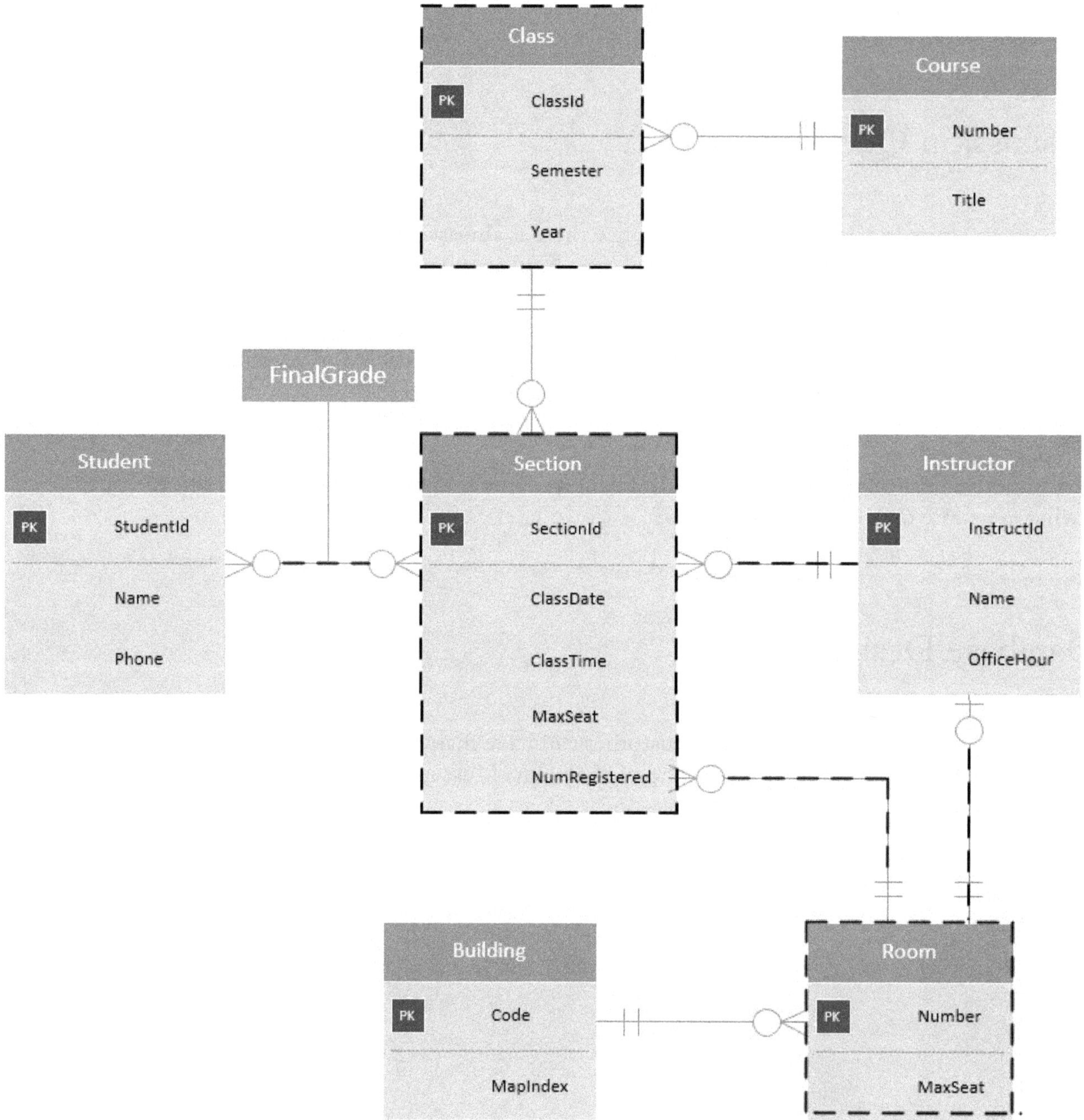


# 5.18 SQL Exercises

Exercise 5.1

Display the average price of all products in the Deliveries table.

| | Average Price |
|---|---|
| 1 | 463.32 |

Exercise 5.2

Display the number of employees who provide a phone number in the employees table.

| | Number of employees with phone number |
|---|---|
| 1 | 5 |

Exercise 5.3

Display the total number of units of products ID 1 delivered. From Appendix B, you may find that product ID 1 is delivered twice: the first one delivered on Oct. 1, 2016 of 2 units. The second was delivered on Nov. 1, 2016 of 5 units for a total of 7 units of product ID 1 delivered.

| | Total units of product id 1 delivered |
|---|---|
| 1 | 7 |

Exercise 5.4

Display the total value for product ID 7 in the deliveries table. Note that Product ID 7 was delivered twice. The first one is on Oct. 11, 2016 -- 12 units of $79.99 per unit. The second one is on Oct. 12, 2016 -- 18 units of $69.99 per unit. The displayed total value for product ID 7 should be 12X79.99 + 18X69.99 = $2219.70.

| | Total value of Product ID 7 delivered |
|---|---|
| 1 | 2219.70 |

Exercise 5.5

Display the lowest priced item on sale. Show the price.

| | Lowest priced item |
|---|---|
| 1 | 59.99 |

Exercise 5.6

Display the total number of units delivered for each product. Show product ID and the corresponding total units delivered, like this:

| | ProductId | Total units delivered |
|---|---|---|
| 1 | 1 | 7 |
| 2 | 2 | 10 |
| 3 | 3 | 10 |
| 4 | 4 | 20 |
| 5 | 5 | 15 |
| 6 | 6 | 25 |
| 7 | 7 | 30 |

Exercise 5.7

Display one of the highest priced items in the deliveries table. Show the product ID and the price.

| | ProductID | Highest priced item |
|---|---|---|

| | | |
|---|---|---|
| 1 | 2 | 1199.99 |

Exercise 5.8

Display the total value delivered for each product. For example, with the following data about Product Id 1,

| | DeliveryId | ProductId | Quantity | Price | DeliveryDate |
|---|---|---|---|---|---|
| 1 | 1 | 1 | 2 | 1099.99 | 2016-10-01 09:30:00.0000000 |
| 2 | 2 | 1 | 5 | 1199.99 | 2016-11-01 10:20:00.0000000 |

The total delivered value of Product Id 1 is 2X1099.99 + 5X1199.99 = 8199.93

Show product ID and corresponding total price

| | ProductId | Delivery total |
|---|---|---|
| 1 | 1 | 8199.93 |
| 2 | 2 | 11999.90 |
| 3 | 3 | 1299.90 |
| 4 | 4 | 1599.80 |
| 5 | 5 | 2099.85 |
| 6 | 6 | 4249.75 |
| 7 | 7 | 2219.70 |

Exercise 5.9

Display all products with a total value delivered of more than $3,000.00. By looking at the result in Exercise 5.8, you can see Product ID 1, 2, and 6 meet this criterion. Display Product ID and the corresponding delivery total.

| | ProductId | Delivery total |
|---|---|---|
| 1 | 1 | 8199.93 |
| 2 | 2 | 11999.90 |
| 3 | 6 | 4249.75 |

Exercise 5.10

Display the total units of each product delivered, but only those with a total unit more than 15. Referring to the results table in Exercise 5.6, you can see that only 3 of the 7 products meet this criterion. Show product ID and the corresponding total units delivered.

| | ProductId | Total units delivered |
|---|---|---|
| 1 | 4 | 20 |
| 2 | 6 | 25 |
| 3 | 7 | 30 |

Exercise 5.11

Display orders that contain three or more units of items that cost more than $150.00 each. Show order ID and the total units of the item.

| | OrderId | Total quantity |
|---|---|---|
| 1 | 2 | 7 |
| 2 | 3 | 4 |
| 3 | 5 | 3 |

Exercise 5.12

Display orders that contain product ID 1 or 3. Show order ID, total quantity of product, and average price (not weighted average price) for each order.

| | OrderId | Total units | Average price |
|---|---|---|---|
| 1 | 1 | 3 | 824.99 |
| 2 | 2 | 1 | 1499.99 |
| 3 | 3 | 2 | 159.99 |
| 4 | 5 | 6 | 149.99 |
| 5 | 6 | 1 | 1499.99 |

Exercise 5.13

Display orders that contain 3 or more units of product ID 1 or 3. Show order ID, total quantity of product, and average price (not weighted average price) of each order. Sort by quantity from high to low.

| | OrderId | Total units | Average price |
|---|---|---|---|
| 1 | 5 | 6 | 149.99 |
| 2 | 1 | 3 | 824.99 |

Exercise 5.14

Display products that are delivered between Oct. 5, 2016 and Oct. 10, 2016. Show product ID.

| | ProductId |
|---|---|
| 1 | 3 |
| 2 | 4 |
| 3 | 5 |

Exercise 5.15

Display suppliers who provide product ID 3, 4, or 5. Show supplier ID.

| | SupplierId |
|---|---|
| 1 | 3 |
| 2 | 5 |
| 3 | 2 |

Exercise 5.16

Display suppliers whose products are delivered between Oct. 5, 2016 and Oct. 10, 2016. Show supplier ID.

| | SupplierId |
|---|---|
| 1 | 3 |
| 2 | 5 |
| 3 | 2 |

**SQL Exercise 5.17**

**Similar to Exercise 5.7, display all highest priced item(s) in the deliveries table. Show the product ID and the** price.

| | ProductId | Highest price |
|---|---|---|

| | | |
|---|---|---|
| 1 | 1 | 1199.99 |
| 2 | 2 | 1199.99 |

## 5.19 Solutions to Review Questions

5.1 C; 5.2 A; 5.3 B; 5.4 A; 5.5 A; 5.6 B; 5.7 C; 5.8 C; 5.9 C; 5.10 D; 5.11 A; 5.12 B; 5.13 C; 5.14 A; 5.15 A; 5.16 A; 5.17 C; 5.18 C; 5.19 B; 5.20 D; 5.21 B; 5.22 A; 5.23 C; 5.24 A; 5.25 C; 5.26 D; 5.27 B; 5.28 D; 5.29 B; 5.30 A; 5.31 D; 5.32 C; 5.33 D; 5.34 D; 5.35 B; 5.36 A; 5.37 D; 5.38 B;

# Chapter 6: Normalization, Denormalization, and SQL Join

## Chapter Learning Objectives

6.1 Explain different types of anomalies.
6.2 Execute normalization on relations.
6.3 Recognize the need for denormalization.
6.4 Critique on entity integrity and referential integrity.
6.5 Retrieve data from multiple tables with JOIN and UNION in SQL.

## 6.1 What Is a Good Relation?

In the last chapter, you learned how to map an ERD to relations. Technically, you can start to write SQL statements to create tables for a database. In fact, there are many types of software that can automatically generate SQL statements and thus create the database for you based on given ERD and relations.

However, just like how there are many ways to construct a four-bedroom house, there are many ways to design a database. Are they all of the same quality? No. Then how do we know which way is better than the others? In this chapter, we will show you how to check if a relation is good and how to make it better through a process called normalization.

A good relation should reflect what's in the ERD, and, of course, the ERD should reflect the mini-world. The relations should contain all the data needed by the business. For example, if the business needs the total years an employee has worked, then the database should have employment history for each employee. All the attributes, entities, and relationships in an ERD should be carried over to relations (how to meet this requirement was covered in the last chapter.)

A good relation should also minimize the data redundancy. When you have the same data stored in more than one place, it takes extra storage, and, more importantly, it can cause inconsistency or data anomalies (for example, you might update the data in one place and forget to update it in another.) Minimizing data redundancy is the topic of this chapter.

Review Question 6.1

You can check if a relation is good and how to make it better through a process called ______.
a. improvement
b. relation enhancement
c. normalization
d. denormalization

Review Question 6.2
Why is normalization introduced in database design?
a. To eliminate the need for ERDs
b. To speed up SQL execution only
c. To evaluate and improve the quality of relations
d. To convert SQL into programming code

Review Question 6.3
What does a good relation do?
a. It reflects what is in the ERD.
b. It allows minimum redundancy.
c. both reflecting what is in the ERD and allowing minimum redundancy.
d. none of the options.

Review Question 6.4
Which of the following is the most serious issue with data redundancy in relations?
a. extra storage.
b. data inconsistency.
c. longer retrieval time.
d. confusion for the user.

## 6.2 What Are Anomalies?

Let's see an example. The following table contains data about employees in a company.

| EmployeeId | FirstName | LastName | Department |
|---|---|---|---|
| 111 | Victoria | Gibson | Accounting |
| 112 | Justin | Smith | Accounting |
| 113 | Melisa | Martin | Marketing |
| 114 | Roy | Rocha | Sales |
| 115 | Jonathan | Williams | Accounting |

Table 6.1 Employees in one table.

Now, assume the company wants to establish a new department, say, Business Intelligence. This new department currently has no employees. The new table will look like this:

| EmployeeId | FirstName | LastName | Department |
|---|---|---|---|
| 111 | Victoria | Gibson | Accounting |
| 112 | Justin | Smith | Accounting |
| 113 | Melisa | Martin | Marketing |
| 114 | Roy | Rocha | Sales |
| 115 | Jonathan | Williams | Accounting |
| Null | Null | Null | Business Intelligence |

Table 6.2 A new department is added to the table.

The problem with this table is that the primary key (EmployeeId) cannot accept null values. However, making up employee IDs, such as 116, to fill in for the null values will also result in issues, in that even though there are only five employees, the table implies that there are six.

This is called an *insertion anomaly* and can be avoided if you use two tables as shown below. Here, you just add a new row called "Business Intelligence" to the department table.

| EmployeeId | FirstName | LastName | DepartmentId |
|---|---|---|---|
| 111 | Victoria | Gibson | 1 |
| 112 | Justin | Smith | 1 |
| 113 | Melisa | Martin | 2 |
| 114 | Roy | Rocha | 3 |
| 115 | Jonathan | Williams | 1 |

Table 6.3 New employee table

| DepartmentId | Department |
|---|---|
| 1 | Accounting |
| 2 | Marketing |
| 3 | Sales |

Table 6.4 New Department table.

Back to Table 6.1, also consider if employee Roy Rocha left the company. We would have to remove his record, and since he is the only employee in Sales, all data on Sales would be gone if using the single table approach. This is called the *deletion anomaly* and can be avoided if you use two tables as shown above.

Let's see one more anomaly. Back to Table 6.1, suppose the accounting department is renamed as the finance department. You would have to update the name in three locations, row 1, 2, and 5, if using the single table approach. The more times you make a correction, the more susceptible you are to making mistakes (note: in terms of SQL, this is a less serious problem since updates can be corrected in one statement, but it is still possible to have a mistake.)

This is called a *modification anomaly* and can be avoided through the two-table approach (Table 6.3 and 6.4). In the two-table approach, you will only need to update one row in the department table.

Review Question 6.5
The following employee table may cause anomalies. You can avoid the problem by ______.

| EmployeeId | FirstName | LastName | Department |
|---|---|---|---|
| 111 | Victoria | Gibson | Accounting |
| 112 | Justin | Smith | Accounting |

a. not inserting abnormal rows
b. not deleting a whole row
c. not providing a null value
d. breaking up the table into an employee table and a department table

Review Question 6.6
Which of the following is not a type of relation anomaly discussed in this chapter?
a. Insertion anomalies
b. Deletion anomalies

c. Modification anomalies
d. Creation anomalies

Review Question 6.7
With the following employee table, an insertion anomaly may happen when __________.

| EmployeeId | FirstName | LastName | Department |
|---|---|---|---|
| 111 | Victoria | Gibson | Accounting |
| 112 | Justin | Smith | Accounting |

a. a new employee without a department is inserted
b. a new employee for a new department is inserted
c. a new department is inserted
d. a new department without any employees is inserted

Review Question 6.8
With the following employee table, a deletion anomaly may happen when ________.

| EmployeeId | FirstName | LastName | Department |
|---|---|---|---|
| 114 | Roy | Rocha | Sales |
| 115 | Jonathan | Williams | Accounting |

a. an employee is deleted
b. when more than one employee is deleted
c. when an employee who is the single person in a department is deleted
d. when more than one employee in the same department is deleted

Review Question 6.9
With the following employee table, a modification anomaly may happen when _________.

| EmployeeId | FirstName | LastName | Department |
|---|---|---|---|
| 114 | Roy | Rocha | Sales |
| 115 | Jonathan | Williams | Accounting |

a. a department changes its name
b. an employee changes his or her last name
c. an employee changes his or her first name
d. an employee changes both his or her first name and last name

## 6.3 Problems with Null Value

There are scenarios in which a value for an attribute cannot be entered into the database. This generally falls into three categories. The first situation is when the attribute is not applicable. For example, if an employee is in their first job, the 'Previous Job Title' attribute does not apply. The second situation is when the value exists but is temporarily unavailable. For example, all employees have a Date of Birth, but for a new hire, that data may not have been collected yet. The third situation is when the value exists but is indefinitely unknown. For example, an employee's Marital Status may remain unknown if they choose not to disclose it. A NULL value in the database indicates the presence of any of these situations.

As a result, the logical operation for null values is different from a known value. When a null value is in the operation, the operation is often called three-valued logic. These operators are often used in the WHERE and HAVING clauses of SQL SELECT statements.

| | The Other Operand value is: | | | |
|---|---|---|---|---|
| One Operand value is: | | *True* | *False* | *Null* |
| | *True* | **True** | **False** | **Null** |
| | *False* | **False** | **False** | **False** |
| | *Null* | **Null** | **False** | **Null** |

Table 6.5 Three-valued AND logical operator

For example, suppose you want to see whether an employee meets a requirement of being born before Jan. 1 1990 and is a Texas resident. If it is true that an employee's date of birth is before Jan. 1, 1990 and their hometown is unknown/null, then it would therefore be unknown/null whether they meet the requirement of being born before Jan. 1 1990 and being a Texas resident.

However, if it is false that an employee's date of birth is before Jan. 1 1990 (meaning they were born after Jan. 1 1990) and their hometown is still unknown/null, it can be confidently declared that they do not meet the requirement of being born before Jan. 1 1990 and being a Texas resident.

Similarly, the following table shows the three-valued OR operator.

| | The Other Operand value is: | | | |
|---|---|---|---|---|
| One Operand value is: | | *True* | *False* | *Null* |
| | *True* | **True** | **True** | **True** |
| | *False* | **True** | **False** | **Null** |
| | *Null* | **True** | **Null** | **Null** |

Table 6.6 Three-valued OR logical operator

Finally, the following table shows the three-logic NOT operator. Keep in mind that the three-valued NOT logical operator can only be used for one variable unlike for the AND and OR operator.

| The Operand value is: | The result of the NOT operation |
|---|---|
| *True* | **False** |
| *False* | **True** |
| *Null* | **Null** |

Table 6.7 Three-valued NOT logical operator

You cannot compare a null value to a Boolean value by using an equal sign. It is either IS NULL or IS NOT NULL. Also, when null values are in the column of a JOIN operation (an SQL topic on combining two tables later in the chapter), the result can be difficult to predict.

Review Question 6.10
When null values are in the column of a JOIN operation, _______.
a. the SQL statement won't work
b. the SQL statement will run slow
c. the result can be difficult to predict
d. the result can contain many more null values

Review Question 6.11
Which of the following is NOT a possible situation for null values in a database?
a. the database server is down
b. the attribute is not applicable for the entity instance.
c. the data has been not entered in the database table
d. the data is not known

Review Question 6.12
What is the result of the following three-valued logic expression?
True AND Null
a. True
b. False
c. Null

Review Question 6.13
What is the result of the following three-valued logic expression?
False AND Null
a. True
b. False
c. Null

Review Question 6.14
What is the result of the following three-valued logic expression?
False OR Null
a. True
b. False
c. Null

Review Question 6.15
What is the result of the following three-valued logic expression?
True OR Null
a. True
b. False
c. Null

Review Question 6.16
In SQL statements, which of the following is the correct way to write the WHERE clause?
a. WHERE SecondPhone = Null
b. WHERE SecondPhone = 'Null'
c. WHERE SecondPhone IS Null
d. WHERE SecondPhone LIKE Null

## 6.4 Functional Dependency in a Relation

Functional dependency refers to when one attribute determines another. Say you have two columns of a relation, Column1 and Column2. If we say that Column2 is functionally dependent on Column1, we mean that if any two rows in Column1 have the same value, then the corresponding two rows in Column2 must also be equal to each other.

For example, if whenever two students have the same ID they also have the same first name, it can be stated that student first name is functionally dependent on student ID. However, if two students have the same first name, they don't necessarily have the same last name, and therefore it can be stated that student last name is not functionally dependent on student first name.

The above functional dependency definition can be extended to include more than one column. In other words, this relationship can exist between two groups of columns, or even a group of columns and one column.

The functional dependency conclusion should not be made based on limited records in a relation. It should be based on the mini-world data. For example,

| Course | Classroom |
|---|---|
| CS101 | Lincoln311 |
| CS102 | Lincoln312 |
| CS103 | Lincoln313 |

Table 6.8 A partial data table.

Based on the limited data sample, you may conclude that Course is functionally dependent on Classroom since with a given classroom, you can find only one course. However, in reality, this is often not true.

Let's see an example of functional dependency in a relation:

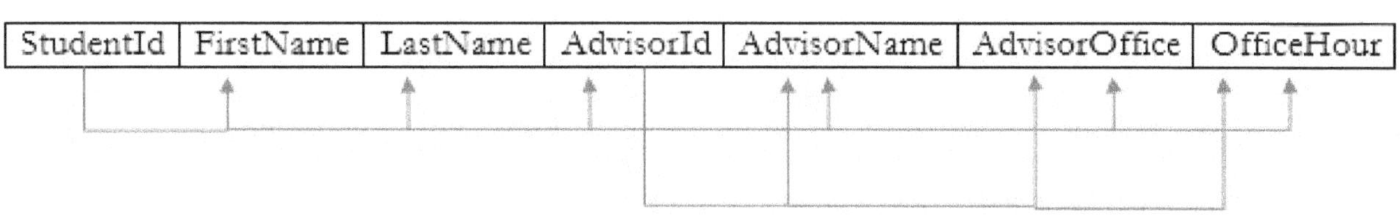


Figure 6.1 Functional dependency diagram

In the above dependency diagram, studentId is called a determinant because if you know the student ID, you can find out all the remaining columns that the arrows point to. AdvisorId is also a determinant, which points to its dependents: AdvisorName, AdvisorOffice, and OfficeHour.

Review Question 6.17
If you want to prove that an attribute is NOT functionally dependent on another attribute, you need ______ examples.
a. one
b. two
c. three
d. many

Review Question 6.18
Say you have two columns of a relation, Column1 and Column2. If two rows in Column1 are equal to each other, then the two corresponding values of Column2 must also be equal to each other. Thus, Column2 is ____________ on Column1.
a. functionally dependent
b. over dependent
c. composite primary key
d. equal

Review Question 6.19
If two students have the same ID, they must have the same first name. Which of the following is true?
a. ID is the primary key
b. ID is a determinant
c. First name is the primary key
d. First name is a determinant

## 6.5 Normalization

As stated in section 6.2, anomalies are caused by duplicated data. There is a process that can reduce the data redundancy called normalization. Normalization is based on functional dependency. The normalization process begins with examining the dependency diagram to break up a relation based on its determinants, thus achieving first normal form. This process can be repeated to achieve second normal form, third normal form, and so on, if necessary.

### 6.5.1 First Normal Form

A relation is a two-dimensional table with unique rows. In practice, any table with a primary key is treated as a relation. A relation is considered to be in First Normal Form (1NF) if all cells are atomic and there are no repeating groups. Let's see an example:

| StudentId | Name | DateBirth | CourseId | Title | Grade | Semester | Location |
|---|---|---|---|---|---|---|---|
| 111 | Alice | 1/4/2001 | CS101, CS211 | Intro CS, Java | A, A | Fall 2017 | Lincoln311, 312 |
| 112 | Tom | 2/6/2000 | CS201, CS211 | Algorithm, Java | B, B | Fall 2017 | Lincoln311, 312 |

Table 6.9 Student registration table without atomic cell values.

Table 6.9 is not in the first normal form because it contains multivalued data. The course id, title, grade, and location fields have more than one value in a cell. One solution to make Table 6.9 in the first normal form is to make each simple value in its own row as shown in Table 6.10.

| StudentId | Name | DateBirth | CourseId | Title | Grade | semester | Location |
|---|---|---|---|---|---|---|---|
| 111 | Alice | 1/4/2001 | CS101 | Intro CS | A | Fall 2017 | Lincoln311 |
| 112 | Tom | 2/6/2000 | CS201 | Algorithm | B | Fall 2017 | Lincoln311 |
| 111 | Alice | 1/4/2001 | CS211 | Java | A | Fall 2017 | Lincoln312 |
| 112 | Tom | 2/6/2000 | CS211 | Java | B | Fall 2017 | Lincoln312 |

Table 6.10 Student registration table with atomic cell values

Table 6.10 is in the first normal form because all cells of the table contain atomic values and any attribute depends on the composite primary key of studentID and courseID.

If you follow the steps for database design from the previous chapters, you won't get a relation like Table 6.9 because multivalued attributes are mapped into a separate relation.

Atomic also means a value is not composite, or that it cannot be further broken down into smaller parts. For example, a student name is not atomic in many cases because the value can be broken down into first name, last name, and middle name. However, sometimes, you may be happy with just a student name. In short, we treat "atomic" as "a single thing". If a school always uses a student name as a single thing, it is ok to treat it as atomic.

## 6.5.2 Second Normal Form

A relation is said to be in the second normal form if it is in the first normal form and every non- primary key attribute is functionally dependent on the whole primary key. Compared to the first normal form, the new part in the second normal form is the "dependent on the whole primary key". For a single attribute primary key relation, this is automatically satisfied because all non-key attributes are dependent on the whole key.

Is the student table of Table 6.10 in the second normal form? No, it has a composite primary key of StudentId and CourseId. The question becomes, "Is every non-primary key attribute functionally dependent on the whole primary key?" The answer is no. For example, Title is not dependent on both StudentId and CourseId. It is dependent on only CourseId. Thus the "dependent on the whole key" is violated.

Let's draw the dependency diagram for Table 6.10.

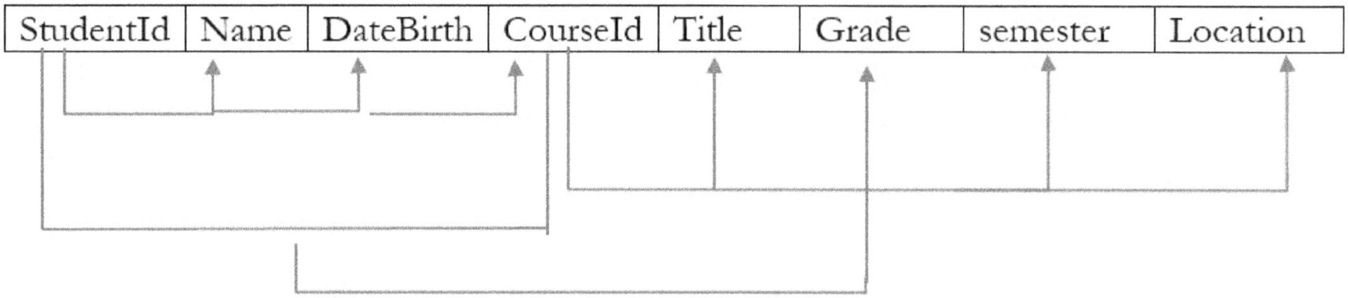


Figure 6.2 Dependency Diagram for Table 6.9

Based on the dependency diagram of Figure 6.2, the relation can be broken into three relations because there are three determinants. The first one is StudentId, the second one is CourseId, and the third one is the composite determinant of StudentId and CourseId.

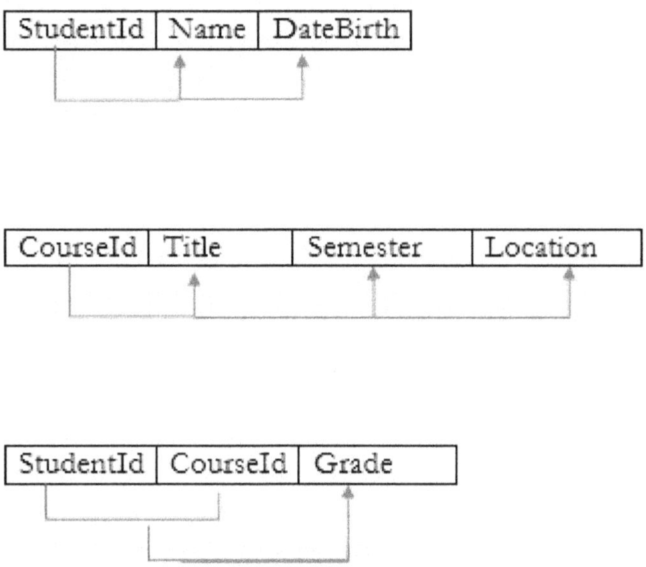


Figure 6.3 Dependency diagram after breakup of a relation.

ALL three relations in Figure 6.3 are in second normal form (actually in third normal form). Let's see another relation that is in the first normal form, but not in the second normal form. Below, you can see that the primary key is both StudentId and CourseId. However, Location does not depend on StudentId (only on CourseId) and so it is in the first normal form but not the second normal form.

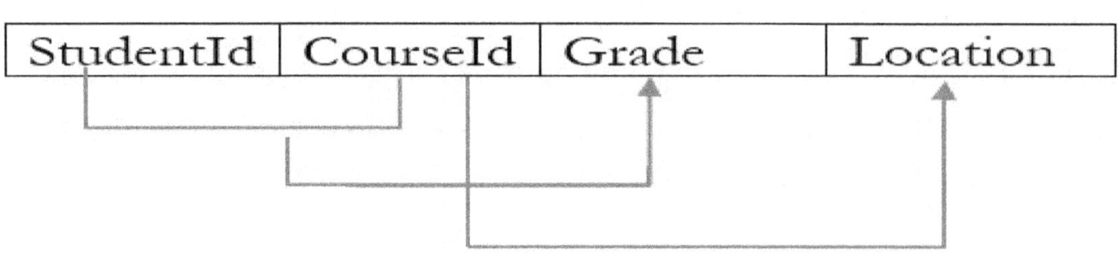


Figure 6.4 Dependency diagram for a relation in first normal form, but not second normal form.

## 6.5.3 Third Normal Form

A relation is in third normal form if it is in second normal form and has no transitive dependency. A transitive dependency is a dependent relationship between two non-primary key attributes.

Suppose a university allows any students to take at most one course for free. They may have a relation like this below:

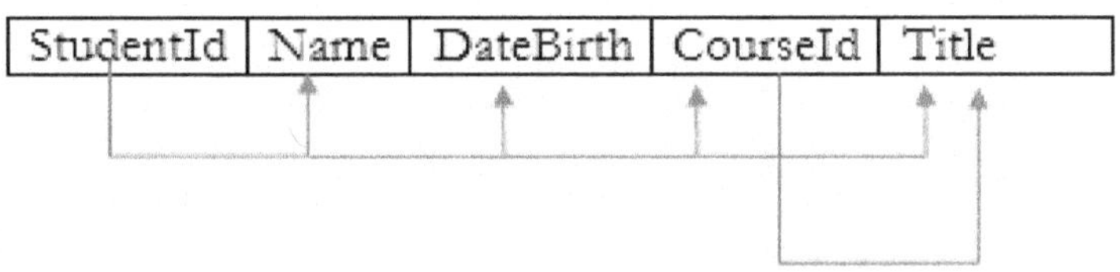


Figure 6.5 A relation with transitive dependency.

In Figure 6.5, the Title attribute is functionally dependent on CourseId, and CourseId is dependent on the StudentId (the primary key of the relation.) This relation is in the second normal form, but not in the third normal form. To convert the relation in Figure 6.5 into third normal form, just break the relation into two based on the determinant of StudentId and CourseId as shown below.

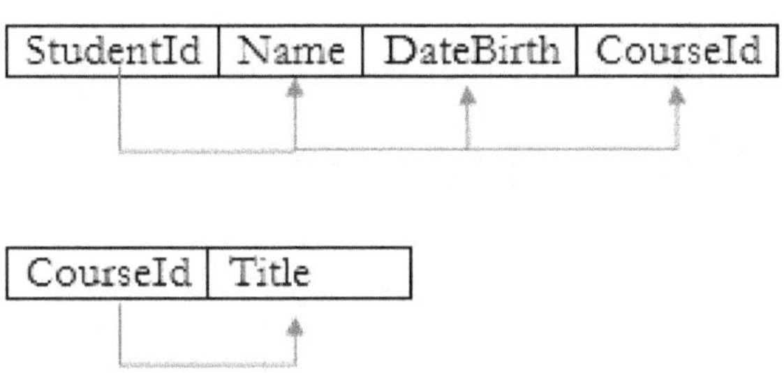


Figure 6.6 Relation in Figure 6.5 now in third normal form.

Also, the three relations in Figure 6.3 contain no transitive dependency and thus are all in 3rd normal form. Here's another example of a relation that is in the 2nd NF, but not in the 3rd NF.

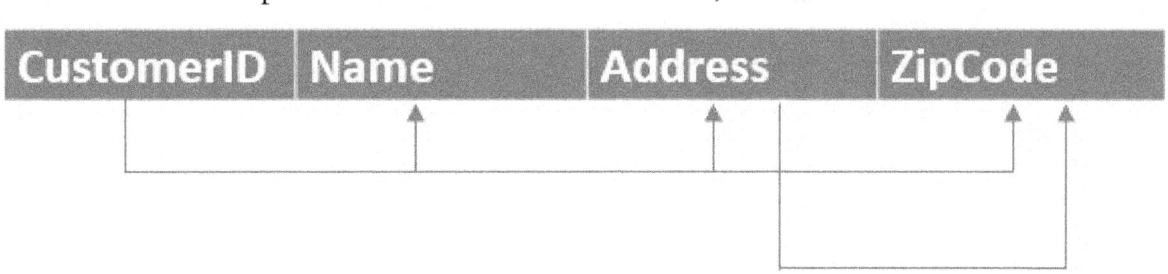


Figure 6.7 A customer relation

The normalization process can go on to higher levels of normalization form. This book only covers up to the third normal form for most practical projects. The higher the normal form the less duplication of the data. However, there's a side effect in this process we will uncover in the next section.

Review Question 6.20
A relation is a two-dimensional table with unique rows. In other words, any table with a _____ is a relation.
a. primary key
b. foreign key
c. numeric column
d. two-dimensional data

Review Question 6.21
The following table is in ______ normal form (pick the highest level).

| StudentId | Name | DateBirth | CourseId | Title | Grade | Semester | Location |
|---|---|---|---|---|---|---|---|
| 111 | Alice | 1/4/2001 | CS101, CS211 | Intro CS, Java | A, A | Fall 2017 | Lincoln311, 312 |
| 112 | Tom | 2/6/2000 | CS201, CS211 | Algorithm, Java | B, B | Fall 2017 | Lincoln311, 312 |

a. first
b. second
c. third
d. not in any normal form

Review Question 6.22
The following table is in ______ normal form (pick the highest level).

| StudentId | Name | DateBirth | CourseId | Title | Grade | semester | Location |
|---|---|---|---|---|---|---|---|
| 111 | Alice | 1/4/2001 | CS101 | Intro CS | A | Fall 2017 | Lincoln311 |
| 112 | Tom | 2/6/2000 | CS201 | Algorithm | B | Fall 2017 | Lincoln311 |
| 111 | Alice | 1/4/2001 | CS211 | Java | A | Fall 2017 | Lincoln312 |
| 112 | Tom | 2/6/2000 | CS211 | Java | B | Fall 2017 | Lincoln312 |

a. first
b. second
c. third
d. not in any normal form

Review Question 6.23
The following relation is in ______ normal form (pick the highest level).
Suppose a university allows any students to take at most one course for free. They may have a relation like this below:

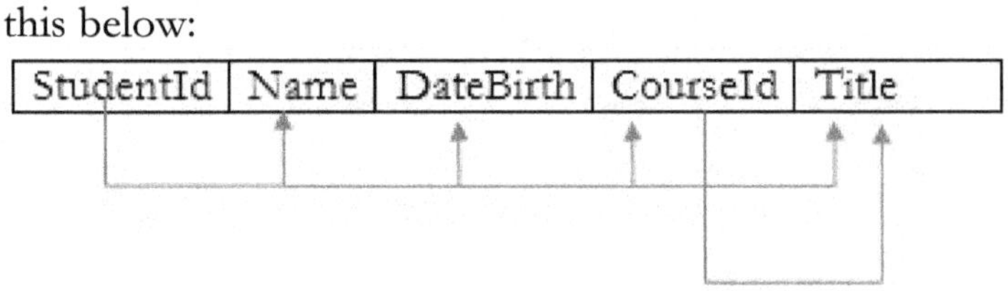


a. first
b. second
c. third

d. not in any normal form

Review Question 6.24
The following relation is in ______ normal form (pick the highest level).

a. first
b. second
c. third
d. not in any normal form

Review Question 6.25
A relation that contains only _________ values in each cell is said in the first normal form.
a. numeric
b. text
c. useful
d. atomic

Review Question 6.26
The process of reducing data redundancy in a relation is called ______________.
a. normalization
b. redundancy minimization
c. redundancy removal
d. redundancy reduction

Review Question 6.27
The normalization process is based on the functional dependency of the attributes. A relation is broken into smaller relations based on its ___________.
a. size
b. determinant
c. structure
d. normal form

Review Question 6.28
A relation is in second normal form if ___________.
a. it is in first normal form
b. all its values are atomic
c. every non-primary key attribute is functionally dependent on the whole primary key
d. it is in first normal form and every non-primary key attribute is functionally dependent on the whole PK

Review Question 6.29
A relation is in the third normal form if ____________.
a. it is in the second normal form
b. every non-primary key attribute is functionally dependent on the whole primary key
c. it contains no transitive dependency

d. it is in the second normal form and it contains no transitive dependency

Review Question 6.30
According to the author, for most business problems, a ______ normal form is good enough for a relation.
a. first
b. second
c. third
d. fourth

## 6.6 Denormalization

In normalization, the higher the normal form, the less duplication in the data. Logically, you would want to go as high as you can. However, when the normal form goes up, the number of relations increases as determinants break them up. When using the data, you will have more tables and thus more joined tables. The process of joining tables is time consuming. This will affect the performance.

As a result, you need to balance the benefit of less data duplication and faster performance. After following the rules to normalize the relations, you may want to do some denormalization. The process of denormalization involves combining relations to avoid joining tables for data retrieval.

There's only one rule for denormalization: data used together should stay together (in other words, they should remain in the same relation.) For example, students and advisors are usually two separate relations. However, if the database always finds the advisor through the student or finds the student through the advisor, then you would want to combine the two relations in one.

In short, the denormalization process is not required, although you may want to use it if performance is a major concern. Remember to balance the benefits between normalization and denormalization.

Review Question 6.31
In normalization, the higher the normal form, the less duplication in the data. Logically, you would want to go ______.
a. to the second normal form
b. to the third normal form
c. to the fourth normal form
d. as high as you can

Review Question 6.32
In normalization, when the normal form goes up, the ______ increases as determinants break them up.

a. number of relations
b. primary key of relations
c. foreign key of relations
d. number of keys

Review Question 6.33
In normalization, when using the data in a higher level of normal form, you will have more tables and thus more joined tables. The process of joining tables is ______. This will affect the ______.
a. fast, data
b. fast, performance
c. time consuming, data
d. time consuming, performance

Review Question 6.34
In normalization, you need to balance the benefit of ______ and ______.
a. quick normalization, faster performance
b. quick normalization, cheaper storage
c. less data duplication, faster performance
d. less data duplication, cheaper storage

Review Question 6.35
A rule for denormalization is to ______________.
a. always keep relations in at least third normal form
b. always keep relations in at least second normal form
c. make sure data used together stay together
d. make sure at least one denormalization occurs for each database

## 6.7 Entity Integrity and Referential Integrity

Each entity should have a primary key so that each row (tuple to be more accurate) can be uniquely identified by the DBMS. Such a requirement is also called entity integrity. The primary key of an entity is kept as the primary key in the relations after mapping.

The relationships between entities in ERD are usually reflected by the use of foreign keys in relations. Adding a foreign key achieves referential integrity. The foreign key actually checks the column value with the primary key of the related relation. The foreign keys are added during the mapping.

For example, as shown in Tables 6.11 and 6.12, a student relation has AdvisorId as a foreign key. The data in the student relation are not valid because Bob has an advisor (advisor 3) that does not exist. As can be seen, the foreign key helps the data quality of the database. Referential integrity keeps data valid.

| StudentId | StudentName | AdvisorId |
|---|---|---|
| 111 | Alice | 1 |
| 222 | Bob | 3 |
| 333 | Tom | 2 |

Table 6.11 Student table

| AdvisorId | AdvisorName |
|---|---|
| 1 | Dr. Xavier |
| 2 | Dr. Young |

Table 6.12 Advisor table

Review Question 6.36
All entities should have a primary key so that each row (tuple to be more accurate) can be uniquely identified by the DBMS. This requirement is called ____________.
a. entity requirement
b. entity integrity
c. entity quality
d. referential integrity

Review Question 6.37
The relationships between entities in ERD are usually reflected by the use of foreign keys in relations. Adding a foreign key achieves _____________.
a. entity requirement
b. entity integrity
c. entity quality
d. referential integrity

# 6.8 SQL INNER JOIN

SQL Example 5.16 from Chapter 5 is repeated below:

Display customers whose orders contain product ID 1. Show customer ID.

You learned how to use subquery to retrieve all the necessary data from more than one table. You cannot use a simple SELECT... FROM on a table because the customer ID and product ID do not appear in the same table.

Often, you will want to retrieve data from multiple tables. You can use INNER JOIN (often shortened to JOIN) to combine the tables and then use SELECT for the data you need. Inner join puts two tables side by side, but only those rows with matching values will appear in the joined table.

For example, if you want to know the total value of each order, you can use the OrderDetails table:

| | OrderId | ProductId | Price | quantity |
|---|---|---|---|---|
| 1 | 1 | 1 | 1499.99 | 1 |
| 2 | 1 | 3 | 149.99 | 2 |
| 3 | 2 | 1 | 1499.99 | 1 |
| 4 | 2 | 2 | 1599.99 | 1 |
| 5 | 2 | 4 | 99.99 | 6 |
| 6 | 2 | 6 | 189.99 | 5 |
| 7 | 3 | 3 | 159.99 | 2 |
| 8 | 3 | 6 | 199.99 | 1 |
| 9 | 3 | 7 | 109.99 | 2 |
| 10 | 3 | 8 | 69.99 | 2 |
| 11 | 3 | 9 | 1449.99 | 1 |
| 12 | 4 | 4 | 99.99 | 2 |
| 13 | 4 | 8 | 69.99 | 1 |
| 14 | 5 | 3 | 149.99 | 6 |
| 15 | 5 | 6 | 199.99 | 3 |
| 16 | 6 | 1 | 1499.99 | 1 |
| 17 | 7 | 2 | 999.99 | 1 |
| 18 | 8 | 7 | 79.99 | 1 |
| 19 | 8 | 8 | 59.99 | 2 |

However, if you also want to know the order date for each order, you have to use the Order table:

| OrderId | CustomerId | EmployeeId | OrderDate |
|---|---|---|---|
| 1 | 1 | 5 | 2017-01-03 |
| 2 | 1 | 3 | 2017-03-05 |
| 3 | 2 | 5 | 2017-02-23 |
| 4 | 4 | 5 | 2017-04-13 |
| 5 | 1 | 4 | 2017-05-03 |
| 6 | 3 | 6 | 2017-05-08 |
| 7 | 5 | 7 | 2016-11-08 |
| 8 | 7 | 2 | 2016-12-23 |

How can you have order total and order date for each order in one single SELECT statement? The answer is to join the tables. You can join the OrderDetails and Orders table according to Order ID -- that is, you put the two tables side by side with the matching values in the OrderId. For example, since OrderId = 1 has two rows in the OrderDetails table and one row in the Orders table, you will have two rows in the new joined table like this:

| | OrderId | ProductId | Price | quantity | OrderId | CustomerId | EmployeeId | OrderDate |
|---|---|---|---|---|---|---|---|---|
| 1 | 1 | 1 | 1499.99 | 1 | 1 | 1 | 5 | 2017-01-03 |
| 2 | 1 | 3 | 149.99 | 2 | 1 | 1 | 5 | 2017-01-03 |

Here's the result of the two tables joined. Spend a few minutes to see how the two tables are used to form this new table.

| | OrderId | ProductId | Price | quantity | OrderId | CustomerId | EmployeeId | OrderDate |
|---|---|---|---|---|---|---|---|---|
| 1 | 1 | 1 | 1499.99 | 1 | 1 | 1 | 5 | 2017-01-03 |
| 2 | 1 | 3 | 149.99 | 2 | 1 | 1 | 5 | 2017-01-03 |
| 3 | 2 | 1 | 1499.99 | 1 | 2 | 1 | 3 | 2017-03-05 |
| 4 | 2 | 2 | 1599.99 | 1 | 2 | 1 | 3 | 2017-03-05 |
| 5 | 2 | 4 | 99.99 | 6 | 2 | 1 | 3 | 2017-03-05 |
| 6 | 2 | 6 | 189.99 | 5 | 2 | 1 | 3 | 2017-03-05 |
| 7 | 3 | 3 | 159.99 | 2 | 3 | 2 | 5 | 2017-02-23 |
| 8 | 3 | 6 | 199.99 | 1 | 3 | 2 | 5 | 2017-02-23 |
| 9 | 3 | 7 | 109.99 | 2 | 3 | 2 | 5 | 2017-02-23 |
| 10 | 3 | 8 | 69.99 | 2 | 3 | 2 | 5 | 2017-02-23 |
| 11 | 3 | 9 | 1449.99 | 1 | 3 | 2 | 5 | 2017-02-23 |
| 12 | 4 | 4 | 99.99 | 2 | 4 | 4 | 5 | 2017-04-13 |
| 13 | 4 | 8 | 69.99 | 1 | 4 | 4 | 5 | 2017-04-13 |
| 14 | 5 | 3 | 149.99 | 6 | 5 | 1 | 4 | 2017-05-03 |
| 15 | 5 | 6 | 199.99 | 3 | 5 | 1 | 4 | 2017-05-03 |
| 16 | 6 | 1 | 1499.99 | 1 | 6 | 3 | 6 | 2017-05-08 |
| 17 | 7 | 2 | 999.99 | 1 | 7 | 5 | 7 | 2016-11-08 |
| 18 | 8 | 7 | 79.99 | 1 | 8 | 7 | 2 | 2016-12-23 |
| 19 | 8 | 8 | 59.99 | 2 | 8 | 7 | 2 | 2016-12-23 |

Let's see another example. Suppose there two tables look like below:

| StudentId | StudentName | AdvisorId |
|---|---|---|
| 1 | Alice | 111 |
| 2 | Bob | 111 |
| 3 | Chuck | 222 |
| 4 | Dan | Null |

Table 6.13 Data for the student table

| AdvisorId | AdvisorName |
|---|---|
| 111 | Xavier |
| 222 | Young |
| 333 | Zach |

Table 6.14 Data for the advisor table

From the data above, you can see that advisor 111 has two students, advisor 222 has one student, and advisor 333 has no students yet. What is the result if you INNER JOIN these two tables based on AdvisorId?

| StudentId | StudentName | AdvisorId | AdivsorId | AdvisorName |
|---|---|---|---|---|
| 1 | Alice | 111 | 111 | Xavier |
| 2 | Alice | 111 | 111 | Xavier |
| 3 | Chuck | 222 | 222 | Young |

Table 6.15 Data for the inner join of the student and advisor tables

We will use INNER JOIN and JOIN interchangeably. The syntax for joining two tables is:

```
SELECT *
FROM Table1Name JOIN Table2Name
ON Table1Name.CommonColumn = Table2Name.CommonColumn
```

The CommonColumn is the column that appears in both tables. In the above example, it is AdvisorId. The equal sign "=" in the ON clause can have other conditions, such as the "<" sign.

If you have more than two tables to join, you join two tables first. Then join the result of the first two tables with the third table and so on.

SQL Example 6.1

Display order details for each order. Show order ID, order date, product ID in the order, quantity, and price of that product.

SQL Example 6.1 Analysis

Because the order ID, order date, product ID, quantity, and price of the products are from two different tables, Orders and OrderDetails tables, you will need to join the two tables. The common column for the two tables is OrderId. Refer to Appendix B for which data are in which table and which field is common between the two tables.

Also, because there are two OrderId columns in the joined table, you should add the table name to qualify the column as shown in the SELECT statement below.

Note that in the SQL Example 6.1 statement below, we show two solutions. The first one shows the minimum qualifier used to avoid ambiguity. The second one shows all SELECT columns with the format of TableName.ColumnName for easy reading.

SQL Example 6.1 statement

```
SELECT Orders.OrderId, OrderDate, ProductId, Quantity, Price
FROM Sales.Orders JOIN Sales.OrderDetails
ON Orders.OrderId = OrderDetails.OrderId;
```

Or

```
SELECT Orders.OrderId, Orders.OrderDate, OrderDetails.ProductId,
OrderDetails.Quantity, OrderDetails.Price
FROM Sales.Orders JOIN Sales.OrderDetails
ON Orders.OrderId = OrderDetails.OrderId;
```

SQL Example 6.1 Output:

| | OrderId | OrderDate | ProductId | quantity | Price |
|---|---|---|---|---|---|
| 1 | 1 | 2017-01-03 | 1 | 1 | 1499.99 |
| 2 | 1 | 2017-01-03 | 3 | 2 | 149.99 |
| 3 | 2 | 2017-03-05 | 1 | 1 | 1499.99 |
| 4 | 2 | 2017-03-05 | 2 | 1 | 1599.99 |
| 5 | 2 | 2017-03-05 | 4 | 6 | 99.99 |
| 6 | 2 | 2017-03-05 | 6 | 5 | 189.99 |
| 7 | 3 | 2017-02-23 | 3 | 2 | 159.99 |
| 8 | 3 | 2017-02-23 | 6 | 1 | 199.99 |
| 9 | 3 | 2017-02-23 | 7 | 2 | 109.99 |
| 10 | 3 | 2017-02-23 | 8 | 2 | 69.99 |
| 11 | 3 | 2017-02-23 | 9 | 1 | 1449.99 |
| 12 | 4 | 2017-04-13 | 4 | 2 | 99.99 |
| 13 | 4 | 2017-04-13 | 8 | 1 | 69.99 |
| 14 | 5 | 2017-05-03 | 3 | 6 | 149.99 |
| 15 | 5 | 2017-05-03 | 6 | 3 | 199.99 |
| 16 | 6 | 2017-05-08 | 1 | 1 | 1499.99 |
| 17 | 7 | 2016-11-08 | 2 | 1 | 999.99 |
| 18 | 8 | 2016-12-23 | 7 | 1 | 79.99 |
| 19 | 8 | 2016-12-23 | 8 | 2 | 59.99 |

SQL Example 6.2

Display order total for each order. Show order ID and order total for each order.

SQL Example 6.2 Analysis

The necessary data are from two tables, so you need to join the two tables as shown in SQL Example 6.1. Take a look at the output of SQL Example 6.1. Can you display the order total with the knowledge you learned from Chapter 5? You will need a SUM() function for the total and GROUP BY clause to combine rows in each order. For example, Order ID 1 has two rows and you should combine them to find the total.

SQL Example 6.2 statement

```
SELECT Orders.OrderId, SUM(Quantity * Price)
 AS "Order total"
FROM Sales.Orders JOIN Sales.OrderDetails
ON Orders.OrderId = OrderDetails.OrderId
GROUP BY Orders.OrderId;
```

SQL Example 6.2 Output:

| | OrderId | Order total |
|---|---|---|
| 1 | 1 | 1799.97 |
| 2 | 2 | 4649.87 |
| 3 | 3 | 2329.92 |
| 4 | 4 | 269.97 |
| 5 | 5 | 1499.91 |
| 6 | 6 | 1499.99 |
| 7 | 7 | 999.99 |
| 8 | 8 | 199.97 |

SQL Example 6.3

Display suppliers and their products. Show supplier name and corresponding product names.

SQL Example 6.3 Analysis

The supplier names are in the suppliers table and the product names are in the products table. You need to join the suppliers and the products table to retrieve all data.

SQL Example 6.3 statement

```
SELECT SupplierName, ProductName
FROM Purchasing.Suppliers JOIN Purchasing.Products
ON Suppliers.SupplierId = Products.supplierid;
```

Example 6.3 Output:

| | SupplierName | ProductName |
|---|---|---|
| 1 | Samsong | 65-Inch 4K Ultra HD Smart TV |
| 2 | Samsong | 60-Inch 4K Ultra HD Smart LED TV |
| 3 | Lonovo | 3200 Lumens LED Home Theater Projector |
| 4 | Canan | Wireless Color Photo Printer |
| 5 | IMB | 6Wireless Compact Laser Printer |
| 6 | IMB | Color Laser Printer |
| 7 | Samsong | 10" 16GB Android Tablet |
| 8 | IMB | GPS Android Tablet PC |
| 9 | Canan | 20.2 MP Digital Camera |

SQL Example 6.4

Display suppliers, their products, and delivery details. Show supplier name and corresponding product names, each delivery quantity, price, and date.

SQL Example 6.4 Analysis

The supplier names are in the suppliers table and the product names are in the products table. Delivery details are from the Deliveries table. You need to join the suppliers, the products, and the deliveries tables to retrieve all data. You can only join two tables at a time. The result of two joined tables is a table that can be used to join another table. The two joined tables must have a common field.

SQL Example 6.4 statement

```
SELECT SupplierName, ProductName, Quantity, Price, DeliveryDate
FROM Purchasing.Suppliers JOIN Purchasing.Products
ON Suppliers.SupplierId = Products.supplierid
JOIN Purchasing.Deliveries
ON Products.ProductId = Deliveries.ProductId;
```

Example 6.4 Output:

| | SupplierName | ProductName | Quantity | Price | DeliveryDate |
|---|---|---|---|---|---|
| 1 | Samsong | 65-Inch 4K Ultra HD Smart TV | 2 | 1099.99 | 2016-10-01 09:30:00.0000000 |
| 2 | Samsong | 65-Inch 4K Ultra HD Smart TV | 5 | 1199.99 | 2016-11-01 10:20:00.0000000 |
| 3 | Samsong | 60-Inch 4K Ultra HD Smart LED TV | 10 | 1199.99 | 2016-10-02 11:10:00.0000000 |
| 4 | Lonovo | 3200 Lumens LED Home Theater Projector | 10 | 129.99 | 2016-10-05 09:15:00.0000000 |
| 5 | Canan | Wireless Color Photo Printer | 20 | 79.99 | 2016-10-07 14:00:00.0000000 |
| 6 | IMB | 6Wireless Compact Laser Printer | 15 | 139.99 | 2016-10-07 15:30:00.0000000 |
| 7 | IMB | Color Laser Printer | 25 | 169.99 | 2016-10-10 10:30:00.0000000 |
| 8 | Samsong | 10" 16GB Android Tablet | 12 | 79.99 | 2016-10-11 11:10:00.0000000 |
| 9 | Samsong | 10" 16GB Android Tablet | 18 | 69.99 | 2016-10-12 09:50:00.0000000 |

SQL Example 6.5

Display suppliers, their products, and total quantity delivered. Show supplier name and corresponding product names and total quantity of that product delivered.

SQL Example 6.5 Analysis

Examine the output table from SQL Example 6.4. All necessary data is in that table. You need to join the three tables to get all the data. You also need to use an aggregate function to determine the total quantity of each product delivered. For example, the Samsong 65-inch 4K Ultra HD Smart TV is delivered twice and the total is 7 (2+5). When you use the aggregate function, you should GROUP BY the non-aggregate columns in the SELECT.

SQL Example 6.5 statement

```
SELECT SupplierName, ProductName, SUM(Quantity) AS "Total delivered"
FROM Purchasing.Suppliers JOIN Purchasing.Products
ON Suppliers.SupplierId = Products.supplierid
JOIN Purchasing.Deliveries
ON Products.ProductId = Deliveries.ProductId
GROUP BY SupplierName, ProductName;
```

Example 6.5 Output:

| | SupplierName | ProductName | Total delivered |
|---|---|---|---|
| 1 | Samsong | 10" 16GB Android Tablet | 30 |
| 2 | Lonovo | 3200 Lumens LED Home Theater Projector | 10 |
| 3 | Samsong | 60-Inch 4K Ultra HD Smart LED TV | 10 |
| 4 | Samsong | 65-Inch 4K Ultra HD Smart TV | 7 |
| 5 | IMB | 6Wireless Compact Laser Printer | 15 |
| 6 | IMB | Color Laser Printer | 25 |
| 7 | Canan | Wireless Color Photo Printer | 20 |

SQL Example 6.6

Display suppliers, their products, and the most recent delivery date of the product. Show supplier name and corresponding product names and the date of the most recent delivery.

SQL Example 6.6 Analysis

Examine the output table from SQL Example 6.4 again. All necessary data is in that table. You need to join the three tables to get all the data. You also need to use an aggregate function, MAX(), to determine the most recent date in the delivery date column. For example, the Samsong 65-inch 4K Ultra HD Smart TV is delivered twice with the delivery dates of Oct 1, 2016 and Nov. 1, 2016. When you use the aggregate function, you should GROUP BY the non-aggregate columns in the SELECT.

SQL Example 6.6 statement

```
SELECT SupplierName, ProductName, MAX(DeliveryDate) AS "Most recent
delivery"
FROM Purchasing.Suppliers JOIN Purchasing.Products
ON Suppliers.SupplierId = Products.supplierid
JOIN Purchasing.Deliveries
ON Products.ProductId = Deliveries.ProductId
GROUP BY SupplierName, ProductName;
```

Example 6.6 Output:

| | SupplierName | ProductName | Most recent delivery |
|---|---|---|---|
| 1 | Samsong | 10" 16GB Android Tablet | 2016-10-12 09:50:00.0000000 |
| 2 | Lonovo | 3200 Lumens LED Home Theater Projector | 2016-10-05 09:15:00.0000000 |
| 3 | Samsong | 60-Inch 4K Ultra HD Smart LED TV | 2016-10-02 11:10:00.0000000 |
| 4 | Samsong | 65-Inch 4K Ultra HD Smart TV | 2016-11-01 10:20:00.0000000 |
| 5 | IMB | 6Wireless Compact Laser Printer | 2016-10-07 15:30:00.0000000 |
| 6 | IMB | Color Laser Printer | 2016-10-10 10:30:00.0000000 |
| 7 | Canan | Wireless Color Photo Printer | 2016-10-07 14:00:00.0000000 |

SQL Example 6.7

Display all suppliers, their products, the most recent delivery date of the product and the quantity of the delivery. Show supplier name and corresponding product names, most recent delivery date and the quantity of that delivery.

SQL Example 6.7 Analysis

Again, all necessary data are in the output table from SQL Example 6.4. Since the only difference from SQL Example 6.6 is the quantity of that delivery, why can't we just add the quantity column to the SELECT statement of Example 6.6? Unfortunately, it will not run because the Quantity column is a non-aggregate column, so you should also add Quantity in the GROUP BY clause as shown below:

```
SELECT SupplierName, ProductName, MAX(DeliveryDate) AS "Most recent delivery", Quantity
FROM Purchasing.Suppliers JOIN Purchasing.Products
ON Suppliers.SupplierId = Products.supplierid
JOIN Purchasing.Deliveries
ON Products.ProductId = Deliveries.ProductId
GROUP BY SupplierName, ProductName, Quantity;
```

And the output will look like this:

| | SupplierName | ProductName | Most recent delivery | Quantity |
|---|---|---|---|---|
| 1 | Canan | Wireless Color Photo Printer | 2016-10-07 14:00:00.0000000 | 20 |
| 2 | IMB | 6Wireless Compact Laser Printer | 2016-10-07 15:30:00.0000000 | 15 |
| 3 | IMB | Color Laser Printer | 2016-10-10 10:30:00.0000000 | 25 |
| 4 | Lonovo | 3200 Lumens LED Home Theater Projector | 2016-10-05 09:15:00.0000000 | 10 |
| 5 | Samsong | 10" 16GB Android Tablet | 2016-10-11 11:10:00.0000000 | 12 |
| 6 | Samsong | 10" 16GB Android Tablet | 2016-10-12 09:50:00.0000000 | 18 |
| 7 | Samsong | 60-Inch 4K Ultra HD Smart LED TV | 2016-10-02 11:10:00.0000000 | 10 |
| 8 | Samsong | 65-Inch 4K Ultra HD Smart TV | 2016-10-01 09:30:00.0000000 | 2 |
| 9 | Samsong | 65-Inch 4K Ultra HD Smart TV | 2016-11-01 10:20:00.0000000 | 5 |

Are the results correct? No, there are only seven products, but the results give nine most recent delivery dates. This problem is caused by the Quantity in the GROUP BY clause.

To solve this problem, move the "Most recent delivery" to a WHERE clause. Then there is no need for Quantity in the GROUP BY clause.

SQL Example 6.7 statement

```
SELECT SupplierName, ProductName, DeliveryDate, Quantity
FROM Purchasing.Suppliers JOIN Purchasing.Products
ON Suppliers.SupplierId = Products.Supplierid
JOIN Purchasing.Deliveries
ON Products.ProductId = Deliveries.ProductId
WHERE DeliveryDate = (SELECT MAX(DeliveryDate) FROM Purchasing.Deliveries
WHERE ProductId = Products.ProductId);
```

Example 6.7 Output:

| | SupplierName | ProductName | DeliveryDate | Quantity |
|---|---|---|---|---|
| 1 | Samsong | 10" 16GB Android Tablet | 2016-10-12 09:50:00.0000000 | 18 |
| 2 | IMB | Color Laser Printer | 2016-10-10 10:30:00.0000000 | 25 |
| 3 | IMB | 6Wireless Compact Laser Printer | 2016-10-07 15:30:00.0000000 | 15 |
| 4 | Canan | Wireless Color Photo Printer | 2016-10-07 14:00:00.0000000 | 20 |
| 5 | Lonovo | 3200 Lumens LED Home Theater Projector | 2016-10-05 09:15:00.0000000 | 10 |
| 6 | Samsong | 60-Inch 4K Ultra HD Smart LED TV | 2016-10-02 11:10:00.0000000 | 10 |
| 7 | Samsong | 65-Inch 4K Ultra HD Smart TV | 2016-11-01 10:20:00.0000000 | 5 |

Review Question 6.38
If the data needed are from more than one table, you can ___________.
a. combine the tables
b. join the tables
c. use WHERE clause
d. use HAVING clause

Review Question 6.39
Inner join puts two tables side by side, _____________.
a. but only those rows with matching values will appear in the joined table.
b. all the rows from both tables will be in the joined table.
c. but the two tables must have the same number of rows.
d. but the two tables must have the same number of columns.

## 6.9 SQL OUTER JOIN

Outer join is similar to the inner join you learned in the last section. It combines two tables side by side into a larger table. The difference is the treatment of rows with no match. In the case of inner join, when there is no match, the rows won't appear in the joined table. However, in case of outer join, when there is no match, some rows will still appear in the joined table depending on the type of outer join. There are three types of outer join: left, right, and full.

LEFT OUTER JOIN puts the left table first in the joined table and then finds any matching rows from the right table. Rows with no match on the left table side should still appear in the joined table. LEFT OUTER JOIN is often shortened as LEFT JOIN. Let's see an example. Use the data from Table 6.13 Student Table and Table 6.14 Advisor Table. Assume the Student Table is the left table (FROM Student LEFT JOIN Advisor). The joined table is this:

| StudentId | StudentName | AdvisorId | AdivsorId | AdvisorName |
|---|---|---|---|---|
| 1 | Alice | 111 | 111 | Xavier |
| 2 | Alice | 111 | 111 | Xavier |
| 3 | Chuck | 222 | 222 | Young |
| 4 | Dan | Null | Null | Null |

Table 6.16 Data for the student left join the advisor

Compare Table 6.16 Left Join with Table 6.15 Inner Join and note the differences. All rows from the left are kept even if there is no match from the right table.

The SQL statement for the left outer join with the above example is:

```
SELECT *
FROM Student LEFT JOIN Advisor
ON Student.AdvisorId = Advisor.AdvisorId;
```

The RIGHT OUTER JOIN is just the opposite of LEFT OUTER JOIN. RIGHT OUTER JOIN puts the right table first in the joined table then finds any matching rows from the left table. Any rows from the right table that have no match should still appear in the joined table. RIGHT OUTER JOIN is often shortened as RIGHT JOIN.

Let's use the same tables of Student and Advisor and see how the right outer join works. Assume the left table is still the Student table and the right table is the Advisor table.

| StudentId | StudentName | AdvisorId | AdivsorId | AdvisorName |
|---|---|---|---|---|
| 1 | Alice | 111 | 111 | Xavier |
| 2 | Alice | 111 | 111 | Xavier |
| 3 | Chuck | 222 | 222 | Young |
| Null | Null | Null | 333 | Zach |

Table 6.17 Data for the Student right join the Advisor

Compare the Table 6.17 RIGHT OUTER JOIN with Table 6.16 LEFT JOIN for differences.

The SQL statement for the RIGHT OUTER JOIN of the above example is:

```
SELECT *
```

```
FROM Student RIGHT JOIN Advisor
ON Student.AdvisorId = Advisor.AdvisorId;
```

You may have a question at this point: if you switch the two tables and change RIGHT JOIN to LEFT JOIN in SQL statement, what is the difference in the result? The answer is that you will get the same table. In the example used in this chapter, the following two SQL statements result in the same joined table:

```
SELECT *
FROM Student LEFT JOIN Advisor
ON Student.AdvisorId = Advisor.AdvisorId;
```

And

```
SELECT *
FROM Advisor RIGHT JOIN Student
ON Student.AdvisorId = Advisor.AdvisorId;
```

As a result, we will rarely use RIGHT JOIN in this book because it can be replaced with LEFT JOIN.

The third type of outer join is the FULL OUTER JOIN, often shortened to FULL JOIN. The full outer join is the combination of LEFT OUTER JOIN and RIGHT OUTER JOIN. The data from both tables are kept in the joined table. If a match is found, use the matching data. If no match is found, use NULL. Let's see an example of the Student and Advisor tables and see how the full join works.

| StudentId | StudentName | AdvisorId | AdivsorId | AdvisorName |
|---|---|---|---|---|
| 1 | Alice | 111 | 111 | Xavier |
| 2 | Alice | 111 | 111 | Xavier |
| 3 | Chuck | 222 | 222 | Young |
| 4 | Dan | Null | Null | Null |
| Null | Null | Null | 333 | Zach |

Table 6.18 Data for the Student full join the Advisor

SQL Example 6.8

Display all suppliers. If a supplier has products on the products table, also display the product names. Otherwise, display null as the product name. Show supplier names and corresponding product names.

SQL Example 6.8 Analysis

The supplier names are in the suppliers table and the product names are in the products table. You need to join the two tables. The inner join will only display the rows with matching supplier ID. The inner join may not display all suppliers if some suppliers do not provide their products yet.

Use LEFT JOIN with the suppliers table as the left table, thus guaranteeing that all suppliers will be displayed.

SQL Example 6.8 statement

```
SELECT SupplierName, ProductName
FROM Purchasing.Suppliers LEFT JOIN Purchasing.Products
ON Suppliers.SupplierId = Products.SupplierId;
```

Example 6.8 Output:

| | SupplierName | ProductName |
|---|---|---|
| 1 | Pine Apple | NULL |
| 2 | IMB | 6Wireless Compact Laser Printer |
| 3 | IMB | Color Laser Printer |
| 4 | IMB | GPS Android Tablet PC |
| 5 | Lonovo | 3200 Lumens LED Home Theater Projector |
| 6 | Samsong | 65-Inch 4K Ultra HD Smart TV |
| 7 | Samsong | 60-Inch 4K Ultra HD Smart LED TV |
| 8 | Samsong | 10" 16GB Android Tablet |
| 9 | Canan | Wireless Color Photo Printer |
| 10 | Canan | 20.2 MP Digital Camera |

SQL Example 6.9

Display all suppliers. If a supplier has delivered any product, also display the most recent delivery date of the supplier. Otherwise, display null. Show supplier name and the corresponding most recent delivery date.

SQL Example 6.9 Analysis

The supplier names are in the suppliers table and the delivery date is in the deliveries table. You need to join the two tables. However, the two tables have no common column. You need a third table that has common columns with each of the two tables. This is the products table. The products table has a common column (SupplierId) with the Suppliers table. The products table also has a common column (ProductId) with the Deliveries table. As a result, you will join three tables even though the data you need are from two tables.

Use LEFT JOIN with the supplier table as the left table, thus guaranteeing that all suppliers will be displayed. However, you cannot simply first LEFT JOIN the Suppliers table with Products table and then JOIN the Deliveries table, because the second INNER JOIN will remove any non-matched rows. The correct way to join is to first join the INNER JOIN of Products table and the Deliveries table, then RIGHT OUTER JOIN with the Suppliers table.

Because Max() is an aggregate function, you need to GROUP BY SupplierName.

SQL Example 6.9 statement

```
SELECT SupplierName, Max(DeliveryDate) AS "Most recent delivery date"
FROM Purchasing.Products JOIN Purchasing.Deliveries
ON Products.ProductId = Deliveries.ProductId
RIGHT JOIN Purchasing.Suppliers
ON Products.supplierid = Suppliers.SupplierId
GROUP BY SupplierName;
```

Example 6.9 Output:

| | SupplierName | Most recent delivery date |
|---|---|---|
| 1 | Canan | 2016-10-07 14:00:00.0000000 |
| 2 | IMB | 2016-10-10 10:30:00.0000000 |
| 3 | Lonovo | 2016-10-05 09:15:00.0000000 |
| 4 | Pine Apple | NULL |
| 5 | Samsong | 2016-11-01 10:20:00.0000000 |

Review Question 6.40
What's the difference between outer join and inner join?
a. INNER JOIN will ignore the non-matching rows while OUTER JOIN will keep non-matching rows.
b. INNER JOIN will keep the non-matching rows while OUTER JOIN will ignore the non-matching rows.
c. Both INNER JOIN and OUTER JOIN will keep the non-matching rows. However, the OUTER JOIN result will depend on the join type.
d. Neither INNER JOIN nor OUTER JOIN will keep the non-matching rows. But, INNER JOIN may keep the non-matching rows depending on the join type.

# 6.10 SQL SELF JOIN

When you need data from two tables, you join the two tables. When you need data from the same table more than once, you use self-join. Self-join is not a new type of join. It is joining the same table with inner or outer join.

The self-join can be used in two situations. One use is when you want to compare two rows of the same table. With the self-join, you can compare the values from two different columns. Two rows of the same table can now be treated as two rows of different tables. Another use of self-join is for a unary relationship.

SQL Example 6.10

Display all customers with the same name. Show customer name and email address.

SQL Example 6.10 Analysis

For your convenience, we reproduced the partial table of the customers here:

| | CustomerId | CustomerName | Email |
|---|---|---|---|
| 1 | 1 | Just Electronics | jwhite@je.com |
| 2 | 2 | Beyond Electronics | green@beil.com |
| 3 | 3 | Beyond Electronics | black1@be.com |
| 4 | 4 | E Fun | bgold@efun.com |
| 5 | 5 | Overstock E | dy@os.com |
| 6 | 6 | E Fun | green@ef.com |
| 7 | 7 | Electronics4U | smith@e4u.com |
| 8 | 8 | Cheap Electronics | NULL |

All the data you need are from the same table: the customers table. However, SQL cannot compare rows within the same column. Thus, you must duplicate the table and put the tables side by side. Then, by manually checking the table, you can easily find that they are Customer ID 2 and 3, then 4 and 6.

The self-joined result looks like:

| CustomerId | CustomerName | Email | CustomerId | CustomerName | Email |
|---|---|---|---|---|---|
| 1 | Just Electronics | jwhite@je.com | 1 | Just Electronics | jwhite@je.com |
| 2 | Beyond Electronics | green@beil.com | 2 | Beyond Electronics | green@beil.com |
| 3 | Beyond Electronics | black1@be.com | 3 | Beyond Electronics | black1@be.com |
| 4 | E Fun | bgold@efun.com | 4 | E Fun | bgold@efun.com |
| 5 | Overstock E | dy@os.com | 5 | Overstock E | dy@os.com |
| 6 | E Fun | green@ef.com | 6 | E Fun | green@ef.com |
| 7 | Electronics4U | smith@e4u.com | 7 | Electronics4U | smith@e4u.com |

Every row has the same customer name in this joined table. However, we are only looking for duplicate customer names. Therefore, look for matching customer names with different customer IDs.

You should use the same customer name but different customer IDs for the join condition.

Because there is only one table called Customers, there is no way to differentiate the two duplicate tables. Thus, we use aliases. In the SQL statement below, we use C1 to represent the first table and C2 to represent the second table.

SQL Example 6.10 statement

```
SELECT DISTINCT C1.CustomerId, C1.CustomerName, C1.Email
FROM Sales.Customers AS C1 JOIN Sales.Customers AS C2
ON (C1.CustomerId != C2.CustomerId)
AND (C1.CustomerName = C2.CustomerName);
```

Example 6.10 Output:

| | CustomerId | CustomerName | Email |
|---|---|---|---|
| 1 | 2 | Beyond Electronics | green@beil.com |
| 2 | 3 | Beyond Electronics | black1@be.com |
| 3 | 4 | E Fun | bgold@efun.com |
| 4 | 6 | E Fun | green@ef.com |

SQL Example 6.11

Display employees with their manager. Show employee name and their corresponding manager's name.

SQL Example 6.11 Analysis

Both the employee's name and the manager's name are in the same table. Duplicate the employees table, one for the employee name and one for the manager's name. Then you just pick the employee name from the employee table and the manager name from the manager table. The join condition is the manager ID from the employee table equals the employee ID from the manager table. Recall that the employees entity has a unary relationship with itself. Because the employees table does not have an employee name column, you can use the first name to concatenate with the last name.

SQL Example 6.11 statement

```
SELECT Employee.FirstName + ' ' + Employee.LastName AS "Employee name",
Manager.FirstName + ' ' + Manager.LastName AS "Manager name"
FROM HR.Employees AS Employee JOIN HR.Employees AS Manager
ON Employee.ManagerId = Manager.EmployeeId;
```

Example 6.11 Output:

| | Employee name | Manager name |
|---|---|---|
| 1 | Dianne Hart | Alex Hall |
| 2 | Maria Law | Alex Hall |
| 3 | Alice Law | Alex Hall |
| 4 | Black Hart | Dianne Hart |
| 5 | Christina Robinson | Dianne Hart |
| 6 | Nicholas Pinkston | Maria Law |

Review Question 6.41

In SQL statements, JOIN usually means ____________.

a. INNER JOIN

b. LEFT JOIN

c. OUTER JOIN

d. SELF JOIN

## 6.11 SQL UNION

While JOIN puts the two tables side by side, UNION puts the two tables top and bottom. Because the two tables are top and bottom, corresponding columns must be similar. For example, suppose you are going to unionize two tables, and each table has two columns. The first table has name and age columns. The second table has a name and a date of birth column. You won't be able to unionize these two tables because the age and the date of birth columns won't match. They have different data types. Two tables must have the same data type in order to unionize. This requirement is called union compatibility.

All corresponding columns of two union tables must be union compatible. Union compatibility means one data type can be converted to the other data type. For example, VARCHAR data type can be converted to CHAR data type so they are union compatible. Another example, NUMERIC and DATE cannot be converted to each other, so the two types are said to be not union compatible. UNION will automatically remove any duplicates. If you want to keep the duplicated rows, use UNION ALL instead.

SQL Example 6.12

Display a mail list for all customers and suppliers. Show company name, street, city, state, country, and postal code.

SQL Example 6.12 Analysis

Examine the corresponding column of the customers table and suppliers table. You will notice that all columns are union compatible.

SQL Example 6.12 statement

```
SELECT CustomerName, StreetAddress, City, State, PostalCode, Country
FROM Sales.Customers
UNION
SELECT SupplierName, StreetAddress, City, State, PostalCode, Country
FROM Purchasing.Suppliers;
```

Example 6.12 Output:

| | CustomerName | StreetAddress | City | State | PostalCode | Country |
|---|---|---|---|---|---|---|
| 1 | Beyond Electronics | 45 Cherry Street | Chicago | IL | 32302 | USA |
| 2 | Beyond Electronics | 6767 GameOver Blvd | Atlanta | GA | 43347 | USA |
| 3 | Canan | 12 Camera St | Ota | Tokyo | 100-0121 | Japan |
| 4 | Cheap Electronics | 1010 Easy St | Ottawa | Ontario | K1A 0B1 | Canada |
| 5 | E Fun | 888 Main Ave. | Seattle | WA | 69356 | USA |
| 6 | E Fun | 915 Market st. | London | England | EC1A 1BB | UK |
| 7 | Electronics4U | 27 Colmore Row | Birmingham | England | B3 2EW | UK |
| 8 | IMB | 123 International Blvd | Los Angeles | CA | 89202 | USA |
| 9 | Just Electronics | 123 Broad way | New York | NY | 12012 | USA |
| 10 | Lonovo | 33 Beijin Square | Beijing | Beijing | 100201 | China |
| 11 | Overstock E | 39 Garden Place | Los Angeles | CA | 32302 | USA |
| 12 | Pine Apple | 1 Pine Apple St. | Idanha | CA | 87201 | USA |
| 13 | Samsong | 1 Electronics Road | Yeongtong | Suwon | 30174 | South Korea |

Review Question 6.42
While JOIN puts the two tables side by side, _________ puts the two tables top and bottom.
a. LEFT JOIN
b. RIGHT JOIN
c. FULL JOIN
d. UNION

## 6.12 Chapter Summary

This chapter covered minimizing data redundancy through normalization. Relations advance from First (1NF) through Second (2NF) to Third Normal Form (3NF) by analyzing functional dependencies and splitting relations. Most business problems require 3NF. You also explored denormalization, adhering to the rule that data used together stay together to optimize performance. In SQL, you learned unionizing and different types of joins, which allow you to have data from more than one table. You can treat the joined tables as one larger table and apply all the knowledge you learned from previous chapters to that table.

## 6.13 Discussion Questions

Discussion 6.1
For beginners, developing a database is about building one or more tables/relations. It is important that your relations are solid. Discuss the characteristics of a good relation.

Discussion 6.2
In this chapter, you learned that duplicating data may cause anomalies. In your own words, explain what anomalies are. Use examples if necessary.

Discussion 6.3
In this chapter, we talked a lot about minimizing data redundancy. Why not simply eliminate all redundancy? In other words, can we completely remove the redundancy in a database? Why or why not?

## 6.14 Database Design Exercises

Exercise One:
The following table is in which normal form ($1^{st}$, $2^{nd}$, or $3^{rd}$ normal form)? If it is not in the third normal form, normalize it to the third normal form. Show the normalization process.

| EmployeeId | FirstName | LastName | DateHired | JobID | JobTitle | FromDate | ToDate |
|---|---|---|---|---|---|---|---|
| 111123 | Alice | Smith | 7/15/2019 | 999<br>888 | Developer,<br>Scrum master | 7/2019<br>6/2020 | 6/2020<br>Current |
| 112123 | Tom | Scott | 2/14/2015 | 888<br>111<br>100 | Scrum master,<br>CTO,<br>COO | 2/2015<br>10.2018<br>3/2020 | 9/2018<br>2/2020<br>Current |

Exercise Two

The following table is in which normal form (1st, 2nd, or 3rd normal form)? If it is not in the third normal form, normalize it to the third normal form. For simplicity, let's assume the Name field is atomic.

| StudentNum | Name | Course1 | Grade1 | Course2 | Grade2 | Course3 | Grade3 |
|---|---|---|---|---|---|---|---|
| 111 | Eliza King | Intro CS | A | Java | B | SQL | A |
| 222 | John Floyd | Intro CS | B | C++ | A | Java | B |
| 113 | Cory Peck | C++ | B | Algorithm | C | Java | B |
| 123 | Ryan Tran | SQL | B | Java | A | Algorithm | C |

# 6.15 SQL Exercises

Exercise 6.1

Display delivery details for each product. Show Product name, delivery ID, quantity, price, and delivery date (without the time part).

| | ProductName | DeliveryId | Quantity | Price | Delivery date |
|---|---|---|---|---|---|
| 1 | 65-Inch 4K Ultra HD Smart TV | 1 | 2 | 1099.99 | 2016-10-01 |
| 2 | 65-Inch 4K Ultra HD Smart TV | 2 | 5 | 1199.99 | 2016-11-01 |
| 3 | 60-Inch 4K Ultra HD Smart LED TV | 3 | 10 | 1199.99 | 2016-10-02 |
| 4 | 3200 Lumens LED Home Theater Projector | 4 | 10 | 129.99 | 2016-10-05 |
| 5 | Wireless Color Photo Printer | 5 | 20 | 79.99 | 2016-10-07 |
| 6 | 6Wireless Compact Laser Printer | 6 | 15 | 139.99 | 2016-10-07 |
| 7 | Color Laser Printer | 7 | 25 | 169.99 | 2016-10-10 |
| 8 | 10" 16GB Android Tablet | 8 | 12 | 79.99 | 2016-10-11 |
| 9 | 10" 16GB Android Tablet | 9 | 18 | 69.99 | 2016-10-12 |

Exercise 6.2

Display product name and total quantity delivered for each product. Show Product ID, Product name, and total quantity delivered for that product.

| | ProductId | ProductName | Delivery total unit |
|---|---|---|---|
| 1 | 1 | 65-Inch 4K Ultra HD Smart TV | 7 |
| 2 | 2 | 60-Inch 4K Ultra HD Smart LED TV | 10 |
| 3 | 3 | 3200 Lumens LED Home Theater Projector | 10 |
| 4 | 4 | Wireless Color Photo Printer | 20 |
| 5 | 5 | 6Wireless Compact Laser Printer | 15 |
| 6 | 6 | Color Laser Printer | 25 |
| 7 | 7 | 10" 16GB Android Tablet | 30 |

Exercise 6.3

Display customers and their orders. Show customer ID, customer name and corresponding order ID and order date.

| | CustomerId | CustomerName | OrderId | OrderDate |
|---|---|---|---|---|
| 1 | 1 | Just Electronics | 1 | 2017-01-03 |
| 2 | 1 | Just Electronics | 2 | 2017-03-05 |
| 3 | 2 | Beyond Electronics | 3 | 2017-02-23 |
| 4 | 4 | E Fun | 4 | 2017-04-13 |

| | | | | |
|---|---|---|---|---|
| 5 | 1 | Just Electronics | 5 | 2017-05-03 |
| 6 | 3 | Beyond Electronics | 6 | 2017-05-08 |
| 7 | 5 | Overstock E | 7 | 2016-11-08 |
| 8 | 7 | Electronics4U | 8 | 2016-12-23 |

Exercise 6.4

Display customers, their orders, and order details in each order. Show customer ID, customer name, and corresponding order ID, order date, product ID, price, and quantity in the order. Sort by customer ID, Order ID, and product ID.

| | CustomerId | CustomerName | OrderId | OrderDate | ProductId | Price | Quantity |
|---|---|---|---|---|---|---|---|
| 1 | 1 | Just Electronics | 1 | 2017-01-03 | 1 | 1499.99 | 1 |
| 2 | 1 | Just Electronics | 1 | 2017-01-03 | 3 | 149.99 | 2 |
| 3 | 1 | Just Electronics | 2 | 2017-03-05 | 1 | 1499.99 | 1 |
| 4 | 1 | Just Electronics | 2 | 2017-03-05 | 2 | 1599.99 | 1 |
| 5 | 1 | Just Electronics | 2 | 2017-03-05 | 4 | 99.99 | 6 |
| 6 | 1 | Just Electronics | 2 | 2017-03-05 | 6 | 189.99 | 5 |
| 7 | 1 | Just Electronics | 5 | 2017-05-03 | 3 | 149.99 | 6 |
| 8 | 1 | Just Electronics | 5 | 2017-05-03 | 6 | 199.99 | 3 |
| 9 | 2 | Beyond Electronics | 3 | 2017-02-23 | 3 | 1499.99 | 2 |
| 10 | 2 | Beyond Electronics | 3 | 2017-02-23 | 6 | 149.99 | 1 |
| 11 | 2 | Beyond Electronics | 3 | 2017-02-23 | 7 | 109.99 | 2 |
| 12 | 2 | Beyond Electronics | 3 | 2017-02-23 | 8 | 69.99 | 2 |
| 13 | 2 | Beyond Electronics | 3 | 2017-02-23 | 9 | 1449.99 | 1 |
| 14 | 3 | Beyond Electronics | 6 | 2017-05-08 | 1 | 1499.99 | 1 |
| 15 | 4 | E Fun | 4 | 2017-04-13 | 4 | 99.99 | 2 |
| 16 | 4 | E Fun | 4 | 2017-04-13 | 8 | 69.99 | 1 |
| 17 | 5 | Overstock E | 7 | 2016-11-08 | 2 | 999.99 | 1 |
| 18 | 7 | Electronics4U | 8 | 2016-12-23 | 7 | 79.99 | 1 |
| 19 | 7 | Electronics4U | 8 | 2016-12-23 | 8 | 59.99 | 2 |

Exercise 6.5

Display customers, their orders, and total value in each order. Show customer ID, customer name, and corresponding order ID, order date, and total value in each order (price * quantity).

| | CustomerId | CustomerName | OrderId | OrderDate | Order total |
|---|---|---|---|---|---|
| 1 | 1 | Just Electronics | 1 | 2017-01-03 | 1799.97 |
| 2 | 1 | Just Electronics | 2 | 2017-03-05 | 4649.87 |
| 3 | 1 | Just Electronics | 5 | 2017-05-03 | 1499.91 |
| 4 | 2 | Beyond Electronics | 3 | 2017-02-23 | 2329.92 |
| 5 | 3 | Beyond Electronics | 6 | 2017-05-08 | 1499.99 |
| 6 | 4 | E Fun | 4 | 2017-04-13 | 269.97 |
| 7 | 5 | Overstock E | 7 | 2016-11-08 | 999.99 |
| 8 | 7 | Electronics4U | 8 | 2016-12-23 | 199.97 |

Exercise 6.6

Display customers, their orders, and the most expensive unit price in the order. Show customer ID, customer name, order ID, order date, and unit price for the most expensive item in the order.

| | CustomerId | CustomerName | OrderId | OrderDate | Highest unit price in order |
|---|---|---|---|---|---|
| 1 | 1 | Just Electronics | 1 | 2017-01-03 | 1499.99 |

| | | | | | |
|---|---|---|---|---|---|
| 2 | 1 | Just Electronics | 2 | 2017-03-05 | 1599.99 |
| 3 | 1 | Just Electronics | 5 | 2017-05-03 | 199.99 |
| 4 | 2 | Beyond Electronics | 3 | 2017-02-23 | 1449.99 |
| 5 | 3 | Beyond Electronics | 6 | 2017-05-08 | 1499.99 |
| 6 | 4 | E Fun | 4 | 2017-04-13 | 99.99 |
| 7 | 5 | Overstock E | 7 | 2016-11-08 | 999.99 |
| 8 | 7 | Electronics4U | 8 | 2016-12-23 | 79.99 |

Exercise 6.7

Display customers, their orders, and the most expensive unit price in the order. Show customer ID, customer name, order ID, order date, unit price for the most expensive item in the order, and how many units ordered with that price in that order.

| | CustomerId | CustomerName | OrderId | OrderDate | Highest unit price in order | Quantity |
|---|---|---|---|---|---|---|
| 1 | 1 | Just Electronics | 1 | 2017-01-03 | 1499.99 | 1 |
| 2 | 1 | Just Electronics | 2 | 2017-03-05 | 1599.99 | 1 |
| 3 | 1 | Just Electronics | 5 | 2017-05-03 | 199.99 | 3 |
| 4 | 2 | Beyond Electronics | 3 | 2017-02-23 | 1449.99 | 1 |
| 5 | 3 | Beyond Electronics | 6 | 2017-05-08 | 1499.99 | 1 |
| 6 | 4 | E Fun | 4 | 2017-04-13 | 39.99 | 2 |
| 7 | 5 | Overstock E | 7 | 2016-11-08 | 999.99 | 1 |
| 8 | 7 | Electronics4U | 8 | 2016-12-23 | 79.99 | 1 |

Exercise 6.8

Display all customers. If a customer has placed one or more orders, include those orders. Otherwise, include null. Show customer ID, customer name, and corresponding order ID and order date.

| | CustomerId | CustomerName | OrderId | OrderDate |
|---|---|---|---|---|
| 1 | 1 | Just Electronics | 1 | 2017-01-03 |
| 2 | 1 | Just Electronics | 2 | 2017-03-05 |
| 3 | 1 | Just Electronics | 5 | 2017-05-03 |
| 4 | 2 | Beyond Electronics | 3 | 2017-02-23 |
| 5 | 3 | Beyond Electronics | 6 | 2017-05-08 |
| 6 | 4 | E Fun | 4 | 2017-04-13 |
| 7 | 5 | Overstock E | 7 | 2016-11-08 |
| 8 | 6 | E Fun | NULL | NULL |
| 9 | 7 | Electronics4U | 8 | 2016-12-23 |
| 10 | 8 | Cheap Electronics | NULL | NULL |

Exercise 6.9

Display all customers. If a customer has placed any orders, also display the highest unit price in any order of that customer. Otherwise, display null. We want to know each customer's highest price item ever ordered. Show customer ID, customer name, and the highest unit price in any order of that customer.

| | CustomerId | CustomerName | Highest unit price |
|---|---|---|---|
| 1 | 1 | Just Electronics | 1599.99 |
| 2 | 2 | Beyond Electronics | 1449.99 |
| 3 | 3 | Beyond Electronics | 1499.99 |
| 4 | 4 | E Fun | 99.99 |
| 5 | 5 | Overstock E | 999.99 |
| 6 | 6 | E Fun | NULL |
| 7 | 7 | Electronics4U | 79.99 |

| 8 | 8 | Cheap Electronics | NULL |
|---|---|---|---|

Exercise 6.10

Display all employees with the same last name. Show their full name and date of birth.

| | Employee name | BirthDate |
|---|---|---|
| 1 | Dianne Hart | 1978-12-03 |
| 2 | Black Hart | 1982-11-09 |
| 3 | Maria Law | 1988-07-13 |
| 4 | Alice Law | 1988-12-13 |

Exercise 6.11

Display all employees. If an employee is a manager, include the supervisees' name. otherwise, display null. Show manager and supervisee full name.

| | Manager | Supervisee |
|---|---|---|
| 1 | Alex Hall | Dianne Hart |
| 2 | Alex Hall | Maria Law |
| 3 | Alex Hall | Alice Law |
| 4 | Dianne Hart | Black Hart |
| 5 | Dianne Hart | Christina Robinson |
| 6 | Maria Law | Nicholas Pinkston |
| 7 | Alice Law | NULL |
| 8 | Black Hart | NULL |
| 9 | Christina Robinson | NULL |
| 10 | Nicholas Pinkston | NULL |

Exercise 6.12

Display all states the LifeStyle has a business (customer or supplier). Show state and country.

| | State | Country |
|---|---|---|
| 1 | Beijing | China |
| 2 | CA | USA |
| 3 | England | UK |
| 4 | GA | USA |
| 5 | IL | USA |
| 6 | NY | USA |
| 7 | Ontario | Canada |
| 8 | Suwon | South Korea |
| 9 | Tokyo | Japan |
| 10 | WA | USA |

# 6.16 Solutions to Review Questions

6.1 C; 6.2 C; 6.3 C; 6.4 B; 6.5 D; 6.6 D; 6.7 D; 6.8 C; 6.9 A; 6.10 C; 6.11 A; 6.12 C; 6.13 B; 6.17 4; 6.15 A; 6.16 C; 6.17 A; 6.18 A; 6.19 B; 6.20 A; 6.21 D; 6.22 A; 6.23 B; 6.24 B; 6.25 D; 6.26 A; 6.27 B; 6.28 D; 6.29 D; 6.30 C; 6.31 D; 6.32 A; 6.33 D; 6.34 C; 6.35 C; 6.36 B; 6.37 D; 6.38 B; 6.39 A; 6.40 A; 6.41 A; 6.42 D;

# Chapter 7: Relational Algebra and SQL Data Manipulation

## Chapter Learning Objectives

7.1 Explain relational algebra.
7.2 Implement data retrieval in both SQL and relational algebra.
7.3 Use SQL INSERT, DELETE, and UPDATE statements.

## 7.1 What Is Relational Algebra?

"Relational" is the adjective form of relations or tables. Algebra means using letters and symbols to represent numbers in mathematical expressions and equations. For example, instead of writing 2+3, you can use algebra to write a + b. The "+" is called an operator. Relational algebra is using letters and symbols to represent relations and operations. The operations are either unary or binary. The unary operation works on just one relation, such as SELECT operation. The binary operation works on two relations, such as JOIN.

In this chapter, you will learn the following unary operations:

```
SELECT, PROJECT, RENAME
```

You will also learn the following binary operations:

```
UNION, INTERSECTION, SET DIFFERENCE, CARTESIAN PRODUCT, JOIN
```

Review Question 7.1
The ______________ uses letters and symbols to represent relations and operations.
a. arithmetic
b. relational algebra
c. relational symbol
d. relational operation

Review Question 7.2
Which of the following is a unary relational operation?
a. JOIN
b. UNION
c. SELECT
d. SET DIFFERENCE

Review Question 7.3

Which of the following is a binary relational operation?
a. SELECT
b. PROJECT
c. RENAME
d. SET DIFFERENCE

## 7.2 Why Should You Learn Relational Algebra?

In the previous chapters, you learned how to write SQL statements to retrieve the data you need. You don't necessarily need to know relational algebra, the mathematics behind SQL, in order to use SQL. However, understanding relational algebra can help you write queries more efficiently and effectively. This is like you know all the arithmetic operations. Do you really need algebra? Let's see an example and let you answer the question yourself.

What is 264*264 + 2*264*736 + 736*736?

Without algebra, you would calculate the answer to be 1000000.

With algebra, you would do this instead: 264*264 +2*264*736+ 736*736 = (264+736)(264+736)=1000*1000=1000000. You get the same answer, but which way takes less time?

In algebra, there is a formula: a*a + 2*a*b + b*b = (a+b)(a+b).

A database administrator told me he wanted to learn relational algebra because one of his colleagues improved his SQL statements significantly by working with relational algebra.

A relation is a set. According to the set theory, element sequence in a set does not make any difference. For example, the following two sets, R and S, are the same:
R = {1, 3, 6}; S = {6, 1, 3};
Additionally, a set won't allow duplicate elements. For example, you cannot have a set like this:
T = {1, 3, 3};
Instead, the T set should be T= {1, 3};

Relational algebra is the theory behind all SQL statements. You learned how to write SQL statements in the previous chapters. This is a good time to summarize what you learned in the previous chapters.

Review Question 7.4
Understanding relational algebra can help you write ______ more efficiently and effectively.
a. SQL queries
b. formulas
c. expressions
d. algebras

Review Question 7.5
A relation in a relational database is NOT a(n) ______.
a. algebra operator
b. set
c. table
d. a set of tuples

Review Question 7.6
According to the set theory, element sequence in a set ______.
a. should be from large to small
b. should be from small to large
c. makes two sets different
d. does not make any differences

Review Question 7.7
Which of the following is NOT a set?
a. {1, 2, 3}
b. {1, 2, c}
c. {1, 2, 1}
d. {any whole number}

Review Question 7.8
The ___________ is the theory behind all SQL statements.
a. relational algebra
b. SQL concept
c. SQL theory
d. SQL foundation

## 7.3 The SELECT Operation

The SELECT operation is used to retrieve rows of data (also called tuples in relational language) that meet certain conditions from a relation. The expression is:

$$\sigma_{\langle \text{selection condition} \rangle}(R)$$

where the $\sigma$ (sigma) symbol is used to denote the SELECT operator and the selection condition is a Boolean expression specified for the attributes of relation R. For example:

Using the practice database in the book (Appendix B has the data,) retrieve all the products of supplier number 5 in relational algebra. The relational expression is:

$$\sigma_{<supplierId\ =\ 5>}\text{Products}$$

For another example, retrieve all deliveries with product quantities of 10 or more units. You will get the following relational expression:

$$\sigma_{<quantity\ >=\ 10>}\ \text{Deliveries}$$

As another example, retrieve all deliveries with product quantity of 10 or more units and unit price of $1000 or more. You will get the following relational expression.

$$\sigma_{<quantity\ >=\ 10\ AND\ price\ >=\ 1000>}\ \text{Deliveries}$$

Let's see the SQL statements from the above three relational expressions:

```
SELECT * FROM Products WHERE SupplierId = 5;
SELECT * FROM Deliveries WHERE Quantity >= 10;
SELECT * FROM Deliveries WHERE Quantity >= 10 AND Price >= 1000;
```

Even though SELECT appears in both relational expressions and SQL statements, they have very different meanings. In the expression, the SELECT operator determines which rows to appear in the result set while the SELECT clause in SQL statements determines which columns to pick. The SELECT of relational expressions is similar to the WHERE clause in SQL statements.

Review Question 7.9
The SELECT of relational expressions is similar to the ______ clause in SQL statements.
a. SELECT
b. FROM
c. ORDER BY
d. WHERE

Review Question 7.10
The ________ operation is used to retrieve rows of data that meet certain conditions from a relation.
a. SELECT
b. PROJECT
c. RENAME
d. UNION

Review Question 7.11
Which SQL statement is equivalent to the following relational algebra expression?

σ <supplierId = 3> Products
a. SELECT * FROM SupplierId = 3;
b. SELECT * FROM Products WHERE SupplierId = 3;
c. SELECT SupplierId FROM Products WHERE SupplierId = 3;
d. SELECT SupplierId, 3 FROM Products;

## 7.4 The PROJECT Operation

The PROJECT operation is used to retrieve columns of data from a relation. The expression is:

π<attribute list>(R)

where the π (pi) symbol represents the PROJECT operator and the columns selected from relation R are in the attribute list.

Let's see an example from the same database used throughout the book. Write the expression to retrieve all product names from the product table

π <ProductName> Products

What happens if there are two products with the same name? If the ProductName is the only attribute retrieved, the duplication product names will be removed. Remember that a set only has unique members (and therefore no duplications.)

Let's see another example. Write the expression to display all products delivered with product ID and delivery date.

π <ProductId, DeliveryDate> Deliveries

How about combining both SELECT and PROJECT operators? Write the expression to retrieve all product names from supplier ID 3.

π <ProductName> σ <supplierId = 3> Products

The expression can become difficult to read, especially when the problem is more complex. We suggest that you use the RENAME operation that will be discussed in the next section.

The corresponding SQL statements for the expressions in this section is:

```
SELECT DISTINCT ProductName FROM Products;
SELECT DISTINCT ProductId, DeliveryDate FROM Deliveries;
SELECT DISTINCT ProductName FROM Deliveries WHERE SupplierId = 3;
```

Review Question 7.12
The PROJECT of relational expressions is similar to the ______ clause in SQL statements.
a. SELECT
b. FROM
c. ORDER BY
d. WHERE

Review Question 7.13
The ________ operation is used to retrieve columns of data from a relation.
a. SELECT
b. PROJECT
c. RENAME
d. UNION

Review Question 7.14
Which SQL statement is equivalent to the following relational algebra expression?

```
π <ProductId, DeliveryDate> Deliveries
```

a. SELECT ProductId, DeliveryDate FROM Deliveries;
b. SELECT * FROM Deliveries;
c. SELECT ProductId FROM Deliveries WHERE DeliveryDate = GETDATE();
d. SELECT * FROM Deliveries WHERE ProductId = @ProductId;

## 7.5 The RENAME Operation

The result of a relational expression is also a relation, but it does not have a name. The RENAME operator is often used to assign a name to that relation.

Let's rewrite the expression to retrieve all product names from supplier ID 3 from last section here with the RENAME operator:

```
Supplier3Product <-- σ <supplierId = 3> Products
Supplier3ProductName <-- π <ProductName> Supplier3Product
```

In the above example, you first RENAME the result of all products from supplier ID 3 as Supplier3Product. The <-- symbol points to the newly assigned name. Next, you use PROJECT on the new relation (Supplier3Product) to keep only the product name and use RENAME to rename the new result as Supplier3ProductName.

Let's see another example.

Retrieve all deliveries with product quantity of 10 or more units. Show ProductId and DeliveryDate.

```
Delivery10OrMore <-- σ <quantity >= 10> Deliveries
Result <-- π <ProductId, DeliveryDate> Deliveriy10OrMore
```

Here's another example:

Write the relational expression to retrieve all deliveries with product quantity of 10 or more units and unit price of 1000 or more. Show DeliveryId, ProductId, and DeliveryDate.

```
Delivery10Unit1000Price <-- σ <quantity >= 10 AND price >= 1000> Deliveries
Result <-- π <DeliveryId, ProductId, DeliveryDate> Delivery10Unit1000Price
```

Keep in mind that these operations may be used in different orders to suit different circumstances.

These are the corresponding SQL statements for the examples in this section:

```
SELECT DISTINCT ProductName FROM Deliveries WHERE SupplierId = 3;
SELECT DISTINCT ProductId, DeliveryDate FROM Deliveries WHERE Quantity >= 10;
SELECT DISTINCT DeliveryId, ProductId, DeliveryDate FROM Deliveries WHERE Quantity
>= 10 AND Price >= 1000;
```

The above examples used RENAME for relations. However, RENAME can also be used for columns. For example:

```
R(DeliveryId, Units_Delivered, Wholesale_Price) <-- π <DeliveryId, Quantity, Price>
Deliveries
```

In the above expression, the columns were renamed Quantity as Units_Delivered and Price as Wholesale_Price in a new relation called R with the same tuples from the Deliveries.

Review Question 7.15

The result of a relational expression is ______.

a. a special relation
b. a nameless relation
c. a special tuple
d. a nameless tuple

Review Question 7.16
What is the following symbol in relational algebra?
<--
a. SELECT
b. PROJECT
c. RENAME
d. UNION

Review Question 7.17
What is the following symbol in relational algebra?
π
a. SELECT
b. PROJECT
c. RENAME
d. UNION

## 7.6 The UNION Operation

The UNION operation includes all rows from both relations with duplications removed. The expression is

```
R1 U R2
```

Where R1 is a relation and R2 is another relation. UNION will include all rows from R1 and R2 with duplicates removed. Similar to the SQL statement, UNION compatibility is also required.

For example, write a relational expression to display all orders handled by Employee 5 or placed after April 1, 2017.

```
OrderByEmployee5 <-- σ <EmployeeId = 5> Orders
OrderAfter04012017 <-- σ <OrderDate > '20170401'> Orders
Result <-- OrderByEmployee5 U OrderAfter04012017;
```

The corresponding SQL statement is

```
SELECT * FROM Orders WHERE EmployId = 5
UNION
SELECT * FROM Orders WHERE OrderDate > '20170401';
```

Review Question 7.18
In the following expression: `R1 U R2`. The two relations R1 and R2 must _______
a. have the same number of attributes

b. have the same number of rows
c. be union compatible
d. be from the same relation

Review Question 7.19
The ___________ operation includes all rows from both relations with duplicates removed.
a. SELECT
b. PROJECT
c. RENAME
d. UNION

Review Question 7.20
Which SQL statement is equivalent to the following relational algebra expression?

```
OrderByEmployee5 <-- σ <EmployeeId = 5> Orders
OrderAfter04012017 <-- σ <OrderDate > '20170401'> Orders
Result <-- OrderByEmployee5 U OrderAfter04012017;
```

a. SELECT * FROM Orders
b. SELECT OrderId FROM Orders UNION SELECT OrderDate FROM Orders;
c. SELECT * FROM Orders WHERE EmployId = 5 UNION SELECT * FROM Orders WHERE OrderDate > '20170401';
d. there's no equivalent in SQL.

## 7.7 The INTERSECTION Operation

The INTERSECTION operation keeps only the common rows between two relations. The expression is

```
R1 ∩ R2
```

Where R1 is a relation and R2 is another relation. The INTERSECTION will include all rows that appear in both R1 and R2. Similar to the SQL statement, UNION compatibility is also required.

For example, write relational expressions to display all orders handled by Employee 5 and placed after April 1, 2017.

```
OrderByEmployee5 <-- σ <EmployeeId = 5> Orders
OrderAfter04012017 <-- σ <OrderDate > '20170401'> Orders
Result <-- OrderByEmployee5 ∩ OrderAfter04012017;
```

The corresponding SQL statement (note that instead of INTERSECTION, use INTERSECT in T-SQL) is:

```
SELECT * FROM Orders WHERE EmployId = 5
INTERSECT
SELECT * FROM Orders WHERE OrderDate > '20170401';
```

Review Question 7.21

In the following expression: `R1 ∩ R2`. The two relations R1 and R2 must ______

a. have the same number of attributes
b. have the same number of rows
c. be union compatible
d. be from the same relation

Review Question 7.22

The ____________ operation keeps only the common rows between two relations.

a. UNION
b. INTERSECTION
c. SET DIFFERENCE
d. CARTESIAN PRODUCT

## 7.8 The SET DIFFERENCE Operation

The SET DIFFERENCE operation keeps only the rows that appear in the first relation and not in the second relation. The expression is

```
R1 - R2
```

where R1 is a relation and R2 is another relation. The SET DIFFERENCE will include all rows that appear in R1 but not in R2. Similar to the SQL statement, UNION compatibility is required.

For example, write relational expressions to display all orders handled by Employee 5 but not placed after April 1, 2017.

```
OrderByEmployee5 <-- σ <EmployeeId = 5> Orders
OrderAfter04012017 <-- σ <OrderDate > '20170401'> Orders
Result <-- OrderByEmployee5 - OrderAfter04012017;
```

The corresponding SQL statement (note that instead of SET DIFFERENCE, use EXCEPT in T-SQL) is:

```
SELECT * FROM Orders WHERE EmployId = 5
EXCEPT
SELECT * FROM Orders WHERE OrderDate > '20170401';
```

Note that INTERSECTION can be expressed in terms of union and set difference as follows, assuming R and S are two relations:

```
R∩S=((R∪S)-(R-S))-(S-R)
```

Review Question 7.23
Which relational algebra operator does NOT require union compatibility?
a. UNION
b. CARTESIAN PRODUCT
c. INTERSECTION
d. SET DIFFERENCE

Review Question 7.24
The corresponding T-SQL clause for SET DIFFERENCE is ______.
a. SELECT
b. UNION
c. DIFFERENCE
d. EXCEPT

Review Question 7.25
The ________ operation keeps only the rows that appear in the first relation and not in the second relation.
a. UNION
b. INTERSECTION
c. SET DIFFERENCE
d. CARTESIAN PRODUCT

Review Question 7.26
Which of the following relational algebra equations is true?
a. R∩S=((R∪S)−(R-S))+(S−R)
b. R∩S=((R∪S)+(R-S))−(S−R)
c. R∩S=((R∪S)−(R-S))−(S−R)
d. R∩S=((R∪S)−(R+S))−(S−R)

## 7.9 The CARTESIAN PRODUCT Operation

Suppose the relation R1 has a1 number of attributes and r1 number of rows and another relation, R2, has a2 attributes and r2 rows. The result of using CARTESIAN PRODUCT on R1 and R2 is a new relation that has a1+ a2 number of attributes and r1×r2 number of rows. Each row from R1 should be combined with each row from R2 for a result of r1×r2 number of rows. The expression is

```
R1 × R2
```

Let's see an example. Write the relational expression to list all possible combinations of suppliers and products.

```
Result <-- Suppliers × Products
```

Refer to Appendix B. The Supplier table has 7 columns and 5 rows and the Products table has 3 columns and 9 rows. So, the Result table will have 10 columns and 45 rows.

You may notice that there are not many cases in which the CARTESIAN PRODUCT operation will be used. However, it is a basic operation for the JOIN operation introduced next.

Review Question 7.27
There are not many cases in which the CARTESIAN PRODUCT operation will be used. However, it is a basic operation for the ______ operation.
a. UNION
b. INTERSECTION
c. SET DIFFERENCE
d. JOIN

Review Question 7.28
Suppose relation R1 has a1 attributes and r1 rows and another relation, R2, has a2 attributes and r2 rows. The result of using CARTESIAN PRODUCT on R1 and R2 is a new relation that has ______ number of attributes.
a. a1 + a2
b. a1 – a2
c. a1 * a2
d. a1 / a2

Review Question 7.28
Suppose relation R1 has a1 attributes and r1 rows and another relation, R2, has a2 attributes and r2 rows. The result of using CARTESIAN PRODUCT on R1 and R2 is a new relation that has ______ number of rows.
a. r1 + r2
b. r1 – r2
c. r1 * r2
d. r1 /r2

Review Question 7.30
Suppose relation R1 has a1 attributes and r1 rows and another relation, R2, has a2 attributes and r2 rows. The result of using _______ on R1 and R2 is a new relation that has a1+a2 number of attributes and r1×r2 number of rows. Each row from R1 should be combined with each row from R2 for a result of r1×r2 number of rows.
a. UNION
b. INTERSECTION
c. SET DIFFERENCE
d. CARTESIAN PRODUCT

## 7.10 The JOIN Operation

So far, you learned seven relational operations. They are SELECT, PROJECT, RENAME, UNION, INTERSECTION, SET DIFFERENCE, and CARTESIAN PRODUCT. We usually consider the operations SELECT, PROJECT, RENAME, UNION, SET DIFFERENCE, and CARTESIAN PRODUCT to be part of a complete set. INTERSECTION is left out. Why is that? It is due to the fact that INTERSECTION can be expressed as UNION and SET DIFFERENCE as shown in Section 7.8.

Similarly, JOIN is not a part of the complete set because it can be expressed as the CARTESIAN PRODUCT followed by the SELECT operation. The expression for JOIN is:

```
R1 ⋈<join condition> R2
```

For example, write a relational expression to display all suppliers and their products. Do not show the suppliers without any products (Join condition is shown as subscript).

```
CurrentSupplierProduct <-- Suppliers ⋈supplierId Products
```

The same result can be achieved by the following two steps:

```
SupplierProduct <-- Suppliers × Products;
CurrentSupplierProduct <-- σ <supplierId = supplierId> SupplierProduct;
```

Review Question 7.31
The INTERSECTION operation is not part of the complete set of six operations because ___________.
a. it can be expressed in terms of UNION and SET DIFFERENCE
b. it is rarely used
c. it is too late to be introduced
d. the complete set of six is a good number

Review Question 7.32
The ______ operation can be expressed as CARTESIAN PRODUCT followed by the SELECT operations.
a. UNION
b. INTERSECTION
c. SET DIFFERENCE
d. JOIN

Review Question 7.33
Select the relational expression that is the same as the following:

```
SupplierProduct <-- Suppliers X Products;
```

```
CurrentSupplierProduct <-- σ <supplierId=supplierId> SupplierProduct;
```

a. CurrentSupplierProduct <-- Suppliers U Products;
b. CurrentSupplierProduct <-- Suppliers ∩ Products;
c. CurrentSupplierProduct <-- Suppliers ⋈ Products
d. CurrentSupplierProduct <-- Suppliers - Products;

## 7.11 The SQL INSERT Statement

The data stored in a database changes all the time. When LifeStyle LLC hires a new employee, a new row for the employee has to be inserted. When a supplier delivers a product, a new row in the deliveries table is inserted. If the delivered product is new, a new row in the products table should also be inserted before the new row in the deliveries table can be inserted. In this section, you will learn ways to insert data.

The syntax for inserting a single row into a table is:

```
INSERT INTO TableName (Column1, Column2, ...) VALUES (Value1, Value2, ...).
```

Not all columns of a table have to be in the INSERT statement unless they are required (NOT NULL) columns. Also, the sequence in the SQL INSERT statement does not have to be the same as that in the table. However, each value in the SQL statement must have a matching data type for the one in the table. Finally, the column and value in the SQL statement must be paired.

The following is the syntax for inserting multiple rows into a table:

```
INSERT INTO TableName(Column1, Column2, ...) VALUES (Row1Value1, Row2Value2, ...),
                                                   (Row2Value1, Row2Value2, ...)
```

Note the comma between rows of values. It is a common typo of omitting that comma.

You can also insert data from another table. The syntax is:

```
INSERT INTO Table1Name(Column1, Column2, ...)
    SELECT ColumnOne, ColumnTwo, ...
    FROM Table2Name;
```

SQL Example 7.1

LifeStyle LLC just hired a new employee. Write an SQL statement to add the employee to the database. The new employee data is shown below:

| FirstName | LastName | BirthDate | HireDate | HomeAddress | City | State | PostalCode | Phone | ManagerId |
|---|---|---|---|---|---|---|---|---|---|

| Ryan | Price | 1991-10-15 | 2015-09-22 | 123 Broadway Blvd | New Canton | VA | 23123 | (434) 290-1223 | 3 |
|---|---|---|---|---|---|---|---|---|---|

SQL Example 7.1 Analysis

You can apply the syntax straightaway to this example. The table name is HR.Employees. All the column names and corresponding values are given.

Note in the SQL statement below, there's the letter N in front of the string value. This is to convert the data type from VARCHAR to NVARCHAR. The default string data type is VARCHAR and the database uses NVARCHAR. The difference between VARCHAR and NVARCHAR is that the latter can hold characters of international language (N stand for National), such as Korean, Japanese, and Chinese).

The INSERT statement is easy to understand. However, typos are also frequent. The column name must be the same as it appears in the table and the column value must be the same data type as in the table.
You should not provide an employee ID because it is an IDENTITY field which means a unique value will be automatically provided by the SQL Server.

SQL Example 7.1 statement

```
INSERT INTO HR.Employees (FirstName, LastName, BirthDate, HireDate,
HomeAddress, City, State, PostalCode, Phone, ManagerId)
    VALUES(N'Ryan', N'Price', '19911015', '20150922', N'123 Broadway Blvd',
N'New Canton', N'VA', 23123, N'(434) 290-1223', 3);
```

SQL Example 7.1 Output:

```
(1 row(s) affected)
```

SQL Example 7.2

LifeStyle LLC just hired a new employee. But this time, you only know the new employee's first name, last name, birth date, and hire date. Write an SQL statement to add the employee to the database. The new employee data is shown below:

| FirstName | LastName | BirthDate | HireDate |
|---|---|---|---|
| James | Anderson | 1990-03-12 | 2015-11-11 |

SQL Example 7.2 Analysis

The INSERT syntax only requires that you provide the data for those columns that do not allow NULL value. In other words, you don't have to provide all values for a row. However, the column names and their corresponding values still must be matched.

SQL Example 7.2 statement

```
INSERT INTO HR.Employees (LastName, FirstName, BirthDate, HireDate) VALUES
(N'Anderson', N'James', '19900312', '20151111');
```

SQL Example 7.2 Output:

(1 row(s) affected)

SQL Example 7.3

LifeStyle LLC just hired two new employees. Write an SQL statement to add both employees to the database. The new employee data is shown below:

| FirstName | LastName | BirthDate | HireDate |
|---|---|---|---|
| Adam | Smith | 1989-02-01 | 2016-09-19 |
| Kyle | Johnson | 1988-12-23 | 2016-09-19 |

SQL Example 7.3 Analysis

This is a straightforward application of the syntax for inserting multiple rows.

SQL Example 7.3 statement

```
INSERT INTO HR.Employees (FirstName, LastName, HireDate, BirthDate) VALUES
    (N'Adam', N'Smith', '20160919', '19890201'),
    (N'Kyle', N'Johnson', '20160919', '19881223');
```

SQL Example 7.3 Output:

(2 row(s) affected)

SQL Example 7.4

Supplier ID 2 becomes a new customer of LifeStyle LLC. To avoid typos, write an SQL statement to copy the data of supplier 2 from the suppliers table into the customers table.

SQL Example 7.4 Analysis

This is also an example where you can apply the syntax directly.

SQL Example 7.4 statement

```
INSERT INTO Sales.Customers (CustomerName, StreetAddress, City, State,
PostalCode, Country)
    SELECT SupplierName, StreetAddress, City, State, PostalCode, Country
    FROM Purchasing.Suppliers
    WHERE SupplierId = 2;
```

SQL Example 7.4 Output:

(1 row(s) affected)

SQL Example 7.5

Twelve units of product ID 1 were just delivered. Write an SQL statement to add the record in the deliveries table.

SQL Example 7.5 Analysis

The purpose of this example is to learn how the default value works. When developers create a new table, they can set certain default values for certain columns. For example, the deliverydate of the deliveries table has a default value of the system's date and time. If you also won't provide a delivery date when inserting a new row of delivery, the SQL Server will insert the timestamp of the moment you inserted the row. Similarly, when you do not provide a price, the default value is $0.

SQL Example 7.5 statement

```
INSERT INTO Purchasing.Deliveries (ProductId, Quantity)
    VALUES (1, 12);
```

SQL Example 7.5 Output:

(1 row(s) affected)

Review Question 7.34
Which of the following is the T-SQL syntax for inserting a single row into a table (data are not from different tables?)
a. INSERT INTO TableName (Column1, Column2, ...) VALUES (Value1, Value2, ...).
b. INSERT INTO TableName(Column1, Column2, ...) VALUES (Row1Value1, Row2Value2, ...),
(Row2Value1, Row2Value2, ...)
c. INSERT INTO Table1Name(Column1, Column2, ...) SELECT ColumnOne, ColumnTwo, ...
FROM Table2Name;

d. INSERT INTO TableName (Value1, Value2, ... ) FOR (Column1, Column2, ... );

Review Question 7.35
Which of the following is the T-SQL syntax for inserting rows of data into a table with data from a different table?
a. INSERT INTO TableName (Column1, Column2, ...) VALUES (Value1, Value2, ...).
b. INSERT INTO TableName(Column1, Column2, ...) VALUES (Row1Value1, Row2Value2, ...),
(Row2Value1, Row2Value2, ...)
c. INSERT INTO Table1Name(Column1, Column2, ...) SELECT ColumnOne, ColumnTwo, ...
FROM Table2Name;
d. INSERT INTO TableName (Value1, Value2, ... ) FOR (Column1, Column2, ... );

## 7.12 The SQL UPDATE Statement

Users will need to edit a row in a table from time to time. For example, when a new employee is hired, he or she may not have a home address yet. You can still enter the employee basic data (e.g. first name, last name, date of birth, and hire date) into the employees table. In a few days, when the employee has a home address, you can update the row with the new data.

The syntax for UPDATE is:

```
UPDATE TableName
SET Column1Name = NewValue1,
      Column2Name = NewValue2,
      ....
    ColumnxName = NewValuex
WHERE Condition;
```

If you omit the WHERE clause, the whole table is updated with the new value for the columns, which is typically not the desired result. So, do not forget the WHERE clause. With the WHERE clause, only those rows that meet the condition will be updated.

SQL Example 7.6
LifeStyle LLC just received the price for the product delivered in SQL Example 7.5. The new price is $1449.99. Write the SQL statement to update the record.

SQL Example 7.6 Analysis
This is an example in which you can apply the syntax directly. Just use the SELECT statement to check the deliveryId before applying the following statement. In the example, we use the ID of 10. Yours may be different.

SQL Example 7.6 statement

```
UPDATE Purchasing.Deliveries
SET Price = 1449.99
WHERE DeliveryId = 10;
```

SQL Example 7.6 Output:

(1 row(s) affected)

SQL Example 7.7

One of the newly hired employee, James Anderson, just submitted the new address below:

| HomeAddress | City | State | PostalCode | Phone |
|---|---|---|---|---|
| 201 Jefferson St. | Buckingham | VA | 23123 | (434) 290-5456 |

Write a SQL statement to update his record in the database.

SQL Example 7.7 Analysis

This is also an example where you can apply the syntax directly. In the following statement, we use the EmployeeId of 9 for James Anderson. The ID for James Anderson may be different in your database because the column has the identity constraint (which means automatically generated). You can use the SELECT statement to find the EmployeeId for James Anderson in your database.

You may notice that the ManagerId column is still Null for James Anderson. That's ok. You can update it again when you know the manager ID later on.

SQL Example 7.7 statement

```
UPDATE HR.Employees
SET HomeAddress = '201 Jefferson St.',
    City = 'Buckingham',
    State = 'VA',
    PostalCode = '23123',
    Phone = '(434) 290-5456'
WHERE EmployeeId = 9;
```

SQL Example 7.7 Output:

(1 row(s) affected)

SQL Example 7.8

Write an SQL statement to add the ManagerId of 3 to all newly hired employees (all new employees you inserted in this chapter).

SQL Example 7.8 Analysis

This example practices how to update multiple rows in one statement. All you need is the WHERE clause. Originally, there are seven employees (See Appendix B). All new employees inserted in this chapter have an employee ID greater than seven. You can use WHERE EmployeeId > 7.

SQL Example 7.8 statement

```
UPDATE HR.Employees
SET ManagerId = 3
WHERE EmployeeId > 7;
```

SQL Example 7.8 Output:

(4 row(s) affected)

SQL Example 7.9

You just realized it is too early to assign the manager ID for those new employees. Write an SQL statement to delete the manager ID for those employees.

SQL Example 7.9 Analysis

You cannot use the DELETE statement (explained in the next section) to delete a partial row. The correct way to delete a partial row is by using the UPDATE statement. Basically, you set those values to NULL.

SQL Example 7.9 statement

```
UPDATE HR.Employees
SET ManagerId = Null
WHERE EmployeeId > 7;
```

SQL Example 7.9 Output:

(4 row(s) affected)

Review Question 7.36

Write an SQL statement to change the price of an OrderDetails table from $2.00 to $2.10 for all quantities under 10.
a. UPDATE OrderDetails SET Price FROM 2.0 TO 2.1 WHERE Quantity < 10;
b. UPDATE OrderDetails SET Price = 2.1 WHERE Quantity < 10;
c. UPDATE OrderDetails CHANGE Price FROM 2.0 TO 2.1 WHERE Quantity < 10;
d. UPDATE OrderDetails SET Price = 2.1 WHERE Price = 2.0 AND Quantity < 10;

## 7.13 The SQL DELETE Statement

When an employee leaves the company or an order is cancelled, you may want to delete the corresponding rows to keep the data updated. The syntax for delete is:

```
DELETE FROM TableName
WHERE condition;
```

The DELETE statement removes complete rows from the table that meet the condition. If you omit the WHERE clause, all data will be removed. The table is still there, but with no data.

SQL Example 7.10

The shipment of twelve units of product ID 1 in Example 7.5 was a mistake by the supplier. It was supposed to ship to a different wholesaler. Write the SQL statement to remove that row.

SQL Example 7.10 Analysis

This example practices how to delete a row. You can use the SELECT statement to find the ID of that delivery:

```
SELECT * FROM Purchasing.Deliveries;
```

In our case, the deliveryID is 10. You can now issue the DELETE statement with the WHERE clause:

```
WHERE DeliveryId = 10;
```

SQL Example 7.10 statement

```
DELETE FROM Purchasing.Deliveries
WHERE DeliveryId = 10;
```

SQL Example 7.10 Output:

(1 row(s) affected)

SQL Example 7.11

Delete all new employees you inserted in this chapter.

SQL Example 7.11 Analysis

The difference between deleting a single row and multiple rows is the WHERE clause. You should be very careful when deleting multiple rows.

SQL Example 7.11 statement

```
DELETE FROM HR.Employees
WHERE EmployeeId > 7;
```

SQL Example 7.11 Output:

(4 row(s) affected)

Review Question 7.37
Which of the following is the SQL syntax for deleting rows of data with matching conditions?
a. DELETE FROM TableName WHERE condition;
b. DELETE ROWS FROM TableName WHERE condition;
c. DELETE condition FROM TableName;
d. DELETE condition ROWS FROM TableName;

# 7.14 Chapter Summary

In this chapter, you learned what relational algebra is and why you should learn it. Eight relational operations were introduced. By now, you should be able to write most relational data retrievals through both SQL statements and relational algebra expressions. In SQL statements, you learned how to insert new rows into the table, update existing rows in the table, and delete all rows of the table that meet certain conditions. This chapter completes the journey of how to develop a database with tables and retrieve and manipulate data in the tables. In the next chapter, you will apply the knowledge learned to a real- world project.

# 7.15. Discussion

Discussion 7.1
You don't have to know relational algebra in order to retrieve data from the database. Throughout the book, you learned that SQL SELECT statements accomplish exactly the same thing. Do you agree with the author that you should learn relational algebra? Why or Why not.

Discussion 7.2
This chapter introduces eight relational operations, but only six of them are part of the complete set. Why are the other two excluded from the complete set?

# 7.16 Relational Algebra Exercise

Write relational expressions to accomplish these tasks. Use the same database from Appendix B.

a. Retrieve the company name, contact, and email of all domestic (USA) customers.
b. Retrieve the company name, contact, and email of all customers who have ever placed an order.
c. Retrieve the company name, contact, email, order date, quantity, and price for all customers with all orders.

# 7. 17 SQL Exercises

Exercise 7.1

LifeStyle LLC has a new customer who provides the following data. Write an SQL statement to add the customer to the database. The new customer data is shown below:

| CustomerName | StreetAddress | City | State | PostalCode | Country | Contact | Email |
|---|---|---|---|---|---|---|---|
| E Store | 11 Pine Pl | Seattle | WA | 69301 | USA | Eric Wade | wade@estore.com |

Exercise 7.2

LifeStyle LLC has another new customer. But, this time, you only know the new customer's name. Write an SQL statement to add the customer to the database. The new customer's data is shown below:

| CustomerName |
|---|
| Magic E |

Exercise 7.3

LifeStyle LLC gains two more customers. Write an SQL statement to add both customers to the database. The new customer data is shown below:

| CustomerName | Contact |
|---|---|
| E4U | Tom Cornell |
| Web E | Daniel Head |

Exercise 7.4

Customer ID 5 becomes a new supplier of LifeStyle LLC. To avoid typos, write an SQL statement to copy the data of customer 5 from the customers table into the suppliers table (because the suppliers do not have contact and email columns, do not copy these two columns from the customers table).

Exercise 7.5

Order ID 8 has a missing product ID 1 because the customer is still negotiating the price. The manager wants to include the data in the OrderDetails table with the default values for the price and quantity. Write an SQL statement to add product ID 1 to the order details table for Order ID 8.

Exercise 7.6

The order details for Order ID 8 of product ID 1 you inserted in Exercise 7.5 now has a known quantity of 10 units. Write an SQL statement to update the record.

Exercise 7.7

One of the newly added customers, Magic E, just submitted the new address below. Write an SQL statement to update the customer's record.

| StreetAddress | City | State | PostalCode | Country |
|---|---|---|---|---|
| 168 Pine Apple Ln | San Francisco | CA | 10101 | USA |

Exercise 7.8

Write an SQL statement to add the email customers@lifestyle.com to all newly added customers (all customers you inserted in this chapter exercises).

Exercise 7.9

You just realized it is a mistake to assign all newly added customers an email of customers@lifestyle.com. Write an SQL statement to delete the emails for those customers.

Exercise 7.10

The customer and the manager cannot reach an agreement on Order ID 8 of Product ID 1. You inserted a row in the OrderDetails table in Exercise 7.5. Now write an SQL statement to delete that row in order details.

Exercise 7.11

Write an SQL statement to delete all new customers you added in this chapter's exercises.

## 7.18 Solutions to Review Questions

7.1 B; 7.2 C; 7.3 D; 7.4 A; 7.5 A; 7.6 D; 7.7 C; 7.8 A; 7.9 D; 7.10 A; 7.11 B; 7.12 A; 7.13 B; 7.14 A; 7.15 B; 7.16 C; 7.17 B; 7.18 C; 7.19 D; 7.20 C; 7.21 C; 7.22 B; 7.23 B; 7.24 D; 7.25 C; 7.26 C; 7.27 D; 7.28 A; 7.29 C; 7.30 D; 7.31 A; 7.32 D; 7.33 C; 7.34 A; 7.35 C; 7.36 D; 7.37 A;

# Chapter 8: A Project and SQL Create Statement

## Chapter Learning Objectives

8.1 Develop a relational database with the given business description.
8.2 Implement physical design with an appropriate Transact-SQL data type.
8.3 Write Transact-SQL statements to create databases and tables with the given physical ERD.

## 8.1 The Panda Language School (PLS) Business Description

The Panda Language School, founded in 1994, is a non-profit organization. The primary mission of PLS is to provide an avenue for students of all ages and ethnic backgrounds to learn the Chinese language, arts, and culture. Most students are children aged 5 to 15.

PLS is operated in its 50,000 square feet facility and its financial support is mainly from tuition and donations from individuals, private businesses, and institutions. Its activities are also supported by volunteers. Each year, it offers 50+ Chinese Language classes for Chinese-speaking and non-Chinese-speaking children and adults. PLS also provides over 100 Chinese Arts/Culture, sports, math and college preparation, and specialty training courses, as well as a variety of club activities.

The school opens from 10:00am to 7:00pm on weekends and most holidays as well as selected evenings from 5:00pm to 7:00pm on weekdays. PLS is the largest Chinese school in the tri-state area. PLS strives to continue serving as the best place for students to learn the Chinese language, arts, and culture.

The following describes how the business is run related to the database they want.

A new family needs to fill out a form like the following (bottom part is cut off due to the size limit)

## The Panda Language School (PLS),
# NEW FAMILY REGISTRATION FORM

| FAMILY INFORMATION | | | |
|---|---|---|---|
| Last name in Chinese | | Date in this address | |
| Phone | | ☐ Chinese American | |
| Cell | | ☐ Other | |
| E-mail | | | |
| Home address<br>City, State ZIP Code | | | |

| GUARDIAN INFORMATION | | | |
|---|---|---|---|
| Guardian 1 name | | Guardian 2 name | |
| Guardian 1 address | | Guardian 2 address | |
| Guardian 1 Phone | | Guardian 2 Phone | |
| Guardian 1 Cell | | Guardian 2 Cell | |
| Guardian 1 E-mail | | Guardian 2 E-mail | |

| STUDENT INFORMATION | | | |
|---|---|---|---|
| First name | | Phone | |
| Last name | | Date of birth | |
| Gender | | E-mail | |
| Relationship to Guardian | | Additional Information | |
| First name | | Phone | |
| Last name | | Date of birth | |
| Gender | | E-mail | |
| Relationship to Guardian | | Additional Information | |
| First name | | Phone | |
| Last name | | Date of birth | |
| Gender | | E-mail | |
| Relationship to Guardian | | Additional Information | |

**AGREEMENT**

1. **By submitting this application, you authorize The Panda Language School (PLS), to contact you for any PLS related activities and events.**
2. **PLS may share your information with other organizations for educational related purposes.**

| SIGNATURES | | | |
|---|---|---|---|
| Signature | | Signature | |
| Name | | Name | |
| Date | | Date | |

Table 8.1 A family registration form for PLS new families.

The application is free. Once accepted, students can fill out the following form for course registration every semester. The registration form will be kept in the cabinet and inside each family folder. The tuition is required at the time of registration but will be handled in a separate software system. Students can fill out multiple forms stapled together if they want to take more than one course. The data on the form will be entered into a spreadsheet by a secretary to share with the school administrators and the instructors.

The Panda Language School (PLS),
COURSE REGISTRATION FORM

| STUDENT INFORMATION | | | |
|---|---|---|---|
| Guardian name | | Phone | |
| Student name | | Date of birth | |
| Gender | | E-mail | |
| Relationship to Guardian | | Additional Information | |
| **COURSE INFORMATION** | | | |
| Course Number | | Start Date | |
| Course Title | | Finish Date | |
| Meet day | | | |
| Meet Time | | | |
| Instructor Name | | | |
| **SCHOOL USE** | | | |
| Approval | | School Note: | |
| Tuition Paid | | | |
| Scholarship Amount | | | |
| Registered | | | |

Table 8.2 A course registration form for PLS students.

The school also keeps the instructor data on a 3 by 5 index card. Basic information includes name, address, phone, email, emergency contact, date hired, and type (paid or volunteer).

For courses offered, there's no official prerequisite. On the registration form, the school will inform the students what class they can or cannot take. The prerequisite is often self explanatory from the course title. For example, Chinese Language 1 is the prerequisite for Chinese Language 2. Parents can always call the school or arrange a free test to see which level the child may best fit in.

All courses are on a list in a spreadsheet. In addition to the information listed in the registration form, each course has a maximum capacity. Seat availability is updated by the secretary who also manages registration. One of the most often asked questions from the administrators is how many students can register for a certain course.

Students receive grades of A, B, C, D, F, P, W for each course, as submitted by the instructor.

PLS wants you to develop the database so they can remove all paperwork to save both employee time and conserve the environment. Specifically, they want to:

1. Be able to manipulate family, instructor, course information.
2. Allow students to register for courses, check registration and grade.
3. Allow instructors to post course grade.

Feel free to contact PLS if you have any questions.

## 8.2 PLS Business Rules

The following is a list of business rules extracted from the business description in Section 8.1 (The business has agreed not to store any payment data in this database):

Each family can have up to 2 parents/guardians. Each guardian is related to exactly one family.
Each family can have one or more children/students. Each child is from exactly one family.
Each student can register for any number of courses. Each course can have several students.
Each course is taught by one instructor. An instructor can teach many courses.
A family has an id, last name, phone, cellphone, email, home address, city, state, and zip code.
A student has an id, first name, last name, gender, relationship, phone, email, birth date, and note.
A course has a number, title, meet day, meet time, start date, end date, and seat capacity.
A guardian has an id, name, address, phone, cell, and email.
An instructor has an id, name, address, phone, email, hire date, and type.
The relationship between the student and course has a grade.

## 8.3 Entity Relationship Diagram

Based on the business rules above, develop a conceptual ERD. Then, with the business description, add all attributes to their corresponding entities and relationships. A conceptual ERD is displayed in Figure 8.1. A logical ERD is displayed in Figure 8.2.

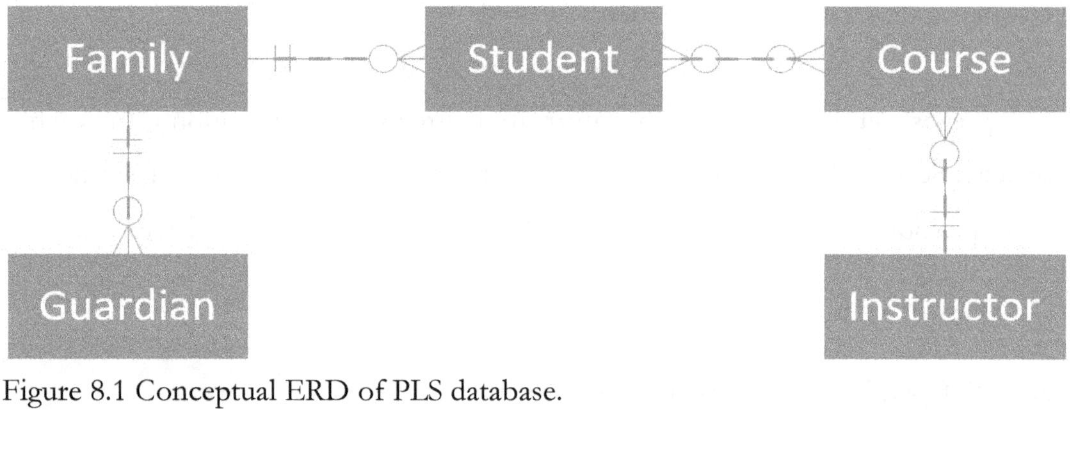


Figure 8.1 Conceptual ERD of PLS database.

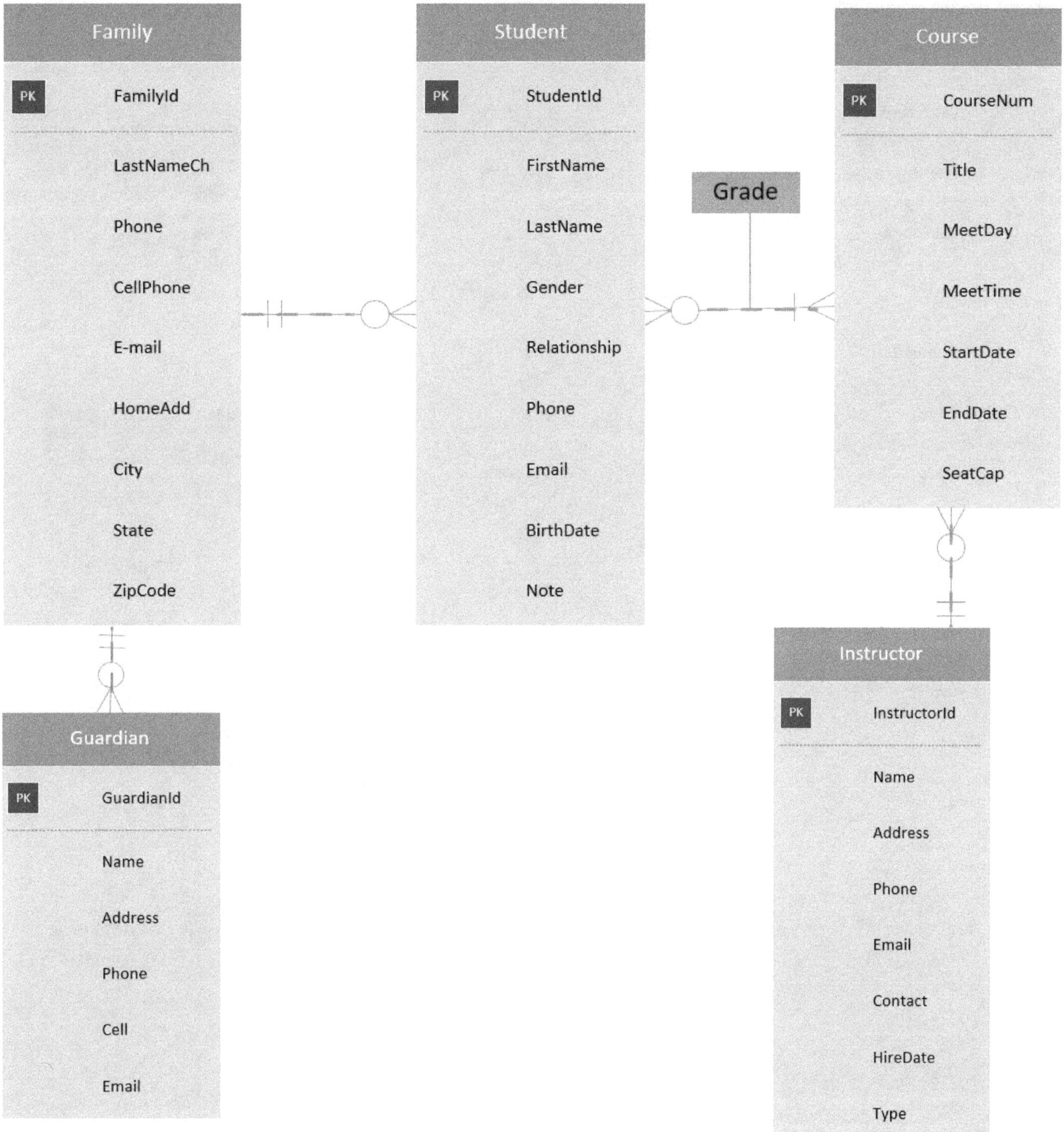


Figure 8.2 Logical ERD of PLS database.

## 8.4 Mapping ERD to Relations

Next, follow ERD to the relations mapping rules outlined in Chapter 5. Figure 8.3 shows the mapping result.

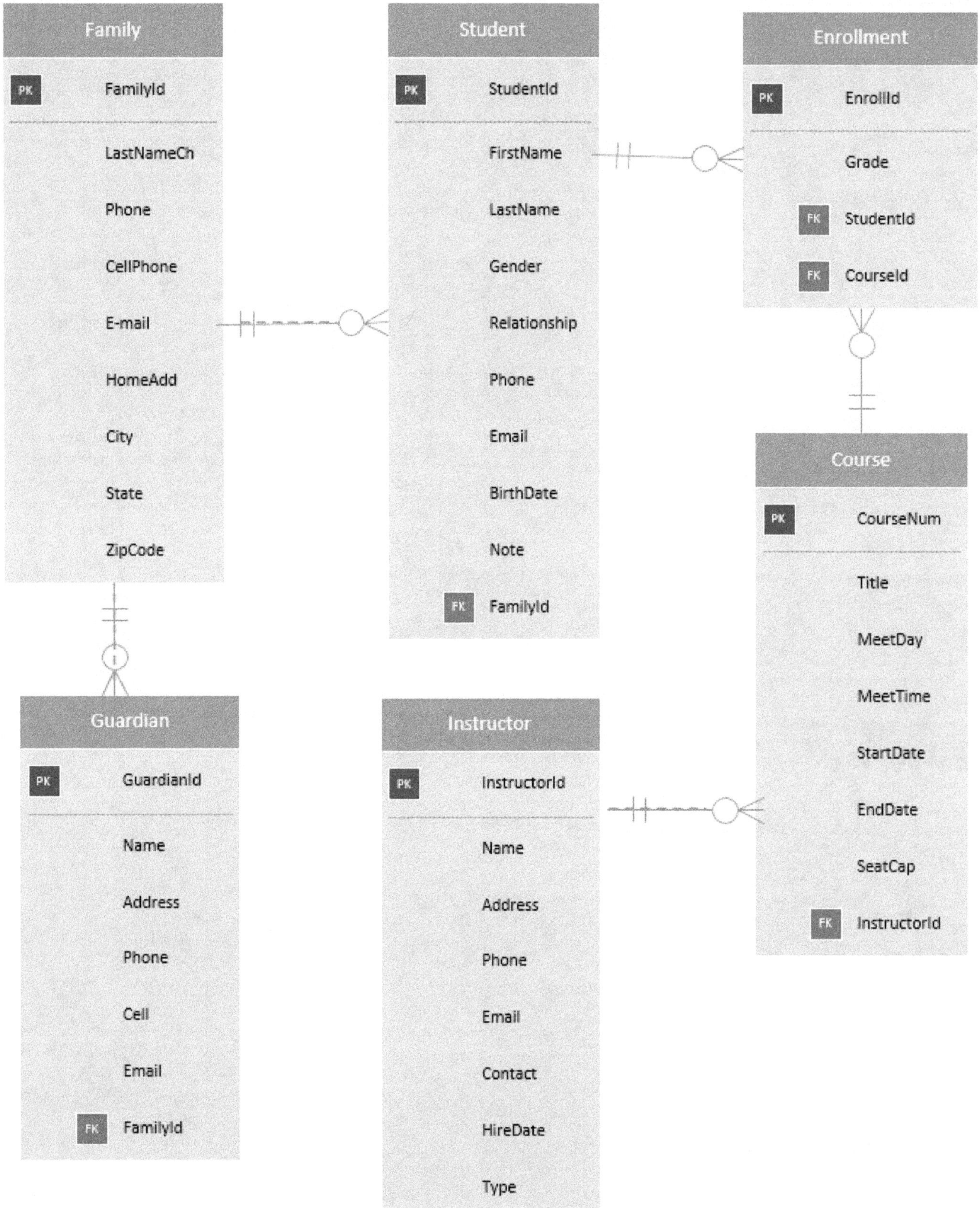


Figure 8.3 Relations that map the logical ERD of PLS database.

## 8.5 Normalization and Denormalization

All relations are in at least 3rd normal form.

Review Question 8.1
You extract business rules from descriptions. What should you focus on?
a. entities and relationships
b. entities, relationships, and attributes
c. how business work
d. make it simple

Review Question 8.2
You construct conceptual ERDs from business rules. What should you focus on?
a. entities and relationships
b. entities, attributes, and relationships
c. primary keys
d. make it simple

Review Question 8.3
You construct logical ERDs from conceptual ERDs. What should you focus on?
a. entities and relationship
b. attributes
c. primary keys
d. attributes and primary keys

Review Question 8.4
You map logical ERD to relations. What should you focus on?
a. foreign keys
b. attributes
c. primary keys
d. attributes and primary keys

## 8.6 Physical Design with Data Type

The design process so far can apply to any DBMSs. In physical design, the PLS decides to go with SQL Server. Next, the data type for each attribute of the relations should be added. Transact-SQL (T-SQL for short) has the following major data type available:

*Character strings / Unicode character strings*

The character strings data type is used to store alphanumeric characters, such as student name and street address among others. The popular character string data types are char and varchar.

Use char if all data in an attribute is the same size. For example, US Zip code is always five digits, so you can set the data type as CHAR(5).

Use varchar if the data of the attribute has variable length, such as first name and last name. You set the maximum length of the attribute. For example, the data type for the first name attribute can be VARCHAR(120), assuming a person's first name will not go over 120 characters.

In either char or varchar, the largest number you can put in the parentheses is 8000. In case the attribute value may be more than 8000 characters, use varchar(max) as the data type, which can hold a value up to 2GB. Note that these limits may change in future versions; this information is provided for general context.

If the attribute values include foreign languages such as Arabic, Japanese, or Korean, instead of using char or varchar, you should use nchar or nvarchar. Adding an "n" in front of char or varchar indicates it is Unicode and can hold foreign languages that take two bytes in each character. The "n" stands for national. In this book, we use the Unicode version so it can hold both English and foreign languages.

*Exact numeric*

The exact numeric data type is used to store numbers with exact value, such as bank account balance, product price, or number of credit hours a student has taken. The more popular exact numeric types include bit, int, money, and numeric.

Use bit if the attribute values are all Boolean with 1 for TRUE and 0 for FALSE.
Use int if the attribute values are whole numbers between approximately -2 million to +2 million.
Use money if the attribute values are currency of any state.
Use numeric if the attribute value is stored with fixed precision and scale. The format is numeric (p, s) where the p stands for precision (which is the total number of digits allowed) and s stands for scale (which is total digits to the right of the decimal place.) The largest number for p is 38 with a default value of 18 and s is any digit between 0 and p with a default value of 0. The value for s cannot be specified if the value for p is not specified, so NUMERIC ( , 3) won't work.

Let's see some examples of how numeric(p, s) works.

NUMERIC (3, 1) will hold a number up to 99.9. The total number of digits is 3, with only one of the three digits allowed to be after the decimal.

NUMERIC (5,3) will hold a number up to 99.999. The total number of digits is 5, with only three of the five digits allowed to be after the decimal.

*Date and Time*

The date and time data type are used to store date and time values. The more popular types are date and datetime2.

Use date data type if the attribute value is a date. The default string literal format is 'YYYY-MM-DD' (such as '2022-12-15'.)

Use datetime2 data type if the attribute value contains both the date and the time of day. It also allows fractional seconds for higher precision. The default string literal format is 'YYYY-MM-DD hh:mm:ss[.fractional seconds]'. The square bracket [] indicates the optional part. An example can be '2012-12-21 07:34:00.1523423'

*Binary Strings*

The binary strings data type is used to store binary data, such as image files. The more popular types are binary and varbinary.

Use binary(n) if the attribute value is a fixed-length binary data of n bytes. The maximum value for n is 8000.

Use varbinary(n) if the attribute value is variable-length binary data of up to n bytes. The maximum value for n is 8000.

Use varbinary(max) if the attribute value is variable-length binary data that exceeds 8000 bytes.

Review Question 8.5
In which step of the relational database design process should you pick a DBMS?
a. conceptual
b. logical
c. physical
d. as early as possible

Review Question 8.6
NCHAR is a data type in SQL Server. What does n in NCHAR stand for?
a. normalization
b. normal
c. national
d. NoSQL

Review Question 8.7
In T-SQL, which of the following is a Unicode character string data type?
a. NVARCHAR
b. CHAR
c. TEXT
d. VARCHAR

Review Question 8.8
In T-SQL, what's the difference between the VARCHAR and NVARCHAR data type?
a. VARCHAR is used for foreign languages.
b. NVARCHAR is used for foreign languages only.
c. VARCHAR can be used for both English and foreign languages.
d. NVARCHAR can be used for both English and foreign languages.

Review Question 8.9
In T-SQL, which data type is used to store values of True or False?
a. Boolean
b. Logic
c. T/F
d. bit

Review Question 8.10
In T-SQL, what precision and scale are needed for a number like 22.345?
a. numeric(2, 3)
b. numeric(2, 5)
c. numeric(5, 3)
d. numeric(3, 2)

Review Question 8.11
In T-SQL, if you need both date and time of the day with fractional seconds, which data type is recommended?
a. date
b. datetime
c. datetime2
d. any of the options

Review Question 8.12
In T-SQL, varbinary data type is often used to store ___________.
a. images
b. variables
c. numbers
d. digits

Review Question 8.13
In T-SQL, which of the following data type can be used to store a name called "Alice"?
a. CHAR(5)
b. CHAR(6)
c. VARCHAR(6)
d. Any of the other three options

Review Question 8.14
In T-SQL, which of the following is NOT a data type for numbers?
a. bit
b. binary
c. money
d. numeric

Review Question 8.15
If you insert '2023-02-05' for the value of a datetime2 data type, what is the actual value stored?
a. 2023-02-05
b. 2023-02-06
c. 2023-02-05 00:00:00 0000000
d. It will cause an error because of a mismatched data type.

Review Question 8.16
The default string literal format for datetime2 is ______.
a. YYYY-MM-DD
b. YYYY-MM-DD hh:mm:ss
c. MM-DD-YYYY
d. MM-DD-YYYY hh:mm:ss

Review Question 8.17
Use ______ data type if the attribute values are whole numbers between approximately -2 million to +2 million.
a. smallint
b. mediumint
c. int
d. largeint

## 8.7 Transact-SQL Code to Create Database and Table

To run SQL code in Visual Studio, the first thing you need is to connect to a database. The statement for connecting is:

```
USE databaseName;
```

Before you create your first database, you should connect to a default database called *master*.

When scripting for a new database, you are unlikely to run all code successfully in just one attempt. When you try the second attempt to run the code, there will be some tables already created in the first attempt that will cause trouble. We suggest adding a deletion line before you create a database so that you can run the script as many times as you need. Every run of the script will first delete the database and then create a fresh one. Do not use the statement for a database in production.

The statement to delete/drop a database is

```
DROP DATABASE databaseName;
```

Add an IF statement to avoid deleting the database the first time you run it, as shown below:

```
DROP DATABASE IF EXISTS databaseName;
```

Now, you are ready to create a database. The statement for creating database is:

```
CREATE DATABASE databaseName;
```

Some statements should be in their own batch. This is like how some products cannot ship with other products, they have to ship in their own container. For T-SQL, some statements require to be in their own batch. One such statement is CREATE DATABASE. Just add the keyword GO to cut the code from the remaining code into different batches.

Next, create schemas for the database objects. You can think of schemas as containers that can be used for better organization of the database objects. In this case, schemas are used for organizing the tables and other objects. A schema should have an authorization setting, like how a container has a lock. The default user account is dbo (the default schema in SQL Server). The schema can allow better security with different authorization settings for different schemas.

The syntax for creating a schema is:

```
CREATE SCHEMA schemaName AUTHORIZATION dbo;
```

Finally, it is time for creating tables. The Create Table syntax is:

```
CREATE TABLE SchemaName.TableName
(
    fieldName dataType Null or NOT Null,
    ......
    CONSTRAINT
);
```

You can add IDENTITY to a field to indicate that the value for the field will be automatically generated by the SQL Server. The IDENTITY is often used together with the primary key field. However, SQL Server only promises the uniqueness of the values, no guarantee of the sequence. This may cause problems for foreign keys. As a result, we sometimes turn it off as shown in the examples of the next section.

There are three types of constraints introduced in this chapter. One is the primary key constraint with the following syntax:

```
CONSTRAINT PK_TableName PRIMARY KEY (primary_key_field);
```

Where, PK_TableName is the name of the primary key and can be any legal name. But, it is conventional to use PK and underscore followed by the table name.

A foreign key constraint has the following syntax:

```
CONSTRAINT FK_TableName_ReferenceTableName FOREIGN KEY (foreign_key_field)
REFERENCES ReferenceTableName (primary_key_of_referenced_table);
```

Recall that a foreign key is a field in the current table which is also a primary key in a referenced table. A Foreign Key Constraint must reference a table that is created before the current one. As a result, tables in the script cannot be created in any order you like.

The CHECK Constraint can ensure certain conditions in fields are met. For example, you can use CHECK to make sure a course start date is before the end date.

The rest of the section lists the complete code for creating the database for PLS.

```
-- Connect to SQL Server master database
USE master;

-- Drop database just in case you need to start all over
DROP DATABASE IF EXISTS PLS;

-- Create database
CREATE DATABASE PLS;
GO

-- Connect to PLS
USE PLS;
GO

-- Create schemas
CREATE SCHEMA Customer AUTHORIZATION dbo;
GO
CREATE SCHEMA School AUTHORIZATION dbo;
GO

-- Create tables
CREATE TABLE Customer.Families
(
    FamilyId      INT              NOT NULL     IDENTITY,
```

```
    LastNameCh   NVARCHAR(20)    NOT NULL,
    Phone        NVARCHAR(15)    NOT NULL,
    CellPhone    NVARCHAR(15)    NULL,
    Email        NVARCHAR(50)    NOT NULL,
    HomeAddress  NVARCHAR(50)    NULL,
    City         NVARCHAR(20)    NULL,
    [State]      NVARCHAR(20)    NULL,
    Zipcode      NVARCHAR(10)    NULL,
    CONSTRAINT PK_Families PRIMARY KEY (FamilyId)
);

CREATE TABLE Customer.Guardians
(
    GuardianId    INT             NOT NULL    IDENTITY,
    [Name]        NVARCHAR(20)    NOT NULL,
    [Address]     NVARCHAR(50)    NULL,
    Phone         NVARCHAR(15)    NOT NULL,
    Cell          NVARCHAR(15)    NULL,
    Email         NVARCHAR(50)    NOT NULL,
    FamilyId      INT             NOT NULL,
    CONSTRAINT PK_Guardians PRIMARY KEY (GuardianId),
    CONSTRAINT FK_Guardians_Families FOREIGN KEY (FamilyId) REFERENCES Customer.Families
(FamilyId)
);

CREATE TABLE Customer.Students
(
    StudentId    INT             NOT NULL    IDENTITY,
    FirstName    NVARCHAR(20)    NOT NULL,
    LastName     NVARCHAR(20)    NOT NULL,
    Gender       NVARCHAR(10)    NULL,
    Relation     NVARCHAR(10)    NOT NULL,
    Phone        NVARCHAR(15)    NULL,
    Email        NVARCHAR(50)    NULL,
    BirthDate    DATE            NOT NULL,
    Note         NVARCHAR(1000)  NULL,
    FamilyId     INT             NOT NULL,
    CONSTRAINT PK_Students PRIMARY KEY (StudentId),
    CONSTRAINT FK_Students_Families FOREIGN KEY (FamilyId) REFERENCES Customer.Families
(FamilyId)
);

CREATE TABLE School.Instructors
(
    InstructorId     INT             NOT NULL    IDENTITY,
    [Name]           NVARCHAR(20)    NOT NULL,
    [Address]        NVARCHAR(50)    NULL,
    Phone            NVARCHAR(15)    NOT NULL,
    Email            NVARCHAR(50)    NOT NULL,
    Contact          NVARCHAR(20)    NOT NULL,
    HireDate         DATE            NOT NULL,
    [Type]           NVARCHAR(10)    NULL,
    CONSTRAINT PK_Instructors PRIMARY KEY (InstructorId)
);

CREATE TABLE School.Courses
(
    CourseNum        INT             NOT NULL    IDENTITY,
    Title            NVARCHAR(30)    NOT NULL,
    MeetDay          NVARCHAR(30)    NULL,
```

```
    MeetTime         NVARCHAR(30)     NULL,
    StartDate        DATE             NULL,
    EndDate          DATE             NULL,
    SeatCap          INT              NULL,
    InstructorId     INT              NULL,
    CONSTRAINT PK_Courses PRIMARY KEY (CourseNum),
    CONSTRAINT FK_Courses_Instructors FOREIGN KEY (InstructorId) REFERENCES School.Instructors
(InstructorId),
    CONSTRAINT CHK_StartEndDate CHECK (StartDate < EndDate)
);

CREATE TABLE Customer.Enrollments
(
    EnrollId         INT              NOT NULL IDENTITY,
    Grade            NCHAR(1)         NULL,
    StudentId        INT              NOT NULL,
    CourseNum        INT              NOT NULL,
    CONSTRAINT PK_Enrollments PRIMARY KEY (EnrollId),
    CONSTRAINT FK_Enrollments_Students FOREIGN KEY (StudentId) REFERENCES Customer.Students
(StudentId),
    CONSTRAINT FK_Enrollments_Courses FOREIGN KEY (CourseNum) REFERENCES School.Courses
(CourseNum)
);
```

Review Question 8.18
The schema can allow better security in relational database with ______.
a. two-factor passwords
b. less passwords to memorize
c. different authorization settings for different schema
d. the up to date technologies

Review Question 8.19
We often use IDENTITY in SQL Server for primary keys. However, there is no guarantee that the value provided will be ______.
a. unique
b. in sequence
c. accurate
d. useful

Review Question 8.20
To run SQL code in Visual Studio, the first thing you need is to connect to a database. The statement for connecting is: ______.
a. CONNECT databaseName;
b. CONNECT TO databaseName;
c. CONNECT TO DATABASE databaseName;
d. USE databaseName;

Review Question 8.21
When scripting for a new database, you are unlikely to run all code successfully in just one attempt. When you try the second attempt to run the code, there will be some tables already created in the first attempt that will cause trouble. We suggest adding a ______ line before you create a database so that you can run the script as many times as you need.
a. new database

b. update database
c. insertion
d. deletion

Review Question 8.22
Some statements should be in their own batch. This is like how some products cannot ship with other products, they have to ship in their own container. Add the keyword ______ to cut the code from the remaining code into different batches.
a. BATCH
b. NEW BATCH
c. GO
d. CUT

Review Question 8.23
A schema should have an authorization setting, like how a container has a lock. The default user account is ______ (the default schema in SQL Server).
a. dbo
b. dba
c. dbms
d. schema

Review Question 8.24
When creating a table, you can add ______ to a field to indicate that the value for the field will be automatically generated by the SQL Server.
a. AUTO_INCREMENT
b. ID
c. AUTO_GENERATE
d. IDENTITY

Review Question 8.25
When creating a table, the ______ field is often used together with the primary key field.
a. FIRST
b. IDENTITY
c. DEFAULT
d. LAST

Review Question 8.26
When creating a table, which of the following is NOT a CONSTRAINT type?
a. PRIMARY KEY
b. FOREIGN KEY
c. RELATION
d. CHECK

Review Question 8.27
In T-SQL localhost, the first step for creating a database for the first time is ________.
a. issuing "CREATE DATABASE" statement
b. connecting to DATABASE
c. connecting to SQL Server master database
d. setting permission for the new database

Review Question 8.28
In T-SQL, a ________ is a container that includes one or more tables of a database.
a. SELECT statement
b. database
c. schema
d. table

Review Question 8.29
At the physical level of database design, a table has one or more fields. Most fields have three parts, _______, ________, and _________.
a. field name, field nickname, and data type
b. field name, data type, and nullable
c. field name, field nickname, and nullable
d. database name, table name, and field name

Review Question 8.30
In addition to fields, a table can have constraints. What are the three constraints we covered in this chapter?
a. Primary Key, check, and Foreign Key
b. Primary Key, check, and Non-primary Key
c. Foreign Key, check, and Non-foreign Key
d. Key, check, and non-key

Review Question 8.31
Suppose a table has the following constraint: `CONSTRAINT FK_Students_Families FOREIGN KEY (FamilyId) REFERENCES Customer.Families (FamilyId)`. Which table(s) can you find a field called "FamilyId"?
a. Families table only
b. The table with the constraint only
c. both Families table and the table with the constraint
d. neither Families table nor the table with the constraint

## 8.8 Sample SQL Statements for Working with the Database

In this section you will write SQL statements to answer the following questions:

1. Insert one family with one guardian and two children.
2. Insert one instructor and two courses taught by that instructor.
3. Enroll students to classes.
4. Display all students who enrolled in a specific course.
5. Assign grades to students who enrolled in a course.
6. Display total number of students enrolled in a specific course.

The rest of the section contains all statements to accomplish the above tasks. Every time you run this code, you must re-execute the script in Section 8.7 to make sure you have a fresh database. It is a good idea to put the two scripts in one file so that you will always have a fresh database to work with.

```
-- Q1. Insert a family with one guardian and two children
SET IDENTITY_INSERT Customer.Families ON;
INSERT INTO Customer.Families (FamilyId, LastNameCh, Phone, CellPhone, Email, HomeAddress,
City, [State], ZipCode)
    VALUES (1, 'Chen', '2021112233', '2021112234', 'chen1234@gmail.com', '101 Chinaberry
St', 'Peking', 'OH', '50505');
SET IDENTITY_INSERT Customer.Families OFF;
INSERT INTO Customer.Guardians ([Name], Phone, Email, FamilyId)
    VALUES ('Li', '2021212134', 'li1234@gmail.com', 1);
SET IDENTITY_INSERT Customer.Students ON;
INSERT INTO Customer.Students (StudentId, FirstName, LastName, Relation, BirthDate,
FamilyId) VALUES
    (1, 'Alice', 'Chen', 'Daughter', '20101010', 1),
    (2, 'Tom', 'Chen', 'Son', '20120922', 1);
SET IDENTITY_INSERT Customer.Students OFF;

-- Q2. Insert one instructor and two courses taught by that instructor
SET IDENTITY_INSERT School.Instructors ON;
INSERT INTO School.Instructors(InstructorId, [Name], Phone, Email, Contact, HireDate)
    VALUES (1, 'Bruce Lee', '2021231234', 'brucelee123@gmail.com', 'Anna Lee',
'20170104');
SET IDENTITY_INSERT School.Instructors OFF;
SET IDENTITY_INSERT School.Courses ON;
INSERT INTO School.Courses(CourseNum, Title, MeetDay, MeetTime, StartDate, EndDate,
SeatCap, InstructorId) VALUES
    (1, 'KongFu Step 1', 'Saturdays', '5:00-5:30PM', '20170701', '20170801', 10, 1),
    (2, 'Chinese Classic Music 1', 'Sundays', '5:30-6:00PM', '20170701', '20170801', 15,
1);
SET IDENTITY_INSERT School.Courses OFF;
-- Q3. Enrol Alice to Bruce Lee's Kongfu Step 1 (coursenum is 1) and Chinese Classic Music
-- (courseNum is 2)
-- Enroll Tom to Bruce Lee's Chinese Classic Music 1 (coursenum is 2)
INSERT INTO Customer.Enrollments (StudentId, CourseNum) VALUES
    (1, 1),
    (1, 2),
    (2, 2);

-- Q4. Display all students from Chinese Classic Music 1 (courseNum is 2);
SELECT Students.StudentId, Students.FirstName + ' ' + Students.LastName AS "Student Name",
Courses.Title
    FROM Customer.Students JOIN Customer.Enrollments
    ON Students.StudentId = Enrollments.StudentId
    JOIN School.Courses
    ON Enrollments.CourseNum = Courses.CourseNum
    WHERE Courses.CourseNum = 2;

-- Q5. Assign grades to students in Chinese Classic Music
-- Alice (Student ID 1) A, Tom (Student ID 2) C
UPDATE Customer.Enrollments
    SET Grade = 'A'
    WHERE StudentId = 1 AND CourseNum = 2;
UPDATE Customer.Enrollments
    SET Grade = 'C'
    WHERE StudentId =2 AND CourseNum = 2;

-- Q6. Display number of students registered for Chinese Classic Music (CourseNum 2)
SELECT COUNT(*) AS "Number of students in Chinese Classic Music"
FROM Customer.Enrollments
WHERE CourseNum = 2;
```

## 8.9 Chapter Summary

In this chapter, you experienced the process of applying database development knowledge to a real-world database project. The chapter starts with a business description of the mini-world, which includes the requirements from the customer. Next, business rules are extracted from the description. With good business rules, it is easy to construct the conceptual and logical ERD. Next, mapping the ERD to relations, normalize and denormalize the relations. In physical ERD, add data type to the attributes of the relations. Finally, write SQL statements and run the statements to create the database with all necessary tables.

## 8.10 Discussion

Discussion 8.1
This book introduces the following major activities for developing relational databases: mini-world business descriptions, business rules, conceptual ERD, logical ERD, map ERD to relations, normalize/denormalize relations, physical design with data type, and generating SQL statements to create databases and tables. In your opinion, how important is the above sequence? Can any activity be executed before another not following that sequence?

Discussion 8.2
The majority of statements in Section 8.7 create tables. Can these tables be created in any order/sequence? Why or why not?

Discussion 8.3
Database development is both an art and science. There is more than one database that can meet the business requirements. For example, in the PLS database, you can denormalize the relations by combining Family and Guardian relations into one relation, which results in a different database. Can you think of another database from the one provided in this chapter for the PLS database?

## 8.11 Project Exercise One

The Tiger State University (TSU) has a tutoring office that would like to replace its current paper-based system with an online application. They would like you to develop the database for them.

The tutoring office has a list of tutors with tutor ID, first name, last name, highest education, course number and course title for which the tutor can help, and their available date and time. Usually a tutor would set up available dates and times 5 to 7 days ahead. The available time slot is automatically set to 30 minutes intervals. So, for example, a tutor's available date and time can be Tuesday, February 16, 2021, 9am, 9:30am, 5pm, 5:30pm, and 6pm.

## *Tutor Form*

| TutorID | First Name | Last Name | Education Level | Course No. | Available Time |
|---|---|---|---|---|---|
| 1 | Justin | Calson | Senior | CHEM101 | M, 2/15/2021, 9:30am, 2pm, T, 2/16/2021, 10am, 4:30pm |
| 2 | Nate | Scott | master | COMP101, COMP102 | T, 2/16/2021, 9am, 1:30am, 5pm, 5:30pm, 6pm |
| 3 | Jeremy | Hayes | bachelor | CHEM 101, COMP101 | W, 2/17/2021, 9:30am, 10am |

Any student at TSU can sign up for tutoring. A student would have to provide student ID, first name and last name, course number, and the title and instructor name and email for the course he or she needs help with. Then, the student picks an available time slot from the tutor form by checking the available date and time on the tutor form and filling out the date and time in the sign-up form.

## *Sign up form*

| Student ID | First Name | Last Name | Course No. | Course Title | Instructor Name | Instructor Email | Check-in |
|---|---|---|---|---|---|---|---|
| 231654 | Tanner | Dawson | CHEMP 101 | Intro to Chemistry | Grace Church | Church2 @tsu.edu | T, 2/16/2021, 4:30pm |
| 231654 | Tanner | Dawson | COMP10 1 | Intro to CS | John Meyer | Meyer22 @tsu.edu | T, 2/16/2021, 5pm |

Both walk-in and scheduled appointments use the same sign up form. In other words, walk in students should also fill out the tutor form and signup form.

For simplicity, the tutoring office's database won't share any data with the university's database.

Your task:

1. Write out all possible business rules.
2. Develop a conceptual ERD.
3. Develop a logical ERD.
4. Map the ERD to relations.
5. Implement any necessary normalization/denormalization.
6. Write SQL statements to create the database and the tables.
7. Write SQL statements to answer the following questions (always use make-up data if not provided).
   a. Add data provided in the tutor form.
   b. Update one tutor's available date and time to a different date and time.
   c. Add data about your database course. Make up a new tutor for the course.
   d. Display all available tutoring time slots for COMP101. Show the slot time and tutor names.
   e. Add data provided in the signup form.
   f. Insert your data for the signup form. You need a tutor for COMP101.
   g. Display how many time slots are filled for tutoring COMP101.

## 8.12 Project Exercise Two

The Tiger State University's (TSU) athletic department wants to keep track of their student athletes' academic performances. They need your help to develop a database to replace their current spreadsheet-based practice.

An athletic student has a student ID, first name, last name, sports played and the corresponding coach's name, office address and phone. The majority of students play only one sport, but occasionally, a student may play two sports or more. There are about 25 sports at TSU. A coach can coach one or more teams.

An athletic student is also required to take between 4 to 6 courses per semester to meet the scholarship requirements. A course has course number, title, credit (an integer between 1 and 5) current semester (fall, spring, and summer) and year, instructor name, instructor office address, phone, and email. The class schedule is also recorded.

The instructors are required to report two grades, one in the middle of the semester and one final grade. For those students who receive a grade of D or below, the department will inform the coach and create a plan for the student to catch up. A plan is just a short paragraph with a date created. When a plan's objectives are achieved, the plan is marked as accomplished.

Your task:

1. Write out all possible business rules.
2. Develop a conceptual ERD.
3. Develop a logical ERD.
4. Map the ERD to relations.
5. Implement any normalization/denormalization.
6. Write SQL statements to create the database and the tables.
7. Write SQL statements to answer the following questions (use made-up data when they are not given).
   a. Add three students who play three different sports. One of the students plays two sports.
   b. Add between 4 to 6 courses to each student. Some of these courses are taken by more than one student.
   c. Assign midterm grades to each course for each student. One student received two Ds and another student received one D. All other grades are C or better.
   d. Display students with grades below C. Show student ID, name, sport(s) played, coach name, the course(s) that have a grade lower than C, and the instructor information.
   e. Display total credit hours for each student for the current semester.

## 8.13 Project Exercise Three

The Vacation Inn is a small family-owned hotel located in the Great Lake Resort area. The owners would like to have a housekeeping tracking software that would allow them to track when a room is cleaned or under cleaning and by whom. They also want the application to calculate the total wages for each contracted janitor by the end of each week. A janitor is paid by the number of rooms he or she cleaned and the type of the room.

A janitor has a first name, last name, street address, city, state, zip code, and phone number. A janitor can clean any type of room in the Vacation Inn.

There are three types of rooms in Vacation Inn. They are suites, one King-size bed, and two Queen-size beds. The wages for each type of room are $7, $5, and $6 accordingly. However, these types and pay rates are changing. For example, just a few years ago, smoking rooms were deleted. Now, the whole hotel is smoke free.

The room numbers for the suites are 201, 202, 203, 204, and 205. The room numbers for the King-size bedrooms are 101, 103, 105, 107, 109, 111, 113, 115, and 117. The room numbers for the two Queen-size bedrooms are 102, 104, 106, 108, 110, 112, 114, 116, and 118. A guest room that needs cleaning should be indicated in the database so that the janitors know which rooms to clean.

Each janitor will have a tablet with all room numbers that need cleaning on the screen. When the janitor touches a room, the clock begins recording. When the job is done, the janitor touches a button on their screen to stop recording. Even though janitors are not paid by the hour. It is required by law to make sure they paid above the state minimum wage.

Your task:

1. Write out all possible business rules.
2. Develop a conceptual ERD
3. Develop a logical ERD.
4. Map the ERD to relations.
5. Implement any normalization/denormalization.
6. Write SQL statements to create the database and the tables.
7. Write SQL statements to answer the following questions (use made-up data when they are not given).
    a. Add all three types of rooms with all room numbers in the database
    b. Add three contracted janitors.

c. Update the room list so that 2 suites, 7 double rooms, and 8 single rooms need cleaning.
d. List all room numbers for rooms that need cleaning.
e. Pick any three rooms from C, and assign three janitors to the rooms. Show that two janitors have finished.
f. Display all rooms that are in the process of cleaning, including the clock in time and the janitor's name.

## 8.14 Solutions to Review Questions

8.1 B; 8.2 A; 8.3 D; 8.4 A; 8.5 C; 8.6 C; 8.7 A; 8.8 D; 8.9 D; 8.10 C; 8.11 C; 8.12 A; 8.13 D; 8.14 B; 8.15 C; 8.16 B; 8.17 C; 8.18 C; 8.19 B; 8.20 D; 8.21 D; 8.22 C; 8.23 A; 8.24 D; 8.25 B; 8.26 C; 8.27 C; 8.28 C; 8.29 B; 8.30 A; 8.31 C;

# Chapter 9: Introduction to NoSQL Database

## Chapter Learning Objectives

9.1 Identify the key characteristics that distinguish NoSQL from relational databases
9.2 Explain the CAP theorem and its implications for database design
9.3 Compare ACID and BASE consistency models

## 9.1 What is NoSQL?

The term "NoSQL" stands for "Not Only SQL" and represents a broad category of DBMS that differ from traditional RDBMS. The name itself is somewhat misleading -- NoSQL doesn't mean the complete absence of SQL or structured query languages. Instead, it signifies a departure from the rigid, table-based relational model that has dominated database technology since the 1970s.

NoSQL databases emerged in the early 2000s as innovative technology companies faced unprecedented challenges in data management. Companies like Google, Amazon, and Facebook were building applications at scales never before imagined, serving hundreds of millions of users and processing petabytes of data. Their requirements quickly surpassed what traditional relational databases could efficiently handle.

A NoSQL database is designed to store and retrieve data using mechanisms that differ from the tabular relations used in relational databases. Rather than organizing data into rows and columns within tables, NoSQL databases employ various data models optimized for specific use cases: documents, key-value pairs, wide columns, or graphs.

*Document stores* organize data into self-contained units, typically formatted as JSON or BSON, which are common, easy-to-read data formats. Each document can possess a unique structure, allowing developers to evolve the schema over time without costly migrations, making them ideal for content management systems and complex user profiles.

*Key-value stores* represent the simplest model, functioning like a massive distributed hash table, which spreads data across multiple servers for fast, reliable access. Data is accessed via a unique key, offering extremely low latency and high throughput, which suits caching mechanisms and session management where quick lookups are prioritized over complex queries.

*Wide-column stores* arrange data into column families rather than fixed rows, enabling efficient storage of sparse data across distributed systems. This model excels at handling massive write volumes and analytical queries over large datasets, providing the scalability required for time-series data and IoT applications.

*Graph databases* focus on the relationships between data points rather than the data itself, using nodes and edges to represent entities and their connections. This structure is uniquely suited for navigating highly connected data, such as social networks, fraud detection systems, and recommendation engines where relationship depth matters.

The key insight behind NoSQL is that not all data fits neatly into tables with predefined schemas, and not all applications require the strict consistency guarantees that relational databases provide. By relaxing some of these traditional constraints, NoSQL databases can achieve remarkable improvements in scalability, flexibility, and performance for certain workloads.

Review Question 9.1
What does the term NoSQL primarily signify?
a. Databases that completely eliminate SQL
b. Databases that reject structured data entirely
c. Databases that move beyond the rigid relational table model
d. Databases designed only for unstructured data

Review Question 9.2
Why did NoSQL databases gain popularity in the early 2000s?
a. Relational databases stopped being supported by vendors
b. Large-scale web companies needed to manage massive and rapidly growing datasets
c. SQL became too difficult for developers to learn
d. Governments required a new database standard

Review Question 9.3
Which NoSQL model is most appropriate for storing highly connected data, such as relationships in a social network?
a. Key-value store
b. Wide-column store
c. Document store
d. Graph database

Review Question 9.4
A company needs extremely fast data retrieval for user session management and caching. Which NoSQL model would best meet this requirement?
a. Graph database

b. Document store
c. Key-value store
d. Wide-column store

## 9.2 The Evolution from SQL to NoSQL

To understand the rise of NoSQL, we must first appreciate the context in which relational databases dominated the landscape.

### 9.2.1 The Relational Era

In 1970, Edgar F. Codd published his seminal paper describing the relational model for database management as discussed in Chapter 1. This model revolutionized how organizations stored and accessed data by introducing the concept of organizing data into tables with rows and columns, linked together through relationships. SQL emerged as the standard language for interacting with these databases.

For decades, relational databases served businesses extremely well, primarily because they offered a disciplined approach to structured data organization. At the heart of this system is the schema, a blueprint that defines exactly what data can be stored before any information is actually saved. By requiring developers to specify data types and constraints upfront, relational databases enforce data integrity. This means that invalid entries, such as text in a date field or orphaned records without a corresponding parent, are rejected at the door, ensuring that the data remains clean, predictable, and trustworthy over time.

Beyond simple storage, relational databases provide powerful query capabilities that allow for complex analysis across multiple tables. Through the process of normalization, data is split into smaller, logical tables to reduce redundancy, but this separation could make retrieval difficult. SQL solves this with join operations, which dynamically reassemble related data from different tables during a query.

Perhaps the most critical feature for enterprise applications is the support for ACID transactions, which ensure data consistency and reliability even during errors or system failures. ACID stands for Atomicity, Consistency, Isolation, and Durability, properties that guarantee that database operations are processed reliably. For example, in a banking application, transferring money involves subtracting from one account and adding to another; ACID ensures that either both actions happen successfully or neither does, preventing scenarios where money disappears or is duplicated. This level of guarantee is essential for systems where data accuracy is non-negotiable.

Finally, the longevity of relational databases has created a mature tools and expertise ecosystem that lowers the barrier to entry. Because the technology has been the industry standard for so long, there is a vast abundance of administrative tools, visualization software, and programming libraries designed to work seamlessly with SQL. Furthermore, the widespread knowledge of relational theory means that finding skilled developers and database administrators is easier compared to newer technologies. This well-established support network reduces operational risk and allows teams to build and maintain systems with confidence.

Together, these strengths made the relational model the undisputed gold standard for business applications throughout the late 20th and early 21st centuries. However, as the internet evolved and applications began to demand massive scalability and flexible data structures, the very features that made relational databases reliable began to present challenges. The rigid schema became difficult to change rapidly, and complex joins became performance bottlenecks at massive scales. The NoSQL databases are not necessarily replacements for these features, but rather alternative solutions designed to solve the specific problems that arise when relational strengths become limitations.

## 9.2.2 The Internet Age Challenge

However, as we entered the 21st century, the landscape began to change dramatically. Several key developments created new challenges that traditional systems struggled to meet.

Massive Scale became a primary concern as web applications like Google's search engine and Amazon's e-commerce platform began serving hundreds of millions and eventually billions of users. The volume of data being generated and accessed grew exponentially beyond the capacity of single servers. Companies found that vertically scaling hardware hit a financial and physical ceiling, forcing them to adopt horizontal scaling strategies like sharding that relational databases were not originally designed to handle efficiently. *Sharding* is splitting a large database into smaller pieces across multiple servers to improve performance and handle more data.

Velocity of Data emerged as a critical factor when real-time data streams from web clickstreams, IoT devices, sensors, and mobile apps created continuous flows of information that needed to be processed immediately. Traditional batch processing approaches became inadequate for use cases like fraud detection or live trending topics where seconds matter. Modern systems now require the ability to ingest and query millions of events per second without lagging behind the incoming flow.

Variety of Data expanded significantly because the internet brought diverse data types beyond traditional structured records. Social media posts, images, videos, log files, and sensor readings flooded systems, and much of this data was unstructured or semi-structured formats like JSON. Trying to force this flexible content into rigid table schemas often resulted in complex joins or wasted space, prompting a shift toward storage solutions that could accommodate evolving data shapes without costly migrations.

Global Distribution became necessary as applications needed to serve users across different geographic regions with low latency. Users expect instant access regardless of whether they are in New York or Tokyo, requiring data to be distributed across multiple data centers worldwide. This shift introduced complexities around data replication and consistency that traditional single-location databases could not resolve without sacrificing performance or availability.

### 9.2.3 The Birth of NoSQL

Between 2006 and 2009, several groundbreaking projects emerged that would define the NoSQL movement: Google published its BigTable paper in 2006 (Chang et al., 2008), describing a distributed storage system for structured data at web scale. Amazon followed in 2007 with a paper on Dynamo, a highly available key-value store that pioneered eventual consistency for services like its shopping cart (DeCandia et al., 2007). Facebook developed Cassandra starting in 2007 for inbox search and released it as open source in 2008. Finally, 10gen (later MongoDB Inc.) released the document-oriented MongoDB in 2009, designed for ease of development and scalability.

These systems shared common characteristics: they were designed for horizontal scalability, embraced eventual consistency where appropriate, and optimized for specific access patterns rather than trying to be general-purpose solutions.

The term 'NoSQL' was popularized in 2009 by Johan Oskarsson at a meetup in San Francisco to describe this emerging category of non-relational, distributed databases. (The term was actually first used in 1998 by Carlo Strozzi, but gained widespread recognition through the 2009 event.)

Review Question 9.5
What is the primary purpose of a schema in relational databases?
a. To encrypt stored data

b. To define data structure before storage
c. To distribute data globally
d. To eliminate duplicate queries

Review Question 9.6
In ACID transactions, what does Atomicity ensure?
a. Data is stored in small units
b. Operations are globally distributed
c. Transactions occur fully or not at all
d. Queries run simultaneously

Review Question 9.7
What challenge made vertical scaling less viable for internet-scale companies?
a. Increasing SQL complexity
b. Financial and physical hardware limits
c. Lack of skilled administrators
d. Decline in structured data

Review Question 9.8
Which factor refers to the need to process continuous streams of real-time data such as clickstreams and sensor inputs?
a. Variety
b. Atomicity
c. Velocity
d. Normalization

# 9.3 Why NoSQL?

Relational databases continue to power financial systems, ERP platforms, and inventory management applications. However, specific workload characteristics in modern cloud-native systems expose architectural trade-offs that motivate the adoption of NoSQL solutions.

## 9.3.1 Scalability Challenges

Relational databases have traditionally relied on vertical scaling -- adding more CPU, RAM, or storage to a single server. At some point, you simply can't buy a larger machine, and even when you can, the cost becomes impractical. The performance improvements are modest and eventually level off.

Horizontal scaling -- also called scaling out -- increases a system's capacity by adding more machines or nodes to the system. One major benefit of this approach is cost: instead of buying a single, extremely powerful (and extremely expensive) server, organizations can add multiple inexpensive, commodity servers as demand grows. Over time, this makes horizontal scaling more affordable and flexible than relying on high-end hardware.

However, horizontal scaling introduces new challenges for relational databases. While techniques like sharding can spread data across multiple servers, they require developers to manually divide data using a shard key such as customer ID or geographic region. Queries that need data from multiple shards -- called cross-shard joins -- must coordinate across the network, which often slows performance significantly. For example, joining user activity stored on different shards may require large data transfers and distributed locking. Many engineering teams find that implementing and maintaining sharding logic at the application level adds substantial complexity and increases long-term maintenance costs.

### 9.3.2 Schema Rigidity

Predefined schemas slow feature deployment in rapidly evolving products. In relational systems, altering a production table with millions of rows often requires migration scripts, index rebuilding, and sometimes temporary downtime. For instance, adding a new required column to a heavily used orders table may lock the table during modification, affecting live transactions. Continuous deployment environments that release updates weekly or daily struggle when schema changes require careful coordination across development, QA, and operations teams.

Diverse data types create inefficient table designs in structured schemas. E-commerce platforms frequently manage products with varying attributes. Electronics may require voltage and processor specifications, clothing requires size and fabric details, and furniture requires material and dimensions. Modeling all product types in a single relational table can produce dozens of nullable columns. Alternatively, heavy normalization introduces multiple auxiliary tables, increasing join complexity. Document-oriented databases allow each product record to store only relevant attributes without redesigning the schema.

### 9.3.3 Join Performance

Relational databases are very good at joining related data from different tables. But as the amount of data grows -- and especially when that data is spread across multiple servers -- join operations become much more expensive. For example, a query that joins five tables stored on different servers may need to move gigabytes of data across the network.

These distributed joins add latency and increase infrastructure costs. On a single machine, relational databases can perform joins quickly when indexes are used correctly. However, when tables are stored on multiple nodes, every join requires communication between those nodes. A query that combines customer profiles, transactions, shipments, and support tickets across different systems can generate a large amount of network traffic. At high volumes, this network overhead becomes a major bottleneck for analytics-heavy workloads such as real-time recommendations or fraud detection.

## 9.3.4 Impedance Mismatch

Developers often think about data as objects in their applications, while relational databases store data as tables. This difference -- called the object-relational impedance mismatch -- creates a gap between how data is modeled in code and how it is stored. Bridging this gap usually requires a mapping layer, which adds extra complexity and can affect performance.

Most modern applications use object-oriented languages like Java, C#, or Python, where data is represented as objects with nested fields. Relational databases, however, require these objects to be broken down into rows spread across multiple tables. Object-Relational Mapping (ORM) tools such as Hibernate or Entity Framework help automate this translation, but they also introduce additional layers that generate SQL, manage loading behavior, and sometimes produce inefficient queries. As a result, developers often spend considerable time tuning ORM-generated SQL to prevent performance issues.

## 9.3.5 CAP Theorem Constraints

As we'll explore in detail later, CAP theorem trade-offs limit relational database availability in distributed systems. The CAP theorem demonstrates that distributed databases cannot simultaneously guarantee consistency, availability, and partition tolerance during network failures. Traditional relational databases emphasize strong consistency, meaning transactions must remain synchronized across replicas. In globally distributed systems, temporary network partitions can cause write operations to block until consistency is restored. High-traffic platforms that require uninterrupted availability during regional outages often adopt architectures that relax strict consistency to maintain responsiveness.

Review Question 9.9
What is a key advantage of horizontal scaling compared to vertical scaling?
a. It removes the need for indexing
b. It allows adding multiple inexpensive servers
c. It guarantees strong consistency
d. It simplifies join operations

Review Question 9.10
How can predefined schemas slow development in agile environments?
a. They prevent horizontal scaling
b. They require coordination and migration for structural changes
c. They eliminate transaction support
d. They automatically duplicate data

Review Question 9.11
Why can storing diverse product types in one relational table be inefficient?
a. It removes foreign keys
b. It eliminates indexing
c. It creates many unused or null fields
d. It prevents transactions

Review Question 9.12
What is the object-relational impedance mismatch?
a. A conflict between indexing and sharding
b. A difference between object models and table structures
c. A failure of ACID guarantees
d. A limitation of horizontal scaling

## 9.4 Key Characteristics of NoSQL Databases

As we transition from the structured, table-driven world of relational databases discussed in the first eight chapters, we enter the diverse and highly adaptable realm of NoSQL. Despite their immense diversity in design and purpose, NoSQL databases share several defining characteristics that make them indispensable for modern, data-intensive applications.

### 9.4.1 Flexible Schema Design

The first major hallmark of NoSQL databases is their flexible schema design. Unlike traditional relational databases that require you to rigidly define tables, columns, and data types before inserting a single record, NoSQL databases typically employ schema-less or schema-flexible architectures. This design choice empowers developers to store data without defining its exact structure in advance, facilitating rapid iteration and agile development.

Consequently, heterogeneous data can coexist peacefully; documents within the exact same collection can possess entirely different structures. This flexibility is particularly practical in dynamic industries like e-commerce, where companies must manage continuously evolving product catalogs. For example, in a document-oriented database like MongoDB, one product document representing a laptop might look like this:

```
{
  "_id": "prod_123",
  "name": "Laptop",
  "category": "Electronics",
  "price": 999.99,
  "specs": {
    "processor": "Intel i7",
    "ram": "16GB",
    "storage": "512GB SSD"
  }
}
```

Meanwhile, another product in that very same collection might represent an item of clothing, featuring a completely different structural layout while living alongside the electronics:

```
{
  "_id": "prod_456",
  "name": "T-Shirt",
  "category": "Clothing",
  "price": 29.99,
  "sizes": ["S", "M", "L", "XL"],
  "material": "Cotton",
  "color": "Blue"
}
```

## 9.4.2 Horizontal Scalability

Another critical characteristic is horizontal scalability. Relational databases traditionally rely on vertical scaling, or "scaling up," which involves purchasing an increasingly expensive, high-end server with more RAM and CPU power to handle growth. In contrast, NoSQL databases are designed from the ground up to scale horizontally, or "scale out," by simply adding more servers to a distributed cluster.

This architecture provides linear scalability, meaning that adding more nodes increases capacity and throughput proportionally. It is also highly cost-effective, as scaling with standard commodity hardware is vastly more economical than relying on specialized enterprise mainframes. Furthermore, it enables elastic scaling. Modern businesses, such as streaming platforms or online retailers during Black Friday, can elastically increase or decrease their database capacity based on sudden traffic demands to prevent application crashes.

## 9.4.3 High Performance

By optimizing for specific data models and access patterns, NoSQL databases can deliver exceptional, low-latency performance that traditional databases often struggle to match at scale. This performance boost is achieved through several operational mechanisms. First, systems like Redis are designed for in-memory operations, storing data entirely in RAM to deliver microsecond-level response times. Second, NoSQL systems feature drastically reduced operational overhead. By utilizing simpler data models, they eliminate the need for resource-intensive SQL join operations and complex query parsing. Finally, many NoSQL databases are deeply optimized for high-throughput write operations. In the real world, this immense performance is leveraged for high-speed financial transactions, live gaming leaderboards, real-time analytics, and managing the relentless flood of data generated by modern IoT devices.

### 9.4.4 High Availability

For enterprises, unexpected downtime translates to lost revenue and a damaged reputation. Consequently, NoSQL systems prioritize high availability through resilient design patterns. They utilize built-in replication, automatically copying data across multiple nodes so that no single piece of critical information exists in just one place. This distributed architecture intentionally eliminates any single point of failure within the database infrastructure. If a server unexpectedly crashes or undergoes routine maintenance, the system relies on automatic failover mechanisms to seamlessly redirect network traffic. Global applications like ride-sharing services and media streaming giants rely heavily on this high availability, ensuring their platforms continue operating smoothly even if an entire regional data center experiences a massive outage.

### 9.4.5 Distributed Architecture

Building closely upon availability, NoSQL databases embrace network distribution as a core architectural principle. Rather than centralizing data in one massive repository, these systems utilize automated data partitioning -- often referred to as sharding -- to distribute information evenly across multiple nodes. This framework also allows for immense geographic distribution, where data can be replicated to multiple data centers worldwide.

For global applications, this means European users access data from European servers, while Asian users connect to local data centers, drastically reducing response latency. Furthermore, these distributed networks are built with network partition tolerance, guaranteeing that systems continue functioning correctly and safely even when severe networking issues temporarily isolate certain nodes from the rest of the cluster.

### 9.4.6 Diverse Data Models

Finally, unlike the one-size-fits-all approach of the traditional relational model, the NoSQL ecosystem offers specialized, diverse data models tailored to specific application use cases. Document stores, such as

MongoDB and CouchDB, store data as flexible, JSON-like documents, making them ideal for content management systems and evolving user profiles. Key-value stores, including Redis and Amazon DynamoDB, utilize simple key-value pairs to deliver blazing-fast lookups for caching, user session management, and online shopping carts. Column-family stores, like Apache Cassandra and HBase, organize data by columns rather than rows, providing the perfect architecture for analytical workloads and heavy telemetry logging. Lastly, Graph databases, such as Neo4j and Amazon Neptune, represent data as interconnected networks of relationships, offering unparalleled efficiency for building complex social networks, powerful recommendation engines, and sophisticated fraud detection systems.

Review Question 9.13
In a document-oriented database, what is possible within a single collection?
a. Only identical record structures
b. Documents with different structures
c. Tables with foreign keys
d. Records without unique IDs

Review Question 9.14
What does horizontal scalability in NoSQL systems primarily involve?
a. Increasing RAM in one server
b. Adding more servers to a cluster
c. Reducing database size
d. Replacing SQL with APIs

Review Question 9.15
Why are systems like Redis able to achieve very low latency?
a. They rely on disk-only storage
b. They use complex joins
c. They store data in memory
d. They avoid replication

Review Question 9.16
How do NoSQL databases improve availability?
a. By storing all data on one server
b. By eliminating write operations
c. By using replication and failover
d. By preventing network partitions

Review Question 9.17
What is the purpose of sharding in distributed NoSQL systems?
a. To normalize data
b. To encrypt transactions
c. To divide data across nodes
d. To enforce schema rules

Review Question 9.18
Which type of NoSQL database is best suited for analyzing relationships in social networks?
a. Column-family store
b. Graph database
c. Key-value store
d. Document store

## 9.5 NoSQL vs SQL: A Comparative Analysis

Understanding when to use NoSQL versus SQL requires examining their fundamental differences across several dimensions. While both paradigms effectively store and manage data, they are engineered to solve entirely different sets of problems in modern application development.

### 9.5.1 Data Model

The most pronounced difference lies in how data is structured and stored. SQL databases strictly organize data into tables containing rows and columns. Each row represents a distinct entity, and columns represent attributes, with relationships established definitively through foreign keys. This relational model is highly effective for interconnected data, such as an e-commerce platform linking customers, orders, and products. Conversely, NoSQL employs varied, specialized data models depending on the system type. Document databases use nested, JSON-like structures; key-value stores use simple pairs; column stores organize data by columns for analytics; and graph databases use nodes and edges to map complex relationships.

### 9.5.2 Schema

SQL databases mandate a predefined, rigid schema. Developers must meticulously define table structures, column data types, and relationships before inserting a single piece of data. Modifying this structure later requires `ALTER TABLE` statements and complex migrations, which can be disruptive to live applications. NoSQL, on the other hand, champions flexible, dynamic schemas. You can insert data with varying structures seamlessly, allowing fields to be added or removed on the fly. In real-world Agile environments, this means a startup can rapidly iterate on a product feature without waiting for database administrators to approve and implement schema changes.

### 9.5.3 Scaling

When an application's user base grows, the database must scale to meet demand. SQL databases primarily scale vertically, which means upgrading the existing hardware by adding more CPU, RAM, or SSD capacity to a single server. While horizontal scaling, or sharding, is possible in SQL, it is notoriously complex and often heavily application-specific. NoSQL databases are designed natively for horizontal scaling. Adding nodes to a distributed cluster is straightforward, and the system automatically partitions and distributes data across commodity servers. This makes NoSQL highly cost-effective and resilient for massive, global-scale applications dealing with massive datasets.

### 9.5.4 Query Language

SQL databases utilize Structured Query Language (SQL), an immensely powerful, declarative, and universally standardized language. SQL is unrivaled for executing complex queries, performing multi-table joins, and computing deep analytical aggregations. In contrast, NoSQL query capabilities vary wildly by database type. While some offer SQL-like languages, most rely on native programming APIs or proprietary, JSON-based query languages. Because NoSQL data is often pre-aggregated or denormalized, join operations are typically limited, discouraged, or entirely absent, trading relational depth for blazing-fast data retrieval.

### 9.5.5 Transactions

For applications where data accuracy is non-negotiable, such as financial banking systems, SQL provides robust ACID (Atomicity, Consistency, Isolation, Durability) transactions. This guarantees data integrity even during complex, multi-table operations. Historically, NoSQL systems sacrificed ACID guarantees in favor of relaxed transaction models to achieve unparalleled availability and performance at scale. However, the gap is closing; modern NoSQL databases now support ACID transactions for specific operations, offering developers a hybrid middle ground for applications that need both scale and reliability.

### 9.5.6 Consistency

Consistency models dictate what users see when accessing data simultaneously. SQL databases guarantee strong consistency: once a transaction commits, all clients querying the database will see the exact same data at the exact same time. NoSQL often employs eventual consistency, prioritizing speed and availability. In distributed NoSQL setups, replicas may temporarily show slightly different, outdated data, but they will eventually converge to the same state. This is acceptable for applications like social media feeds, where a slightly delayed "like" count is harmless, but it would be disastrous for calculating a live bank balance.

### 9.5.7 Use Cases

Choosing the right database hinges entirely on the project's use case. SQL is the definitive choice for applications requiring strict data integrity (like financial software and inventory management), complex query requirements with multiple joins, structured business intelligence reporting, and scenarios where immediate data consistency is critical. NoSQL is ideal for large-scale, high-throughput applications handling massive volumes of unstructured or semi-structured data. Real-world examples include high-speed logging for Internet of Things (IoT) devices, real-time gaming, globally distributed mobile apps, and environments where data models evolve rapidly.

### 9.5.8 Performance Comparison

In terms of performance, SQL excels at complex analytical queries involving multiple related tables. However, it can encounter severe bottlenecks and slow down significantly when dealing with extremely large datasets or massive write volumes, as the overhead of maintaining strong consistency takes a toll. NoSQL delivers exceptional, low-latency performance for simple queries like key lookups and single-document retrieval. It handles high-velocity write volumes with efficiency. Yet, because of its limited join support, retrieving highly relational data in NoSQL often requires executing multiple application-level queries.

### 9.5.9 Development Experience

Finally, the development experience differs significantly. SQL boasts a deeply mature ecosystem with decades of extensive tools, frameworks, and community support. However, it presents a steeper learning curve regarding complex normalization, often requiring Object-Relational Mapping (ORM) tools to bridge the impedance mismatch between relational tables and object-oriented code. NoSQL is widely considered highly developer-friendly. Its data models map naturally and directly to modern programming language objects. This enables faster initial development and prototyping, though developers must be mindful that tooling and standardization in the NoSQL space are sometimes less mature than their SQL counterparts.

Review Question 9.19
How do SQL databases typically scale when demand increases?
a. By adding more nodes automatically
b. By splitting data into documents
c. By upgrading a single server
d. By eliminating joins

Review Question 9.20
Why are join operations often limited in NoSQL systems?
a. Because SQL is unsupported
b. Because data is usually denormalized
c. Because hardware is weaker

d. Because transactions are disabled

Review Question 9.21
What is a major advantage of SQL transactions in financial systems?
a. They reduce hardware costs
b. They eliminate replication
c. They guarantee ACID properties
d. They support eventual consistency

Review Question 9.22
What does eventual consistency in NoSQL systems imply?
a. Data is permanently inconsistent
b. All users always see identical data instantly
c. Updates may appear slightly delayed across replicas
d. Transactions cannot be committed

Review Question 9.23
Which scenario is best suited for NoSQL rather than SQL?
a. Banking account balance calculations
b. Structured financial reporting
c. Multi-table relational analytics
d. High-speed IoT logging

Review Question 9.24
Why might developers find NoSQL easier for early-stage prototyping?
a. It eliminates distributed systems
b. Its data models map naturally to objects
c. It guarantees strong consistency
d. It requires normalization

## 9.6 The CAP Theorem

The CAP theorem is a foundational principle for anyone designing, building, or managing distributed database systems. Proposed initially by computer scientist Eric Brewer in 2000 and formally proven by MIT professors Seth Gilbert and Nancy Lynch in 2002, this theorem defines the absolute physical and logical limits of distributed data stores (Gilbert & Lynch, 2012). As organizations move away from single-server relational databases toward globally distributed NoSQL architectures, understanding the CAP theorem becomes essential for making informed architectural compromises.

### 9.6.1 Understanding the Three Properties

The theorem states that a distributed data store can provide at most two of three specific guarantees simultaneously: Consistency, Availability, and Partition Tolerance. To grasp the theorem's implications, we must first clearly define these three properties.

Consistency (C) in the context of the CAP theorem means that every read from the database receives the most recent write or an error. Regardless of which specific node in a distributed cluster a client connects to, they will all see the exact same data at the exact same time. For this to happen, when data is written to one node, it must be immediately and synchronously forwarded or replicated to all other nodes before the database confirms the write was successful.

Availability (A) guarantees that every request receives a non-error response. The system continues to operate and respond to client requests even if some nodes within the cluster are down, undergoing maintenance, or unreachable. However, this guarantee comes without the promise that the response contains the absolute most recent write.

Finally, Partition Tolerance (P) means the system continues to operate despite arbitrary message loss or network failures between nodes. In a distributed system, a "partition" occurs when a network connection breaks, leaving nodes unable to communicate with one another. A partition-tolerant system survives this network split and keeps functioning.

## 9.6.2 The Trade-off

When first learning the CAP theorem, it is tempting to view it as a simple "choose any two" menu. However, in practical distributed systems, network partitions are an absolute inevitability. Hardware fails, routers crash, cables are accidentally cut, and entire data centers can become isolated due to severe weather. Because network failures cannot be magically prevented, Partition Tolerance (P) is not optional -- it is a mandatory requirement for any distributed system. Therefore, the practical reality of the CAP theorem is that when a network partition occurs, engineers must make a definitive choice between preserving Consistency or preserving Availability.

## 9.6.3 CA Systems (Consistency + Availability)

A CA system attempts to provide both consistency and availability but cannot physically tolerate network partitions. Because network partitions are unavoidable in distributed environments, true CA systems are essentially non-distributed, single-node databases. A traditional, single-server SQL database sitting in a local server room falls perfectly into this category. It is highly available and strictly consistent, but the moment the network cable to that single server is cut, the entire system is inaccessible. In the realm of globally distributed NoSQL networks, aiming for a CA architecture simply does not make practical sense.

### 9.6.4 CP Systems (Consistency + Partition Tolerance)

When a system chooses Consistency and Partition Tolerance, it intentionally sacrifices Availability during network failures. If a network split occurs, a CP system will protect data accuracy at all costs. It may actively reject read and write requests, return error messages, or completely shut down isolated nodes until the network is fully restored and synchronized.

Practical examples of CP systems include MongoDB (when configured with majority read/write concerns), HBase, and Redis in specific clustering setups. These systems are typically chosen for use cases where returning stale or incorrect data is catastrophic. Consider a financial banking application or a strict inventory management system. If a network partition isolates an ATM from the central bank servers, the system cannot verify the user's true balance. In this CP scenario, it is infinitely better to reject the withdrawal request (sacrificing availability) than to risk dispensing funds the user does not actually have (sacrificing consistency).

### 9.6.5 AP Systems (Availability + Partition Tolerance)

Conversely, AP systems prioritize Availability and Partition Tolerance, accepting "eventual consistency" as a trade-off. During a network partition, an AP system remains highly available, cheerfully accepting reads and writes on whatever nodes the user can reach. The system allows different nodes to temporarily hold conflicting or outdated data. Once the network partition is resolved, the database employs background protocols to eventually reconcile differences and synchronize the data.

Prominent AP systems include Cassandra, Amazon DynamoDB, CouchDB, and Riak. These databases are the backbone of applications where uptime is paramount and slight data delays are harmless. A classic example is a social media platform. If a user in Tokyo "likes" a photograph, it is perfectly acceptable if a user in New York doesn't see that updated like count for a few seconds. The application prioritizes staying online and interactive for all users globally, even if the data state is temporarily fragmented.

### 9.6.6 Beyond the Basics

Years after his original proposition, Eric Brewer clarified that the CAP theorem is not as rigidly binary as the initial "choose two" interpretation implies (Brewer, 2012). First, network partitions are relatively rare in modern infrastructure. During normal operations -- when there is no partition -- a well-designed system can effectively provide both consistency and availability.

Furthermore, modern databases offer highly tunable trade-offs. Systems like Cassandra allow developers to tune the balance per query. A critical financial operation in an app might be coded to demand strict consistency, while loading a user's avatar image favors availability. Finally, computer scientists introduced the PACELC theorem as a practical extension to CAP. PACELC states that in the case of a Partition, a system must choose between Availability and Consistency; Else (when the system is running normally without partitions), the system must choose between Latency and Consistency. This advanced framework better reflects the day-to-day reality of database engineering, where minimizing response time (latency) often requires sacrificing perfect, instant data synchronization.

Review Question 9.25
According to the CAP theorem, a distributed system can guarantee at most how many of the three properties simultaneously?
a. One
b. Two
c. All three
d. None

Review Question 9.26
What does Consistency mean in the CAP context?
a. Every read returns the latest write or an error
b. Every node stores different data
c. Writes are processed asynchronously
d. The system never fails

Review Question 9.27
What typically happens in a CP system during a network partition?
a. The system returns outdated data
b. The system rejects some requests
c. The system ignores the partition
d. The system increases latency

Review Question 9.28
What key clarification did Eric Brewer later provide about CAP?
a. Partitions never occur
b. Systems must always sacrifice availability
c. The trade-offs are not strictly binary
d. Consistency is optional

Review Question 9.29
According to the PACELC theorem, what trade-off exists when there is no partition?
a. Latency versus Consistency

b. Availability versus Storage
c. Consistency versus Security
d. Partition Tolerance versus Durability

## 9.7 ACID vs BASE Consistency Models

As we dive deeper into distributed systems, we encounter two competing consistency models that represent fundamentally different philosophies for managing data: ACID and BASE. Choosing between these models is not merely a technical decision; it dictates how your application behaves under heavy load, how it responds to network failures, and what kind of user experience it ultimately delivers.

### 9.7.1 The ACID Properties

ACID has been the gold standard for traditional relational databases since their inception. The acronym represents a set of four rigid properties designed to guarantee the reliable processing of database transactions, even in the event of severe system crashes or power failures. The first property, *Atomicity*, dictates that all operations within a transaction must succeed or fail together as a single, indivisible unit. There is strictly no partial completion. For example, when transferring money between two bank accounts, the database must process both the debit from the sender and the credit to the receiver. If the system crashes after the debit but before the credit, atomicity ensures the entire transaction is rolled back, leaving the database completely unchanged.

The second property, *Consistency*, ensures that a transaction only brings the database from one valid state to another. It maintains all predefined rules, constraints, cascades, and triggers. If a financial database enforces a strict rule that checking account balances cannot be negative, consistency guarantees that no transaction can ever leave an account with a negative balance, not even temporarily during processing.

The third pillar is *Isolation*. In the real world, thousands of users access databases simultaneously. Isolation ensures that concurrent transactions execute completely independently without interfering with each other, producing the exact same result as if the transactions had been executed sequentially. If two customers are simultaneously trying to purchase the last concert ticket in stock, isolation prevents a race condition, ensuring only one purchase succeeds while the other is rejected.

Finally, *Durability* guarantees that once a transaction successfully commits, the changes persist permanently. Even if the server suffers a catastrophic power outage a millisecond after confirming the commit, the committed data is safely written to non-volatile storage (often utilizing mechanisms like Write-Ahead Logging) and will survive the crash.

### 9.7.2 The BASE Properties

In contrast to the strictness of SQL, NoSQL databases often follow the BASE model. Born out of the massive scalability requirements of Web 2.0 and guided by the realities of the CAP theorem, BASE intentionally prioritizes high availability and partition tolerance over strict, immediate consistency.

The first property, *Basically Available*, means the system guarantees availability for querying and updating most of the time. Even if specific nodes or servers experience catastrophic failures, the database remains online to serve requests, though the response it provides might not reflect the absolute latest write. A practical example is a massive social media application; the platform remains accessible for browsing feeds and posting updates even if a regional data center goes offline.

The second property is *Soft State*. Unlike ACID systems where the state only changes when a transaction occurs, the state of a BASE system may change over time without any external input. Because the system doesn't enforce immediate, synchronous consistency across all global replicas, data is continuously replicating in the background. If you view a "like" count on a viral post, that number might fluctuate and show different values to different users across the globe for a short period as updates passively ripple through the distributed network.

The final property is *Eventual Consistency*. This is the core promise of the BASE model: given enough time without new updates, all replicas will eventually converge to the exact same state. When you update your profile picture on a global platform, users in Europe might see the old picture for a few minutes while users in Asia see the new one. However, the system guarantees that eventually, once background replication completes, all users worldwide will see the updated image.

### 9.7.3 Comparing ACID and BASE

When comparing these two paradigms side-by-side, the trade-offs become clear. Regarding consistency guarantees, ACID provides immediate, strict accuracy, whereas BASE offers eventual consistency over an undefined period. This directly impacts their availability priorities: an ACID system will gladly sacrifice availability (rejecting your request or locking the database) to maintain perfect consistency, whereas a BASE system prioritizes keeping the application highly available, even if it means serving slightly outdated data.

Performance characteristics also differ heavily. ACID databases often suffer from higher latency due to the immense coordination overhead required to lock rows and synchronize nodes across a network. BASE models, freed from these heavy locking mechanisms, generally offer vastly superior write performance and horizontal scalability. Consequently, their use cases align differently. ACID is mandatory for critical data like financial ledgers, billing systems, and medical records. BASE shines in handling user-generated content, massive telemetry logging, social interactions, and real-time analytics.

Finally, they shift complexity to different areas. ACID makes reasoning about the data state remarkably simple for developers because the database is always correct. BASE shifts that burden; developers must write complex application logic to handle potential data conflicts, out-of-order events, and temporary inconsistencies.

## 9.7.4 The Convergence of Models

In modern software engineering, the rigid distinction between ACID and BASE has significantly blurred. We are no longer strictly bound to choosing one extreme or the other. Many modern NoSQL databases now offer tunable consistency, allowing developers to request stronger, ACID-like consistency for specific, high-value queries while leaving the rest of the application eventually consistent. Furthermore, NoSQL giants like MongoDB introduced multi-document ACID transactions starting in version 4.0, bridging a massive historical gap.

Simultaneously, a new category called "Distributed SQL" (featuring databases like Google Spanner and CockroachDB) has emerged, specifically engineered to provide robust ACID guarantees across globally distributed, horizontal architectures. Today, the most effective approach is often a hybrid microservices architecture, utilizing polyglot persistence -- where an application seamlessly uses a strictly ACID relational database for its billing service, while simultaneously leveraging a blazing-fast BASE NoSQL database for its product recommendation engine.

Review Question 9.30
What does Atomicity in ACID guarantee?
a. Transactions are processed faster under heavy load
b. All operations in a transaction succeed or fail together
c. The database is always available
d. Data is replicated across all servers

Review Question 9.31
Which ACID property ensures that the database moves only between valid states?
a. Isolation
b. Durability
c. Consistency
d. Atomicity

Review Question 9.32
Which ACID property prevents race conditions when two users attempt the same action simultaneously?
a. Durability
b. Isolation
c. Consistency
d. Atomicity

Review Question 9.33
What does Durability ensure after a transaction commits?
a. The transaction can be reversed manually
b. The data will eventually replicate
c. The data persists even after a crash
d. The database remains online

Review Question 9.34
Which property is part of the BASE model?
a. Atomic State
b. Strong Isolation
c. Eventual Consistency
d. Deterministic Execution

Review Question 9.35
What does "Soft State" mean in the BASE model?
a. Data changes only after user transactions
b. System state may change over time without new input
c. The system never crashes
d. Transactions are permanently logged

Review Question 9.36
How does BASE differ from ACID in terms of availability?
a. BASE sacrifices availability for strict consistency
b. BASE prioritizes availability even if data is outdated
c. BASE eliminates replication
d. BASE guarantees zero latency

Review Question 9.37
Why do ACID systems often experience higher latency?
a. They avoid data validation
b. They minimize storage usage
c. They require heavy coordination and locking
d. They reject concurrent transactions

Review Question 9.38
Which type of applications typically require ACID guarantees?
a. Social media "like" counters
b. Telemetry logging systems
c. Financial ledgers
d. Product recommendation engines

## 9.8 Chapter Summary

This chapter introduces NoSQL databases, designed for internet-scale applications prioritizing scalability and flexibility over traditional guarantees. Key concepts include flexible schemas, horizontal scalability via commodity hardware, and the CAP theorem's consistency-availability trade-offs. The ACID vs. BASE distinction highlights differing consistency philosophies. Ultimately, choose the right tool: neither SQL nor NoSQL is universally superior; each excels in different scenarios.

## 9.9 Discussion Questions

Discussion 9.1
Some people claim that the name "NoSQL" is misleading. Do you agree? Why or why not?

Discussion 9.2
Compare ACID and BASE consistency models. When would you prefer each?

Discussion 9.3
What are the four main types of NoSQL databases? Provide an example use case for each.

## 9.10 References

Brewer, E. (2012). CAP twelve years later: How the" rules" have changed. *Computer*, *45*(2), 23-29.
Chang, F., Dean, J., Ghemawat, S., Hsieh, W. C., Wallach, D. A., Burrows, M., ... & Gruber, R. E. (2008). Bigtable: A distributed storage system for structured data. ACM Transactions on Computer Systems (TOCS), 26(2), 1-26.
DeCandia, G., Hastorun, D., Jampani, M., Kakulapati, G., Lakshman, A., Pilchin, A., ... & Vogels, W. (2007). Dynamo: Amazon's highly available key-value store. ACM SIGOPS operating systems review, 41(6), 205-220.
Gilbert, S., & Lynch, N. (2012). Perspectives on the CAP Theorem. Computer, 45(2), 30-36.

## 9.11 Solutions to the Review Questions

9.1 C; 9.2 B; 9.3 D; 9.4 C; 9.5 B; 9.6 C; 9.7 B; 9.8 C; 9.9 B; 9.10 B; 9.11 C; 9.12 B; 9.13 B; 9.14 B; 9.15 C; 9.16 C; 9.17 C; 9.18 B; 9.19 C; 9.20 B; 9.21 C; 9.22 C; 9.23 D; 9.24 B; 9.25 B; 9.26 A; 9.27 B; 9.28 C; 9.29 A; 9.30 B; 9.31 C; 9.32 B; 9.33 C; 9.34 C; 9.35 B; 9.36 B; 9.37 C; 9.38 C;

# Chapter 10: NoSQL Database Types

## Chapter Learning Objectives

10.1 Explain the four main types of NoSQL databases and their characteristics
10.2 Identify appropriate use cases for each NoSQL database type
10.3 Compare the strengths and trade-offs of different NoSQL database types

## 10.1 Introduction to NoSQL Database Categories

As our previous survey, NoSQL databases are not a single, monolithic technology. Instead, "NoSQL" encompasses a rich, diverse family of distributed database systems, with each category meticulously optimized for specific data models and distinct access patterns. Because NoSQL abandons the one-size-fits-all relational structure, understanding these different underlying architectures is crucial for selecting the right database to meet your application's unique performance and scaling needs.

In this chapter, we will dive deeper into the four primary categories that dominate the NoSQL landscape. First, Document-Oriented Databases store data as flexible, semi-structured documents, typically using JSON or BSON formats. Because these nested documents map naturally to object-oriented programming structures, they are highly developer-friendly. They excel in scenarios requiring agile, evolving schemas, such as content management systems, complex e-commerce product catalogs, and highly variable user profiles.

Second, Key-Value Stores represent the simplest yet arguably the most powerful data model in terms of raw, unadulterated performance. They store data as a massive dictionary of opaque values retrieved by a single, unique key. By stripping away query complexity and often operating entirely in-memory, key-value stores deliver predictable, microsecond-level latency. They are the industry standard for high-speed caching, web session management, and storing transient data like live online shopping carts.

Third, Column-Family Stores organize data into wide columns rather than traditional rows. Unlike relational databases, these columns are sparse and grouped into "families," allowing the system to handle massive volumes of distributed data with incredible write efficiency. They are engineered natively for horizontal scale across multiple servers and are heavily utilized for write-intensive workloads like massive IoT telemetry gathering, event logging, and analyzing vast amounts of time-series data.

Finally, Graph Databases model data as interconnected networks consisting of nodes (the entities) and edges (the relationships between them). Rather than relying on expensive, compute-heavy SQL joins to connect disparate tables, graph databases treat the relationships themselves as first-class, queried citizens. This makes them uniquely powerful for rapidly traversing highly connected data, making them indispensable for building modern social networks, complex product recommendation engines, and real-time fraud detection systems.

In practice, these four categories are rarely mutually exclusive. Modern enterprise applications frequently use multiple NoSQL databases in combination alongside traditional SQL systems -- a highly effective architectural practice known as polyglot persistence. For example, a modern global e-commerce platform might use a Document store to house its vast product catalog, a Key-Value store to rapidly cache user sessions, a Graph database to power its "customers also bought" recommendation engine, and a robust SQL database to securely process the final financial checkout.

In the following sections, let's explore each of these four NoSQL categories in greater depth, unpacking their specific architectures, technical limitations, and practical implementations.

Review Question 10.1
Which NoSQL category stores data as flexible JSON or BSON-like documents?
a. Column-Family Stores
b. Graph Databases
c. Document-Oriented Databases
d. Key-Value Stores

Review Question 10.2
Which NoSQL model is best known for microsecond-level latency and high-speed caching?
a. Graph Databases
b. Key-Value Stores
c. Column-Family Stores
d. Document Databases

Review Question 10.3
Which type of NoSQL database is most suitable for time-series data and IoT telemetry workloads?
a. Column-Family Stores
b. Graph Databases
c. Document Databases
d. Key-Value Stores

Review Question 10.4
Why are Graph Databases particularly powerful for recommendation engines?

a. They eliminate the need for indexing
b. They enforce strict relational schemas
c. They treat relationships as first-class entities
d. They store only structured tables

## 10.2 Document-Oriented Databases

Instead of forcing data into rigid rows and columns, document-oriented databases store information in self-contained documents. If you think of a relational database as a highly organized spreadsheet, a document database is more like a digital filing cabinet. You can toss a highly detailed tax return into one folder, and a simple handwritten sticky note into the next. Both live in the same drawer, but they have completely different structures. In the digital world, these documents are typically formatted similarly to JSON (JavaScript Object Notation) or XML. Each document is a complete, self-contained unit of data that can have a different structure from other documents stored right next to it in the same collection.

### 10.2.1 Core Structure and Concepts

To grasp how document databases operate, it helps to map their core concepts to the relational database terms you already know. The foundation of this system is the *document* itself. A document is a complex data structure that can contain primitive values (like text and numbers), arrays (lists of items), and even nested objects (documents within documents). Developers love this approach because these documents usually take the form of JSON or BSON (Binary JSON). In modern programming languages like Python, JavaScript, or C#, data is already manipulated as "objects" in the code. Document databases allow developers to save these objects directly to the database without having to chop them up and translate them into multiple relational tables -- a common headache known in the industry as the "object-relational impedance mismatch."

Documents are organized into *collections*. You can think of a collection as roughly analogous to a table in a relational database, but with a crucial twist: collections do not enforce a fixed schema. In a SQL database, if your "Users" table has columns for First Name, Last Name, and Age, every single record must follow that blueprint. In a document database collection, one document might contain just a username and an email address, while the very next document in the same collection might contain a username, a physical address, a list of favorite hobbies, and a nested history of recent purchases.

Inside these documents are *fields*, which consist of field-value pairs. Fields are similar to columns in a relational table, but because they are defined dynamically within each individual document rather than strictly at the collection level, you have ultimate flexibility. Finally, just like a primary key in a SQL table, every document must have a unique *identifier*. This is typically a field automatically named `_id`, which serves as the document's primary key and ensures that no matter how messy or diverse the data gets, every single document can be uniquely located and retrieved.

## 10.2.2 MongoDB: The Leading Document Database

When discussing document databases in the real world, the conversation almost always centers on MongoDB. MongoDB is far and away the most popular document-oriented database on the market today. It is beloved by developers for its intuitive approach to data modeling and its incredibly rich feature set. While we use JSON as a mental model, MongoDB actually stores data under the hood in BSON (Binary JSON). This is a highly optimized, binary representation of JSON that extends the format to include specific data types that standard JSON lacks, such as native dates, floating-point numbers, and binary data.

To understand MongoDB's power, we need to look at its architecture, which is built from the ground up to handle massive scale. At the highest level, MongoDB organizes data into *databases*, similar to how a SQL server manages multiple database instances. Each database then holds multiple *collections*, which, as we discussed, act as flexible containers for *documents*. A single document in MongoDB can hold a massive amount of information -- up to 16MB in size. To put that in perspective, a 16MB text document could hold the entire text of the Harry Potter series with room to spare.

Of course, storing data is only half the battle; retrieving it quickly is just as important. Like relational databases, MongoDB utilizes *indexes* to optimize query performance. Instead of scanning every single document in a collection to find a specific user, an index acts like a book's glossary. MongoDB supports standard single-field indexes, compound indexes, and even specialized indexes like geospatial indexes for location-based apps (like finding the nearest rideshare driver) and text indexes for search engines.

Where MongoDB truly steps away from traditional relational systems is in its approach to high availability and scaling. In the internet era, a database going down means a company loses money every second. MongoDB solves this with *Replica Sets*. A replica set is a cluster of MongoDB servers that all maintain the exact same dataset. There is one "Primary" node that handles all the active reads and writes, and multiple "Secondary" nodes that constantly copy the data. If the server hosting the primary node suddenly catches fire or loses power, the secondary nodes instantly hold an automated "election" to promote a new primary node. The application stays online, and the users never know a catastrophic hardware failure just occurred.

Furthermore, as a company grows from thousands of users to millions, a single database server -- no matter how powerful -- will eventually run out of RAM and storage. Relational databases traditionally scale "vertically," meaning you have to buy a more expensive, beefier server. MongoDB excels at horizontal scaling through a process called Sharding. Sharding automatically distributes your data across multiple different servers. Imagine an address book so large it breaks the binding; sharding splits it up, putting last names A-M on server one, and N-Z on server two. By partitioning data based on a "shard key," MongoDB can scale to hold hundreds of terabytes of data across dozens of cheap, standard servers.

## 10.2.3 Key Features and Capabilities

MongoDB's popularity isn't just due to its architecture; its feature set fundamentally changes how teams build software. The most immediate benefit is the *flexible schema.* In agile software development, applications change rapidly. If an engineering team wants to add a new "loyalty points" feature to user profiles, doing so in a heavily populated relational database might require a massive migration script that locks the database and causes hours of downtime. In MongoDB, the application simply starts saving the "loyalty points" field into new documents. The database doesn't complain, and there is zero downtime.

To retrieve this data, MongoDB uses a *rich query language.* Instead of writing complex SQL `SELECT` statements, developers pass JSON-like query objects. It supports everything you'd expect: exact matches, range queries (e.g., price greater than $50), regular expressions, and deep searches into nested arrays. When you need to do heavy data analysis -- like calculating the average sales per region over the last month -- MongoDB offers the *Aggregation Framework.* This works like an assembly line for data. Documents pass through a "pipeline" of stages, where they can be filtered, grouped, reshaped, and summarized before the final result is returned to the user.

For edge cases that exceed normal limits, MongoDB has built-in solutions. If you need to store user-uploaded videos or massive high-resolution images that exceed the 16MB document limit, MongoDB provides *GridFS.* GridFS automatically chops large files into smaller chunks, stores them as separate documents, and seamlessly reassembles them when you request the file. Additionally, while early NoSQL databases were criticized for sacrificing data safety for speed, modern MongoDB supports multi-document ACID transactions. This means if you are transferring money from Account A to Account B, and the database crashes halfway through, MongoDB guarantees that either the entire transaction succeeds, or the whole thing is canceled. You will never be left with half-updated, corrupted data.

### 10.2.4 A Practical Data Model Example

To bring this all together, let's look at how data is represented in a document database compared to a relational one. Consider a modern e-commerce application storing a product catalog. In the relational databases you studied in chapters 1 through 8, managing a single product would likely require five or six different tables: one for the core product info, one for technical specifications, a junction table for search tags, another table for user reviews, and another for warehouse inventory. Pulling that data together would require complex, resource-heavy `JOIN` statements.

In MongoDB, all of that information can be stored in a single, elegantly structured document:

```
{
  "_id": ObjectId("507f1f77bcf86cd799439011"),
  "name": "Professional Camera",
  "category": "Electronics",
  "price": 1299.99,
  "currency": "USD",
  "inStock": true,
  "specifications": {
    "sensor": "Full Frame",
    "resolution": "45.7 MP",
    "iso_range": [100, 102400],
    "video": "8K at 30fps"
  },
  "tags": ["photography", "professional", "mirrorless"],
  "reviews": [
    {
      "user": "photo_enthusiast",
      "rating": 5,
      "comment": "Exceptional image quality",
      "date": ISODate("2024-11-15T10:30:00Z")
    },
    {
      "user": "video_creator",
      "rating": 4,
      "comment": "Great for video work",
      "date": ISODate("2024-11-20T14:22:00Z")
    }
  ],
  "inventory": {
    "warehouse_A": 15,
    "warehouse_B": 23,
    "warehouse_C": 8
  },
  "created_at": ISODate("2024-10-01T09:00:00Z"),
  "updated_at": ISODate("2024-12-10T16:45:00Z")
}
```

Notice how intuitive this is. The document uses an embedded object for the `specifications` and `inventory`. It uses simple arrays to hold strings for the `tags`. Most impressively, it uses an array of embedded documents to hold the `reviews`. When the application queries the database for this camera, the database performs a single read operation and returns the entire, fully-formed object. The application doesn't have to piece anything together.

## 10.2.5 Use Cases for Document Databases

Because of this speed and flexibility, document databases excel in several massive industries. They are the backbone of modern Content Management Systems (CMS). Blogs, news sites, and wikis need flexible schemas because a text-based article requires entirely different data fields than a photo gallery or a podcast episode. A document database easily stores all of these distinct content types in a single "Posts" collection.

Similarly, E-commerce Catalogs thrive on this architecture. A store selling both t-shirts and televisions would struggle with a rigid SQL database, as shirts need fields for "size" and "fabric," while TVs need "screen resolution" and "refresh rate." Document models allow each product document to have its own unique set of attributes without cluttering the database with hundreds of empty, unused columns.

They are also the standard for User Profiles in social networks and gaming platforms, where users might unlock different achievements, link different third-party social accounts, or choose varying privacy settings over time. For Real-time Analytics and IoT (Internet of Things) Data Collection, document databases are unmatched. Smart thermostats, fitness trackers, and factory sensors stream massive amounts of differently formatted data every second. Document databases can ingest these event logs continuously without rigid schemas blocking the flow, allowing data scientists to analyze the information in real time. Finally, because the JSON-like format maps so naturally to the code used in iOS and Android development, document databases greatly simplify back-end architecture for Mobile Applications.

Review Question 10.5
Which format is most commonly associated with document databases?
a. CSV
b. YAML
c. JSON
d. SQL

Review Question 10.6
What problem do document databases help eliminate for developers?

a. Network latency
b. Horizontal scaling
c. Object-relational impedance mismatch
d. Index fragmentation

Review Question 10.7
In a document database, collections differ from SQL tables because they:
a. Do not allow indexing
b. Enforce strict schemas
c. Require primary keys
d. Do not enforce fixed schemas

Review Question 10.8
What format does MongoDB use internally to store data?
a. Plain text JSON
b. XML
c. BSON
d. CSV

Review Question 10.9
What is the purpose of an index in MongoDB?
a. To split data across servers
b. To improve query performance
c. To enforce schema rules
d. To compress documents

Review Question 10.10
In a replica set, which node handles active reads and writes?
a. Secondary node
b. Arbiter node
c. Primary node
d. Shard node

Review Question 10.11
What process allows MongoDB to scale horizontally?
a. Replication
b. Indexing
c. Vertical partitioning
d. Sharding

Review Question 10.12
What does the Aggregation Framework in MongoDB do?
a. Encrypts documents
b. Caches frequently used queries
c. Processes data through a pipeline for analysis
d. Splits large files into chunks

Review Question 10.13
What feature allows MongoDB to store files larger than 16MB?
a. Replica Sets

b. GridFS
c. BSON compression
d. Compound indexes

Review Question 10.14
Why are document databases ideal for e-commerce catalogs?
a. They require complex JOIN queries
b. They enforce strict column consistency
c. They allow each product to have different attributes
d. They prevent nested data structures

Review Question 10.15
What is a key advantage of storing related product data in a single document?
a. Reduced storage cost
b. Elimination of all indexing
c. Automatic schema enforcement
d. Single read returns the full object

## 10.3 Key-Value Stores

While document databases allow you to query within the data structure itself, key-value stores simplify this model by treating the stored data as an opaque object. Imagine a digital coat check. You hand the attendant a unique ticket number (the key), and they hand you back your specific coat (the value). The attendant doesn't care if the item is a heavy winter parka, an umbrella, or a light jacket; they just match the key to the item and hand it over. They do not look inside the pockets. That is exactly how a Key-Value Store works.

### 10.3.1 Characteristics of Key-Value Stores

Because the database treats the stored value as an "opaque blob" -- meaning it doesn't interpret or care about the structure of the data inside -- these databases offer blindingly fast, microsecond-level latency. When the database engine doesn't have to parse tables, check foreign key constraints, or run complex `JOIN` operations, retrieving data is practically instantaneous.

They also scale horizontally with ease. By using a mathematical technique called consistent hashing, a key-value store can effortlessly distribute millions of keys across dozens of different server nodes. However, this raw speed comes with a major trade-off: there is no query language. You cannot ask a simple key-value store, "Find all users older than 25" or "Calculate the average price of items." You can only retrieve data if you know its exact, unique key.

## 10.3.2 Redis: The King of In-Memory Storage

When software engineers talk about key-value stores in the real world, they are almost always talking about Redis (Remote Dictionary Server). Redis consistently ranks as one of the most loved databases in global developer surveys, and its secret weapon is that it is an in-memory database.

While traditional relational databases (like SQL Server or PostgreSQL) read and write data to a physical hard drive or SSD, Redis stores its data directly in the server's RAM. Accessing RAM is exponentially faster than accessing a disk. This allows Redis to deliver sub-millisecond response times.

In web architecture, Redis rarely replaces a relational database; instead, it works alongside it as a cache. Imagine an e-commerce site with a complex SQL query that calculates the top 10 best-selling products. If that query takes two seconds to run, executing it for every single homepage visitor would crash the database. Instead, the application runs the SQL query once, stores the resulting data in Redis with a key like `homepage_best_sellers`, and serves that pre-calculated data instantly from RAM to the next million visitors.

## 10.3.3 Durability, Scaling, and Advanced Features

You might be wondering: "If Redis stores everything in RAM, doesn't it lose all its data if the server loses power or restarts?" Not necessarily. Redis offers two main persistence options to save your data to a permanent disk. RDB (Redis Database) takes point-in-time snapshots of your data at specific intervals. Alternatively, AOF (Append Only File) continuously logs every single write operation to disk, so the exact dataset can be safely reconstructed after a crash.

To handle enterprise-level traffic, Redis utilizes Master-Slave Replication, automatically copying data from a primary active server to backup replica instances. If you outgrow a single server's RAM limits, Redis Cluster provides automatic data sharding across multiple nodes, allowing you to scale horizontally.

Beyond just storing data, Redis is a powerhouse for building interactive features. It includes Pub/Sub (Publish/Subscribe) messaging, which developers use to build live chat rooms and real-time notifications. It supports server-side Lua Scripting for running complex scripts directly on the database, and handles basic Transactions (using MULTI/EXEC commands) to ensure a group of commands executes safely together without interruption.

Review Question 10.16
How does a key-value store treat the data it stores?
a. As structured relational tables
b. As nested JSON documents
c. As indexed rows with constraints
d. As opaque values linked to unique keys

Review Question 10.17
What is the primary performance advantage of key-value stores?
a. Complex query optimization
b. Microsecond-level latency
c. Automatic schema validation
d. Built-in JOIN operations

Review Question 10.18
Why can't you query "all users older than 25" in a simple key-value store?
a. It lacks a query language
b. It cannot store numbers
c. It enforces strict schemas
d. It limits key length

Review Question 10.19
What is the purpose of AOF persistence in Redis?
a. To shard data across nodes
b. To take periodic memory snapshots
c. To continuously log write operations
d. To compress stored values

Review Question 10.20
What feature in Redis enables horizontal scaling across multiple nodes?
a. Pub/Sub
b. Redis Cluster
c. Lua scripting
d. MULTI/EXEC

## 10.4 Column-Family Stores

In the previous sections of this chapter, you explored the flexible filing cabinets of document stores and the lightning-fast simplicity of key-value stores. Now, imagine you need to build a system that can ingest millions of data points every single second -- like the temperature readings from every smart thermostat in a country, or the messaging history for millions of active Discord users. You need a database that scales across thousands of servers without ever going down. This is the exact problem column-family databases/wide-column databases were invented to solve. Instead of organizing data strictly by rows, column-family databases store data by columns. To a beginner, this sounds like a minor semantic difference, but it completely changes how the database writes and reads information across a massive cluster of computers.

## 10.4.1 Understanding the Column-Family Model

At the highest level, data is organized into a Keyspace. This is roughly analogous to a "database" in a relational system. The keyspace is where you define your high-level rules, such as how many copies of your data should exist across your servers. Inside the keyspace, you have Column Families, which are similar to relational tables. However, this is where the strict rules of SQL disappear.

In a column family, you have Rows, each identified by a unique row key. But unlike a SQL table where every row must have the exact same columns, a row in a column family can have entirely different columns from its neighbor. In fact, a single row can contain millions of columns, hence the term "wide-column store."

The smallest building block is the Column itself. In this model, a column isn't just a header at the top of a table; it is a self-contained unit consisting of a name (the key), a value, and a timestamp. That timestamp is important in a distributed system because if two users try to update the same piece of data on two different servers at the exact same time, the database uses the timestamp to determine which update "wins." (Note: You might occasionally read about "Super Columns" in older documentation, which were columns that contained nested columns, but these have been deprecated in modern versions as the technology evolved).

## 10.4.2 Apache Cassandra: The Distributed Powerhouse

When we talk about wide-column stores in the industry, we are almost exclusively talking about Apache Cassandra. Originally developed by Facebook to power its inbox search feature, Cassandra was open-sourced and has since become the backbone of companies like Netflix, Apple, and Uber.

Cassandra's superpower is its Peer-to-Peer Architecture. In traditional databases, you often have a "Master" node that handles writes and "Slave" nodes that handle reads. If the Master node crashes, the system halts until a new Master is elected. Cassandra throws this concept out the window. Every single node (server) in a Cassandra cluster is entirely equal. There is no master, and therefore, there is no single point of failure.

To distribute data across these equal nodes, Cassandra uses a mathematical concept called Consistent Hashing, organizing the servers into a giant "ring." When a piece of data comes in, a hash function determines exactly where on the ring that data belongs. Furthermore, Cassandra ensures data survival through automated Replication. If you set a replication factor of 3, Cassandra automatically stores a copy of every piece of data on three different servers. If one server catches fire and a second one loses power, your application stays online because the third server still has the data.

Because data lives in multiple places, Cassandra offers Tunable Consistency. As a developer, you can choose to prioritize speed (acknowledging a write as soon as one server gets it) or extreme accuracy (waiting until a majority of the servers confirm they have saved the new data) on a query-by-query basis.

### 10.4.3 The Secret to Massive Ingestion: The Write Path

To understand how Cassandra can ingest millions of records a second, you have to look at its write path. Traditional relational databases often struggle with heavy write loads because they must continuously seek out specific locations on a hard drive to update rows and re-balance indexes. Cassandra bypasses this bottleneck entirely by making disk writes sequential and append-only.

When a write request hits a Cassandra node, two things happen almost simultaneously. First, the data is appended to a Commit Log on the physical disk. This is a sequential log that acts as a fail-safe; if the server suddenly loses power, the Commit Log ensures the newly arrived data is not lost. Second, the data is written to an in-memory data structure called a Memtable. Because writing to RAM is exponentially faster than seeking and writing to a specific block on a hard drive, the node can acknowledge the write as successful the moment the data hits the Memtable and Commit Log. There is no waiting for complex on-disk indexing to finish.

But memory is finite. Once the Memtable reaches a certain size threshold, Cassandra "flushes" the data to the hard drive, saving it as a Sorted String Table, or SSTable. This is where Cassandra's unique rules come into play: SSTables are completely immutable. Once an SSTable is written to the disk, it is never modified. If an application updates a user's record or deletes a message, Cassandra doesn't open the old SSTable to overwrite the data. It simply writes the new data (or a deletion marker called a "tombstone") into a new Memtable, which eventually flushes into an entirely new SSTable.

### 10.4.4 Reading the Data and Compaction

Because writes are optimized to be incredibly fast, reading data in a wide-column store requires a bit more coordination. When you query Cassandra, the database cannot simply look in one single location. The most up-to-date version of a row might be sitting in the in-memory Memtable, or its history might be spread across several different SSTables on the disk.

To return the correct result, Cassandra checks the Memtable and the relevant SSTables. It compares the timestamps of the requested columns, merges this information, discards older values in favor of the newer ones, and returns a single, unified result to the application.

You might be wondering: if Cassandra never deletes or updates old data in place, won't the hard drive eventually fill up with millions of obsolete SSTables? To solve this, Cassandra runs an automated background process called Compaction. Compaction periodically reads multiple smaller SSTables, merges them together, keeps only the newest data based on the timestamps, and permanently throws away the outdated information and tombstones. This produces a new, highly optimized SSTable and reclaims disk space, ensuring that the read path remains fast over time.

Ultimately, this architecture -- combining peer-to-peer nodes, tunable consistency, and a memory-first write path -- is what makes column-family stores the premier choice for planet-scale applications. When you need a system that never sleeps and can absorb a relentless firehose of data, wide-column databases stand ready.

### 10.4.5 A Paradigm Shift in Database Design

Because of how it stores data, designing for Cassandra requires unlearning some relational database habits. In SQL, you model your data first (normalizing it to avoid duplication) and then you write complex queries to stitch it together.

Cassandra uses Query-Driven Design. You must define exactly what questions your application will ask before you create your tables. If you need to view users by their email, and also view users by their recent activity, you will literally create two separate tables and duplicate the data across both. Denormalization is encouraged. The golden rule of wide-column stores is One Table Per Query. You want your query to hit exactly one partition on one server. If you choose partition keys that distribute your data evenly, you avoid "hotspots" (where one server does all the work while the others sit idle), allowing your database to scale infinitely.

Because of these unique traits, column-family stores dominate specific use cases. They are the industry standard for Time-Series Data like IoT sensors and metrics that are constantly appended. They handle massive Event Logging for audit trails. They power the global Recommendation Engines that serve you movies on Netflix, and they manage the high-velocity Financial Services data used in modern stock trading.

Review Question 10.21
What core problem were column-family databases designed to solve?
a. Managing small, static datasets
b. Running complex JOIN queries
c. Ingesting massive volumes of distributed data
d. Enforcing strict relational schemas

Review Question 10.22
In a column-family database, what is a Keyspace roughly equivalent to in relational databases?
a. A table
b. An index
c. A row
d. A database

Review Question 10.23
What additional element does each column contain besides a name and value?
a. A foreign key
b. A schema definition
c. A timestamp
d. A shard ID

Review Question 10.24
What architectural feature ensures Cassandra has no single point of failure?
a. Master-Slave architecture
b. Vertical scaling
c. Peer-to-Peer architecture
d. Centralized coordinator node

Review Question 10.25
How does Cassandra distribute data across servers?
a. Manual partitioning
b. Consistent hashing
c. Foreign key mapping
d. Vertical sharding

Review Question 10.26
What is the first step in Cassandra's write process?
a. Writing to an SSTable
b. Writing to a memtable
c. Appending to the commit log
d. Running compaction

Review Question 10.27
What happens when a memtable becomes full?

a. It deletes old records
b. It converts into an index
c. It flushes data to an SSTable
d. It triggers replication

Review Question 10.28
What is the guiding design principle for Cassandra data modeling?
a. Normalize everything
b. One table per query
c. Avoid data duplication
d. Use JOINs frequently

## 10.5 Graph Databases

If you have ever watched a detective movie, you have likely seen the classic "investigator's corkboard." The detective pins photos of suspects, locations, and evidence to the board, and then connects them with a tangled web of red string to show who knows whom, who was where, and how the crimes are linked.

A Graph Database is the digital equivalent of that corkboard. Instead of forcing data into rigid rows and columns, it represents data as a sprawling network of interconnected entities. While a relational database has to work hard to calculate deep relationships (imagine writing a SQL query to find "the friends of the friends of the friends of Alice"), a graph database traverses those connections instantly because the "red string" is physically stored in the database.

### 10.5.1 Core Concepts of Graph Databases

To understand how graph databases work, we need to define the digital pushpins and red strings that make up the network. The terminology is straightforward but fundamentally different from tables and rows.

Nodes (The Pushpins): Nodes represent individual entities. A node could be a person, a product, a city, a company, or a specific user account.
Labels: To keep things organized, nodes are categorized using labels. For example, a node representing you might have the label `Person`, while a node representing your smartphone might have the label `Product`.
Properties: Nodes hold data in the form of key-value pairs called properties. A `Person` node might have properties like `{name: "Alice", age: 28, city: "New York"}`.

Relationships (The Red String): Relationships are the connections between two nodes. In a graph database, a relationship is a first-class citizen; it is just as important as the node itself.
Direction: Every relationship must have a start node and an end node, indicating the flow of the connection (e.g., Alice `FOLLOWS` Bob).
Type: Relationships are explicitly named to define the nature of the connection, such as `FRIENDS_WITH`, `PURCHASED`, or `LOCATED_IN`.
Properties: Just like nodes, relationships can hold their own data! This is incredibly powerful. A `FRIENDS_WITH` relationship might have a property like `{since: 2020}`. Doing this in a relational database usually requires creating an entirely separate, cumbersome "junction table."

When you string these elements together -- moving from one node, across a relationship, to another node -- you create a Path. Graph databases are entirely optimized around finding and traversing these paths as quickly as possible.

## 10.5.2 Neo4j: The Leading Graph Database

When developers and data scientists talk about graph databases, they are almost universally talking about Neo4j. Neo4j is the undisputed market leader in this space. It is renowned for combining the mathematical power of graph theory with the enterprise-grade reliability you would expect from a traditional SQL database.

Unlike some NoSQL databases that sacrifice data integrity for speed, Neo4j is fully ACID compliant. This means that if you are processing a financial transaction that involves updating several nodes and relationships at once, Neo4j guarantees that the entire transaction will succeed or fail as a single unit. You will never be left with partially updated, corrupted data.

The secret to Neo4j's speed is a concept called Index-Free Adjacency. In a traditional relational database, if you want to find all of Alice's friends, the database has to scan a massive "index" (like a giant phonebook) to find matching foreign keys. If the database has a billion rows, that index lookup takes time. In Neo4j, relationships are physically stored as memory pointers on the disk. Each node literally points to its neighbors. Traversing from Alice to her friends doesn't require an index lookup; the database simply walks through the predefined door. Because of this, traversing a graph takes the exact same amount of time whether your database has a thousand nodes or ten billion nodes.

### 10.5.3 Cypher: Drawing Your Queries

To interact with this web of data, Neo4j created a highly visual, declarative query language called Cypher. If you know SQL, picking up Cypher is surprisingly intuitive, but with a fun twist: Cypher uses ASCII-art syntax to physically draw the graph patterns you are looking for.

Here is how you draw in Cypher:
Nodes are drawn using parentheses to look like circles: `(n)`
Relationships are drawn using arrows to show direction: `-->` or `<--`
Labels are prefixed with a colon: `(:Person)`
Properties are enclosed in curly braces: `{name: 'Alice'}`

Let's look at a basic Cypher pattern:
`(a:Person {name: 'Alice'})-[:KNOWS]->(b:Person)`

Even if you have never written a line of code in your life, you can likely read that statement. It translates to: Find a Person node named Alice, who has a "KNOWS" relationship pointing to another Person node. Cypher's visual nature makes querying complex networks incredibly natural.

### 10.5.4 Practical Graph Use Cases

Because graph databases excel at uncovering hidden patterns and deep connections, they are the backbone of many modern digital experiences.

1. Recommendation Engines
If you have ever shopped online and seen a section labeled "Customers who bought this item also bought...", you are likely looking at the output of a graph database. Graph databases can instantly traverse the path: Find User A -> Follow Relationship "Purchased" -> Find Product X -> Follow Relationship "Purchased By" backwards -> Find User B -> Follow Relationship "Purchased" -> Find Product Y. By finding what User B bought, the system can instantly recommend Product Y to User A.

2. Fraud Detection
Financial institutions use graph databases to uncover sophisticated crime rings. Traditional SQL databases struggle to detect "circular money transfers" (where Person A sends money to B, who sends it to C, who

sends it back to A) because the queries are too complex and slow. A graph database can spot these circular paths instantly, allowing banks to flag money laundering or credit card fraud in real time.

3. Social Networks

This is the most natural fit. Mapping users, their friendships, who follows whom, and who liked whose post is literally a graph. When LinkedIn tells you that someone is a "3rd-degree connection," it is simply traversing a graph path three hops deep.

4. IT Network and Operations

Large companies use graph databases to map their entire IT infrastructure. If a specific server router goes down, a graph database can instantly trace the physical connections and software dependencies to tell the IT team exactly which applications and users will be affected by the outage.

Review Question 10.29
In the text, what real-world object is used to describe how graph databases model data?
a. A filing cabinet
b. A spreadsheet
c. A corkboard with red string
d. A library catalog

Review Question 10.30
In a graph database, what represents an individual entity such as a person or product?
a. Table
b. Node
c. Column
d. Index

Review Question 10.31
Why are graph databases faster at finding “friends of friends” compared to relational databases?
a. They use more RAM
b. They avoid primary keys
c. They store relationships directly
d. They remove all indexes

Review Question 10.32
Which graph database is widely considered the market leader?
a. MongoDB
b. Redis
c. Neo4j
d. Cassandra

Review Question 10.33

What does ACID compliance in Neo4j guarantee?
a. Instant horizontal scaling
b. Full-text search by default
c. Automatic sharding
d. Reliable transaction integrity

Review Question 10.34
What is Index-Free Adjacency?
a. A caching mechanism
b. Relationships stored as direct pointers
c. A distributed indexing model
d. A background compaction process

Review Question 10.35
Why are graph databases particularly effective for fraud detection?
a. They compress financial data
b. They eliminate transaction logs
c. They enforce strict schemas
d. They detect circular relationship paths quickly

## 10.6 Comparison of NoSQL Database Types

Over the last few sections, you've seen how NoSQL steps away from the strict, tabular grids of relational databases to offer specialized solutions for data problems. But with four different options -- Document, Key-Value, Column-Family, and Graph -- how do software engineers actually choose which one to use? This decision comes down to understanding the trade-offs of each system. There is no single "best" database; there is only the best database for your specific problem. Let's compare them across the dimensions that matter most to developers.

### 10.6.1 Complexity, Queries, and the Learning Curve

If you are optimizing for simplicity and raw speed, Key-Value stores are unmatched. They are the easiest to learn because they only do one thing: map a unique key to a blob of data. However, this simplicity means their query capabilities are limited -- you cannot search inside the data.

Document databases sit in the "Goldilocks zone" for most developers. Because they use familiar JSON-like structures, the learning curve is gentle. They offer a good balance, allowing you to build rich, complex queries (like searching for specific nested fields) without the rigid setup of a SQL table.

On the more complex end, Column-Family stores require a fundamental mental shift. You must know the exact queries your application will run before you design your tables, which can be challenging for beginners. Finally, Graph databases have the steepest learning curve. You have to stop thinking about data as isolated records and start thinking entirely about relationships, but they reward that effort with unparalleled power for tracing deep connections.

## 10.6.2 Performance and Scalability

When a company goes viral, its database needs to scale. Key-Value and Column-Family databases are the champions of horizontal scaling. You can add cheap commodity servers to the network indefinitely to handle massive spikes in traffic or continuous avalanches of write-heavy data (like IoT sensor readings).

Document databases also scale quite well using sharding, making them great general-purpose workhorses. Graph databases, however, face a unique challenge here. Because their entire value relies on the interconnected "red string" between data points, splitting a graph across multiple servers is mathematically difficult and can slow down performance. They excel at deep traversal queries but are generally slower for bulk data operations.

## 10.6.3 The Real-World Cheat Sheet

In modern architecture, large companies practice polyglot persistence -- a fancy industry term meaning "using multiple different database types in the same application." An app like Netflix or Amazon doesn't pick just one; they use the right tool for each specific feature.

Here is a quick cheat sheet for when to reach for each type:

| Database Type | Best Feature | Real-World Use Cases | Popular Example |
|---|---|---|---|
| **Document** | Flexible schemas, rich queries. | E-commerce catalogs, Content Management (CMS), User profiles. | MongoDB |
| **Key-Value** | Blistering fast, simple lookups. | Caching, shopping carts, session storage. | Redis, DynamoDB |
| **Column-Family** | Massive scale, write-heavy data. | Time-series data, event logging, IoT sensors. | Cassandra |
| **Graph** | Deep relationship tracing. | Social networks, recommendation engines, fraud detection. | Neo4j |

Table 10.1 Cheat sheet for the comparison of NoSQL.

Review Question 10.43
Which NoSQL database type is the simplest to learn but offers very limited query capabilities?
a. Document
b. Column-Family
c. Key-Value
d. Graph

Review Question 10.44
Which database type is described as being in the “Goldilocks zone” for most developers?
a. Graph
b. Document
c. Column-Family
d. Key-Value

Review Question 10.45
Why do Graph databases face challenges with horizontal scaling?
a. They cannot store large files
b. They lack indexing support
c. They require fixed schemas
d. Their interconnected structure is difficult to split across servers

Review Question 10.46
Which database types are considered the strongest for horizontal scaling and handling massive write-heavy workloads?
a. Key-Value and Column-Family
b. Document and Graph
c. Graph and Key-Value
d. Document and Column-Family

Review Question 10.47
Which database is listed in the text as a popular example of a Column-Family store?
a. MongoDB
b. Redis
c. Cassandra
d. Neo4j

## 10.7 Chapter Summary

This chapter explored the four main types of NoSQL databases, each designed for specific data models and use cases: document databases, key-value stores, column-family stores, and graph databases. Understanding these database types, their strengths, and trade-offs enables you to select the right tool for each specific requirement in your application architecture. Modern applications often employ multiple NoSQL databases in polyglot persistence architectures, leveraging each database's unique capabilities.

## 10.8 Discussion Questions

Discussion 10.1
What are the four main types of NoSQL databases surveyed in the chapter? Provide one example system for each type. Explain how they differ from relational databases.

Discussion 10.2
What is the purpose of a partition key in Cassandra, and why is it important for performance?

Discussion 10.3
Why are graph databases particularly well-suited for social network applications?

Discussion 10.4
Compare query capabilities across document, key-value, column-family, and graph databases. What factors should you consider when choosing between MongoDB and Cassandra for a new application?

## 10.9 Solutions to the Review Questions

10.1 C; 10.2 B; 10.3 A; 10.4 C; 10.5 C; 10.6 C; 10.7 D; 10.8 C; 10.9 B; 10.10 C; 10.11 D; 10.12 C; 10.13 B; 10.14 C; 10.15 D; 10.16 D; 10.17 B; 10.18 A; 10.19 C; 10.20 B; 10.21 C; 10.22 D; 10.23 C; 10.24 C; 10.25 B; 10.26 C; 10.27 C; 10.28 B; 10.29 C; 10.30 B; 10.31 C; 10.32 C; 10.33 D; 10.34 B; 10.35 D; 10.36 C; 10.37 B; 10.38 D; 10.39 A; 10.40 C;

# Chapter 11: Data Modeling and Schema Design

## Chapter Learning Objectives

11.1 Apply fundamental principles of NoSQL data modeling
11.2 Make informed decisions between embedding and referencing data
11.3 Implement MongoDB schema design patterns for common scenarios
11.4 Design denormalized schemas for optimal read performance

## 11.1 Data Modeling Fundamentals for NoSQL

If you feel like everything you learned about data modeling in the first eight chapters is about to be thrown out the window, you are entirely right. Data modeling in NoSQL requires a fundamental, sometimes uncomfortable, shift in thinking. Relational databases prioritize saving storage space and keeping data perfectly consistent. NoSQL databases prioritize raw speed, massive scalability, and the agility to change your application on the fly. Let's break down how you actually design data in this new paradigm.

### 11.1.1 The Paradigm Shift: The Great Unlearning

To succeed in NoSQL data modeling, you have to unlearn some of the most sacred rules of SQL. This shift is generally categorized into three major mindset changes.

1. From Normalization to Denormalization

In relational databases, you normalize data to eliminate redundancy. If you have a user's address, you store it in exactly one place (a `Locations` table) and point to it using foreign keys. You do this so that if the user moves, you only have to update the database in one single spot.

NoSQL actually encourages the exact opposite: denormalization. Because joining tables together is computationally expensive and slow, NoSQL databases prefer you to store related information together, even if it means duplicating data. Yes, you read that right. In NoSQL, it is perfectly acceptable -- and often encouraged -- to duplicate data to make your application run faster.

2. From Schema-First to Query-First

When you built your SQL databases, you likely started with a whiteboard. You drew your entities (Users, Products, Orders), defined how they related to each other, built your strict tables, and then figured out how to write the SQL `SELECT` queries to pull the data out. This is a schema-first approach. It's like building a kitchen based purely on where the appliances fit best.

NoSQL design completely inverts this process. You must use a *query-first* approach. Before you even think about creating a database collection, you must know exactly what questions your application will ask. You look at the user interface of your app, figure out what data needs to be displayed on the screen at exactly the same time, and then you design your database documents to serve that exact query instantly. It's like building a kitchen based entirely on the specific meals you plan to cook.

3. From Strict ACID to Raw Performance

While relational databases prioritize strict ACID transactions (guaranteeing that every piece of data is perfectly accurate and updated simultaneously across the whole system), NoSQL often trades some of those guarantees for better performance. In a global, highly scaled application, NoSQL accepts "eventual consistency." This means if you update a profile picture, it might take a few milliseconds for that new picture to replicate to servers on the other side of the world. For most modern applications, that tiny delay is a worthwhile trade-off for the ability to handle millions of users at once.

| Feature | Relational (SQL) Mindset | NoSQL Mindset |
|---|---|---|
| **Primary Goal** | Data integrity and zero duplication. | Query speed and massive scale. |
| **Design Flow** | Design the schema -> Write the queries. | Know the queries -> Design the schema. |
| **Data Storage** | Highly normalized (split into many tables). | Highly denormalized (kept together) |
| **Retrieval** | Complex `JOIN` operations. | Single, fast read operations. |

Table 11.1 Mindset: SQL vs NoSQL

## 11.1.2 Core Principles of NoSQL Data Modeling

Once you have adopted the NoSQL mindset, you can start building. While NoSQL doesn't have the strict "Normal Forms" (like 1NF, 2NF) of SQL, the industry relies on five core principles to guide good design.

Principle 1: Data Accessed Together Should Stay Together

This is the golden rule of NoSQL design. If your application frequently needs multiple pieces of information simultaneously to load a single webpage or app screen, those pieces of information should be stored in the exact same document or incredibly close together.

Imagine you are building an e-commerce product page. To load the screen, you need the product's name, its price, the top three customer reviews, and the URLs for the product images. In a relational database, this requires `JOIN` operations across four different tables. In NoSQL (like MongoDB), you simply embed the reviews and the image URLs directly inside the main Product document. The database does one single read, grabs the document, and the page loads instantly.

Principle 2: Design for Your Access Patterns

Because NoSQL lacks the flexible querying of SQL, your database structure must mirror your application's behavior. Before designing anything, you must document your access patterns. You need to know:

What data will be read together?

Which queries will happen 10,000 times a second, and which will only happen once a month?

What data relationships are the most critical to the user experience?

If you design a NoSQL database without knowing your access patterns first, you will end up with a database that is both slow and frustrating to update.

Principle 3: Embrace Controlled Redundancy

As we mentioned in the paradigm shift, redundancy is your friend in NoSQL, but it must be controlled. Let's say you are building a blogging platform like Medium. You have a `Users` collection and a `Posts` collection. When displaying a post, you want to show the author's name and their avatar image next to the title. Instead of doing a secondary lookup to the `Users` collection every time someone reads the article, you simply duplicate the author's name and avatar URL directly into the `Post` document.

This eliminates an expensive join. But why is it "controlled"? Because you have to ask yourself: How often does a user change their name or avatar? Rarely. And if they do, is it a disaster if their old articles show their old avatar for a few minutes while a background script updates them? Usually, no. You are trading a tiny bit of update complexity for a massive boost in read speed.

Principle 4: Optimize for Reads or Writes

Every database workload leans either toward being read-heavy or write-heavy. Different NoSQL schema designs optimize for different operations.

If you are building a news website, an article is written once but read by millions of people. You should denormalize heavily, embed all related data (like tags and author info), and duplicate data so the database only has to do one quick fetch to serve the reader. This schema design is read-optimized.

If you are building a system to collect temperature data from millions of IoT weather sensors every second, you don't care about reading the data quickly; you just need to write it to the disk before the system crashes. In this case, you minimize duplication, keep documents very small, and accept that when a data scientist eventually wants to read that data, they might have to run a slower, more complex query. This is write-optimized.

Principle 5: Consider the Data Lifecycle

Data is not static; it changes over time, and your schema must account for this. You have to ask yourself how the data grows.

A common beginner mistake in NoSQL is the "unbounded array." Imagine you embed comments directly into a YouTube video's document. If the video gets 50 comments, it's incredibly fast to load. But what if the video goes viral and gets 50,000 comments? The document becomes too massive to load into memory, and your application crashes. Understanding the lifecycle of your data means knowing when to embed data (like a limited set of product tags) and when to split data out into separate references (like an infinite stream of user comments).

Review Question 11.1
What is the primary goal of NoSQL databases compared to relational databases?
a. Eliminating all data redundancy
b. Perfect ACID compliance
c. Query speed and massive scale
d. Minimizing storage costs

Review Question 11.2
What does “denormalization” mean in NoSQL design?
a. Splitting data into many smaller tables
b. Removing foreign keys
c. Encrypting duplicate records
d. Storing related data together, even if duplicated

Review Question 11.3
In a query-first approach, what must be known before designing the schema?
a. The storage engine type
b. The exact queries the application will run
c. The maximum disk size
d. The number of database administrators

Review Question 11.4
Why is controlled redundancy considered beneficial in NoSQL?

a. It reduces hardware requirements
b. It simplifies indexing
c. It improves read performance
d. It guarantees strict consistency

Review Question 11.5
In a write-heavy IoT sensor system, what is prioritized?
a. Large embedded documents
b. Immediate analytical queries
c. Minimizing duplication and keeping documents small
d. Complex join operations

Review Question 11.6
When is aggressive data duplication acceptable in NoSQL?
a. When the system is read-heavy
b. When storage costs are high
c. When consistency is legally required
d. When schema changes are forbidden

## 11.2 Embedding vs Referencing

Now that you have shifted your mindset from the rigid grids of relational databases to the flexible, query-driven world of NoSQL, you are ready to face the single most important decision a NoSQL architect makes.

If you are designing a document database (like MongoDB), every time you look at two pieces of related data, you have to ask yourself one critical question: Should I embed this data, or should I reference it? Getting this choice right means your application will be fast and able to scale to millions of users. Getting it wrong usually results in sluggish performance, crashing servers, and a database that is impossibly tangled. Let's explore both approaches in depth, look at some real-world examples, and build a mental framework for exactly when to use each.

### 11.2.1 The Heavyweight Champion: Embedding (Denormalization)

Embedding is the act of storing related data within the same document, creating a nested, tree-like structure. If you recall our previous chapter, this is the NoSQL equivalent of denormalization --grouping everything together so the database doesn't have to look anywhere else. Because NoSQL databases use flexible formats like JSON, embedding feels natural. You simply put curly braces inside of other curly braces.

Let's look at an example of a customer placing an order. If we choose to embed the data, the entire transaction lives inside a single document:

```json
{
  "_id": "order_12345",
  "order_date": "2025-12-15",
  "status": "shipped",
  "customer": {
    "customer_id": "cust_789",
    "name": "Sarah Johnson",
    "email": "sarah@example.com",
    "shipping_address": {
      "street": "123 Main St",
      "city": "Boston",
      "state": "MA",
      "zip": "02101"
    }
  },
  "items": [
    {
      "product_id": "prod_456",
      "name": "Wireless Headphones",
      "quantity": 1,
      "price": 79.99
    }
  ],
  "total": 79.99
}
```

## 11.2.2 Why We Love Embedding

The biggest advantage of embedding is Single Query Performance. In a relational database, generating an order receipt requires joining the `Orders` table, the `Customers` table, and the `OrderDetails` table. In NoSQL, the database simply reaches into the hard drive, grabs document `order_12345`, and hands it to the application. It requires exactly one database operation. This concept is called Data Locality -- because all the related data is physically stored right next to each other on the disk, reading it is practically instantaneous.

Embedding also provides a massive safety net called Atomic Operations. "Atomicity" means that an operation either completely succeeds or completely fails; there is no in-between. Because all the order data is in one document, if the system crashes while updating the order status, you won't be left with a corrupted database where the customer was charged but the items weren't recorded.

Finally, embedding matches how programmers actually write code. The nested JSON document maps perfectly to the objects used in Python, JavaScript, or C#, meaning developers spend less time translating database rows into application variables.

### 11.2.3 The Dangers of Embedding

However, embedding is not a silver bullet. The biggest trap beginners fall into is the Unbounded Array. Imagine you are building a blog, and you decide to embed user comments directly inside the `Blog_Post` document. If the post gets 10 comments, it loads instantly. But what if the post goes viral and gets 50,000 comments? The document will grow indefinitely. Most NoSQL databases have strict hard limits on document size to protect RAM. MongoDB, for example, will completely reject any document larger than 16 Megabytes. If your embedded array hits that ceiling, your application will crash and users will be unable to leave new comments.

Furthermore, embedding heavily duplicates data. If Sarah Johnson updates her email address, she shouldn't have to update it on every past order she ever made. If you embedded her email in 50 order documents, a simple profile update suddenly becomes an expensive operation that has to scan and rewrite 50 different files.

### 11.2.4 The Old Friend: Referencing (Normalization)

If embedding sounds dangerous for your specific feature, you pivot to Referencing. Referencing means storing relationships between documents using unique identifiers. If this sounds exactly like using Foreign Keys in a relational SQL database, you are absolutely correct!

Let's look at how that exact same order from above looks if we use referencing. Instead of one massive document, the data is split across three different collections (tables):

The Orders Collection:

```
{
  "_id": "order_12345",
  "order_date": "2024-12-15",
  "status": "shipped",
  "customer_id": "cust_789",
  "total": 79.99
}
```

The Customers Collection:

```
{
  "_id": "cust_789",
  "name": "Sarah Johnson",
  "email": "sarah@example.com"
}
```

The OrderDetails Collection:

```
{
  "_id": "item_001",
  "order_id": "order_12345",
  "product_id": "prod_456",
  "quantity": 1,
  "price": 79.99
}
```

### 11.2.5 Why We Use Referencing

Referencing completely solves the unbounded array problem. If a blog post gets a million comments, it doesn't matter, because each comment is its own tiny, isolated document in a separate `Comments` collection that simply points back to the `post_id`. The main blog post document remains small and lightning-fast to load.

It also eliminates data duplication. Sarah's email address exists in exactly one place: her Customer document. If she updates her email, you change it once, and every single order she has ever placed points to the correct, updated information. You also gain the ability to load data selectively. If you only want to display a list of order dates and totals on a dashboard, you don't have to force the database to also load all the heavy customer and product data into memory.

### 11.2.6 The Cost of Referencing

The primary drawback of referencing is Network Latency and Application Complexity. Remember, NoSQL databases generally do not support complex `JOIN` commands.

If you want to display the full order receipt to the user, the database can't do it in one step. Your application code (e.g., your Node.js server) must first query the `Orders` collection. Then, it has to look at the `customer_id` and send a second query to the `Customers` collection. Then it looks at the items and sends a third query to the `OrderDetails` collection. These multiple round trips to the database take time. If your database server is in Virginia and your application server is in Ohio, the time it takes for data to travel back and forth over the network multiple times can make your application feel sluggish to the end user.

### 11.2.7 The Golden Mean: Extended References (The Hybrid Approach)

In the real world of enterprise software development, we rarely choose 100% embedding or 100% referencing. We usually use a highly optimized hybrid approach known as Extended References (or Partial Embedding).

Think about a physical receipt you get from a grocery store. It lists the name of the milk you bought and the price you paid on that specific day. It doesn't list the name of the dairy farm, the store's wholesale cost, or the product's aisle number. It only embeds the exact details needed for that specific interaction.

We do the same thing in NoSQL. We embed the frequently accessed, read-heavy fields, while keeping a reference ID to the full, heavy document.

```
{
  "_id": "order_12345",
  "order_date": "2024-12-15",
  "customer": {
    "customer_id": "cust_789",
    "name": "Sarah Johnson"  // Embedded for instant dashboard display
  },
  "items": [
    {
      "product_id": "prod_456",
      "name": "Wireless Headphones",
      "price": 79.99  // Embedded as a historical point-in-time snapshot
    }
  ]
}
```

This hybrid approach provides the fast, single-query performance of embedding, because the application has enough information (Sarah's name and the product name) to render an "Order History" screen instantly. However, if the user clicks "View Full Product Details," the application uses the referenced `product_id` to fetch the massive product document.

Furthermore, embedding the `price` here is actually a massive feature, not a bug. If the store raises the price of the headphones to $99.99 tomorrow, Sarah's historical receipt shouldn't change. By embedding the price at the time of purchase, we preserve the integrity of historical data while still referencing the live product catalog!

## 11.2.8 The Developer's Decision Framework

When you sit down to build a new feature, how do you actually decide? Here is a practical cheat sheet used by NoSQL developers:

*Choose to Embed When:*

The data is a "One-to-One" or "One-to-Few" relationship: A user and their account preferences (theme: dark mode, language: English). This data is small, bounded, and rarely changes.
The child data cannot exist without the parent: A shipping address makes no sense without the customer it belongs to.
You always view the data together: If a user profile always displays a bio and an avatar, store them together.

*Choose to Reference When:*
The data is "One-to-Many" and the "Many" is huge: A popular user on a social network might have millions of followers. You must reference them, or the document will break.
The data is "Many-to-Many": Students enrolling in multiple classes, and classes having multiple students.
The child data is accessed independently: An e-commerce product exists in the catalog, gets searched by users, and appears in marketing campaigns entirely independent of the "Orders" it belongs to.

*Choose Extended References (Hybrid) When:*
You need high performance but face massive data: You embed just the username and avatar of the person who left a comment, but reference their full user profile ID so you don't load their entire account history on every blog post.

Transitioning from SQL's strict normalization to NoSQL's flexible denormalization takes practice, but once you master it, you can build systems that serve millions of users with zero lag.

Review Question 11.7
What is the central design decision in a document database like MongoDB?
a. Whether to use SQL or NoSQL
b. Whether to embed or reference related data
c. Whether to encrypt documents
d. Whether to use ACID transactions

Review Question 11.8
What is the biggest performance advantage of embedding?
a. Lower disk costs
b. Single-query performance
c. Automatic indexing
d. Unlimited document growth

Review Question 11.9
Why are atomic operations easier with embedding?
a. Because documents cannot fail

b. Because updates affect one document
c. Because NoSQL disables crashes
d. Because arrays cannot grow

Review Question 11.10
Referencing in NoSQL is most similar to what concept in SQL?
a. Index scanning
b. Foreign keys
c. Table partitioning
d. Stored procedures

Review Question 11.11
What is the primary performance cost of referencing?
a. Increased disk usage
b. Reduced storage limits
c. Multiple network round trips
d. Loss of atomicity entirely

Review Question 11.12
Which problem does referencing completely solve?
a. Atomic updates
b. Unbounded arrays
c. Query planning
d. Data locality

Review Question 11.13
What is Extended References (Hybrid Approach)?
a. A strict normalization strategy
b. Embedding only indexes
c. Fully duplicating all data
d. Embedding key fields while keeping reference IDs

Review Question 11.14
Why embed the product price in an order document in the hybrid model?
a. To reduce indexing costs
b. To preserve historical accuracy
c. To eliminate product collections
d. To avoid foreign keys

Review Question 11.15
When should you choose embedding?
a. When the relationship is one-to-few and bounded
b. When the child data grows infinitely
c. When the relationship is many-to-many
d. When data must be accessed independently

Review Question 11.16
According to the text, when is referencing the better choice?
a. When data always appears together
b. When child data is massive or many-to-many

c. When atomic updates are required
d. When performance is irrelevant

## 11.3 MongoDB Schema Design Patterns

When you build a house, you don't invent a new way to frame a door or lay a foundation. You rely on architectural patterns that have been proven to work over decades. Software engineering is exactly the same. Over the years, the engineers at MongoDB and other major NoSQL providers have watched thousands of companies build applications. They noticed that developers kept running into the exact same challenges, so they documented standardized, proven solutions. We call these Schema Design Patterns. Because you are just starting out, we are going to focus on the four most common and powerful patterns. We will leave out some of the advanced, administrative patterns for now, and focus on the patterns you will actually use to build your first applications.

### 11.3.1 The Attribute Pattern

The Problem:
Imagine you are building the database for a massive e-commerce platform like Amazon. You have a single `Products` collection. However, the items you sell have completely different characteristics. A laptop has a `processor`, `ram`, and `screen_size`. A t-shirt has a `size`, `color`, and `fabric_type`. A book has an `isbn`, `author`, and `page_count`.

If you were using a relational SQL database, this would be a nightmare. You would either have to create a table with hundreds of empty columns (where the t-shirt row has a `NULL` value for `processor`), or you would have to build a highly complex, slow-running "Entity-Attribute-Value" table architecture.

In NoSQL, because documents are flexible, your first instinct might be to just throw the fields directly into the document:

```
{
  "_id": "prod_laptop_123",
  "name": "Professional Laptop",
  "category": "electronics",
  "processor": "Intel i7",
  "ram": "16GB",
  "storage": "512GB SSD"
}
```

This works perfectly -- until a user tries to search your website.

To make searches fast, databases use "indexes". If you build your documents like the example above, you would have to tell the database to create a specific index for `processor`, another for `ram`, another for `color`, and so on. MongoDB actually has a hard limit on how many indexes you can create per collection. You would quickly hit that limit, and searches for un-indexed fields would force the database to scan every single product one by one, bringing your app to a grinding halt.

The Solution:
The Attribute Pattern solves this by moving all of these unpredictable, varied fields into a single, predictable array of key-value pairs.

```
{
  "_id": "prod_laptop_123",
  "name": "Professional Laptop",
  "category": "electronics",
  "specs": [
    { "k": "processor", "v": "Intel i7" },
    { "k": "ram", "v": "16GB" },
    { "k": "storage", "v": "512GB SSD" }
  ]
}
```

By structuring the data this way, you only need to create one single index on the `specs.k` (key) and `specs.v` (value) fields. Suddenly, your database can instantly search across thousands of different product attributes without changing the schema or adding new indexes. Whenever the business decides to start selling a new category of products -- say, car parts with entirely new specifications -- your database is already equipped to handle it, search it, and filter it instantly.

## 11.3.2 The Bucket Pattern

The Problem:
The modern world is filled with devices that constantly generate data. Imagine you are building the backend for a smart home company that sells internet-connected thermostats. Every single minute, the thermostat sends the current temperature of the room to your database.

If you create a new document for every single reading, it looks like this:

```
{ "_id": 1, "sensor_id": "sensor_001", "timestamp": "2024-12-15T00:00:00Z", "temp": 72.3 }
{ "_id": 2, "sensor_id": "sensor_001", "timestamp": "2024-12-15T00:01:00Z", "temp": 72.4 }
```

At one reading per minute, one thermostat generates 1,440 documents a day. If your company sells 100,000 thermostats, your database is suddenly trying to write and store 144 million documents every single day.

The problem here isn't just the temperature data; it's the overhead. In the example above, the actual data we care about (`72.3`) is tiny. The vast majority of the storage space is being wasted on repeating the `sensor_id`, the `_id`, and the field names over and over again. Your database will run out of memory, and querying "What was the average temperature today?" will require the database to scan thousands of individual documents.

The Solution:

The Bucket Pattern groups (or "buckets") data together based on a specific time frame -- for example, one hour. Instead of creating a new document every minute, you create one document per hour. When a new minute's reading comes in, you simply update the document by pushing the new reading into an embedded array.

```
{
  "_id": "sensor_001_2024-12-15-00",
  "sensor_id": "sensor_001",
  "start_time": "2024-12-15T00:00:00Z",
  "end_time": "2024-12-15T00:59:59Z",
  "measurement_count": 60,
  "measurements": [
    { "time": "00:00", "temp": 72.3 },
    { "time": "00:01", "temp": 72.4 }
    // ... 58 more measurements stored here
  ],
  "summary": {
    "avg_temp": 72.5,
    "min_temp": 71.8,
    "max_temp": 73.2
  }
}
```

This pattern reduces the number of documents your database has to manage by 60x. Furthermore, notice the `summary` block at the bottom. Every time you push a new temperature into the array, you can have the database automatically update the daily average, minimum, and maximum. When a user opens their mobile app to see their daily chart, the database doesn't have to calculate the math on the fly; it just hands them the pre-calculated `summary`, making the app feel fast.

## 11.3.3 The Subset Pattern

The Problem:

In the previous section on "Embedding vs. Referencing," we talked about the danger of the unbounded array. Embedding data is fast, but if you embed too much (like thousands of comments on a viral video), your document will hit the 16MB size limit and crash.

However, choosing to use Referencing for everything has its own downsides. If you put all the comments in a separate collection, the database has to perform a secondary query just to load the main webpage.

Think about how you actually browse the internet. When you click on a YouTube video or an Amazon product, do you read all 10,000 comments? No. You look at the top 10 most recent or most helpful reviews, and 99% of the time, you never click the "Load More Comments" button.

The Solution:

The Subset Pattern perfectly aligns your database structure with real-world user behavior. Instead of choosing between 100% embedding or 100% referencing, you do both. You embed a subset of the data (the part the user is most likely to need immediately) and reference the rest.

```
// The Movie Document (Loaded instantly when the page opens)
{
  "_id": "movie_123",
  "title": "The Matrix",
  "rating_summary": { "average": 4.8, "count": 14500 },
  "recent_reviews": [
    { "user": "neo_fan", "rating": 5, "text": "Still a masterpiece.", "date": "2024-12-14" },
    // ... exactly 9 more recent reviews embedded here
  ]
}
```

When a user loads the movie page, the database fetches a single document. That document contains everything needed to render the screen: the title, the overall average rating, and the 10 most recent reviews. It is blindingly fast.

Meanwhile, behind the scenes, you have a completely separate `Reviews` collection holding all 14,500 historical reviews. If a user actually clicks "Read All Reviews," then your application runs the secondary query to fetch them. The Subset Pattern ensures that your primary documents stay small and fast, while still allowing your application to handle massive amounts of data.

## 11.3.4 The Extended Reference Pattern

The Problem:

If you recall from our last chapter, fully normalizing data (separating everything into its own collection and referencing it via IDs) is the standard way to build a SQL database. In NoSQL, doing this forces your application to do a lot of heavy lifting.

Let's look at an e-commerce order. If your `Orders` collection only contains a `customer_id` and a `product_id`, your application has to run three separate database queries just to show the user a simple "Order Confirmation" screen (one query for the order, one to get the customer's name, and one to get the product's name). This network traffic slows your application down.

The Solution:

The Extended Reference Pattern (which we briefly introduced as the "Hybrid Approach" earlier) formalizes the solution: you duplicate only the specific fields that are accessed most frequently, while relying on the reference ID for everything else.

```
{
  "_id": "order_123",
  "order_date": "2024-12-15",
  "status": "shipped",
  "customer": {
    "id": "cust_789",
    "name": "Sarah Johnson",
    "email": "sarah@example.com"
  },
  "items": [
    {
      "product_id": "prod_456",
      "name": "Wireless Headphones",
      "price_at_purchase": 79.99,
      "image_url": "/images/prod_456.jpg"
    }
  ],
  "total": 79.99
}
```

Notice what we did here. We didn't embed Sarah's entire profile (like her password hash, her notification preferences, or her secondary shipping addresses). We only embedded her name and email -- the exact data needed to send a receipt. We didn't embed the headphone's manufacturer details or warehouse location; we only embedded the name and the thumbnail image.

This pattern provides the ultimate read performance. A single query gets you everything you need to draw the user interface.

Furthermore, this pattern solves a critical business logic problem. Notice the `price_at_purchase` field. If we had purely referenced the `Products` collection, and the store manager raised the price of the headphones to $99.99 the next day, Sarah's historical receipt would suddenly look like she paid $99.99. By embedding (duplicating) the price into the order document at the exact moment of checkout, we create a permanent historical snapshot that protects the integrity of our financial records, while still keeping a reference to the main product catalog!

Learning to identify when to use these patterns takes practice, but once you master them, you can design databases that are flexible, highly performant, and capable of scaling to millions of users.

Review Question 11.17
What are Schema Design Patterns in NoSQL?
a. Random structures created per project
b. Strict normalization rules
c. Proven solutions to recurring database design problems
d. Built-in MongoDB commands

Review Question 11.18
The Attribute Pattern is primarily designed to solve what problem?
a. Large document sizes
b. Too many unpredictable product fields
c. Slow network latency
d. Write-heavy workloads

Review Question 11.19
Why would directly storing fields like `processor`, `ram`, and `color` create indexing issues in MongoDB?
a. MongoDB prohibits indexing text fields
b. Each attribute would require its own index
c. Indexes slow down writes completely
d. JSON does not support nested fields

Review Question 11.20
In the Attribute Pattern, how are flexible attributes stored?
a. In separate collections
b. As foreign keys
c. As a single key-value array
d. In binary format

Review Question 11.21
What is the main problem addressed by the Bucket Pattern?
a. Schema migrations
b. Massive streams of time-series data
c. Many-to-many relationships

d. Product search filtering

Review Question 11.22
What additional benefit does the `summary` section in a bucket provide?
a. Encryption
b. Pre-calculated metrics
c. Index removal
d. Automatic sharding

Review Question 11.23
The Subset Pattern is primarily a compromise between which two approaches?
a. Indexing and sharding
b. Embedding and referencing
c. ACID and BASE
d. Compression and encryption

Review Question 11.24
What problem does the Subset Pattern prevent?
a. Infinite recursion
b. Index corruption
c. Network outages
d. The unbounded array issue

Review Question 11.25
What is the primary drawback of fully normalized referencing in NoSQL?
a. Data duplication
b. Limited indexing
c. Multiple database queries
d. Reduced storage flexibility

Review Question 11.26
The Extended Reference Pattern duplicates which type of data?
a. Entire related documents
b. Frequently accessed fields only
c. All historical records
d. Index definitions

Review Question 11.27
Why is embedding `price_at_purchase` in an order document important?
a. To reduce index size
b. To prevent product deletion
c. To preserve historical accuracy
d. To eliminate foreign keys

## 11.4 Denormalization Strategies

In the relational SQL world, duplication is considered a cardinal sin. If a user changes their name, you only want to update that name in one single table. But as we transition deeper into NoSQL, you are learning that the rules have changed. In the world of massive scale -- think Netflix, Amazon, or X (formerly Twitter) -- joining tables together on the fly is simply too slow. To make web pages load instantly, NoSQL embraces denormalization: the deliberate duplication and grouping of data to optimize for read performance.

This isn't a careless mistake; it is a highly calculated architectural strategy. Let's look at when to use it, the four ways to do it, and how to keep your database from descending into chaos when duplicated data needs to change.

## 11.4.1 The Golden Rules: When to Denormalize

Before you start copying and pasting data everywhere, you need to understand your application's Read-to-Write Ratio. On platforms like X, millions of people might view a viral tweet, but only one person wrote it. That is a massive read-to-write ratio (perhaps 10,000 to 1). In these scenarios, you must denormalize. You willingly make the database work a little harder during the one single "write" so that the 10,000 "reads" are blindingly fast. You should also denormalize when related data is always displayed together on the screen, or when the data you are duplicating rarely changes (like a birthdate or a published article).

Conversely, do not denormalize if your data is highly volatile. If a piece of data changes every five seconds (like a live stock market price), and you have duplicated that price across fifty different documents, your database will spend all its processing power frantically trying to update all fifty copies, bringing your system to a halt.

## 11.4.2 Four Practical Strategies for Denormalization

When you decide to denormalize, there are four techniques used by software engineers.

Strategy 1. Complete Duplication (The "Copy/Paste" Method)
This is the simplest form of denormalization. You take an entire document and embed it directly inside another document.

Imagine a blog post. Instead of just putting an `author_id` on the post and making the database look up the author later, you copy the author's entire profile -- their name, their bio, their social media links, and their avatar -- directly into the blog post document. This is perfect for small pieces of data that are relatively stable. When a reader clicks the article, the database does one quick fetch, and the entire page loads instantly.

Strategy 2. Selective Duplication (The "Teaser Trailer" Method)
Complete duplication is great, but what if the related document is massive? If your user profiles contain hundreds of settings, purchase history, and private messages, you don't want to embed all of that into a public blog post!

Instead, you use Selective Duplication. You duplicate only the specific fields needed to render the screen. On a blog post, you might duplicate just the `author_name` and `author_avatar_url`, while keeping a reference ID to the full user profile. This gives you the speed of denormalization without bloating your document size.

Strategy 3. Computed Values (The "Math in Advance" Method)
In a relational database, if you want to know the average review score of a pair of headphones, you write a SQL query like `SELECT AVG(rating) FROM Reviews WHERE product_id = 123`. The database then grinds through thousands of reviews, calculates the math, and returns a `4.3`. Doing this math every single time a customer views the product page is a massive waste of CPU power.

In NoSQL, we denormalize this by pre-computing the value. We add fields directly to the main Product document for `average_rating` and `total_review_count`. When a user loads the page, no math is done; the database just reads the static number `4.3` and displays it.

Strategy 4. Snapshot Data (The "Carbon Copy" Method)
Sometimes, denormalization isn't just for speed; it is required for legal or business logic. Imagine an e-commerce order. If you buy a laptop today for $1,000, your order receipt needs to reflect that forever. If the store uses a relational database and only references the `product_id`, and the store manager raises the price of the laptop to $1,200 tomorrow, your historical receipt will suddenly look like you paid $1,200!
By duplicating the `price_at_purchase` and the `item_name` directly into the order document at the exact moment of checkout, you create a permanent "snapshot." This data should never be updated, even if the source data changes.

## 11.4.3 The Catch: Maintaining the Clones

Denormalization sounds like a cheat code for fast applications, but it introduces the hardest problem in NoSQL: Data Synchronization. If you duplicate a user's name across 50 documents, and they get married and change their last name, how do you update all 50 copies without breaking your app?

1. Update-on-Write (The Brute Force Approach)
The most straightforward method is to update everything instantly. When the user changes their name, your application code immediately reaches into the `Users` collection to update their profile, and then searches the `Comments`, `Posts`, and `Orders` collections to overwrite their name everywhere it appears.

This ensures your data is perfectly accurate everywhere, immediately. However, it makes the "Save" button feel very slow for the user, because the database is doing a ton of work behind the scenes.

2. Periodic Batch Updates (The "Night Shift")
Instead of doing the heavy lifting instantly, you can schedule it for when the servers are quiet. Think back to our "Computed Values" example with the average product ratings. It doesn't actually matter if an Amazon product's average rating is accurate down to the very second. Engineers will write "Cron Jobs" -- automated scripts that wake up at 3:00 AM when web traffic is low. The script scans all the new reviews from the past 24 hours, calculates the new averages, and updates the main Product documents in one big batch.

This keeps your website fast during the day. The trade-off is temporary inconsistency; a user might leave a 1-star review at noon, but the product's overall average won't drop until the next morning.

3. Event-Driven Updates (The "Domino Effect")
In modern, advanced applications, engineers use a concept called "Message Queues" (like Kafka or RabbitMQ). When a user updates their profile picture, the application updates their main profile and then shouts into a digital megaphone: "Hey everyone, User 123 changed their picture!" The application immediately returns a "Success" message to the user, so the app feels lightning fast. Meanwhile, in the background, invisible worker servers hear that megaphone announcement and quietly scramble to update the old picture in the forums, the blog posts, and the chat messages.

This is the industry standard for massive apps because it handles high volume perfectly without slowing down the user experience. However, it requires setting up extra infrastructure.

4. Accept Staleness (The "Good Enough" Principle)

Sometimes, the best strategy is simply to do nothing. If you have ever watched a new, viral YouTube video, you might have noticed the view count randomly freezing at "301 views" for several hours, even though thousands of people are watching it. This is YouTube actively choosing to accept stale data. Updating the central view counter for every single view would crash their servers. So, they just cache the number `301`, show that to everyone to keep the page loading fast, and catch up on the real math later.

For non-critical data (like avatars on old forum posts, or view counters), allowing the data to be slightly stale or outdated is acceptable and saves computing power.

Review Question 11.28
Why is duplication traditionally discouraged in relational SQL databases?
a. It reduces query flexibility
b. It increases storage costs
c. It requires updating data in multiple places
d. It prevents table joins

Review Question 11.29
Why do large-scale platforms like Netflix and Amazon often prefer denormalization?
a. Storage is cheaper than compute
b. Table joins are too slow at massive scale
c. SQL does not support joins
d. Their data rarely changes

Review Question 11.30
When should you avoid denormalizing data?
a. When related data is always displayed together
b. When data rarely changes
c. When writes are infrequent
d. When data changes very frequently

Review Question 11.31
In Selective Duplication, what is typically duplicated in a blog post?
a. The entire user profile
b. Only the database ID
c. Just the necessary display fields
d. All historical activity

Review Question 11.32
Snapshot Data is particularly important for which scenario?
a. Temporary cache storage
b. Live sports scores
c. Historical transaction records
d. Session authentication

Review Question 11.33
What is the main drawback of the Update-on-Write approach?
a. It allows inconsistent data
b. It delays background processing
c. It makes the user's save action slower
d. It requires message queues

Review Question 11.34
Event-Driven Updates commonly rely on technologies like Apache Kafka. What is their main advantage?
a. They eliminate data duplication
b. They make updates synchronous
c. They maintain responsiveness while updating in the background
d. They remove the need for indexing

Review Question 11.35
Why might platforms like YouTube intentionally allow stale view counts?
a. To reduce storage costs
b. To prevent server overload
c. To improve data accuracy
d. To simplify database schemas

# 11.5 Chapter Summary

This chapter outlines NoSQL data modeling, emphasizing design for access patterns over abstract entities. It advocates storing related data together, embracing controlled redundancy, and choosing embedding versus referencing based on cardinality. Key schema patterns like Attribute and Bucket optimize specific use cases, while denormalization strategies enhance read performance. Together, they set the stage for practical implementation in the next chapter.

# 11.6 Discussion Questions

Discussion 11.1
When should you choose embedding over referencing? Provide three specific criteria.

Discussion 11.2
Explain the MongoDB Schema Design Patterns covered in this chapter and describe a use case for each pattern where it would be beneficial. Additionally, describe what types of applications benefit most from it.

Discussion 11.3
Describe the strategies discussed in the chapter for maintaining denormalized data and trade-offs of each.

# 11.7 Solutions to the Review Questions

11.1 C; 11.2 D; 11.3 B; 11.4 C; 11.5 C; 11.6 A; 11.7 B; 11.8 B; 11.9 B; 11.10 B; 11.11 C; 11.12 B; 11.13 D; 11.14 B; 11.15 A; 11.16 B; 11.17 C; 11.18 B; 11.19 B; 11.20 C; 11.21 B; 11.22 B; 11.23 B; 11.24 D; 11.25 C; 11.26 B; 11.27 C; 11.28 C; 11.29 B; 11.30 D; 11.31 C; 11.32 C; 11.33 C; 11.34 C; 11.35 B;

# Chapter 12 A Hands-On Introduction to MongoDB

## Chapter Learning Objectives

12.1 Insert documents into a collection using insertOne() and insertMany().
12.2 Query documents with filters, projections, comparison operators, and logical operators.
12.3 Sort and limit query results to control what data is returned.
12.4 Update and Delete documents using common operators.

## 12.1 Introduction

In previous chapters you learned about NoSQL databases in general -- their motivation, categories, and the CAP theorem trade-offs that differentiate them from traditional relational systems. You have also worked extensively with relational databases and SQL, so you understand concepts such as tables, rows, primary keys, foreign keys, and joins. This chapter builds a bridge between those two worlds by introducing MongoDB, the most widely used document-oriented NoSQL database in the world. Rather than working with a completely new data set, we will take a familiar relational schema -- the LifeStyleDB database you may recognize from earlier SQL chapters -- and reshape it into MongoDB's flexible document model.

MongoDB stores data as documents written in a format called BSON (Binary JSON). Unlike a row in a relational table, a BSON document is a self-describing, hierarchical structure that can hold nested sub-documents and arrays. A collection of documents is roughly analogous to a table, and a database in MongoDB is a named container for collections. Because there is no fixed schema enforced by the database engine, two documents in the same collection can have completely different fields, giving you the flexibility to evolve your data model without running ALTER TABLE statements.

MongoDB provides a rich query language, powerful aggregation pipelines, full-text search, and geospatial capabilities -- but for this introductory chapter, we will focus exclusively on the four fundamental data-manipulation operations: Create, Read, Update, and Delete (CRUD).

The chapter is organized into five main sections. We begin with setting up the environment so that you have a working MongoDB installation and the MongoDB Compass interface. We then examine the design decisions involved in converting the relational LifeStyleDB schema into MongoDB collections. The three sections that follow cover each CRUD category in turn, pairing each concept with a numbered example drawn directly from the LifeStyleDB data and a corresponding exercise so that you can practice immediately. By the end of the chapter you will be comfortable using MongoDB Compass -- the graphical interface -- to manage data in a real database.

Review Question 12.1
How does a MongoDB collection compare to a relational database structure?
a. It is equivalent to a database view
b. It is roughly analogous to a table
c. It functions as a foreign key
d. It replaces the need for rows

Review Question 12.2
What key characteristic distinguishes BSON documents from relational table rows?
a. They require predefined schemas
b. They cannot store arrays
c. They are limited to flat structures
d. They can contain nested and hierarchical data

Review Question 12.3
Which tool will you use in this book to manage MongoDB data?
a. MongoDB Compass
b. SQL Developer
c. mongosh
d. phpMyAdmin

## 12.2 Setting Up the Environment

This section guides you through setting up your MongoDB development environment. You'll install the free MongoDB Community Server and MongoDB Compass, the official graphical user interface (GUI), then establish your first connection. By the end, you'll have a fully functional local database instance ready for the hands-on, visual examples in this chapter.

### 12.2.1 Installing MongoDB Community Server

MongoDB is available in several editions. For learning and development purposes, the free MongoDB Community Server is everything you need. Navigate to https://www.mongodb.com/try/download/community and choose the installer that matches your operating system. As of the current release, MongoDB 8.2.5 is the latest stable branch. The examples in this chapter were tested on MongoDB 8.2.5, though the core features are compatible with versions 6.x and later.

Since this book uses Visual Studio for the first eight chapters, we assume you are using Windows. However, MongoDB can be installed on macOS and Linux. Download the `.msi` installer and run it. The setup wizard will ask whether you want to install "complete" or "custom"; click on "complete." Next, it will ask if you want to run MongoDB as a Windows Service; accepting this default means the database server starts automatically every time Windows boots. Crucially, the installer also offers to install *MongoDB Compass*. Ensure this option is checked, as Compass will be our primary tool for interacting with the database throughout this chapter.

After installation, verify that the MongoDB daemon (`mongod`) is running by checking its status. On Windows, open the Services panel (`services.msc`) and confirm that the MongoDB service shows as Running.

### 12.2.2 Exploring MongoDB Compass

Instead of relying on a command-line shell, we will use MongoDB Compass for all database interactions. Compass is a powerful, user-friendly graphical interface that allows you to explore your data, build complex queries with a simple point-and-click environment, and visualize your database schema without needing to memorize MongoDB's query language right away. If you accidentally unchecked Compass during the server installation, you can easily download it separately from the official MongoDB website. Once installed, simply locate MongoDB Compass in your Start menu or Applications folder and launch it.

### 12.2.3 Connecting to the MongoDB Server

With the `mongod` service running and Compass open, you are ready to establish your first connection. Upon launching Compass, you will be greeted by the "New Connection" screen. Click on the "Add new connection" button. By default, the Connection String (URI) field is usually pre-filled with `mongodb://localhost:27017`. This is the exact local address and port where your freshly installed server is listening. Type "Book" in the name field and Click the "Save & Connect"

Once connected, the Compass interface will display a list of default databases, such as `admin`, `config`, and `local` under Book connection. These are safe system spaces that you can ignore for now.

Throughout this chapter, we will use our own database named `lifestyledb`. You do not need to execute a command to create this database explicitly; in MongoDB Compass, you can simply click the "+" icon

(Create Database) to set up a new database and collection.

If your database server is not running on the default host and port, or if you are using a cloud-hosted MongoDB Atlas cluster, you can easily adapt. For Atlas clusters, the web dashboard will generate a full connection string (e.g., `mongodb+srv://...`) which you can copy and paste directly into the Compass connection bar before clicking connect.

Review Question 12.4
What is the purpose of MongoDB Compass?
a. To automatically back up databases
b. To provide a graphical interface for interacting with MongoDB
c. To replace the MongoDB server process
d. To compile BSON files into JSON

Review Question 12.5
What does the default connection string `mongodb://localhost:27017` represent?
a. A remote cloud cluster
b. A backup database location
c. The local server address and port
d. A temporary test environment

Review Question 12.6
How can the `lifestyledb` database be created in MongoDB with compass?
a. By running a command-line CREATE DATABASE statement
b. By using the Create Database button
c. Automatically during installation
d. By modifying the configuration file

## 12.3. Modeling LifeStyleDB in MongoDB

Having spent the first eight chapters building and querying LifeStyleDB as a relational database, you are now ready to re-imagine this system within a document-oriented architecture. This section guides you through the process of schema design for MongoDB, using the familiar LifeStyleDB entities as our foundation. Transitioning from SQL to NoSQL demands a strategic shift in how we think about data relationships and storage based on access patterns. We will analyze the existing relational relationships and make deliberate design choices about embedding versus referencing to optimize the database for MongoDB's architecture.

### 12.3.1 Reviewing the Relational Schema

LifeStyleDB contains seven tables across three schemas. The HR schema holds an Employees table that includes a self-referencing ManagerId foreign key. The Purchasing schema contains Suppliers, Products, and Deliveries tables, where Products references Suppliers and Deliveries references Products. The Sales schema holds Customers, Orders, and OrderDetails tables, with Orders referencing both Customers and Employees, and OrderDetails referencing both Orders and Products.

## 12.3.2 Embedding vs. Referencing

As you learned in Chapter 11, embedding places related data directly inside a parent document as a nested sub-document or array. Referencing stores a piece of identifying information (typically an _id value) in one document that points to another document in a different collection, similar to a foreign key. The general guidance in MongoDB design is: "Embed when you access the data together; reference when you access the data independently."

For LifeStyleDB we will make the following choices. OrderDetails will be embedded inside each Order document as an array of line-item sub-documents, because an order and its details are almost always retrieved together and order details have no meaningful existence outside their parent order. All other entities -- Customers, Employees, Suppliers, Products, and Deliveries -- will remain as separate collections, and we will reference them by their numeric id field. This hybrid approach is typical of real-world MongoDB applications.

One important difference from a relational database is that MongoDB automatically assigns every inserted document a unique identifier stored in the _id field. By default, _id is an ObjectId -- a 12-byte value that is globally unique and includes an embedded timestamp. For learning purposes we will override the default by providing our own integer _id values that match the original primary keys from the relational database. This makes it easier to compare the MongoDB data against the SQL data you already know.

## 12.3.3 Collection Overview

After applying these design decisions, our MongoDB version of LifeStyleDB will have six collections. The customers collection holds one document per customer, with address fields stored as a nested address sub-document. The employees collection holds one document per employee; the managerId field stores the integer _id of the manager, serving as a manual reference. The suppliers collection holds one document per supplier with an embedded address. The products collection holds one document per product and references its supplier via a supplierId field. The deliveries collection holds one document per delivery event referencing a productId. Finally, the orders collection holds one document per order, embedding an array called orderDetails that contains one sub-document per line item. The diagram below summarizes the six collections and their key fields.

Review Question 12.7
What is a key difference between relational databases and MongoDB regarding relationships?

a. MongoDB enforces stricter foreign keys
b. Relational databases do not support JOINs
c. MongoDB does not natively enforce foreign key constraints
d. Relational databases require embedded documents

Review Question 12.8
According to general MongoDB design guidance, when should you embed related data?
a. When the data changes frequently
b. When the data is always accessed together
c. When storage space is limited
d. When documents exceed 12 bytes

Review Question 12.9
In the MongoDB version of LifeStyleDB, how are OrderDetails handled?
a. Stored in a separate collection with references
b. Converted into supplier documents
c. Embedded inside each Order document
d. Removed to simplify the schema

Review Question 12.10
What is the default type of the `_id` field in MongoDB?
a. Integer
b. UUID string
c. ObjectId
d. Auto-increment value

# 12.4 CRUD Operations: Create

Creating data in MongoDB means inserting documents into a collection. MongoDB provides two methods for this purpose: insertOne() inserts a single document, and insertMany() inserts an array of documents in a single operation. Both methods are called on a collection object, and both return a result object that tells you whether the operation succeeded and what _id values were assigned.

## 12.4.1 Opening a Database Session

NoSQL Example 12.1: Launching MongoDB Compass and Connecting to the Server

Before performing any database operations you must start an interactive MongoDB Compass session. Open the application, connect to your server clicking the “Book” connection you added early in the chapter, and open the embedded shell (mongosh) at the top right of the screen. MongoDB will display a welcome message and place you at the test> prompt.

Once connected, you can issue the db command to confirm which database is currently active. You can also run show dbs to list all databases that currently contain data. To practice, type the following at the prompt:

```
db
```

This will shows current database name which is "test"

Next, type the following at the prompt:

```
show dbs
```

This will lists all databases with their size

At this point you are connected to the test database, which is MongoDB's default. In the next example, we will switch to our working database.

### 12.4.2 Creating the LifeStyleDB Database

NoSQL Example 12.2: Switching to (and Creating) the lifestyledb Database

In MongoDB the *use* command switches the current context to a named database. If the database does not yet exist, MongoDB will create it the first time you write any data to it. Type the
following at the MongoDB Compass prompt:

```
use lifestyledb
```

The shell responds with *switched to db lifestyledb* and your prompt changes to **lifestyledb>**. The database does not physically exist on disk yet -- MongoDB is lazily waiting until you insert at least one document. You can verify this by running show dbs, which will not yet show lifestyledb in the list. After the first insert in the next example, the database will appear.

### 12.4.3 Inserting a Single Document with insertOne()

NoSQL Example 12.3: Inserting One Customer Document

The insertOne() method accepts a single JavaScript object (document) and inserts it into the specified collection. The syntax is db.collectionName.insertOne({ field: value, ... }). If the collection does not exist, MongoDB creates it automatically. Let us insert the first customer from our data set:

```
db.customers.insertOne({_id: 1, customerName: "Just Electronics",
address: {street: "123 Broad way", city: "New York", state: "NY", postalCode: "12012",
country: "USA"},
contact: "John White",
email: "jwhite@je.com"
})
```

Notice several things about this document. First, we explicitly set _id to the integer 1, matching the original CustomerId from the relational table. This is not required -- if you omit _id, MongoDB generates an

ObjectId automatically -- but using the original keys makes the data easier to reason about while you are learning. Second, the four address-related columns from the SQL table (StreetAddress, City, State, PostalCode, Country) have been consolidated into a nested address sub-document. This is a common MongoDB pattern: fields that are logically related and always
retrieved together work well as an embedded sub-document. After running insertOne(), MongoDB responds with an acknowledgment object similar to:

```
{
acknowledged: true,
insertedId: 1
}
```

The acknowledged field confirms that the write was received and stored, and insertedId shows the _id of the newly inserted document. Now run show dbs again -- you will see lifestyledb has appeared in the list, confirming that the database was created.

## 12.4.4 Inserting Multiple Documents with insertMany()

NoSQL Example 12.4: Inserting All Customers with insertMany()

While insertOne() is convenient for a single document, insertMany() is far more efficient when you need to load multiple documents at once. It accepts an array of document objects and inserts them all in a single network round-trip. Let us insert the remaining seven customers. Note that customer 8 (Cheap Electronics) has no contact or email in the original data, so we simply omit those fields -- MongoDB imposes no requirement that every document contain the same fields.

```
db.customers.insertMany([{ _id: 2, customerName: "Beyond Electronics",
address: { street: "45 Cherry Street", city:"Chicago", state: "IL", postalCode:
"32302", country: "USA" },
contact: "Scott Green", email: "green@beil.com" },
{ _id: 3, customerName: "Beyond Electronics",
address: { street: "6767 GameOver Blvd", city:"Atlanta", state: "GA", postalCode:
"43347", country: "USA" },
contact: "Alice Black", email: "black1@be.com" },
{ _id: 4, customerName: "E Fun",
address: { street: "888 Main Ave.", city: "Seattle", state: "WA", postalCode: "69356",
country: "USA" },
contact: "Ben Gold", email: "bgold@efun.com" },
{ _id: 5, customerName: "Overstock E",
address: { street: "39 Garden Place", city: "Los Angeles", state: "CA", postalCode:
"32302", country: "USA" },
contact: "Daniel Yellow", email: "dy@os.com" },
{ _id: 6, customerName: "E Fun",
address: { street: "915 Market st.", city: "London", state: "England", postalCode:
"EC1A 1BB", country: "UK" },
```

```
contact: "Frank Green", email: "green@ef.com" },
{ _id: 7, customerName: "Electronics4U",
address: { street: "27 Colmore Row", city: "Birmingham", state: "England", postalCode:
"B3 2EW", country: "UK" },
contact: "Grace Smith", email: "smith@e4u.com" },
{ _id: 8, customerName: "Cheap Electronics",
address: { street: "1010 Easy St", city: "Ottawa", state: "Ontario", postalCode: "K1A
0B1", country: "Canada" } }
])
```

insertMany() returns an object containing acknowledged: true and an insertedIds map that lists the _id of every inserted document. If any single document in the array fails to insert (for example, because its _id already exists in the collection), MongoDB stops inserting at that point by default and reports the error. You can change this behavior by passing the option { ordered: false }, which tells MongoDB to continue inserting the remaining documents even after encountering an error.

## 12.4.5 Inserting Employees

NoSQL Example 12.5: Inserting Employee Documents with a Self-Reference

The Employees table in the relational schema contains a self-referencing ManagerId foreign key. In MongoDB, we represent this as a plain managerId field that stores the integer _id of the manager document. There is no built-in enforcement of this reference – MongoDB will not prevent you from inserting a managerId that does not correspond to any existing employee document -- but the reference is meaningful to your application code. Employee 1 (Alex Hall) is the top-level manager, so his managerId field is set to null.

```
db.employees.insertMany([{ _id: 1, firstName: "Alex", lastName: "Hall", birthDate: new
Date("1990-02-03"), hireDate: new Date("2015-08-09"), address: { street: "85 Main Ln",
city: "New Canton", state: "VA", postalCode: "23123"}, phone: "(434) 290-3322",
managerId: null },
{ _id: 2, firstName: "Dianne", lastName: "Hart", birthDate: new Date("1978-12-03"),
hireDate: new Date("2010-08-01"), address: { street: "209 Social Hall Blvd", city:
"New Canton", state: "VA", postalCode: "23123" }, phone: "(434) 290-1122", managerId:
1 },
{ _id: 3, firstName: "Maria", lastName: "Law", birthDate: new Date("1988-07-13"),
hireDate: new Date("2012-08-21"), address: { street: "258 Blinkys St", city: "New
Canton", state: "VA", postalCode: "23123" }, phone: "(434) 531-5673", managerId: 1 },
{ _id: 4, firstName: "Alice", lastName: "Law", birthDate: new Date("1988-12-13"),
hireDate: new Date("2012-04-22"), address: { street: "300 Vista Valley Blvd", city:
"Buckingham", state: "VA", postalCode: "23123" }, phone: "(434) 531-1010", managerId:
1 },
{ _id: 5, firstName: "Black", lastName: "Hart", birthDate: new Date("1982-11-09"),
hireDate: new Date("2015-04-12"), address: { street: "1 Old Fifteen St", city:
"Buckingham", state: "VA", postalCode: "23123" }, phone: "(434) 531-1034", managerId:
2 },
```

```
{ _id: 6, firstName: "Christina", lastName: "Robinson", birthDate: new Date("1978-07-
13"), hireDate: new Date("2014-06-15"), address: { street: "217 Chapel St", city: "New
Canton", state: "VA", postalCode: "23123" }, managerId: 2 },
{ _id: 7, firstName: "Nicholas", lastName: "Pinkston", birthDate: new Date("1977-10-
05"), hireDate: new Date("2013-05-22"), address: { street: "26 N James Madison Rd",
city: "Buckingham", state: "VA", postalCode: "23123" }, managerId: 3 }
])
```

Pay close attention to how dates are stored. In MongoDB Compass you create a JavaScript Date object using the new Date() constructor with an ISO 8601 string. MongoDB stores this as a BSON Date type, which is an integer count of milliseconds since the Unix epoch. Storing dates as BSON Date values rather than plain strings is important because it allows MongoDB to perform date-based comparisons and range queries correctly. Employee 6 (Christina Robinson) has no phone number in the original data, so we simply omit the phone field from her document -- a demonstration of MongoDB's flexible, schema-less design.

## 12.4.6 Inserting Suppliers and Products

NoSQL Example 12.6: Inserting Product Documents that Reference Suppliers

First, populate the suppliers collection. Because the insert statements are structurally identical to what you have already seen, we show only two representative documents here and leave the rest to Exercise 6 at the end of the chapter.

```
db.suppliers.insertMany(
[{ _id: 1, supplierName: "Pine Apple", address: { street: "1 Pine Apple St.", city:
"Idanha", state: "CA", postalCode: "87201", country: "USA" } },
{ _id: 2, supplierName: "IMB", address: { street: "123 International Blvd", city:
"Los Angeles", state: "CA", postalCode: "89202", country: "USA" } }
])
```

Now insert the nine products. Each product document contains a supplierId field that references the _id of a document in the suppliers collection. MongoDB does not enforce this reference, but your application code (or a validation rule you define) can check its integrity when needed.

```
db.products.insertMany([
{ _id: 1, productName: "65-Inch 4K Ultra HD Smart TV", supplierId: 4 },
{ _id: 2, productName: "60-Inch 4K Ultra HD Smart LED TV", supplierId: 4 },
{ _id: 3, productName: "3200 Lumens LED Home Theater Projector", supplierId:3},
{ _id: 4, productName: "Wireless Color Photo Printer", supplierId: 5 },
{ _id: 5, productName: "6Wireless Compact Laser Printer", supplierId: 2 },
{ _id: 6, productName: "Color Laser Printer", supplierId: 2 },
{ _id: 7, productName: "10" 16GB Android Tablet", supplierId: 4 },
{ _id: 8, productName: "GPS Android Tablet PC", supplierId: 2 },
{ _id: 9, productName: "20.2 MP Digital Camera", supplierId: 5 }
])
```

## 12.4.7 Inserting Orders with Embedded Order Details

NoSQL Example 12.7: Inserting Order Documents with an Embedded orderDetails Array

This is the most structurally interesting insert in our data set. In the relational schema, an order and its line items were stored in two separate tables: Sales.Orders and Sales.OrderDetails. In MongoDB, we embed the line items directly inside each order document as an array named orderDetails. Each element of the array is a sub-document with three fields: productId, price, and quantity. This denormalized design means that retrieving a complete order -- including all its line items -- requires only one database lookup instead of a JOIN. The trade-off is that if the price of a product changes in the products collection, the historical price embedded in completed orders is not automatically updated, which is actually desirable behavior for order management systems since you want to preserve the price at the time of sale.

```
db.orders.insertMany([
{ _id: 1, customerId: 1, employeeId: 5, orderDate: new Date("2017-01-03"),
orderDetails: [
{ productId: 1, price: 1499.99, quantity: 1 }, { productId: 3, price: 149.99,
quantity: 2 }
]},
{ _id: 2, customerId: 1, employeeId: 3, orderDate: new Date("2017-03-05"),
orderDetails: [
{ productId: 1, price: 1499.99, quantity: 1 }, { productId: 4, price: 99.99,
quantity: 6 },
{ productId: 6, price: 189.99, quantity: 5 },
{ productId: 2, price: 1599.99, quantity: 1 }
]},
{ _id: 3, customerId: 2, employeeId: 5, orderDate: new Date("2017-02-23"),
orderDetails: [
{ productId: 6, price: 199.99, quantity: 1 },
{ productId: 7, price: 109.99, quantity: 2 },
{ productId: 8, price: 69.99, quantity: 2 },
{ productId: 3, price: 159.99, quantity: 2 },
{ productId: 9, price: 1449.99,quantity: 1 }
]},
{ _id: 4, customerId: 4, employeeId: 5, orderDate: new Date("2017-04-13"),
orderDetails: [
{ productId: 8, price: 69.99, quantity: 1 },
{ productId: 4, price: 99.99, quantity: 2 }
]},
{ _id: 5, customerId: 1, employeeId: 4, orderDate: new Date("2017-05-03"),
orderDetails: [
{ productId: 6, price: 199.99, quantity: 3 },
{ productId: 3, price: 149.99, quantity: 6 }
]},
{ _id: 6, customerId: 3, employeeId: 6, orderDate: new Date("2017-05-08"),
orderDetails: [
```

```
{ productId: 1, price: 1499.99, quantity: 1 }
]},
{ _id: 7, customerId: 5, employeeId: 7, orderDate: new Date("2016-11-08"),
orderDetails: [
{ productId: 2, price: 999.99, quantity: 1 }
]},
{ _id: 8, customerId: 7, employeeId: 2, orderDate: new Date("2016-12-23"),
orderDetails: [
{ productId: 7, price: 79.99, quantity: 1 },
{ productId: 8, price: 59.99, quantity: 2 }
]}
])
```

With all seven insertMany() operations complete, you now have a fully populated LifeStyleDB in MongoDB. You can confirm by running `show collections`, which should list customers, employees, suppliers, products, deliveries, and orders. You can also run db.customers.countDocuments() to confirm that 8 documents were inserted, and db.orders.countDocuments() to confirm 8 orders.

Review Question 12.11
Which command lists all databases that currently contain data in the MongoDB shell?
a. `list dbs`
b. `db.show()`
c. `show dbs`
d. `display databases`

Review Question 12.12
What database is active by default when you first connect to MongoDB?
a. admin
b. system
c. local
d. test

Review Question 12.13
What happens when you run `use lifestyledb` if the database does not yet exist?
a. MongoDB creates the database immediately
b. The command fails with an error
c. The database is created only after data is inserted
d. MongoDB deletes the current database

Review Question 12.14
If a document inserted with `insertOne()` does not include an `_id` field, what does MongoDB do?
a. Rejects the insert
b. Generates an automatic identifier
c. Sets `_id` to zero
d. Uses the collection name as `_id`

Review Question 12.15

Why were address fields grouped into a nested sub-document in the customer example?
a. To reduce document size
b. To enforce relational constraints
c. Because related data is often retrieved together
d. Because MongoDB requires nested documents

Review Question 12.16
What happens by default if one document fails during an `insertMany()` operation?
a. MongoDB deletes previously inserted documents
b. MongoDB skips the error and continues
c. MongoDB stops inserting further documents
d. MongoDB automatically fixes the error

Review Question 12.17
How is the self-referencing manager relationship represented in the employees collection?
a. Using an embedded employee document
b. Using a managerId field referencing another employee's `_id`
c. Using a JOIN query
d. Using an array of manager documents

Review Question 12.18
Why are employee birth dates and hire dates stored using `new Date()`?
a. To reduce storage space
b. To allow MongoDB to perform date comparisons and queries
c. To convert them into text fields
d. To avoid BSON formatting

Review Question 12.19
Why are order line items embedded inside the `orderDetails` array in the orders collection?
a. To eliminate the need for database connections
b. To allow multiple customers per order
c. To avoid retrieving product data
d. To retrieve an entire order with one database query

## 12.5 CRUD Operations: Read

Reading data in MongoDB is done primarily with the find() method. At its simplest, find() with no arguments retrieves all documents in a collection. By adding a filter document as the first argument, you narrow the results to only those documents that match the specified criteria. A second optional argument called a projection controls which fields appear in the result. Additional cursor methods like sort() and limit() can be chained to control ordering and the maximum number of results returned.

In this context, the `find()` method returns a cursor object rather than the documents themselves. Acting as an iterator or pointer to the result set, the cursor allows the database to process queries efficiently without loading all matching data into memory at once. This structure is what enables the chaining of methods like `sort()` and `limit()` to refine the query before you iterate over the cursor to retrieve the actual documents.

## 12.5.1 Retrieving All Documents

NoSQL Example 12.8: Finding All Customers

The most basic read operation retrieves every document in a collection. Call find() with no arguments on the customers collection (issue use lifestyledb command if needed):

```
db.customers.find()
```

MongoDB returns all eight customer documents. In mongosh, the output is formatted as pretty-printed JSON by default. If you are working in a context where the output is not automatically formatted, you can chain the .pretty() cursor method, although in modern versions of mongosh pretty-printing is the default behavior. Notice that each document contains the address sub-document nested within it, exactly as we inserted it. MongoDB does not flatten nested documents during retrieval.

You can also use findOne() when you are interested in only the first matching document. With no filter, db.customers.findOne() returns the first document MongoDB encounters in natural storage order, which for a freshly populated collection will typically be the document with _id: 1.

## 12.5.2 Filtering Documents

NoSQL Example 12.9: Finding Customers Located in the USA

To filter documents you pass a query filter -- a document that describes the criteria a matching document must satisfy -- as the first argument to find(). For equality comparisons, the filter document has the same shape as the field you want to match. To find all customers whose country is "USA", you match against the nested address.country field using dot notation:

```
db.customers.find({ "address.country": "USA" })
```

Dot notation is how you navigate into nested sub-documents in MongoDB queries. The field path "address.country" refers to the country field inside the address sub-document. MongoDB will return the five customer documents where address.country equals the string "USA". Note that the comparison is case-sensitive; "USA" and "usa" would return different results.

Dot notation also works for arrays. If you want to find all orders that include a specific productId in their orderDetails array, you use dot notation into the array: db.orders.find({ "orderDetails.productId": 1 }). MongoDB automatically iterates over array elements when evaluating the filter.

### 12.5.3 Projections

NoSQL Example 12.10: Returning Only Selected Fields

By default, find() returns every field in the matching documents. A projection document, passed as the second argument, lets you include or exclude specific fields. Setting a field to 1 includes it; setting it to 0 excludes it. When selecting which fields to display, you must choose one of two styles: either list the fields you want to see (inclusion) or list the fields you don't want to see (exclusion). You cannot combine these two styles in the same query. However, there is one special exception: you are always allowed to hide the `_id` field, even if you are otherwise choosing specific fields to include.

The following query retrieves all customers but returns only the customerName and email fields. We also explicitly suppress _id by setting it to 0:

```
db.customers.find(
  {},
  { customerName: 1, email: 1, _id: 0 }
)
```

The first argument is an empty filter document {}, which matches all documents. The second argument is the projection. The result contains one document per customer showing only the customerName and email fields. For customer 8, which has no email, MongoDB simply omits the email field from the output because null/missing fields are never included in projection output.

Now consider a query that uses an exclusion projection to return everything except the address sub-document -- useful when you want compact output and the address is not relevant:

```
db.customers.find(
  {},
  { address: 0 }
)
```

This returns all fields in every customer document except for the nested address sub-document.

## 12.5.4 Query Operators

NoSQL Example 12.11: Using Comparison and Logical Operators

Equality filters cover many use cases, but real queries often need range comparisons, membership tests, or logical combinations. MongoDB provides a rich set of query operators, all of which follow the convention of a dollar-sign prefix. The most commonly used comparison operators are $gt (greater than), $gte (greater than or equal), $lt (less than), $lte (less than or equal), $ne (not equal), and $in (value is in a given array). Logical operators $and and $or allow you to combine multiple conditions.

Let us query the orders collection to find all orders placed on or after January 1, 2017:

```
db.orders.find({
  orderDate: { $gte: new Date("2017-01-01") }
})
```

The filter document now uses an operator sub-document instead of a plain value. The pattern { field: { $operator: value } } is the standard syntax for operator-based comparisons in MongoDB. This query returns the six order documents where orderDate is January 1, 2017 or later.

To find orders placed by employee 5 (Black Hart) in 2017, combine two conditions with an implicit AND -- simply include both fields in the same filter document:

```
db.orders.find({
  employeeId: 5,
  orderDate: { $gte: new Date("2017-01-01") }
})
```

When you list multiple conditions in the same filter document, MongoDB treats them as a logical AND. The explicit $and operator produces the same result but is rarely necessary for simple cases:

```
db.orders.find({
  $and: [
    { employeeId: 5 },
    { orderDate: { $gte: new Date("2017-01-01") } }
  ]
})
```

The $in operator tests whether a field's value appears in a specified array. To find all customers located in either the USA or Canada:

```
db.customers.find({
  "address.country": { $in: ["USA", "Canada"] }
})
```

The $or operator evaluates to true when at least one of its sub-conditions is true. To find all employees who are managed by employee 1 or employee 2:

```
db.employees.find({
  $or: [
    { managerId: 1 },
    { managerId: 2 }
  ]
})
```

## 12.5.5 Sorting and Limiting Results

NoSQL Example 12.12: Sorting Orders by Date and Limiting Results

The find() returns a cursor, and you can chain additional methods onto that cursor to control how results are presented. The sort() method accepts a document that specifies which fields to sort on and the direction: 1 for ascending and -1 for descending. The limit() method restricts the cursor to at most a specified number of documents. The skip() method, not demonstrated here, is similarly useful for pagination.

To retrieve the three most recent orders, sorted from newest to oldest:

```
db.orders.find().sort({ orderDate: -1 }).limit(3)
```

The query returns the three orders with the most recent orderDate values. Because we chained sort() before limit(), MongoDB first conceptually sorts all eight orders by date descending, then returns only the top three. In practice, MongoDB may use an index to avoid sorting the entire collection, but the logical result is the same.

You can also combine filtering with sorting and limiting. To find all 2017 orders and display them in chronological order:

```
db.orders.find(
  { orderDate: { $gte: new Date("2017-01-01") } }
).sort({ orderDate: 1 })
```

Review Question 12.20
Which MongoDB method is primarily used to retrieve documents from a collection?
a. retrieve()
b. retrieveDocument()
c. find()
d. retrieveCollection()

Review Question 12.21
What does the `find()` method return in MongoDB before documents are actually retrieved?
a. A JSON object
b. A cursor object
c. A schema definition
d. A temporary collection

Review Question 12.22
Which query correctly retrieves customers whose country is "USA" when the country field is inside the address sub-document?
a. db.customers.find({ country: "USA" })
b. db.customers.find({ address_country: "USA" })
c. db.customers.find({ "address.country": "USA" })
d. db.customers.find({ address: "USA" })

Review Question 12.23
Which statement about MongoDB equality comparisons is correct?
a. They ignore capitalization differences.
b. They are case-sensitive.
c. They automatically convert text to lowercase.
d. They require a special operator.

Review Question 12.24
What is the purpose of a projection in a MongoDB query?
a. To modify the stored documents
b. To control which fields appear in the query results
c. To validate document structure
d. To convert documents to arrays

Review Question 12.25
In a MongoDB projection document, what does setting a field value to `1` indicate?
a. The field will be removed from the database
b. The field will be included in the query result
c. The field will be converted to numeric format
d. The field will be sorted first

Review Question 12.26
Which field can be excluded even when using an inclusion-style projection?
a. orderDate
b. address
c. customerName
d. _id

Review Question 12.27
When multiple conditions are listed in the same MongoDB filter document, how are they evaluated by default?
a. As a logical OR
b. As a logical AND
c. As independent queries
d. As optional filters

Review Question 12.28
What does the following query return?
`db.orders.find().sort({ orderDate: -1 }).limit(3)`
a. The three earliest orders in ascending order
b. The three most recent orders
c. All orders sorted alphabetically
d. The first three orders stored in the collection

## 12.6 CRUD Operations: Update

MongoDB provides several methods for modifying existing documents. The two most commonly used for beginners are updateOne(), which modifies the first document that matches the filter, and updateMany(), which modifies all matching documents. Both methods require two arguments: a filter document that identifies which document(s) to change, and an update document that specifies what changes to make. The update document almost always uses one or more update operators rather than a plain replacement document.

The most important update operators are $set, which sets the value of a field (creating the field if it does not exist); $unset, which removes a field entirely; $inc, which increments a numeric field by a specified amount; $push, which appends an element to an array field; and $pull, which removes matching elements from an array field. Providing a plain document without any operators as the second argument replaces the entire document (except _id), which is rarely what you want and is an easy mistake to make.

### 12.6.1 Updating a Single Document

NoSQL Example 12.13: Updating One Customer's Email Address

Suppose customer 5 (Overstock E) has changed their contact email address. We want to update only the email field without disturbing any other data in the document. Using $set, we can modify a single field while leaving the rest of the document untouched:

```
db.customers.updateOne(
  { _id: 5 },
  { $set: { email: "overstock@os.com" } }
)
```

MongoDB responds with a result object indicating how many documents were matched and modified:

```
{
  acknowledged: true,
```

```
  insertedId: null,
  matchedCount: 1,
  modifiedCount: 1,
  upsertedCount: 0
}
```

matchedCount: 1 confirms that one document matched the filter { _id: 5 }, and modifiedCount: 1 confirms that one document was actually changed. If the new email were identical to the existing value, matchedCount would be 1 but modifiedCount would be 0 because MongoDB detects that nothing actually changed.

The $set operator can also create a new field. If we want to add a creditLimit field to customer 1 that did not previously exist in the document:

```
db.customers.updateOne(
  { _id: 1 },
  { $set: { creditLimit: 50000 } }
)
```

This is one of MongoDB's most useful features: because there is no fixed schema, you can add new fields to specific documents without migrating the entire collection. Other customer documents remain unaffected and have no creditLimit field.

## 12.6.2 Updating Multiple Documents

NoSQL Example 12.14: Adding a country Field to All US Customers

updateMany() applies the same update to every document that matches the filter. This is equivalent to an UPDATE ... WHERE statement in SQL. Imagine that our business decides to add a top-level country field (separate from the one inside the address sub-document) to make certain queries faster, and we want to start by setting this field on all customers in the USA. We can filter by address.country and set the new country field simultaneously:

```
db.customers.updateMany(
  { "address.country": "USA" },
  { $set: { country: "USA" } }
)
```

The response will show matchedCount: 5 and modifiedCount: 5, reflecting the five US-based customers. The three non-US customers remain unchanged.

As another practical example, suppose a new business policy requires that all orders from 2016 be flagged with a status field of "archived". We can apply this to all matching orders in a single operation:

```
db.orders.updateMany(
  {
    orderDate: { $gte: new Date("2016-01-01"), $lt: new Date("2017-01-01") }
  },
  { $set: { status: "archived" } }
)
```

Notice that the comparison operators $gte and $lt are placed inside the same sub-document for the orderDate field, which MongoDB interprets as a range condition equivalent to BETWEEN in SQL. This query will match and update the two orders from 2016 (orders 7 and 8).

Review Question 12.29
What are the two required arguments when using `updateOne()` or `updateMany()` in MongoDB?
a. A projection document and a sort document
b. A filter document and an update document
c. A cursor object and a projection document
d. A collection name and a document ID

Review Question 12.30
Which MongoDB update operator removes a field completely from a document?
a. $pull
b. $set
c. $unset
d. $push

Review Question 12.31
What happens if a plain document without update operators is provided as the second argument in an update operation?
a. MongoDB ignores the update request.
b. MongoDB replaces the entire document except the `_id` field.
c. MongoDB updates only the fields that differ.
d. MongoDB merges the new fields with existing ones automatically.

Review Question 12.32
When the `$set` operator is used to assign a value to a field that does not already exist in a document, what occurs?
a. MongoDB creates the field with the specified value.
b. The update fails due to schema mismatch.
c. MongoDB stores the value in a temporary field.
d. The field is ignored unless previously defined.

Review Question 12.33
In the following query, what type of condition is applied to the `orderDate` field?
`{ orderDate: { $gte: new Date("2016-01-01"), $lt: new Date("2017-01-01") } }`
a. A membership test for multiple dates

b. A logical OR condition
c. A range condition similar to BETWEEN in SQL
d. A text pattern search

## 12.7 CRUD Operations: Delete

Deleting documents in MongoDB is done with deleteOne(), which deletes the first document that matches the filter, and deleteMany(), which deletes all matching documents. Like SQL without foreign key constraints, MongoDB does not cascade deletes -- if you delete a product document, any orders that embed or reference that product are not automatically updated. Your application code must manage referential integrity when it matters to your use case.

### 12.7.1 Deleting a Single Document

NoSQL Example 12.15: Deleting a Specific Customer Document

Suppose customer 8 (Cheap Electronics) has been removed from the system because no orders were ever placed for them. We use deleteOne() with a filter that uniquely identifies the document:

```
db.customers.deleteOne({ _id: 8 })
```

MongoDB returns a result object with a deletedCount field:

```
{
    acknowledged: true,
    deletedCount: 1
 }
```

A deletedCount of 1 confirms that the document was found and removed. If the filter had not matched any document, deletedCount would be 0 and no error would be raised. Verify the deletion with:

```
db.customers.find({ _id: 8 })
```

The result should be an empty cursor, confirming that the document no longer exists in the collection.

### 12.7.2 Deleting Multiple Documents

NoSQL Example 12.16: Deleting All Deliveries for a Given Product

deleteMany() removes every document that matches the filter. This is the MongoDB equivalent of a

DELETE ... WHERE statement in SQL. Suppose that product 7 (10" 16GB Android Tablet) has been discontinued and all delivery records for it need to be purged from the deliveries collection. First, insert the deliveries for product 7 so the example is meaningful:

```
// Insert the deliveries first if not already present
db.deliveries.insertMany([
  { _id: 8, productId: 7, quantity: 12, price: 79.99,
    deliveryDate: new Date("2016-10-11T11:10:00") },
  { _id: 9, productId: 7, quantity: 18, price: 69.99,
    deliveryDate: new Date("2016-10-12T09:50:00") }
])
// Now delete all deliveries for product 7
db.deliveries.deleteMany({ productId: 7 })
```

The response should show deletedCount: 2, reflecting the two delivery records that referenced product 7. If you wanted to delete all documents in a collection while keeping the collection itself intact, you would pass an empty filter: db.deliveries.deleteMany({}). To drop the entire collection including its metadata and indexes, you would instead call db.deliveries.drop().

Review Question 12.34
What happens in MongoDB if you delete a document that is referenced by other documents?
a. All related documents are automatically updated.
b. MongoDB blocks the deletion to preserve relationships.
c. MongoDB automatically deletes the related documents.
d. MongoDB does not enforce cascading deletes.

Review Question 12.35
What does a `deletedCount` value of 0 indicate after executing a delete operation?
a. The database connection failed.
b. No documents matched the filter.
c. The deletion was partially successful.
d. The collection was dropped.

Review Question 12.36
What is the effect of executing the following command?
`db.deliveries.deleteMany({})`
a. It deletes all documents in the deliveries collection but keeps the collection.
b. It deletes only the oldest document in the deliveries collection.
c. It removes the deliveries collection and all its indexes.
d. It deletes only documents with empty fields.

# 12.8 Additional Useful Shell Commands

Before closing this chapter, it is worth knowing a handful of utility commands that you will use regularly in mongosh. The countDocuments() method returns the number of documents in a collection that match a given filter, or all documents if the filter is empty:

```
db.customers.countDocuments()            // total customers
db.customers.countDocuments({ "address.country": "USA" })  // USA customers
```

The distinct() method returns an array of unique values for a specified field across all documents in a collection (or those matching an optional filter). For example, to see all distinct countries in the customers collection:

```
db.customers.distinct("address.country")
```

To see all collections in the current database, use show collections. To drop the entire lifestyledb database and remove all its data from disk, use db.dropDatabase(). Use the latter command with care -- there is no confirmation prompt.

Finally, you can create an index on a field to speed up queries. Indexes in MongoDB work similarly to indexes in relational databases. To create an ascending index on the customerName field:

```
db.customers.createIndex({ customerName: 1 })
```

Index creation is an important performance topic that is covered in depth in our advanced database book. For now, simply know that indexes exist and are created with createIndex().

Review Question 12.39
What is the purpose of the `countDocuments()` method in MongoDB?
a. To count the number of fields in a document
b. To return the number of documents matching a filter
c. To list all collections in a database
d. To remove duplicate documents

Review Question 12.40
Which command permanently removes an entire database in MongoDB?
a. show collections
b. db.deleteDatabase()
c. db.removeDatabase()
d. db.dropDatabase()

## 12.9 Chapter Summary

This chapter introduced MongoDB through a hands-on conversion of the relational LifeStyleDB schema into a document-oriented model. After installing MongoDB, we explored the embedding-versus-referencing design trade-off and built six collections: customers, employees, suppliers, products, deliveries, and orders. We then practiced all four CRUD operations -- insertOne() and insertMany() for creating data; find() with filters, projections, and operators for reading; updateOne() and updateMany() with $set for modifying data; and deleteOne() and deleteMany() for removing documents. These foundational skills prepare you for more advanced MongoDB topics such as aggregation pipelines and index optimization.

## 12.10 Discussion Questions

Discussion 12.1
In the LifeStyleDB conversion, we chose to embed orderDetails inside orders but kept products as a separate collection. What factors drove that decision? Can you think of a scenario where it would make more sense to embed products inside orders as well? Be specific to LifeStyleDB.

Discussion 12.2
MongoDB does not enforce referential integrity the way relational databases do with foreign keys. What are the practical implications of this for the LifeStyleDB scenario? How might an application developer compensate for this limitation?

Discussion 12.3
Explain why MongoDB stores dates as BSON Date objects rather than strings. What problems could arise if dates were stored as plain strings like "2017-01-03"?

## 12.11 NoSQL Exercises

Exercise 12.1 Launch compass and connect to the default MongoDB instance running on localhost. Run the command to show which database is currently active, then list all available databases.

Exercise 12.2 Switch to a new database named exerciseDB. Insert any single document into a collection named test_col, then confirm it exists. Finally, drop the test_col collection.

Exercise 12.3 Switch back to lifestyledb and insert a new customer with _id: 9, customerName "Tech Universe", located at 500 Innovation Drive, Austin, TX, 78701, USA, with contact "Sarah Blue" and email "sblue@techu.com". After inserting, verify the document was created.

Exercise 12.4 Insert three new fictional companies of your own invention into the customers collection. Intentionally omit the email field from one of them. After inserting, verify that the total count has increased by three. Then delete these three test records using one command with a filter that targets only the _id values you assigned to them.

Exercise 12.5 Write the complete statement that inserts all seven employees from the LifeStyleDB data set into a fresh employees collection. Before inserting, drop any existing employees collection. After inserting, verify and confirm that document count equals 7.

Exercise 12.6 The NoSQL Example 12.6 showed only suppliers 1 and 2. Write the complete statement that inserts all five suppliers into the suppliers collection. Then write a separate query that retrieves only the suppliers located in the USA.

Exercise 12.7 Write the statement to insert all nine deliveries from the original LifeStyleDB data into the deliveries collection. After inserting, confirm all nine deliveries are present.

Exercise 12.8 Retrieve all documents in the employees collection. Then retrieve the first employee document.

Exercise 12.9 Write three separate queries against the customers collection using dot notation: (a) find all UK customers, (b) find all customers in the city of "New Canton" from the employees collection, and (c) find all orders that include productId 6 in their embedded orderDetails array.

Exercise 12.10 Write a find() query on the customers collection that returns only the customerName, contact, and email fields for all customers. Then write a second find() that returns all fields for all customers except the address sub-document. Compare the output of both queries and explain in a sentence what type of projection each one uses (inclusion vs. exclusion).

Exercise 12.11 Write the following four queries against the lifestyledb collections: (a) find all deliveries with a price between $79.99 and $129.99 (inclusive); (b) find all products whose supplierId is 2, 4, or 5; (c) find all orders placed by either employeeId 5 or employeeId 7; (d) find all 2017 orders for customerId 1. Display only the relevant fields in your output using a projection.

Exercise 12.12 Write three queries: (a) retrieve the five most expensive deliveries sorted by price in descending order; (b) retrieve the two oldest employees by birthDate in ascending order, returning only their firstName, lastName, and birthDate; (c) retrieve the most recent order placed in 2016.

Exercise 12.13 Perform the following modifications: (a) change the phone number of employee 4 (Alice Law) to "(434) 555-9090"; (b) add a new field called region with the value "Northeast" to customer 1 (Just Electronics) only; (c) remove the country field you added to US customers in Example 14 from the customers collection. After each operation, confirm the change was made correctly.

Exercise 12.14 (a) set a field called region to "Domestic" for all customers whose address.country is "USA", and to "International" for all customers whose address.country is not "USA"; (b) set a field called isActive to true for all employees whose managerId is 1. Verify the results of each update.

Exercise 12.15 Delete the test customer you inserted in Exercise 12.3 (customer _id: 9). Verify the deletion. Then delete all customers in the "International" region (the field you added in Exercise 14). Verify that the correct number of documents were removed.

Exercise 12.16 Write a statement that removes all deliveries where the deliveryDate is before October 10, 2016. Check how many documents were deleted. Then, drop the entire deliveries collection.

## 12.7 Solutions to the Review Questions

12.1 B; 12.2 D; 12.3 A; 12.4 B; 12.5 C; 12.6 B; 12.7 C; 12.8 B; 12.9 C; 12.10 C; 12.11 C; 12.12 D; 12.13 C; 12.14 B; 12.15 C; 12.16 C; 12.17 B; 12.18 B; 12.19 D; 12.20 C; 12.21 B; 12.22 C; 12.23 B; 12.24 B; 12.25 B; 12.26 D; 12.27 B; 12.28 B; 12.29 B; 12.30 C; 12.31 B; 12.32 A; 12.33 C; 12.34 D; 12.35 B; 12.36 A; 12.37 B; 12.38 D;

# APPENDIX A: SQL SCRIPT FOR GENERATING LIFESTYLE DATABASE

```
USE master;

IF DB_ID(N'LifeStyleDB') IS NOT NULL DROP DATABASE LifeStyleDB;

CREATE DATABASE LifeStyleDB;
GO

USE LifeStyleDB;
GO

CREATE SCHEMA HR AUTHORIZATION dbo;
GO
CREATE SCHEMA Sales AUTHORIZATION dbo;
GO
CREATE SCHEMA Purchasing AUTHORIZATION dbo;
GO

CREATE TABLE Sales.Customers
(
 CustomerId       INT        NOT NULL IDENTITY,
 CustomerName     NVARCHAR(50) NOT NULL,
 StreetAddress    NVARCHAR(50) NULL,
 City             NVARCHAR(20) NULL,
 [State]          NVARCHAR(20) NULL,
 PostalCode       NVARCHAR(10) NULL,
 Country          NVARCHAR(20) NULL,
 Contact          NVARCHAR(50) NULL,
 Email            NVARCHAR(50) NULL,
 CONSTRAINT PK_Customers PRIMARY KEY(CustomerId)
);

CREATE TABLE HR.Employees
(
 EmployeeId  INT        NOT NULL IDENTITY,
 FirstName        NVARCHAR(50) NOT NULL,
 LastName         NVARCHAR(50) NOT NULL,
 BirthDate        DATE       NOT NULL,
 HireDate         DATE       NOT NULL,
 HomeAddress      NVARCHAR(50) NULL,
 City             NVARCHAR(20) NULL,
 [State]          NVARCHAR(20) NULL,
 PostalCode       NVARCHAR(10) NULL,
 Phone            NVARCHAR(20) NULL,
 ManagerId        INT               NULL,
 CONSTRAINT PK_Employees PRIMARY KEY(EmployeeId),
```

```
 CONSTRAINT FK_Employees_Employees FOREIGN KEY(ManagerId)
   REFERENCES HR.Employees(EmployeeId),
 CONSTRAINT CHK_BirthDate CHECK(BirthDate <= CAST(SYSDATETIME() AS DATE)),
 CONSTRAINT CHK_HireDate CHECK(BirthDate < HireDate)
);

CREATE TABLE Purchasing.Suppliers
(
 SupplierId        INT          NOT NULL IDENTITY,
 SupplierName      NVARCHAR(50) NOT NULL,
 StreetAddress     NVARCHAR(50) NULL,
 City              NVARCHAR(20) NULL,
 [State]           NVARCHAR(20) NULL,
 PostalCode        NVARCHAR(10) NULL,
 Country           NVARCHAR(20) NULL,
 CONSTRAINT PK_Supplier PRIMARY KEY(SupplierId)
);

CREATE TABLE Purchasing.Products
(
 ProductId         INT          NOT NULL IDENTITY,
 ProductName       NVARCHAR(40) NOT NULL,
 supplierid        INT          NOT NULL,
 CONSTRAINT PK_Products PRIMARY KEY(ProductId),
 CONSTRAINT FK_Products_Suppliers FOREIGN KEY(SupplierId)
   REFERENCES Purchasing.Suppliers(SupplierId)
);

CREATE TABLE Purchasing.Deliveries
(
     DeliveryId        INT            NOT NULL IDENTITY,
     ProductId         INT            NOT NULL,
     Quantity          INT            NOT NULL,
     Price             MONEY          NOT NULL
          CONSTRAINT DF_Deliveries_price DEFAULT(0),
     DeliveryDate  DateTime2     NOT NULL
          CONSTRAINT DF_Deliveries_DeliveryDate DEFAULT(SYSDATETIME()),
     CONSTRAINT PK_Deliveries PRIMARY KEY (DeliveryId),
     CONSTRAINT FK_Deliveries_Products FOREIGN KEY(ProductId)
          REFERENCES Purchasing.Products(ProductId),
     CONSTRAINT CHK_Deliveries_Price CHECK (Price >= 0)
);

CREATE TABLE Sales.Orders
(
 OrderId       INT       NOT NULL IDENTITY,
 CustomerId    INT       NOT NULL,
 EmployeeId    INT       NOT NULL,
 OrderDate     DATE      NOT NULL,
 CONSTRAINT PK_Orders PRIMARY KEY(OrderId),
```

```
 CONSTRAINT FK_Orders_Customers FOREIGN KEY(CustomerId)
   REFERENCES Sales.Customers(CustomerId),
 CONSTRAINT FK_Orders_Employees FOREIGN KEY(EmployeeId)
   REFERENCES HR.Employees(EmployeeId)
);

CREATE TABLE Sales.OrderDetails
(
 OrderId       INT            NOT NULL,
 ProductId     INT            NOT NULL,
 Price         MONEY         NOT NULL
   CONSTRAINT DF_OrderDetails_price DEFAULT(0),
 quantity  SMALLINT         NOT NULL
   CONSTRAINT DF_OrderDetails_qty DEFAULT(1),
 CONSTRAINT PK_OrderDetails PRIMARY KEY(Orderid, Productid),
 CONSTRAINT FK_OrderDetails_Orders FOREIGN KEY(OrderId)
   REFERENCES Sales.Orders(OrderId),
 CONSTRAINT FK_OrderDetails_Products FOREIGN KEY(ProductId)
   REFERENCES Purchasing.Products(ProductId),
 CONSTRAINT CHK_quantity  CHECK (quantity > 0),
 CONSTRAINT CHK_price CHECK (price >= 0)
);

SET IDENTITY_INSERT Sales.Customers ON;
INSERT INTO Sales.Customers(CustomerId, CustomerName, StreetAddress, City, [State], PostalCode, Country,
Contact, Email)
      VALUES(1, 'Just Electronics', '123 Broad way', 'New York', 'NY', '12012', 'USA', 'John White',
'jwhite@je.com');
INSERT INTO Sales.Customers(CustomerId, CustomerName, StreetAddress, City, [State], PostalCode, Country,
Contact, Email)
      VALUES(2, 'Beyond Electronics', '45 Cherry Street', 'Chicago', 'IL', '32302', 'USA', 'Scott Green',
'green@beil.com');
INSERT INTO Sales.Customers(CustomerId, CustomerName, StreetAddress, City, [State], PostalCode, Country,
Contact, Email)
      VALUES(3, 'Beyond Electronics', '6767 GameOver Blvd', 'Atlanta', 'GA', '43347', 'USA', 'Alice Black',
'black1@be.com');
INSERT INTO Sales.Customers(CustomerId, CustomerName, StreetAddress, City, [State], PostalCode, Country,
Contact, Email)
      VALUES(4, 'E Fun', '888  Main Ave.', 'Seattle', 'WA', '69356', 'USA', 'Ben Gold', 'bgold@efun.com');
INSERT INTO Sales.Customers(CustomerId, CustomerName, StreetAddress, City, [State], PostalCode, Country,
Contact, Email)
      VALUES(5, 'Overstock E', '39 Garden Place', 'Los Angeles', 'CA', '32302', 'USA', 'Daniel Yellow', 'dy@os.com');
INSERT INTO Sales.Customers(CustomerId, CustomerName, StreetAddress, City, [State], PostalCode, Country,
Contact, Email)
      VALUES(6, 'E Fun', '915 Market st.', 'London', 'England', 'EC1A 1BB', 'UK', 'Frank Green', 'green@ef.com');
INSERT INTO Sales.Customers(CustomerId, CustomerName, StreetAddress, City, [State], PostalCode, Country,
Contact, Email)
      VALUES(7, 'Electronics4U', '27 Colmore Row', 'Birmingham', 'England', 'B3 2EW', 'UK', 'Grace Smith',
'smith@e4u.com');
INSERT INTO Sales.Customers(CustomerId, CustomerName, StreetAddress, City, [State], PostalCode, Country)
```

```
    VALUES(8, 'Cheap Electronics', '1010 Easy St', 'Ottawa', 'Ontario', 'K1A 0B1', 'Canada');
SET IDENTITY_INSERT Sales.Customers OFF;

SET IDENTITY_INSERT HR.Employees ON;
INSERT INTO HR.Employees(EmployeeId, FirstName, LastName, BirthDate, HireDate, HomeAddress, City, [State],
PostalCode, Phone, ManagerId)
    VALUES(1, 'Alex', 'Hall', '19900203', '20150809', '85 Main Ln', 'New Canton', 'VA', '23123', '(434) 290-3322',
NULL);
INSERT INTO HR.Employees(EmployeeId, FirstName, LastName, BirthDate, HireDate, HomeAddress, City, [State],
PostalCode, Phone, ManagerId)
    VALUES(2, 'Dianne', 'Hart', '19781203', '20100801', '209 Social Hall Blvd', 'New Canton', 'VA', '23123', '(434)
290-1122', 1);
INSERT INTO HR.Employees(EmployeeId, FirstName, LastName, BirthDate, HireDate, HomeAddress, City, [State],
PostalCode, Phone, ManagerId)
    VALUES(3, 'Maria', 'Law', '19880713', '20120821', '258 Blinkys St', 'New Canton', 'VA', '23123', '(434) 531-
5673', 1);
INSERT INTO HR.Employees(EmployeeId, FirstName, LastName, BirthDate, HireDate, HomeAddress, City, [State],
PostalCode, Phone, ManagerId)
    VALUES(4, 'Alice', 'Law', '19881213', '20120422', '300 Vista Valley Blvd', 'Buckingham', 'VA', '23123', '(434)
531-1010', 1);
INSERT INTO HR.Employees(EmployeeId, FirstName, LastName, BirthDate, HireDate, HomeAddress, City, [State],
PostalCode, Phone, ManagerId)
    VALUES(5, 'Black', 'Hart', '19821109', '20150412', '1 Old Fifteen St', 'Buckingham', 'VA', '23123', '(434) 531-
1034', 2);
INSERT INTO HR.Employees(EmployeeId, FirstName, LastName, BirthDate, HireDate, HomeAddress, City, [State],
PostalCode, ManagerId)
    VALUES(6, 'Christina', 'Robinson', '19780713', '20140615', '217 Chapel St', 'New Canton', 'VA', '23123', 2);
INSERT INTO HR.Employees(EmployeeId, FirstName, LastName, BirthDate, HireDate, HomeAddress, City, [State],
PostalCode, ManagerId)
    VALUES(7, 'Nicholas', 'Pinkston', '19771005', '20130522', '26 N James Madison Rd', 'Buckingham', 'VA',
'23123', 3);
SET IDENTITY_INSERT HR.Employees OFF;

SET IDENTITY_INSERT Purchasing.Suppliers ON;
INSERT INTO Purchasing.Suppliers(SupplierId, SupplierName, StreetAddress, City, [State], PostalCode, Country)
    VALUES(1, 'Pine Apple', '1 Pine Apple St.', 'Idanha', 'CA', '87201', 'USA');
INSERT INTO Purchasing.Suppliers(SupplierId, SupplierName, StreetAddress, City, [State], PostalCode, Country)
    VALUES(2, 'IMB', '123 International Blvd', 'Los Angeles', 'CA', '89202', 'USA');
INSERT INTO Purchasing.Suppliers(SupplierId, SupplierName, StreetAddress, City, [State], PostalCode, Country)
    VALUES(3, 'Lonovo', '33 Beijin Square', 'Beijing', 'Beijing', '100201', 'China');
INSERT INTO Purchasing.Suppliers(SupplierId, SupplierName, StreetAddress, City, [State], PostalCode, Country)
    VALUES(4, 'Samsong', '1 Electronics Road', 'Yeongtong', 'Suwon', '30174', 'South Korea');
INSERT INTO Purchasing.Suppliers(SupplierId, SupplierName, StreetAddress, City, [State], PostalCode, Country)
    VALUES(5, 'Canan', '12 Camera St', 'Ota', 'Tokyo', '100-0121', 'Japan');
SET IDENTITY_INSERT Purchasing.Suppliers OFF;


SET IDENTITY_INSERT Purchasing.Products ON;
INSERT INTO Purchasing.Products(ProductId, ProductName, supplierid)
    VALUES(1, '65-Inch 4K Ultra HD Smart TV', 4);
```

```
INSERT INTO Purchasing.Products(ProductId, ProductName, supplierid)
      VALUES(2, '60-Inch 4K Ultra HD Smart LED TV', 4);
INSERT INTO Purchasing.Products(ProductId, ProductName, supplierid)
      VALUES(3, '3200 Lumens LED Home Theater Projector', 3);
INSERT INTO Purchasing.Products(ProductId, ProductName, supplierid)
      VALUES(4, 'Wireless Color Photo Printer', 5);
INSERT INTO Purchasing.Products(ProductId, ProductName, supplierid)
      VALUES(5, '6Wireless Compact Laser Printer', 2);
INSERT INTO Purchasing.Products(ProductId, ProductName, supplierid)
      VALUES(6, 'Color Laser Printer', 2);
INSERT INTO Purchasing.Products(ProductId, ProductName, supplierid)
      VALUES(7, '10" 16GB Android Tablet', 4);
INSERT INTO Purchasing.Products(ProductId, ProductName, supplierid)
      VALUES(8, 'GPS Android Tablet PC', 2);
INSERT INTO Purchasing.Products(ProductId, ProductName, supplierid)
      VALUES(9, '20.2 MP Digital Camera', 5);
SET IDENTITY_INSERT Purchasing.Products OFF;

SET IDENTITY_INSERT Purchasing.Deliveries ON;
INSERT INTO Purchasing.Deliveries(DeliveryId, ProductId, Quantity, Price, DeliveryDate)
      VALUES(1, 1, 2, 1099.99, '20161001 9:30');
INSERT INTO Purchasing.Deliveries(DeliveryId, ProductId, Quantity, Price, DeliveryDate)
      VALUES(2, 1, 5, 1199.99, '20161101 10:20');
INSERT INTO Purchasing.Deliveries(DeliveryId, ProductId, Quantity, Price, DeliveryDate)
      VALUES(3, 2, 10, 1199.99, '20161002 11:10');
INSERT INTO Purchasing.Deliveries(DeliveryId, ProductId, Quantity, Price, DeliveryDate)
      VALUES(4, 3, 10, 129.99, '20161005 9:15');
INSERT INTO Purchasing.Deliveries(DeliveryId, ProductId, Quantity, Price, DeliveryDate)
      VALUES(5, 4, 20, 79.99, '20161007 14:00');
INSERT INTO Purchasing.Deliveries(DeliveryId, ProductId, Quantity, Price, DeliveryDate)
      VALUES(6, 5, 15, 139.99, '20161007 15:30');
INSERT INTO Purchasing.Deliveries(DeliveryId, ProductId, Quantity, Price, DeliveryDate)
      VALUES(7, 6, 25, 169.99, '20161010 10:30');
INSERT INTO Purchasing.Deliveries(DeliveryId, ProductId, Quantity, Price, DeliveryDate)
      VALUES(8, 7, 12, 79.99, '20161011 11:10');
INSERT INTO Purchasing.Deliveries(DeliveryId, ProductId, Quantity, Price, DeliveryDate)
      VALUES(9, 7, 18, 69.99, '20161012 9:50');
SET IDENTITY_INSERT Purchasing.Deliveries OFF;


SET IDENTITY_INSERT Sales.Orders ON;
INSERT INTO Sales.Orders(OrderId, CustomerId, EmployeeId, OrderDate)
      VALUES(1, 1, 5, '20170103');
INSERT INTO Sales.Orders(OrderId, CustomerId, EmployeeId, OrderDate)
      VALUES(2, 1, 3, '20170305');
INSERT INTO Sales.Orders(OrderId, CustomerId, EmployeeId, OrderDate)
      VALUES(3, 2, 5, '20170223');
INSERT INTO Sales.Orders(OrderId, CustomerId, EmployeeId, OrderDate)
      VALUES(4, 4, 5, '20170413');
INSERT INTO Sales.Orders(OrderId, CustomerId, EmployeeId, OrderDate)
```

```
    VALUES(5, 1, 4, '20170503');
INSERT INTO Sales.Orders(OrderId, CustomerId, EmployeeId, OrderDate)
    VALUES(6, 3, 6, '20170508');
INSERT INTO Sales.Orders(OrderId, CustomerId, EmployeeId, OrderDate)
    VALUES(7, 5, 7, '20161108');
INSERT INTO Sales.Orders(OrderId, CustomerId, EmployeeId, OrderDate)
    VALUES(8, 7, 2, '20161223');
SET IDENTITY_INSERT Sales.Orders OFF;


INSERT INTO Sales.OrderDetails(OrderId, ProductId, Price, quantity)
    VALUES(1, 1, 1499.99, 1);
INSERT INTO Sales.OrderDetails(OrderId, ProductId, Price, quantity)
    VALUES(1, 3, 149.99, 2);
INSERT INTO Sales.OrderDetails(OrderId, ProductId, Price, quantity)
    VALUES(2, 1, 1499.99, 1);
INSERT INTO Sales.OrderDetails(OrderId, ProductId, Price, quantity)
    VALUES(2, 4, 99.99, 6);
INSERT INTO Sales.OrderDetails(OrderId, ProductId, Price, quantity)
    VALUES(2, 6, 189.99, 5);
INSERT INTO Sales.OrderDetails(OrderId, ProductId, Price, quantity)
    VALUES(2, 2, 1599.99, 1);
INSERT INTO Sales.OrderDetails(OrderId, ProductId, Price, quantity)
    VALUES(3, 6, 199.99, 1);
INSERT INTO Sales.OrderDetails(OrderId, ProductId, Price, quantity)
    VALUES(3, 7, 109.99, 2);
INSERT INTO Sales.OrderDetails(OrderId, ProductId, Price, quantity)
    VALUES(3, 8, 69.99, 2);
INSERT INTO Sales.OrderDetails(OrderId, ProductId, Price, quantity)
    VALUES(3, 3, 159.99, 2);
INSERT INTO Sales.OrderDetails(OrderId, ProductId, Price, quantity)
    VALUES(3, 9, 1449.99, 1);
INSERT INTO Sales.OrderDetails(OrderId, ProductId, Price, quantity)
    VALUES(4, 8, 69.99, 1);
INSERT INTO Sales.OrderDetails(OrderId, ProductId, Price, quantity)
    VALUES(4, 4, 99.99, 2);
INSERT INTO Sales.OrderDetails(OrderId, ProductId, Price, quantity)
    VALUES(5, 6, 199.99, 3);
INSERT INTO Sales.OrderDetails(OrderId, ProductId, Price, quantity)
    VALUES(5, 3, 149.99, 6);
INSERT INTO Sales.OrderDetails(OrderId, ProductId, Price, quantity)
    VALUES(6, 1, 1499.99, 1);
INSERT INTO Sales.OrderDetails(OrderId, ProductId, Price, quantity)
    VALUES(7, 2, 999.99, 1);
INSERT INTO Sales.OrderDetails(OrderId, ProductId, Price, quantity)
    VALUES(8, 7, 79.99, 1);
INSERT INTO Sales.OrderDetails(OrderId, ProductId, Price, quantity)
    VALUES(8, 8, 59.99, 2);
```

# APPENDIX B: LIFESTYLE DATABASE TABLES

## Sales.Customers Table

| CustomerId | CustomerName | StreetAddress | City | State | PostalCode | Country | Contact | Email |
|---|---|---|---|---|---|---|---|---|
| 1 | Just Electronics | 123 Broad way | New York | NY | 12012 | USA | John White | jwhite@je.com |
| 2 | Beyond Electronics | 45 Cherry Street | Chicago | IL | 32302 | USA | Scott Green | green@beil.com |
| 3 | Beyond Electronics | 6767 GameOver Blvd | Atlanta | GA | 43347 | USA | Alice Black | black1@be.com |
| 4 | E Fun | 888 Main Ave. | Seattle | WA | 69356 | USA | Ben Gold | bgold@efun.com |
| 5 | Overstock E | 39 Garden Place | Los Angeles | CA | 32302 | USA | Daniel Yellow | dy@os.com |
| 6 | E Fun | 915 Market st. | London | England | EC1A 1BB | UK | Frank Green | green@ef.com |
| 7 | Electronics4U | 27 Colmore Row | Birmingham | England | B3 2EW | UK | Grace Smith | smith@e4u.com |
| 8 | Cheap Electronics | 1010 Easy St | Ottawa | Ontario | K1A 0B1 | Canada | NULL | NULL |

## HR.Employees Table

| EmployeeId | FirstName | LastName | BirthDate | HireDate | HomeAddress | City | State | PostalCode | Phone | ManagerId |
|---|---|---|---|---|---|---|---|---|---|---|
| 1 | Alex | Hall | 1990-02-03 | 2015-08-09 | 85 Main Ln | New Canton | VA | 23123 | (434) 290-3322 | NULL |
| 2 | Dianne | Hart | 1978-12-03 | 2010-08-01 | 209 Social Hall Blvd | New Canton | VA | 23123 | (434) 290-1122 | 1 |
| 3 | Maria | Law | 1988-07-13 | 2012-08-21 | 258 Blinkys St | New Canton | VA | 23123 | (434) 531-5673 | 1 |
| 4 | Alice | Law | 1988-12-13 | 2012-04-22 | 300 Vista Valley Blvd | Buckingham | VA | 23123 | (434) 531-1010 | 1 |
| 5 | Black | Hart | 1982-11-09 | 2015-04-12 | 1 Old Fifteen St | Buckingham | VA | 23123 | (434) 531-1034 | 2 |
| 6 | Christina | Robinson | 1978-07-13 | 2014-06-15 | 217 Chapel St | New Canton | VA | 23123 | NULL | 2 |
| 7 | Nicholas | Pinkston | 1977-10-05 | 2013-05-22 | 26 N James Madison Rd | Buckingham | VA | 23123 | NULL | 3 |

## Purchasing.Suppliers Table

| SupplierId | SupplierName | StreetAddress | City | State | PostalCode | Country |
|---|---|---|---|---|---|---|
| 1 | Pine Apple | 1 Pine Apple St. | Idanha | CA | 87201 | USA |
| 2 | IMB | 123 International Blvd | Los Angeles | CA | 89202 | USA |
| 3 | Lonovo | 33 Beijin Square | Beijing | Beijing | 100201 | China |
| 4 | Samsong | 1 Electronics Road | Yeongtong | Suwon | 30174 | South Korea |
| 5 | Canan | 12 Camera St | Ota | Tokyo | 100-0121 | Japan |

## Purchasing.Products Table

| ProductId | ProductName | supplierId |
|---|---|---|
| 1 | 65-Inch 4K Ultra HD Smart TV | 4 |
| 2 | 60-Inch 4K Ultra HD Smart LED TV | 4 |
| 3 | 3200 Lumens LED Home Theater Projector | 3 |
| 4 | Wireless Color Photo Printer | 5 |
| 5 | 6Wireless Compact Laser Printer | 2 |
| 6 | Color Laser Printer | 2 |
| 7 | 10" 16GB Android Tablet | 4 |
| 8 | GPS Android Tablet PC | 2 |
| 9 | 20.2 MP Digital Camera | 5 |

## Purchasing.Deliveries Table

| DeliveryId | ProductId | Quantity | Price | DeliveryDate |
|---|---|---|---|---|
| 1 | 1 | 2 | 1099.99 | 2016-10-01 09:30:00.0000000 |
| 2 | 1 | 5 | 1199.99 | 2016-11-01 10:20:00.0000000 |
| 3 | 2 | 10 | 1199.99 | 2016-10-02 11:10:00.0000000 |
| 4 | 3 | 10 | 129.99 | 2016-10-05 09:15:00.0000000 |
| 5 | 4 | 20 | 79.99 | 2016-10-07 14:00:00.0000000 |
| 6 | 5 | 15 | 139.99 | 2016-10-07 15:30:00.0000000 |
| 7 | 6 | 25 | 169.99 | 2016-10-10 10:30:00.0000000 |
| 8 | 7 | 12 | 79.99 | 2016-10-11 11:10:00.0000000 |
| 9 | 7 | 18 | 69.99 | 2016-10-12 09:50:00.0000000 |

## Sales.Orders Table

| OrderId | CustomerId | EmployeeId | OrderDate |
|---|---|---|---|
| 1 | 1 | 5 | 2017-01-03 |
| 2 | 1 | 3 | 2017-03-05 |
| 3 | 2 | 5 | 2017-02-23 |
| 4 | 4 | 5 | 2017-04-13 |
| 5 | 1 | 4 | 2017-05-03 |
| 6 | 3 | 6 | 2017-05-08 |
| 7 | 5 | 7 | 2016-11-08 |
| 8 | 7 | 2 | 2016-12-23 |

## Sales.OrderDetails Table

| | OrderId | ProductId | Price | quantity |
|---|---|---|---|---|
| 1 | 1 | 1 | 1499.99 | 1 |
| 2 | 1 | 3 | 149.99 | 2 |
| 3 | 2 | 1 | 1499.99 | 1 |
| 4 | 2 | 2 | 1599.99 | 1 |
| 5 | 2 | 4 | 99.99 | 6 |
| 6 | 2 | 6 | 189.99 | 5 |
| 7 | 3 | 3 | 159.99 | 2 |
| 8 | 3 | 6 | 199.99 | 1 |
| 9 | 3 | 7 | 109.99 | 2 |
| 10 | 3 | 8 | 69.99 | 2 |
| 11 | 3 | 9 | 1449.99 | 1 |
| 12 | 4 | 4 | 99.99 | 2 |
| 13 | 4 | 8 | 69.99 | 1 |
| 14 | 5 | 3 | 149.99 | 6 |
| 15 | 5 | 6 | 199.99 | 3 |
| 16 | 6 | 1 | 1499.99 | 1 |
| 17 | 7 | 2 | 999.99 | 1 |
| 18 | 8 | 7 | 79.99 | 1 |
| 19 | 8 | 8 | 59.99 | 2 |

## ABOUT THE AUTHOR

Lucy Scott was born in Mason City Iowa. She currently resides in Boston Massachusetts and lives with her husband Leonard and their two Labrador retrievers, Lola and Buddy.

www.ingramcontent.com/pod-product-compliance
Lightning Source LLC
LaVergne TN
LVHW060025210926
848481LV00013B/3791